‖·‖·‖·
CISCO.

D1597321

Course Booklet

Introduction to Networks

CCNAv7

Cisco Press

‖·‖·‖·‖· Networking
CISCO Academy

Introduction to Networks Course Booklet (CCNAv7)

Published by:
Cisco Press
Hoboken, New Jersey

9 2024

Library of Congress Control Number: 2020936828

ISBN-13: 978-0-13-663295-5

ISBN-10: 0-13-663295-5

Warning and Disclaimer

This book is designed to provide information about Introduction to Networks. Every effort has been made to make this book as complete and as accurate as possible, but no warranty or fitness is implied.

The information is provided on an "as is" basis. The authors, Cisco Press, and Cisco Systems, Inc. shall have neither liability nor responsibility to any person or entity with respect to any loss or damages arising from the information contained in this book or from the use of the discs or programs that may accompany it.

The opinions expressed in this book belong to the author and are not necessarily those of Cisco Systems, Inc.

Editor-in-Chief
Mark Taub

**Alliances Manager,
Cisco Press**
Arezou Gol

Product Line Manager
Brett Bartow

Senior Editor
James Manly

Managing Editor
Sandra Schroeder

Senior Project Editor
Tonya Simpson

Editorial Assistant
Cindy Teeters

Cover Designer
Chuti Prasertsith

Composition
codeMantra

Indexer
Cheryl Ann Lenser

This book is part of the Cisco Networking Academy® series from Cisco Press. The products in this series support and complement the Cisco Networking Academy curriculum. If you are using this book outside the Networking Academy, then you are not preparing with a Cisco trained and authorized Networking Academy provider.

For more information on the Cisco Networking Academy or to locate a Networking Academy, Please visit www.netacad.com

CISCO

Trademark Acknowledgments

All terms mentioned in this book that are known to be trademarks or service marks have been appropriately capitalized. Cisco Press or Cisco Systems, Inc., cannot attest to the accuracy of this information. Use of a term in this book should not be regarded as affecting the validity of any trademark or service mark.

Special Sales

For information about buying this title in bulk quantities, or for special sales opportunities (which may include electronic versions; custom cover designs; and content particular to your business, training goals, marketing focus, or branding interests), please contact our corporate sales department at corpsales@pearsoned.com or (800) 382-3419.

For government sales inquiries, please contact governmentsales@pearsoned.com.

For questions about sales outside the U.S., please contact intlcs@pearson.com.

Feedback Information

At Cisco Press, our goal is to create in-depth technical books of the highest quality and value. Each book is crafted with care and precision, undergoing rigorous development that involves the unique expertise of members from the professional technical community.

Readers' feedback is a natural continuation of this process. If you have any comments regarding how we could improve the quality of this book, or otherwise alter it to better suit your needs, you can contact us through email at feedback@ciscopress.com. Please make sure to include the book title and ISBN in your message.

We greatly appreciate your assistance.

Americas Headquarters	Asia Pacific Headquarters	Europe Headquarters
Cisco Systems, Inc.	Cisco Systems (USA) Pte. Ltd.	Cisco Systems International BV Amsterdam,
San Jose, CA	Singapore	The Netherlands

Cisco has more than 200 offices worldwide. Addresses, phone numbers, and fax numbers are listed on the Cisco Website at **www.cisco.com/go/offices**.

Cisco and the Cisco logo are trademarks or registered trademarks of Cisco and/or its affiliates in the U.S. and other countries. To view a list of Cisco trademarks, go to this URL: www.cisco.com/go/trademarks. Third party trademarks mentioned are the property of their respective owners. The use of the word partner does not imply a partnership relationship between Cisco and any other company. (1110R)

Contents at a Glance

Contents

Command Syntax Conventions

The conventions used to present command syntax in this book are the same conventions used in the IOS Command Reference. The Command Reference describes these conventions as follows:

- **Boldface** indicates commands and keywords that are entered literally as shown. In actual configuration examples and output (not general command syntax), boldface indicates commands that are manually input by the user (such as a **show** command).

- *Italic* indicates arguments for which you supply actual values.

- Vertical bars (|) separate alternative, mutually exclusive elements.

- Square brackets ([ ]) indicate an optional element.

- Braces ({ }) indicate a required choice.

- Braces within brackets ([{ }]) indicate a required choice within an optional element.

About This Course Booklet

Your Cisco Networking Academy Course Booklet is designed as a study resource you can easily read, highlight, and review on the go, wherever the Internet is not available or practical:

- The text is extracted directly, word-for-word, from the online course so you can highlight important points and take notes in the "Your Chapter Notes" section.

- Headings with the exact page correlations provide a quick reference to the online course for your classroom discussions and exam preparation.

- An icon system directs you to the online curriculum to take full advantage of the images embedded within the Networking Academy online course interface and reminds you to do the labs, interactive activities, packet tracer activities, watch videos, and take the chapter quizzes.

The Course Booklet is a basic, economical paper-based resource to help you succeed with the Cisco Networking Academy online course.

Introduction

Networking Academy CCNAv7

Welcome to the first course of the Cisco Networking Academy CCNAv7 curriculum, Introduction to Networks (ITN). This is the first of three courses that are aligned to the CCNA Certification Exam. ITN contains 17 modules, each with a series of topics.

In Introduction to Networks, you will gain a basic understanding of the way networks operate. You will learn about network components and their functions, as well as how a network is structured, and the architectures used to create networks, including the internet.

But ITN is about more than learning networking concepts. By the end of this course, you will be able to build local area networks (LANs), configure basic settings on routers and switches, and implement internet protocol (IP).

In ITN, every concept that you learn and skill that you develop will be used in the rest of the CCNA curriculum. Now is the time to supercharge your networking career and let Cisco Networking Academy help you to reach your goal!

CHAPTER 1

Networking Today

Introduction - 1.0

Why should I take this module? - 1.0.1

Welcome to Networking Today!

Congratulations! This module starts you on your path to a successful career in Information Technology by giving you a foundational understanding of the creation, operation, and maintenance of networks. As a bonus, you get to dive into networking simulations using Packet Tracer. We promise you will really enjoy it!

What will I learn to do in this module? - 1.0.2

Module Title: Networking Today

Module Objective: Explain the advances in modern network technologies.

Topic Title	Topic Objective
Networks Affect our Lives	Explain how networks affect our daily lives.
Network Components	Explain how host and network devices are used.
Network Representations and Topologies	Explain network representations and how they are used in network topologies.
Common Types of Networks	Compare the characteristics of common types of networks.
Internet Connections	Explain how LANs and WANs interconnect to the internet.
Reliable Networks	Describe the four basic requirements of a reliable network.
Network Trends	Explain how trends such as BYOD, online collaboration, video, and cloud computing are changing the way we interact.
Network Security	Identify some basic security threats and solution for all networks.
The IT Professional	Explain employment opportunities in the networking field.

Networks Affect our Lives - 1.1

Networks Connect Us - 1.1.1

Among all of the essentials for human existence, the need to interact with others ranks just below our need to sustain life. Communication is almost as important to us as our reliance on air, water, food, and shelter.

In today's world, through the use of networks, we are connected like never before. People with ideas can communicate instantly with others to make those ideas a reality. News events and discoveries are known worldwide in seconds. Individuals can even connect and play games with friends separated by oceans and continents.

Refer to **Video** in online course

Video - The Cisco Networking Academy Learning Experience - 1.1.2

World changers aren't born. They are made. Since 1997 Cisco Networking Academy has been working towards a single goal: the educating and skill building of the next generation of talent required for the digital economy.

Click Play to how Cisco Networking Academy to learn how we use technology to make the world a better place.

Refer to **Online Course** for Illustration

No Boundaries - 1.1.3

Advancements in networking technologies are perhaps the most significant changes in the world today. They are helping to create a world in which national borders, geographic distances, and physical limitations become less relevant, presenting ever-diminishing obstacles.

The internet has changed the manner in which our social, commercial, political, and personal interactions occur. The immediate nature of communications over the internet encourages the creation of global communities. Global communities allow for social interaction that is independent of location or time zone.

The creation of online communities for the exchange of ideas and information has the potential to increase productivity opportunities across the globe.

The creation of the cloud lets us store documents and pictures and access them anywhere, anytime. So whether we are on a train, in a park, or standing on top of a mountain, we can seamlessly access our data and applications on any device.

Network Components - 1.2

Refer to **Online Course** for Illustration

Host Roles - 1.2.1

If you want to be a part of a global online community, your computer, tablet, or smart phone must first be connected to a network. That network must be connected to the internet. This topic discusses the parts of a network. See if you recognize these components in your own home or school network!

All computers that are connected to a network and participate directly in network communication are classified as hosts. Hosts can be called end devices. Some hosts are also called clients. However, the term hosts specifically refers to devices on the network that are assigned a number for communication purposes. This number identifies the host within a particular network. This number is called the Internet Protocol (IP) address. An IP address identifies the host and the network to which the host is attached.

Servers are computers with software that allow them to provide information, like email or web pages, to other end devices on the network. Each service requires separate server software. For example, a server requires web server software in order to provide web services to the network. A computer with server software can provide services simultaneously to many different clients.

As mentioned before, clients are a type of host. Clients have software for requesting and displaying the information obtained from the server, as shown in the figure.

An example of client software is a web browser, like Chrome or FireFox. A single computer can also run multiple types of client software. For example, a user can check email and view a web page while instant messaging and listening to an audio stream. The table lists three common types of server software.

Type	Description
Email	The email server runs email server software. Clients use mail client software, such as Microsoft Outlook, to access email on the server.
Web	The web server runs web server software. Clients use browser software, such as Windows Internet Explorer, to access web pages on the server.
File	The file server stores corporate and user files in a central location. The client devices access these files with client software such as the Windows File Explorer.

Refer to **Online Course** for Illustration

Peer-to-Peer - 1.2.2

Client and server software usually run on separate computers, but it is also possible for one computer to be used for both roles at the same time. In small businesses and homes, many computers function as the servers and clients on the network. This type of network is called a peer-to-peer network.

Refer to **Interactive Graphic** in online course

End Devices - 1.2.3

The network devices that people are most familiar with are end devices. To distinguish one end device from another, each end device on a network has an address. When an end device initiates communication, it uses the address of the destination end device to specify where to deliver the message.

An end device is either the source or destination of a message transmitted over the network.

Click Play in the figure to see an animation of data flowing through a network.

Refer to
Online Course
for Illustration

Intermediary Devices - 1.2.4

Intermediary devices connect the individual end devices to the network. They can connect multiple individual networks to form an internetwork. These intermediary devices provide connectivity and ensure that data flows across the network.

Intermediary devices use the destination end device address, in conjunction with information about the network interconnections, to determine the path that messages should take through the network. Examples of the more common intermediary devices and a list of functions are shown in the figure.

Refer to
Online Course
for Illustration

Network Media - 1.2.5

Communication transmits across a network on media. The media provides the channel over which the message travels from source to destination.

Modern networks primarily use three types of media to interconnect devices, as shown in the figure:

- **Metal wires within cables** - Data is encoded into electrical impulses.

- **Glass or plastic fibers within cables (fiber-optic cable)** - Data is encoded into pulses of light.

- **Wireless transmission** - Data is encoded via modulation of specific frequencies of electromagnetic waves.

Different types of network media have different features and benefits. Not all network media have the same characteristics, nor are they all appropriate for the same purpose.

Go to the online course to take the quiz and exam.

Check Your Understanding - Network Components - 1.2.6

Network Representations and Topologies - 1.3

Refer to
Online Course
for Illustration

Network Representations - 1.3.1

Network architects and administrators must be able to show what their networks will look like. They need to be able to easily see which components connect to other components, where they will be located, and how they will be connected. Diagrams of networks often use symbols, like those shown in the figure, to represent the different devices and connections that make up a network.

A diagram provides an easy way to understand how devices connect in a large network. This type of "picture" of a network is known as a topology diagram. The ability to recognize the logical representations of the physical networking components is critical to being able to visualize the organization and operation of a network.

In addition to these representations, specialized terminology is used to describe how each of these devices and media connect to each other:

- **Network Interface Card (NIC)** - A NIC physically connects the end device to the network.

- **Physical Port** - A connector or outlet on a networking device where the media connects to an end device or another networking device.

- **Interface** - Specialized ports on a networking device that connect to individual networks. Because routers connect networks, the ports on a router are referred to as network interfaces.

Note: Often, the terms port and interface are used interchangeably.

Refer to
Online Course
for Illustration

Topology Diagrams - 1.3.2

Topology diagrams are mandatory documentation for anyone working with a network. They provide a visual map of how the network is connected. There are two types of topology diagrams, physical and logical.

Physical Topology Diagrams

Physical topology diagrams illustrate the physical location of intermediary devices and cable installation, as shown in the figure. You can see that the rooms in which these devices are located are labeled in this physical topology.

Logical Topology Diagrams

Logical topology diagrams illustrate devices, ports, and the addressing scheme of the network, as shown in the figure. You can see which end devices are connected to which intermediary devices and what media is being used.

The topologies shown in the physical and logical diagrams are appropriate for your level of understanding at this point in the course. Search the internet for "network topology diagrams" to see some more complex examples. If you add the word "Cisco" to your search phrase, you will find many topologies using icons that are similar to what you have seen in these figures.

Go to the online course to take the quiz and exam.

Check Your Understanding - Network Representations and Topologies - 1.3.3

Common Types of Networks - 1.4

Refer to
Interactive Graphic
in online course

Refer to
Online Course
for Illustration

Networks of Many Sizes - 1.4.1

Now that you are familiar with the components that make up networks and their representations in physical and logical topologies, you are ready to learn about the many different types of networks.

Networks come in all sizes. They range from simple networks consisting of two computers, to networks connecting millions of devices.

Simple home networks let you share resources, such as printers, documents, pictures, and music, among a few local end devices.

Small office and home office (SOHO) networks allow people to work from home, or a remote office. Many self-employed workers use these types of networks to advertise and sell products, order supplies, and communicate with customers.

Businesses and large organizations use networks to provide consolidation, storage, and access to information on network servers. Networks provide email, instant messaging, and collaboration among employees. Many organizations use their network's connection to the internet to provide products and services to customers.

The internet is the largest network in existence. In fact, the term internet means a "network of networks". It is a collection of interconnected private and public networks.

In small businesses and homes, many computers function as both the servers and clients on the network. This type of network is called a peer-to-peer network.

Click each button for more information.

Small Home Networks

Small home networks connect a few computers to each other and to the internet.

Small Office and Home Office Networks

The SOHO network allows computers in a home office or a remote office to connect to a corporate network, or access centralized, shared resources.

Medium to Large Networks

Medium to large networks, such as those used by corporations and schools, can have many locations with hundreds or thousands of interconnected hosts.

World Wide Networks

The internet is a network of networks that connects hundreds of millions of computers world-wide.

Refer to
Online Course
for Illustration

LANs and WANs - 1.4.2

Network infrastructures vary greatly in terms of:

- Size of the area covered
- Number of users connected
- Number and types of services available
- Area of responsibility

The two most common types of network infrastructures are Local Area Networks (LANs), and Wide Area Networks (WANs). A LAN is a network infrastructure that provides access to users and end devices in a small geographical area. A LAN is typically used in a department within an enterprise, a home, or a small business network. A WAN is a network infrastructure that provides access to other networks over a wide geographical area, which is typically owned and managed by a larger corporation or a telecommunications service provider. The figure shows LANs connected to a WAN.

LANs

A LAN is a network infrastructure that spans a small geographical area. LANs have specific characteristics:

- LANs interconnect end devices in a limited area such as a home, school, office building, or campus.

- A LAN is usually administered by a single organization or individual. Administrative control is enforced at the network level and governs the security and access control policies.

- LANs provide high-speed bandwidth to internal end devices and intermediary devices, as shown in the figure.

WANs

The figure shows a WAN which interconnects two LANs. A WAN is a network infrastructure that spans a wide geographical area. WANs are typically managed by service providers (SPs) or Internet Service Providers (ISPs).

WANs have specific characteristics:

- WANs interconnect LANs over wide geographical areas such as between cities, states, provinces, countries, or continents.

- WANs are usually administered by multiple service providers.

- WANs typically provide slower speed links between LANs.

Refer to
Online Course
for Illustration

The Internet - 1.4.3

The internet is a worldwide collection of interconnected networks (internetworks, or internet for short). The figure shows one way to view the internet as a collection of interconnected LANs and WANs.

Some of the LAN examples are connected to each other through a WAN connection. WANs are then connected to each other. The red WAN connection lines represent all the varieties of ways we connect networks. WANs can connect through copper wires, fiber-optic cables, and wireless transmissions (not shown).

The internet is not owned by any individual or group. Ensuring effective communication across this diverse infrastructure requires the application of consistent and commonly recognized technologies and standards as well as the cooperation of many network administration agencies. There are organizations that were developed to help maintain the structure and standardization of internet protocols and processes. These organizations include the Internet Engineering Task Force (IETF), Internet Corporation for Assigned Names and Numbers (ICANN), and the Internet Architecture Board (IAB), plus many others.

Refer to
Online Course
for Illustration

Intranets and Extranets - 1.4.4

There are two other terms which are similar to the term internet: intranet and extranet.

Intranet is a term often used to refer to a private connection of LANs and WANs that belongs to an organization. An intranet is designed to be accessible only by the organization's members, employees, or others with authorization.

An organization may use an extranet to provide secure and safe access to individuals who work for a different organization but require access to the organization's data. Here are some examples of extranets:

- A company that is providing access to outside suppliers and contractors

- A hospital that is providing a booking system to doctors so they can make appointments for their patients

- A local office of education that is providing budget and personnel information to the schools in its district

The figure illustrates the levels of access that different groups have to a company intranet, a company extranet, and the internet.

Go to the online
course to take the
quiz and exam.

Check Your Understanding - Common Types of Networks - 1.4.5

Internet Connections - 1.5

Internet Access Technologies - 1.5.1

So, now you have a basic understanding of what makes up a network and the different types of networks. But, how do you actually connect users and organizations to the internet? As you may have guessed, there are many different ways to do this.

Home users, remote workers, and small offices typically require a connection to an ISP to access the internet. Connection options vary greatly between ISPs and geographical locations. However, popular choices include broadband cable, broadband digital subscriber line (DSL), wireless WANs, and mobile services.

Organizations usually need access to other corporate sites as well as the internet. Fast connections are required to support business services including IP phones, video conferencing, and data center storage. SPs offer business-class interconnections. Popular business-class services include business DSL, leased lines, and Metro Ethernet.

Refer to
Online Course
for Illustration

Home and Small Office Internet Connections - 1.5.2

The figure illustrates common connection options for small office and home office users.

- **Cable** - Typically offered by cable television service providers, the internet data signal transmits on the same cable that delivers cable television. It provides a high bandwidth, high availability, and an always-on connection to the internet.

- **DSL** - Digital Subscriber Lines also provide high bandwidth, high availability, and an always-on connection to the internet. DSL runs over a telephone line. In general, small office and home office users connect using Asymmetrical DSL (ADSL), which means that the download speed is faster than the upload speed.

- **Cellular** - Cellular internet access uses a cell phone network to connect. Wherever you can get a cellular signal, you can get cellular internet access. Performance is limited by the capabilities of the phone and the cell tower to which it is connected.

- **Satellite** - The availability of satellite internet access is a benefit in those areas that would otherwise have no internet connectivity at all. Satellite dishes require a clear line of sight to the satellite.

- **Dial-up Telephone** - An inexpensive option that uses any phone line and a modem. The low bandwidth provided by a dial-up modem connection is not sufficient for large data transfer, although it is useful for mobile access while traveling.

The choice of connection varies depending on geographical location and service provider availability.

Refer to
Online Course
for Illustration

Businesses Internet Connections - 1.5.3

Corporate connection options differ from home user options. Businesses may require higher bandwidth, dedicated bandwidth, and managed services. Connection options that are available differ depending on the type of service providers located nearby.

The figure illustrates common connection options for businesses.

- **Dedicated Leased Line** - Leased lines are reserved circuits within the service provider's network that connect geographically separated offices for private voice and/ or data networking. The circuits are rented at a monthly or yearly rate.

- **Metro Ethernet** - This is sometimes known as Ethernet WAN. In this module, we will refer to it as Metro Ethernet. Metro ethernets extend LAN access technology into the WAN. Ethernet is a LAN technology you will learn about in a later module.

- **Business DSL** - Business DSL is available in various formats. A popular choice is Symmetric Digital Subscriber Line (SDSL) which is similar to the consumer version of DSL but provides uploads and downloads at the same high speeds.

- **Satellite** - Satellite service can provide a connection when a wired solution is not available.

The choice of connection varies depending on geographical location and service provider availability.

Refer to
Online Course
for Illustration

The Converging Network - 1.5.4

Traditional Separate Networks

Consider a school built thirty years ago. Back then, some classrooms were cabled for the data network, telephone network, and video network for televisions. These separate networks could not communicate with each other. Each network used different technologies to carry the communication signal. Each network had its own set of rules and standards to ensure successful communication. Multiple services ran on multiple networks.

Converged Networks

Today, the separate data, telephone, and video networks converge. Unlike dedicated networks, converged networks are capable of delivering data, voice, and video between many different types of devices over the same network infrastructure. This network infrastructure uses the same set of rules, agreements, and implementation standards. Converged data networks carry multiple services on one network.

Refer to **Video** in online course

Video - Download and Install Packet Tracer - 1.5.5

This video will show you how to download and install Packet Tracer. You will use Packet Tracer to simulate creating and testing networks on your computer. Packet Tracer is a fun, take-home, flexible software program that will give you the opportunity to use the network representations and theories that you have just learned to build network models and explore relatively complex LANs and WANs.

Students commonly use Packet Tracer to:

- Prepare for a certification exam.

- Practice what they learn in networking courses.

- Sharpen their skills for a job interview.

- Examine the impact of adding new technologies into existing network designs.

- Build their skills for jobs in the Internet of Things.

- Compete in Global Design Challenges (take a look at the 2017 PT 7 Design Challenge on Facebook).

Packet Tracer is an essential learning tool used in many Cisco Networking Academy courses.

To obtain and install your copy of Cisco Packet Tracer follow these steps:

Step 1. Log into your Cisco Networking Academy "I'm Learning" page.

Step 2. Select Resources.

Step 3. Select Download Packet Tracer.

Step 4. Select the version of Packet Tracer you require.

Step 5. Save the file to your computer.

Step 6. Launch the Packet Tracer install program.

Click Play in the video for a detailed walk-through of the Packet Tracer download and installation process.

Refer to **Video** in online course

Video - Getting Started in Cisco Packet Tracer - 1.5.6

Packet Tracer is a tool that allows you to simulate real networks. It provides three main menus:

- You can add devices and connect them via cables or wireless.

- You can select, delete, inspect, label, and group components within your network.

- You can manage your network by opening an existing/sample network, saving your current network, and modifying your user profile or preferences.

If you have used any program such as a word processor or spreadsheet, you are already familiar with the File menu commands located in the top menu bar. The Open, Save, Save As, and Exit commands work as they would for any program, but there are two commands that are special to Packet Tracer.

The Open Samples command will display a directory of prebuilt examples of features and configurations of various network and Internet of Things devices included within Packet Tracer.

The Exit and Logout command will remove the registration information for this copy of Packet Tracer and require the next user of this copy of Packet Tracer to do the login procedure again.

Click Play in the video to learn how to use the menus and how to create your first Packet Tracer network.

Refer to **Packet Tracer Activity** for this chapter

Packet Tracer - Network Representation - 1.5.7

In this activity, you will explore how Packet Tracer serves as a modeling tool for network representations.

Reliable Networks - 1.6

Network Architecture - 1.6.1

Have you ever been busy working online, only to have "the internet go down"? As you know by now, the internet did not go down, you just lost your connection to it. It is very frustrating. With so many people in the world relying on network access to work and learn, it is imperative that networks are reliable. In this context, reliability means more than your connection to the internet. This topic focuses on the four aspects of network reliability.

The role of the network has changed from a data-only network to a system that enables the connections of people, devices, and information in a media-rich, converged network environment. For networks to function efficiently and grow in this type of environment, the network must be built upon a standard network architecture.

Networks also support a wide range of applications and services. They must operate over many different types of cables and devices, which make up the physical infrastructure. The term network architecture, in this context, refers to the technologies that support the infrastructure and the programmed services and rules, or protocols, that move data across the network.

As networks evolve, we have learned that there are four basic characteristics that network architects must address to meet user expectations:

- Fault Tolerance
- Scalability
- Quality of Service (QoS)
- Security

Refer to
Online Course
for Illustration

Fault Tolerance - 1.6.2

A fault tolerant network is one that limits the number of affected devices during a failure. It is built to allow quick recovery when such a failure occurs. These networks depend on multiple paths between the source and destination of a message. If one path fails, the messages are instantly sent over a different link. Having multiple paths to a destination is known as redundancy.

Implementing a packet-switched network is one way that reliable networks provide redundancy. Packet switching splits traffic into packets that are routed over a shared network. A single message, such as an email or a video stream, is broken into multiple message blocks, called packets. Each packet has the necessary addressing information of the source and destination of the message. The routers within the network switch the packets based on the condition of the network at that moment. This means that all the packets in a single message could take very different paths to the same destination. In the figure, the user is unaware and unaffected by the router that is dynamically changing the route when a link fails.

Refer to
Online Course
for Illustration

Scalability - 1.6.3

A scalable network expands quickly to support new users and applications. It does this without degrading the performance of services that are being accessed by existing users. The figure shows how a new network is easily added to an existing network. These networks are scalable because the designers follow accepted standards and protocols. This lets software and hardware vendors focus on improving products and services without having to design a new set of rules for operating within the network.

Refer to
Online Course
for Illustration

Quality of Service - 1.6.4

Quality of Service (QoS) is an increasing requirement of networks today. New applications available to users over networks, such as voice and live video transmissions, create higher expectations for the quality of the delivered services. Have you ever tried to watch a video with constant breaks and pauses? As data, voice, and video content continue to converge onto the same network, QoS becomes a primary mechanism for managing congestion and ensuring reliable delivery of content to all users.

Congestion occurs when the demand for bandwidth exceeds the amount available. Network bandwidth is measured in the number of bits that can be transmitted in a single second, or bits per second (bps). When simultaneous communications are attempted across the network, the demand for network bandwidth can exceed its availability, creating network congestion.

When the volume of traffic is greater than what can be transported across the network, devices will hold the packets in memory until resources become available to transmit them. In the figure, one user is requesting a web page, and another is on a phone call. With a QoS policy in place, the router can manage the flow of data and voice traffic, giving priority to voice communications if the network experiences congestion.

Refer to **Online Course** for Illustration

Network Security - 1.6.5

The network infrastructure, services, and the data contained on network-attached devices are crucial personal and business assets. Network administrators must address two types of network security concerns: network infrastructure security and information security.

Securing the network infrastructure includes physically securing devices that provide network connectivity and preventing unauthorized access to the management software that resides on them, as shown in the figure.

Network administrators must also protect the information contained within the packets being transmitted over the network, and the information stored on network attached devices. In order to achieve the goals of network security, there are three primary requirements.

- **Confidentiality** - Data confidentiality means that only the intended and authorized recipients can access and read data.

- **Integrity** - Data integrity assures users that the information has not been altered in transmission, from origin to destination.

- **Availability** - Data availability assures users of timely and reliable access to data services for authorized users.

Go to the online course to take the quiz and exam.

Check Your Understanding - Reliable Networks - 1.6.6

Network Trends - 1.7

Recent Trends - 1.7.1

You know a lot about networks now, what they are made of, how they connect us, and what is needed to keep them reliable. But networks, like everything else, continue to change. There are a few trends in networking that you, as a NetAcad student, should know about.

As new technologies and end-user devices come to market, businesses and consumers must continue to adjust to this ever-changing environment. There are several networking trends that affect organizations and consumers:

- Bring Your Own Device (BYOD)

- Online collaboration

- Video communications

- Cloud Computing

Refer to
Online Course
for Illustration

Bring Your Own Device (BYOD) - 1.7.2

The concept of any device, for any content, in any manner, is a major global trend that requires significant changes to the way we use devices and safely connect them to networks. This is called Bring Your Own Device (BYOD).

BYOD enables end users the freedom to use personal tools to access information and communicate across a business or campus network. With the growth of consumer devices, and the related drop in cost, employees and students may have advanced computing and networking devices for personal use. These include laptops, notebooks, tablets, smart phones, and e-readers. These may be purchased by the company or school, purchased by the individual, or both.

BYOD means any device, with any ownership, used anywhere.

Refer to
Online Course
for Illustration

Online Collaboration - 1.7.3

Individuals want to connect to the network, not only for access to data applications, but also to collaborate with one another. Collaboration is defined as "the act of working with another or others on a joint project." Collaboration tools, like Cisco WebEx, shown in the figure, give employees, students, teachers, customers, and partners a way to instantly connect, interact, and achieve their objectives.

Collaboration is a critical and strategic priority that organizations are using to remain competitive. Collaboration is also a priority in education. Students need to collaborate to assist each other in learning, to develop the team skills used in the workforce, and to work together on team-based projects.

Cisco Webex Teams is a multifunctional collaboration tool that lets you send instant messages to one or more people, post images, and post videos and links. Each team 'space' maintains a history of everything that is posted there.

Video Communications - 1.7.4

Another facet of networking that is critical to the communication and collaboration effort is video. Video is used for communications, collaboration, and entertainment. Video calls are made to and from anyone with an internet connection, regardless of where they are located.

Video conferencing is a powerful tool for communicating with others, both locally and globally. Video is becoming a critical requirement for effective collaboration as organizations extend across geographic and cultural boundaries.

Refer to **Video**
in online course

Video - Cisco Webex for Huddles - 1.7.5

Click Play in the figure to view how Cisco Webex is incorporated into everyday life and business.

Cloud Computing - 1.7.6

Cloud computing is one of the ways that we access and store data. Cloud computing allows us to store personal files, even backup an entire drive on servers over the internet. Applications such as word processing and photo editing can be accessed using the cloud.

For businesses, Cloud computing extends the capabilities of IT without requiring investment in new infrastructure, training new personnel, or licensing new software. These services are available on-demand and delivered economically to any device that is anywhere in the world without compromising security or function.

Cloud computing is possible because of data centers. Data centers are facilities used to house computer systems and associated components. A data center can occupy one room of a building, one or more floors, or an entire warehouse-sized building. Data centers are typically very expensive to build and maintain. For this reason, only large organizations use privately built data centers to house their data and provide services to users. Smaller organizations that cannot afford to maintain their own private data center can reduce the overall cost of ownership by leasing server and storage services from a larger data center organization in the cloud.

For security, reliability, and fault tolerance, cloud providers often store data in distributed data centers. Instead of storing all the data of a person or an organization in one data center, it is stored in multiple data centers in different locations.

There are four primary types of clouds: Public clouds, Private clouds, Hybrid clouds, and Community clouds, as shown in the table.

Cloud Types

Cloud Type	Description
Public clouds	Cloud-based applications and services offered in a public cloud are made available to the general population. Services may be free or are offered on a pay-per-use model, such as paying for online storage. The public cloud uses the internet to provide services.
Private clouds	Cloud-based applications and services offered in a private cloud are intended for a specific organization or entity, such as a government. A private cloud can be set up using the organization's private network, though this can be expensive to build and maintain. A private cloud can also be managed by an outside organization with strict access security.
Hybrid clouds	A hybrid cloud is made up of two or more clouds (example: part private, part public), where each part remains a distinct object, but both are connected using a single architecture. Individuals on a hybrid cloud would be able to have degrees of access to various services based on user access rights.
Community clouds	A community cloud is created for exclusive use by specific entities or organizations. The differences between public clouds and community clouds are the functional needs that have been customized for the community. For example, healthcare organizations must remain compliant with policies and laws (e.g., HIPAA) that require special authentication and confidentiality. Community clouds are used by multiple organizations that have similar needs and concerns. Community clouds are similar to a public cloud environment, but with set levels of security, privacy, and even regulatory compliance of a private cloud.

Technology Trends in the Home - 1.7.7

Refer to Online Course for Illustration

Networking trends are not only affecting the way we communicate at work and at school, but also changing many aspects of the home. The newest home trends include 'smart home technology'.

Smart home technology integrates into every-day appliances, which can then connect with other devices to make the appliances more 'smart' or automated. For example, you could prepare food and place it in the oven for cooking prior to leaving the house for the day. You program your smart oven for the food you want it to cook. It would also be connected to your 'calendar of events' so that it could determine what time you should be available to eat and adjust start times and length of cooking accordingly. It could even adjust cooking times and temperatures based on changes in schedule. Additionally, a smart phone or tablet connection lets you connect to the oven directly, to make any desired adjustments. When the food is ready, the oven sends an alert message to you (or someone you specify) that the food is done and warming.

Smart home technology is currently being developed for all rooms within a house. Smart home technology will become more common as home networking and high-speed internet technology expands.

Refer to
Online Course
for Illustration

Powerline Networking - 1.7.8

Powerline networking for home networks uses existing electrical wiring to connect devices, as shown in the figure.

Using a standard powerline adapter, devices can connect to the LAN wherever there is an electrical outlet. No data cables need to be installed, and there is little to no additional electricity used. Using the same wiring that delivers electricity, powerline networking sends information by sending data on certain frequencies.

Powerline networking is especially useful when wireless access points cannot reach all the devices in the home. Powerline networking is not a substitute for dedicated cabling in data networks. However, it is an alternative when data network cables or wireless communications are not possible or effective.

Refer to
Online Course
for Illustration

Wireless Broadband - 1.7.9

In many areas where cable and DSL are not available, wireless may be used to connect to the internet.

Wireless Internet Service Provider

A Wireless Internet Service Provider (WISP) is an ISP that connects subscribers to a designated access point or hot spot using similar wireless technologies found in home wireless local area networks (WLANs). WISPs are more commonly found in rural environments where DSL or cable services are not available.

Although a separate transmission tower may be installed for the antenna, typically the antenna is attached to an existing elevated structure, such as a water tower or a radio tower. A small dish or antenna is installed on the subscriber's roof in range of the WISP transmitter. The subscriber's access unit is connected to the wired network inside the home. From the perspective of the home user, the setup is not much different than DSL or cable service. The main difference is that the connection from the home to the ISP is wireless instead of a physical cable.

Wireless Broadband Service

Another wireless solution for the home and small businesses is wireless broadband, as shown in the figure.

This solution uses the same cellular technology as a smart phone. An antenna is installed outside the house providing either wireless or wired connectivity for devices in the home. In many areas, home wireless broadband is competing directly with DSL and cable services.

Go to the online course to take the quiz and exam.

Check Your Understanding - Network Trends - 1.7.10

Network Security - 1.8

Refer to **Online Course** for Illustration

Security Threats - 1.8.1

You have, no doubt, heard or read news stories about a company network being breached, giving threat actors access to the personal information of thousands of customers. For this reason, network security is always going to be a top priority of administrators.

Network security is an integral part of computer networking, regardless of whether the network is in a home with a single connection to the internet or is a corporation with thousands of users. Network security must consider the environment, as well as the tools and requirements of the network. It must be able to secure data while still allowing for the quality of service that users expect of the network.

Securing a network involves protocols, technologies, devices, tools, and techniques in order to protect data and mitigate threats. Threat vectors may be external or internal. Many external network security threats today originate from the internet.

There are several common external threats to networks:

- **Viruses, worms, and Trojan horses** - These contain malicious software or code running on a user device.

- **Spyware and adware** - These are types of software which are installed on a user's device. The software then secretly collects information about the user.

- **Zero-day attacks** - Also called zero-hour attacks, these occur on the first day that a vulnerability becomes known.

- **Threat actor attacks** - A malicious person attacks user devices or network resources.

- **Denial of service attacks** - These attacks slow or crash applications and processes on a network device.

- **Data interception and theft** - This attack captures private information from an organization's network.

- **Identity theft** - This attack steals the login credentials of a user in order to access private data.

It is equally important to consider internal threats. There have been many studies that show that the most common data breaches happen because of internal users of the network.

This can be attributed to lost or stolen devices, accidental misuse by employees, and in the business environment, even malicious employees. With the evolving BYOD strategies, corporate data is much more vulnerable. Therefore, when developing a security policy, it is important to address both external and internal security threats, as shown in the figure.

Refer to **Online Course** for Illustration

Security Solutions - 1.8.2

No single solution can protect the network from the variety of threats that exist. For this reason, security should be implemented in multiple layers, using more than one security solution. If one security component fails to identify and protect the network, others may succeed.

A home network security implementation is usually rather basic. Typically, you implement it on the end devices, as well as at the point of connection to the internet, and can even rely on contracted services from the ISP.

These are the basic security components for a home or small office network:

- **Antivirus and antispyware** - These applications help to protect end devices from becoming infected with malicious software.

- **Firewall filtering** - Firewall filtering blocks unauthorized access into and out of the network. This may include a host-based firewall system that prevents unauthorized access to the end device, or a basic filtering service on the home router to prevent unauthorized access from the outside world into the network.

In contrast, the network security implementation for a corporate network usually consists of many components built into the network to monitor and filter traffic. Ideally, all components work together, which minimizes maintenance and improves security. Larger networks and corporate networks use antivirus, antispyware, and firewall filtering, but they also have other security requirements:

- **Dedicated firewall systems** - These provide more advanced firewall capabilities that can filter large amounts of traffic with more granularity.

- **Access control lists (ACL)** - These further filter access and traffic forwarding based on IP addresses and applications.

- **Intrusion prevention systems (IPS)** - These identify fast-spreading threats, such as zero-day or zero-hour attacks.

- **Virtual private networks (VPN)** - These provide secure access into an organization for remote workers.

Network security requirements must consider the environment, as well as the various applications, and computing requirements. Both home and business environments must be able to secure their data while still allowing for the quality of service that users expect of each technology. Additionally, the security solution implemented must be adaptable to the growing and changing trends of the network.

The study of network security threats and mitigation techniques starts with a clear understanding of the underlying switching and routing infrastructure used to organize network services.

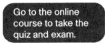
Go to the online course to take the quiz and exam.

Check Your Understanding - Network Security - 1.8.3

The IT Professional - 1.9

CCNA - 1.9.1

As a NetAcad student, you may already have a career in IT, or are still educating yourself to prepare for your career. In either case, it is good to know about the skills needed to match the types of jobs that are available in IT.

The role and skills required of network engineers are evolving and are more vital than ever. The Cisco Certified Network Associate (CCNA) certification demonstrates that you have a knowledge of foundational technologies and ensures you stay relevant with skill sets needed for the adoption of next-generation technologies.

A consolidated and updated CCNA for networking engineers is three courses and one exam which covers the fundamental topics for all network technologies. The new CCNA focuses on IP foundation and security topics along with wireless, virtualization, automation, and network programmability.

There are new DevNet certifications at the associate, specialist and professional levels, to validate your software development skills.

There are specialist certification options to validate your skills in line with your job role and interests. This includes the Cisco Enterprise Advanced Infrastructure Specialist certification.

You can start where you want. There are no prerequisites to start earning your associate, specialist, professional, or expert level certification. Continuing education credits for recertification and ongoing development are now available for CCNA.

Networking Jobs - 1.9.2

Your CCNA certification will prepare you for a variety of jobs in today's market. At www.netacad.com you can click the Careers menu and then select Employment opportunities. You can find employment opportunities where you live by using the new program, the Talent Bridge Matching Engine. Search for jobs with Cisco, as well as Cisco partners and distributors seeking Cisco Networking Academy students and alumni.

You can also search for IT jobs using online search engines such as Indeed, Glassdoor, and Monster. Use search terms such as IT, network administrator, network architects, and computer systems administrator. You can also search using the term Cisco CCNA.

Refer to Lab Activity for this chapter

Lab - Research IT and Networking Job Opportunities - 1.9.3

In this lab, you will complete the following objectives:

- Part 1: Research Job Opportunities
- Part 2: Reflect on Research

Module Practice and Quiz - 1.10

What did I learn in this module? - 1.10.1

Networks Affect our Lives

In today's world, through the use of networks, we are connected like never before. People with ideas can communicate instantly with others to make those ideas a reality. The creation of online communities for the exchange of ideas and information has the potential to increase productivity opportunities across the globe. The creation of the cloud lets us store documents and pictures and access them anywhere, anytime.

Network Components

All computers that are connected to a network and participate directly in network communication are classified as hosts. Hosts can be called end devices. Some hosts are also called clients. Many computers function as the servers and clients on the network. This type of network is called a peer-to-peer network. An end device is either the source or destination of a message transmitted over the network. Intermediary devices connect the individual end devices to the network and can connect multiple individual networks to form an internetwork. Intermediary devices use the destination end device address, in conjunction with information about the network interconnections, to determine the path that messages should take through the network. The media provides the channel over which the message travels from source to destination.

Network Representations and Topologies

Diagrams of networks often use symbols to represent the different devices and connections that make up a network. A diagram provides an easy way to understand how devices connect in a large network. This type of "picture" of a network is known as a topology diagram. Physical topology diagrams illustrate the physical location of intermediary devices and cable installation. Logical topology diagrams illustrate devices, ports, and the addressing scheme of the network.

Common Types of Networks

Small home networks connect a few computers to each other and to the internet. The small office/home office (SOHO) network allows computers in a home office or a remote office to connect to a corporate network, or access centralized, shared resources. Medium to large networks, such as those used by corporations and schools, can have many locations with hundreds or thousands of interconnected hosts. The internet is a network of networks that connects hundreds of millions of computers world-wide. The two most common types of network infrastructures are Local Area Networks (LANs), and Wide Area Networks (WANs). A LAN is a network infrastructure that spans a small geographical area. A WAN is a network infrastructure that spans a wide geographical area. Intranet refers to a private connection of LANs and WANs that belongs to an organization. An organization may use an extranet to provide secure and safe access to individuals who work for a different organization but require access to the organization's data.

Internet Connections

SOHO internet connections include cable, DSL, Cellular, Satellite, and Dial-up telephone. Business internet connections include Dedicated Leased Line, Metro Ethernet, Business DSL, and Satellite. The choice of connection varies depending on geographical location and service provider availability. Traditional separate networks used different technologies, rules, and standards. Converged networks deliver data, voice, and video between many different types of devices over the same network infrastructure. This network infrastructure uses the same set of rules, agreements, and implementation standards. Packet Tracer is a flexible software program that lets you use network representations and theories to build network models and explore relatively complex LANs and WANs.

Reliable Networks

The term network architecture refers to the technologies that support the infrastructure and the programmed services and rules, or protocols, that move data across the network. As networks evolve, we have learned that there are four basic characteristics that network architects must address to meet user expectations: Fault Tolerance, Scalability, Quality of Service (QoS), and Security. A fault tolerant network is one that limits the number of affected devices during a failure. Having multiple paths to a destination is known as redundancy. A scalable network expands quickly to support new users and applications. Networks are scalable because the designers follow accepted standards and protocols. QoS is a primary mechanism for managing congestion and ensuring reliable delivery of content to all users. Network administrators must address two types of network security concerns: network infrastructure security and information security. To achieve the goals of network security, there are three primary requirements: Confidentiality, Integrity, and Availability.

Network Trends

There are several recent networking trends that affect organizations and consumers: Bring Your Own Device (BYOD), online collaboration, video communications, and cloud computing. BYOD means any device, with any ownership, used anywhere. Collaboration tools, like Cisco WebEx give employees, students, teachers, customers, and partners a way to instantly connect, interact, and achieve their objectives. Video is used for communications, collaboration, and entertainment. Video calls are made to and from anyone with an internet connection, regardless of where they are located. Cloud computing allows us to store personal files, even backup an entire drive on servers over the internet. Applications such as word processing and photo editing can be accessed using the cloud. There are four primary types of Clouds: Public Clouds, Private Clouds, Hybrid Clouds, and Custom Clouds. Smart home technology is currently being developed for all rooms within a house. Smart home technology will become more common as home networking and high-speed internet technology expands. Using the same wiring that delivers electricity, powerline networking sends information by sending data on certain frequencies. A Wireless Internet Service Provider (WISP) is an ISP that connects subscribers to a designated access point or hot spot using similar wireless technologies found in home wireless local area networks (WLANs).

Network Security

There are several common external threats to networks:

- Viruses, worms, and Trojan horses

- Spyware and adware

- Zero-day attacks
- Threat Actor attacks
- Denial of service attacks
- Data interception and theft
- Identity theft

These are the basic security components for a home or small office network:

- Antivirus and antispyware
- Firewall filtering

Larger networks and corporate networks use antivirus, antispyware, and firewall filtering, but they also have other security requirements:

- Dedicated firewall systems
- Access control lists (ACL)
- Intrusion prevention systems (IPS)
- Virtual private networks (VPN)

The IT Professional

The Cisco Certified Network Associate (CCNA) certification demonstrates that you have a knowledge of foundational technologies and ensures you stay relevant with skill sets needed for the adoption of next-generation technologies. Your CCNA certification will prepare you for a variety of jobs in today's market. At www.netacad.com you can click the Careers menu and then select Employment opportunities. You can find employment opportunities where you live by using the Talent Bridge Matching Engine. Search for jobs with Cisco as well as Cisco partners and distributors seeking Cisco Networking Academy students and alumni.

Go to the online
course to take the
quiz and exam.

Chapter Quiz - Networking Today

Your Chapter Notes

CHAPTER 2

Basic Switch and End Device Configuration

Introduction - 2.0

Why should I take this module? - 2.0.1

Welcome to Basic Switch and End Device Configuration!

As part of your career in networking, you might have to set up a new network or maintain and upgrade an existing one. In either case, you'll configure switches and end devices so that they are secure and perform effectively based on your requirements.

Out of the box, switches and end devices come with some general configuration. But for your particular network, switches and end devices require your specific information and instructions. In this module, you will learn how to access Cisco IOS network devices. You will learn basic configuration commands and use them to configure and verify a Cisco IOS device and an end device with an IP address.

Of course, there is much more to network administration, but none of that can happen without first configuring switches and end devices. Let's get started!

What will I learn to do in this module? - 2.0.2

Module Title: Basic Switch and End Device Configuration

Module Objective: Implement initial settings including passwords, IP addressing, and default gateway parameters on a network switch and end devices.

Topic Title	Topic Objective
Cisco IOS Access	Explain how to access a Cisco IOS device for configuration purposes.
IOS Navigation	Explain how to navigate Cisco IOS to configure network devices.
The Command Structure	Describe the command structure of Cisco IOS software.
Basic Device Configuration	Configure a Cisco IOS device using CLI.
Save Configurations	Use IOS commands to save the running configuration.
Ports and Addresses	Explain how devices communicate across network media.
Configure IP Addressing	Configure a host device with an IP address.
Verify Connectivity	Verify connectivity between two end devices.

Cisco IOS Access - 2.1

Operating Systems - 2.1.1

Refer to
Online Course
for Illustration

All end devices and network devices require an operating system (OS). As shown in the figure, the portion of the OS that interacts directly with computer hardware is known as the kernel.

The portion that interfaces with applications and the user is known as the shell. The user can interact with the shell using a command-line interface (CLI) or a graphical user interface (GUI).

When using a CLI, the user interacts directly with the system in a text-based environment by entering commands on the keyboard at a command prompt, as shown in the example. The system executes the command, often providing textual output. The CLI requires very little overhead to operate. However, it does require that the user have knowledge of the underlying command structure that controls the system.

```
analyst@secOps ~]$ ls

Desktop   Downloads   lab.support.files   second_drive

[analyst@secOps ~]$
```

Refer to
Online Course
for Illustration

GUI - 2.1.2

A GUI such as Windows, macOS, Linux KDE, Apple iOS, or Android allows the user to interact with the system using an environment of graphical icons, menus, and windows. The GUI example in the figure is more user-friendly and requires less knowledge of the underlying command structure that controls the system. For this reason, most users rely on GUI environments.

However, GUIs may not always be able to provide all the features available with the CLI. GUIs can also fail, crash, or simply not operate as specified. For these reasons, network devices are typically accessed through a CLI. The CLI is less resource intensive and very stable when compared to a GUI.

The family of network operating systems used on many Cisco devices is called the Cisco Internetwork Operating System (IOS). Cisco IOS is used on many Cisco routers and switches regardless of the type or size of the device. Each device router or switch type uses a different version of Cisco IOS. Other Cisco operating systems include IOS XE, IOS XR, and NX-OS.

Note: The operating system on home routers is usually called *firmware*. The most common method for configuring a home router is by using a web browser-based GUI.

Refer to
Online Course
for Illustration

Purpose of an OS - 2.1.3

Network operating systems are similar to a PC operating system. Through a GUI, a PC operating system enables a user to do the following:

- Use a mouse to make selections and run programs
- Enter text and text-based commands
- View output on a monitor

A CLI-based network operating system (e.g., the Cisco IOS on a switch or router) enables a network technician to do the following:

- Use a keyboard to run CLI-based network programs
- Use a keyboard to enter text and text-based commands
- View output on a monitor

Cisco networking devices run particular versions of the Cisco IOS. The IOS version is dependent on the type of device being used and the required features. While all devices come with a default IOS and feature set, it is possible to upgrade the IOS version or feature set to obtain additional capabilities.

The figure displays a list of IOS software releases for a Cisco Catalyst 2960 Switch.

Access Methods - 2.1.4

A switch will forward traffic by default and does not need to be explicitly configured to operate. For example, two configured hosts connected to the same new switch would be able to communicate.

Regardless of the default behavior of a new switch, all switches should be configured and secured.

Method	Description
Console	This is a physical management port that provides out-of-band access to a Cisco device. Out-of-band access refers to access via a dedicated management channel that is used for device maintenance purposes only. The advantage of using a console port is that the device is accessible even if no networking services are configured, such as performing the initial configuration. A computer running terminal emulation software and a special console cable to connect to the device are required for a console connection.
Secure Shell (SSH)	SSH is an in-band and recommended method for remotely establishing a secure CLI connection, through a virtual interface, over a network. Unlike a console connection, SSH connections require active networking services on the device, including an active interface configured with an address. Most versions of Cisco IOS include an SSH server and an SSH client that can be used to establish SSH sessions with other devices.
Telnet	Telnet is an insecure, in-band method of remotely establishing a CLI session, through a virtual interface, over a network. Unlike SSH, Telnet does not provide a secure, encrypted connection and should only be used in a lab environment. User authentication, passwords, and commands are sent over the network in plaintext. The best practice is to use SSH instead of Telnet. Cisco IOS includes both a Telnet server and Telnet client.

Note: Some devices, such as routers, may also support a legacy auxiliary port that was used to establish a CLI session remotely over a telephone connection using a modem. Similar to a console connection, the AUX port is out-of-band and does not require networking services to be configured or available.

Refer to
Interactive Graphic
in online course

Refer to
Online Course
for Illustration

Terminal Emulation Programs - 2.1.5

There are several terminal emulation programs you can use to connect to a networking device either by a serial connection over a console port, or by an SSH/Telnet connection. These programs allow you to enhance your productivity by adjusting window sizes, changing font sizes, and changing color schemes.

Click each program name to see a screen capture of the interface.

PuTTY

Tera Term

SecureCRT

Go to the online course to take the quiz and exam.

Check Your Understanding - Cisco IOS Access - 2.1.6

IOS Navigation - 2.2

Primary Command Modes - 2.2.1

In the previous topic, you learned that all network devices require an OS and that they can be configured using the CLI or a GUI. Using the CLI may provide the network administrator with more precise control and flexibility than using the GUI. This topic discusses using CLI to navigate the Cisco IOS.

As a security feature, the Cisco IOS software separates management access into the following two command modes:

- **User EXEC Mode** - This mode has limited capabilities but is useful for basic operations. It allows only a limited number of basic monitoring commands but does not allow the execution of any commands that might change the configuration of the device. The user EXEC mode is identified by the CLI prompt that ends with the > symbol.

- **Privileged EXEC Mode** - To execute configuration commands, a network administrator must access privileged EXEC mode. Higher configuration modes, like global configuration mode, can only be reached from privileged EXEC mode. The privileged EXEC mode can be identified by the prompt ending with the # symbol.

The table summarizes the two modes and displays the default CLI prompts of a Cisco switch and router.

Command Mode	Description	Default Device Prompt
User Exec Mode	• Mode allows access to only a limited number of basic monitoring commands. • It is often referred to as "view-only" mode.	Switch> Router>
Privileged EXEC Mode	• Mode allows access to all commands and features. • The user can use any monitoring commands and execute configuration and management commands.	Switch# Router#

Configuration Mode and Subconfiguration Modes - 2.2.2

To configure the device, the user must enter global configuration mode, which is commonly called global config mode.

From global config mode, CLI configuration changes are made that affect the operation of the device as a whole. Global configuration mode is identified by a prompt that ends with (config)# after the device name, such as **Switch(config)#**.

Global configuration mode is accessed before other specific configuration modes. From global config mode, the user can enter different subconfiguration modes. Each of these modes allows the configuration of a particular part or function of the IOS device. Two common subconfiguration modes include:

- **Line Configuration Mode** - Used to configure console, SSH, Telnet, or AUX access.

- **Interface Configuration Mode** - Used to configure a switch port or router network interface.

When the CLI is used, the mode is identified by the command-line prompt that is unique to that mode. By default, every prompt begins with the device name. Following the name, the remainder of the prompt indicates the mode. For example, the default prompt for line configuration mode is **Switch(config-line)#** and the default prompt for interface configuration mode is **Switch(config-if)#**.

Refer to **Video** in online course

Video - IOS CLI Primary Command Modes - 2.2.3

Click Play in the figure to view a video demonstration of navigating between IOS modes.

Navigate Between IOS Modes - 2.2.4

Various commands are used to move in and out of command prompts. To move from user EXEC mode to privileged EXEC mode, use the **enable** command. Use the **disable** privileged EXEC mode command to return to user EXEC mode.

Note: Privileged EXEC mode is sometimes called *enable mode*.

To move in and out of global configuration mode, use the **configure terminal** privileged EXEC mode command. To return to the privileged EXEC mode, enter the **exit** global config mode command.

There are many different subconfiguration modes. For example, to enter line subconfiguration mode, you use the **line** command followed by the management line type and number you wish to access. Use the **exit** command to exit a subconfiguration mode and return to global configuration mode.

```
Switch(config)# line console 0
Switch(config-line)# exit
Switch(config)#
```

To move from any subconfiguration mode of the global configuration mode to the mode one step above it in the hierarchy of modes, enter the **exit** command.

To move from any subconfiguration mode to the privileged EXEC mode, enter the **end** command or enter the key combination **Ctrl+Z**.

```
Switch(config-line)# end
Switch#
```

You can also move directly from one subconfiguration mode to another. Notice how after selecting an interface, the command prompt changes from **(config-line)#** to **(config-if)#**.

```
Switch(config-line)# interface FastEthernet 0/1
Switch(config-if)#
```

Refer to **Video** in online course

Video - Navigate Between IOS Modes - 2.2.5

Click Play in the figure to view a video demonstration of how to move between various IOS CLI modes.

A Note About Syntax Checker Activities - 2.2.6

When you are learning how to modify device configurations, you might want to start in a safe, non-production environment before trying it on real equipment. NetAcad gives you different simulation tools to help build your configuration and troubleshooting skills. Because these are simulation tools, they typically do not have all the functionality of real equipment. One such tool is the Syntax Checker. In each Syntax Checker, you are given a set of instructions to enter a specific set of commands. You cannot progress in Syntax Checker unless the exact and full command is entered as specified. More advanced simulation tools, such as Packet Tracer, let you enter abbreviated commands, much as you would do on real equipment.

Refer to **Interactive Graphic** in online course

Syntax Checker - Navigate Between IOS Modes - 2.2.7

Use the Syntax Checker activity to navigate between IOS command lines on a switch.

Go to the online course to take the quiz and exam.

Check Your Understanding - IOS Navigation - 2.2.8

The Command Structure - 2.3

Refer to **Online Course** for Illustration

Basic IOS Command Structure - 2.3.1

This topic covers the basic structure of commands for the Cisco IOS. A network administrator must know the basic IOS command structure to be able to use the CLI for device configuration.

A Cisco IOS device supports many commands. Each IOS command has a specific format, or syntax, and can only be executed in the appropriate mode. The general syntax for a command, shown in the figure, is the command followed by any appropriate keywords and arguments.

- **Keyword** - This is a specific parameter defined in the operating system (in the figure, **ip protocols**).

- **Argument** - This is not predefined; it is a value or variable defined by the user (in the figure, **192.168.10.5**).

After entering each complete command, including any keywords and arguments, press the **Enter** key to submit the command to the command interpreter.

IOS Command Syntax Check - 2.3.2

A command might require one or more arguments. To determine the keywords and arguments required for a command, refer to the command syntax. The syntax provides the pattern, or format, that must be used when entering a command.

As identified in the table, boldface text indicates commands and keywords that are entered as shown. Italic text indicates an argument for which the user provides the value.

Convention	Description
boldface	Boldface text indicates commands and keywords that you enter literally as shown.
italics	Italic text indicates arguments for which you supply values.
[x]	Square brackets indicate an optional element (keyword or argument).
{x}	Braces indicate a required element (keyword or argument).
[x {y | z }]	Braces and vertical lines within square brackets indicate a required choice within an optional element. Spaces are used to clearly delineate parts of the command.

For instance, the syntax for using the **description** command is **description** *string*. The argument is a *string* value provided by the user. The **description** command is typically used to identify the purpose of an interface. For example, entering the command, **description Connects to the main headquarter office switch**, describes where the other device is at the end of the connection.

The following examples demonstrate conventions used to document and use IOS commands:

- **ping** *ip-address* - The command is **ping** and the user-defined argument is the *ip-address* of the destination device. For example, **ping 10.10.10.5**.

- **traceroute** *ip-address* - The command is **traceroute** and the user-defined argument is the *ip-address* of the destination device. For example, **traceroute 192.168.254.254**.

If a command is complex with multiple arguments, you may see it represented like this:

```
Switch(config-if)# switchport port-security aging { static | time time |
type {absolute | inactivity}}
```

The command will typically be followed we a detailed description of the command and each argument.

The Cisco IOS Command Reference is the ultimate source of information for a particular IOS command.

IOS Help Features - 2.3.3

The IOS has two forms of help available: context-sensitive help and command syntax check.

Context-sensitive help enables you to quickly find answers to these questions:

- Which commands are available in each command mode?

- Which commands start with specific characters or group of characters?

- Which arguments and keywords are available to particular commands?

To access context-sensitive help, simply enter a question mark, ?, at the CLI.

Command syntax check verifies that a valid command was entered by the user. When a command is entered, the command line interpreter evaluates the command from left to right. If the interpreter understands the command, the requested action is executed, and the CLI returns to the appropriate prompt. However, if the interpreter cannot understand the command being entered, it will provide feedback describing what is wrong with the command.

Video - Context Sensitive Help and Command Syntax Check - 2.3.4

Refer to **Video** in online course

Click Play in the figure to view a video demonstration of context-sensitive help and command syntax check.

Hot Keys and Shortcuts - 2.3.5

The IOS CLI provides hot keys and shortcuts that make configuring, monitoring, and troubleshooting easier.

Commands and keywords can be shortened to the minimum number of characters that identify a unique selection. For example, the **configure** command can be shortened to **conf** because **configure** is the only command that begins with **conf**. An even shorter version, **con**, will not work because more than one command begins with **con**. Keywords can also be shortened.

The table lists keystrokes to enhance command line editing.

Keystroke	Description
Tab	Completes a partial command name entry.
Backspace	Erases the character to the left of the cursor.
Ctrl+D	Erases the character at the cursor.
Ctrl+K	Erases all characters from the cursor to the end of the command line.
Esc D	Erases all characters from the cursor to the end of the word.
Ctrl+U or Ctrl+X	Erases all characters from the cursor back to the beginning of the command line.
Ctrl+W	Erases the word to the left of the cursor.
Ctrl+A	Moves the cursor to the beginning of the line.
Left Arrow or Ctrl+B	Moves the cursor one character to the left.
Esc B	Moves the cursor back one word to the left.
Esc F	Moves the cursor forward one word to the right.
Right Arrow or Ctrl+F	Moves the cursor one character to the right.
Ctrl+E	Moves the cursor to the end of command line.
Up Arrow or Ctrl+P	Recalls the commands in the history buffer, beginning with the most recent commands.
Ctrl+R or Ctrl+I or Ctrl+L	Redisplays the system prompt and command line after a console message is received.

Note: While the **Delete** key typically deletes the character to the right of the prompt, the IOS command structure does not recognize the Delete key.

When a command output produces more text than can be displayed in a terminal window, the IOS will display a "**--More--**" prompt. The following table describes the keystrokes that can be used when this prompt is displayed.

Keystroke	Description
Enter Key	Displays the next line.
Space Bar	Displays the next screen.
Any other key	Ends the display string, returning to privileged EXEC mode.

This table lists commands used to exit out of an operation.

Keystroke	Description
Ctrl-C	When in any configuration mode, ends the configuration mode and returns to privileged EXEC mode. When in setup mode, aborts back to the command prompt.
Ctrl-Z	When in any configuration mode, ends the configuration mode and returns to privileged EXEC mode.
Ctrl-Shift-6	All-purpose break sequence used to abort DNS lookups, traceroutes, pings, etc.

Video - Hot Keys and Shortcuts - 2.3.6

Click Play in the figure to view a video demonstration of the various hotkeys and shortcuts.

Packet Tracer - Navigate the IOS - 2.3.7

In this activity, you will practice skills necessary for navigating the Cisco IOS, including different user access modes, various configuration modes, and common commands used on a regular basis. You will also practice accessing the context-sensitive help by configuring the clock command.

Lab - Navigate the IOS by Using Tera Term for Console Connectivity - 2.3.8

In this lab, you will complete the following objectives:

- Part 1: Access a Cisco Switch through the Serial Console Port
- Part 2: Display and Configure Basic Device Settings
- Part 3: (Optional) Access a Cisco Router Using a Mini-USB Console Cable

Basic Device Configuration - 2.4

Refer to
Online Course
for Illustration

Device Names - 2.4.1

You have learned a great deal about the Cisco IOS, navigating the IOS, and the command structure. Now, you are ready to configure devices! The first configuration command on any device should be to give it a unique device name or hostname. By default, all devices are assigned a factory default name. For example, a Cisco IOS switch is "Switch."

The problem is if all switches in a network were left with their default names, it would be difficult to identify a specific device. For instance, how would you know that you are connected to the right device when accessing it remotely using SSH? The hostname provides confirmation that you are connected to the correct device.

The default name should be changed to something more descriptive. By choosing names wisely, it is easier to remember, document, and identify network devices. Here are some important naming guidelines for hosts:

- Start with a letter
- Contain no spaces
- End with a letter or digit
- Use only letters, digits, and dashes
- Be less than 64 characters in length

An organization must choose a naming convention that makes it easy and intuitive to identify a specific device. The hostnames used in the device IOS preserve capitalization and lowercase characters. For example, the figure shows that three switches, spanning three different floors, are interconnected together in a network. The naming convention that was used incorporated the location and the purpose of each device. Network documentation should explain how these names were chosen so additional devices can be named accordingly.

When the naming convention has been identified, the next step is to use the CLI to apply the names to the devices. As shown in the example, from the privileged EXEC mode, access the global configuration mode by entering the **configure terminal** command. Notice the change in the command prompt.

```
Switch# configure terminal

Switch(config)# hostname Sw-Floor-1
Sw-Floor-1(config)#
```

From global configuration mode, enter the command **hostname** followed by the name of the switch and press **Enter**. Notice the change in the command prompt name.

Note: To return the switch to the default prompt, use the **no hostname** global config command.

Always make sure the documentation is updated each time a device is added or modified. Identify devices in the documentation by their location, purpose, and address.

Password Guidelines - 2.4.2

The use of weak or easily guessed passwords continues to be the biggest security concern of organizations. Network devices, including home wireless routers, should always have passwords configured to limit administrative access.

Cisco IOS can be configured to use hierarchical mode passwords to allow different access privileges to a network device.

All networking devices should limit administrative access by securing privileged EXEC, user EXEC, and remote Telnet access with passwords. In addition, all passwords should be encrypted and legal notifications provided.

When choosing passwords, use strong passwords that are not easily guessed. There are some key points to consider when choosing passwords:

- Use passwords that are more than eight characters in length.
- Use a combination of upper and lowercase letters, numbers, special characters, and/or numeric sequences.
- Avoid using the same password for all devices.
- Do not use common words because they are easily guessed.

Use an internet search to find a password generator. Many will allow you to set the length, character set, and other parameters.

Note: Most of the labs in this course use simple passwords such as **cisco** or **class**. These passwords are considered weak and easily guessable and should be avoided in production environments. We only use these passwords for convenience in a classroom setting, or to illustrate configuration examples.

Configure Passwords - 2.4.3

When you initially connect to a device, you are in user EXEC mode. This mode is secured using the console.

To secure user EXEC mode access, enter line console configuration mode using the **line console 0** global configuration command, as shown in the example. The zero is used to represent the first (and in most cases the only) console interface. Next, specify the user EXEC mode password using the **password** *password* command. Finally, enable user EXEC access using the **login** command.

```
Sw-Floor-1# configure terminal

Sw-Floor-1(config)# line console 0

Sw-Floor-1(config-line)# password cisco

Sw-Floor-1(config-line)# login

Sw-Floor-1(config-line)# end

Sw-Floor-1#
```

Console access will now require a password before allowing access to the user EXEC mode.

To have administrator access to all IOS commands including configuring a device, you must gain privileged EXEC mode access. It is the most important access method because it provides complete access to the device.

To secure privileged EXEC access, use the **enable secret** *password* global config command, as shown in the example.

```
Sw-Floor-1# configure terminal
Sw-Floor-1(config)# enable secret class
Sw-Floor-1(config)# exit
Sw-Floor-1#
```

Virtual terminal (VTY) lines enable remote access using Telnet or SSH to the device. Many Cisco switches support up to 16 VTY lines that are numbered 0 to 15.

To secure VTY lines, enter line VTY mode using the **line vty 0 15** global config command. Next, specify the VTY password using the **password** *password* command. Lastly, enable VTY access using the **login** command.

An example of securing the VTY lines on a switch is shown.

```
Sw-Floor-1# configure terminal
Sw-Floor-1(config)# line vty 0 15
Sw-Floor-1(config-line)# password cisco
Sw-Floor-1(config-line)# login
Sw-Floor-1(config-line)# end
Sw-Floor-1#
```

Encrypt Passwords - 2.4.4

The startup-config and running-config files display most passwords in plaintext. This is a security threat because anyone can discover the passwords if they have access to these files.

To encrypt all plaintext passwords, use the **service password-encryption** global config command as shown in the example.

```
Sw-Floor-1# configure terminal
Sw-Floor-1(config)# service password-encryption
Sw-Floor-1(config)#
```

The command applies weak encryption to all unencrypted passwords. This encryption applies only to passwords in the configuration file, not to passwords as they are sent over the network. The purpose of this command is to keep unauthorized individuals from viewing passwords in the configuration file.

Use the **show running-config** command to verify that passwords are now encrypted.

```
Sw-Floor-1(config)# end
Sw-Floor-1# show running-config
```

```
!

!
line con 0
password 7 094F471A1A0A
login
!
line vty 0 4
password 7 03095A0F034F38435B49150A1819
login
!
!
end
```

Banner Messages - 2.4.5

Although requiring passwords is one way to keep unauthorized personnel out of a network, it is vital to provide a method for declaring that only authorized personnel should attempt to access the device. To do this, add a banner to the device output. Banners can be an important part of the legal process in the event that someone is prosecuted for breaking into a device. Some legal systems do not allow prosecution, or even the monitoring of users, unless a notification is visible.

To create a banner message of the day on a network device, use the **banner motd #** *the message of the day* **#** global config command. The "#" in the command syntax is called the delimiting character. It is entered before and after the message. The delimiting character can be any character as long as it does not occur in the message. For this reason, symbols such as the "#" are often used. After the command is executed, the banner will be displayed on all subsequent attempts to access the device until the banner is removed.

The following example shows the steps to configure the banner on Sw-Floor-1.

```
Sw-Floor-1# configure terminal
Sw-Floor-1(config)# banner motd #Authorized Access Only#
```

Refer to **Video** in online course

Video - Secure Administrative Access to a Switch - 2.4.6

Click Play in the figure to view a video demonstration of how to secure administrative access to a switch.

Refer to **Interactive Graphic** in online course

Syntax Checker - Basic Device Configuration - 2.4.7

Secure management access to a switch.

- Assign a device name.
- Secure user EXEC mode access.
- Secure privileged EXEC mode access.

- Secure VTY access.
- Encrypt all plaintext passwords.
- Display a login banner.

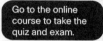

Check Your Understanding - Basic Device Configuration - 2.4.8

Save Configurations - 2.5

Configuration Files - 2.5.1

You now know how to perform basic configuration on a switch, including passwords and banner messages. This topic will show you how to save your configurations.

There are two system files that store the device configuration:

- **startup-config** - This is the saved configuration file that is stored in NVRAM. It contains all the commands that will be used by the device upon startup or reboot. Flash does not lose its contents when the device is powered off.

- **running-config** - This is stored in Random Access Memory (RAM). It reflects the current configuration. Modifying a running configuration affects the operation of a Cisco device immediately. RAM is volatile memory. It loses all of its content when the device is powered off or restarted.

The **show running-config** privileged EXEC mode command is used to view the running config. As shown in the example, the command will list the complete configuration currently stored in RAM.

```
Switch# show running-config

Building configuration...

Current configuration : 1351 bytes

!

! Last configuration change at 00:01:20 UTC Mon Mar 1 1993

!

version 15.0
no service pad
service timestamps debug datetime msec
service timestamps log datetime msec
no service password-encryption

!
```

To view the startup configuration file, use the **show startup-config** privileged EXEC command.

If power to the device is lost, or if the device is restarted, all configuration changes will be lost unless they have been saved. To save changes made to the running configuration to the startup configuration file, use the **copy running-config startup-config** privileged EXEC mode command.

Alter the Running Configuration - 2.5.2

If changes made to the running config do not have the desired effect and the running-config has not yet been saved, you can restore the device to its previous configuration. Remove the changed commands individually, or reload the device using the **reload** privileged EXEC mode command to restore the startup-config.

The downside to using the **reload** command to remove an unsaved running config is the brief amount of time the device will be offline, causing network downtime.

When a reload is initiated, the IOS will detect that the running config has changes that were not saved to the startup configuration. A prompt will appear to ask whether to save the changes. To discard the changes, enter **n** or **no**.

Alternatively, if undesired changes were saved to the startup config, it may be necessary to clear all the configurations. This requires erasing the startup config and restarting the device. The startup config is removed by using the **erase startup-config** privileged EXEC mode command. After the command is issued, the switch will prompt you for confirmation. Press **Enter** to accept.

After removing the startup config from NVRAM, reload the device to remove the current running config file from RAM. On reload, a switch will load the default startup config that originally shipped with the device.

Video - Alter the Running Configuration - 2.5.3

Refer to **Video** in online course

Click Play in the figure to view a video demonstration on how to save switch configuration files.

Capture Configuration to a Text File - 2.5.4

Refer to **Online Course** for Illustration

Configuration files can also be saved and archived to a text document. This sequence of steps ensures that a working copy of the configuration file is available for editing or reuse later.

For example, assume that a switch has been configured, and the running config has been saved on the device.

Step 1.   Open terminal emulation software, such as PuTTY or Tera Term, that is already connected to a switch.

Step 2.   Enable logging in the terminal software and assign a name and file location to save the log file. The figure displays that **All session output** will be captured to the file specified (i.e., MySwitchLogs).

Step 3.   Execute the **show running-config** or **show startup-config** command at the privileged EXEC prompt. Text displayed in the terminal window will be placed into the chosen file.

```
Switch# show running-config

Building configuration...
```

Step 4.   Disable logging in the terminal software. The figure shows how to disable logging by choosing the **None** session logging option.

The text file created can be used as a record of how the device is currently implemented. The file could require editing before being used to restore a saved configuration to a device.

To restore a configuration file to a device:

Step 1.   Enter global configuration mode on the device.

Step 2.   Copy and paste the text file into the terminal window connected to the switch.

The text in the file will be applied as commands in the CLI and become the running configuration on the device. This is a convenient method of manually configuring a device.

Refer to **Packet Tracer Activity** for this chapter

Packet Tracer - Configure Initial Switch Settings - 2.5.5

In this activity, you will perform basic switch configurations. You will secure access to the CLI and console ports using encrypted and plaintext passwords. You will learn how to configure messages for users logging into the switch. These banners are also used to warn unauthorized users that access is prohibited.

Ports and Addresses - 2.6

Refer to **Online Course** for Illustration

IP Addresses - 2.6.1

Congratulations, you have performed a basic device configuration! Of course, the fun is not over yet. If you want your end devices to communicate with each other, you must ensure that each of them has an appropriate IP address and is correctly connected. You will learn about IP addresses, device ports and the media used to connect devices in this topic.

The use of IP addresses is the primary means of enabling devices to locate one another and establish end-to-end communication on the internet. Each end device on a network must be configured with an IP address. Examples of end devices include these:

- Computers (work stations, laptops, file servers, web servers)
- Network printers
- VoIP phones
- Security cameras
- Smart phones
- Mobile handheld devices (such as wireless barcode scanners)

The structure of an IPv4 address is called dotted decimal notation and is represented by four decimal numbers between 0 and 255. IPv4 addresses are assigned to individual devices connected to a network.

Note: IP in this course refers to both the IPv4 and IPv6 protocols. IPv6 is the most recent version of IP and is replacing the more common IPv4.

With the IPv4 address, a subnet mask is also necessary. An IPv4 subnet mask is a 32-bit value that differentiates the network portion of the address from the host portion. Coupled with the IPv4 address, the subnet mask determines to which subnet the device is a member.

The example in the figure displays the IPv4 address (192.168.1.10), subnet mask (255.255.255.0), and default gateway (192.168.1.1) assigned to a host. The default gateway address is the IP address of the router that the host will use to access remote networks, including the internet.

IPv6 addresses are 128 bits in length and written as a string of hexadecimal values. Every four bits is represented by a single hexadecimal digit; for a total of 32 hexadecimal values. Groups of four hexadecimal digits are separated by a colon (:) . IPv6 addresses are not case-sensitive and can be written in either lowercase or uppercase.

Interfaces and Ports - 2.6.2

Refer to **Online Course** for Illustration

Network communications depend on end user device interfaces, networking device interfaces, and the cables that connect them. Each physical interface has specifications, or standards, that define it. A cable connecting to the interface must be designed to match the physical standards of the interface. Types of network media include twisted-pair copper cables, fiber-optic cables, coaxial cables, or wireless, as shown in the figure.

Different types of network media have different features and benefits. Not all network media have the same characteristics. Not all media are appropriate for the same purpose. These are some of the differences between various types of media:

- Distance the media can successfully carry a signal

- Environment in which the media is to be installed

- Amount of data and the speed at which it must be transmitted

- Cost of the media and installation

Not only does each link on the internet require a specific network media type, but each link also requires a particular network technology. For example, Ethernet is the most common local-area network (LAN) technology used today. Ethernet ports are found on end-user devices, switch devices, and other networking devices that can physically connect to the network using a cable.

Cisco IOS Layer 2 switches have physical ports for devices to connect. These ports do not support Layer 3 IP addresses. Therefore, switches have one or more switch virtual interfaces (SVIs). These are virtual interfaces because there is no physical hardware on the device associated with it. An SVI is created in software.

The virtual interface lets you remotely manage a switch over a network using IPv4 and IPv6. Each switch comes with one SVI appearing in the default configuration "out-of-the-box." The default SVI is interface VLAN1.

Note: A Layer 2 switch does not need an IP address. The IP address assigned to the SVI is used to remotely access the switch. An IP address is not necessary for the switch to perform its operations.

Go to the online course to take the quiz and exam.

Check Your Understanding - Ports and Addresses - 2.6.3

Configure IP Addressing - 2.7

Refer to **Online Course** for Illustration

Manual IP Address Configuration for End Devices - 2.7.1

Much like you need your friends' telephone numbers to text or call them, end devices in your network need an IP address so that they can communicate with other devices on your network. In this topic, you will implement basic connectivity by configuring IP addressing on switches and PCs.

IPv4 address information can be entered into end devices manually, or automatically using Dynamic Host Configuration Protocol (DHCP).

To manually configure an IPv4 address on a Windows host, open the **Control Panel > Network Sharing Center > Change adapter settings** and choose the adapter. Next right-click and select **Properties** to display the **Local Area Connection Properties**, as shown in the figure.

Highlight Internet Protocol Version 4 (TCP/IPv4) and click **Properties** to open the **Internet Protocol Version 4 (TCP/IPv4) Properties** window, shown in the figure. Configure the IPv4 address and subnet mask information, and default gateway.

Note: IPv6 addressing and configuration options are similar to IPv4.

Note: The DNS server addresses are the IPv4 and IPv6 addresses of the Domain Name System (DNS) servers, which are used to translate IP addresses to domain names, such as www.cisco.com.

Refer to **Online Course** for Illustration

Automatic IP Address Configuration for End Devices - 2.7.2

End devices typically default to using DHCP for automatic IPv4 address configuration. DHCP is a technology that is used in almost every network. The best way to understand why DHCP is so popular is by considering all the extra work that would have to take place without it.

In a network, DHCP enables automatic IPv4 address configuration for every end device that is DHCP-enabled. Imagine the amount of time it would take if every time you connected to the network, you had to manually enter the IPv4 address, the subnet mask, the default gateway, and the DNS server. Multiply that by every user and every device in an organization and you see the problem. Manual configuration also increases the chance of misconfiguration by duplicating another device's IPv4 address.

As shown in the figure, to configure DHCP on a Windows PC, you only need to select **Obtain an IP address automatically** and **Obtain DNS server address automatically**. Your PC will search out a DHCP server and be assigned the address settings necessary to communicate on the network.

Note: IPv6 uses DHCPv6 and SLAAC (Stateless Address Autoconfiguration) for dynamic address allocation.

Refer to
Interactive Graphic
in online course

Syntax Checker - Verify Windows PC IP Configuration - 2.7.3

It is possible to display the IP configuration settings on a Windows PC by using the **ipconfig** command at the command prompt. The output will show the IPv4 address, subnet mask, and gateway information received from the DHCP server.

Enter the command to display the IP configuration on a Windows PC.

Switch Virtual Interface Configuration - 2.7.4

To access the switch remotely, an IP address and a subnet mask must be configured on the SVI. To configure an SVI on a switch, use the **interface vlan 1** global configuration command. Vlan 1 is not an actual physical interface but a virtual one. Next assign an IPv4 address using the **ip address** *ip-address subnet-mask* interface configuration command. Finally, enable the virtual interface using the **no shutdown** interface configuration command.

After these commands are configured, the switch has all the IPv4 elements ready for communication over the network.

```
Switch# configure terminal
Switch(config)# interface vlan 1
Switch(config-if)# ip address 192.168.1.20 255.255.255.0
Switch(config-if)# no shutdown
```

Refer to
Interactive Graphic
in online course

Syntax Checker - Configure a Switch Virtual Interface - 2.7.5

Refer to Packet
Tracer Activity
for this chapter

Packet Tracer - Implement Basic Connectivity - 2.7.6

In this activity, you will first perform basic switch configurations. Then you will implement basic connectivity by configuring IP addressing on switches and PCs. When the IP addressing configuration is complete, you will use various **show** commands to verify configurations and use the **ping** command to verify basic connectivity between devices.

Verify Connectivity - 2.8

Refer to Video
in online course

Video Activity - Test the Interface Assignment - 2.8.1

In the previous topic, you implemented basic connectivity by configuring IP addressing on switches and PCs. Then you verified your configurations and connectivity, because, what is the point of configuring a device if you do not verify that the configuration is working? You will continue this process in this topic. Using the CLI, you will verify the interfaces and the addresses of the switches and routers in your network.

In the same way that you use commands and utilities like **ipconfig** to verify the network configuration of a PC host, you also use commands to verify the interfaces and address settings of intermediary devices like switches and routers.

Click Play in the figure to view a video demonstration of the **show ip interface brief** command. This command is useful for verifying the condition of the switch interfaces.

Follow Along in Packet Tracer

Download the same PKT file that is used in the video. Practice using the **ipconfig** and **show ip interface brief** commands, as shown in the video.

Refer to **Video** in online course

Video Activity - Test End-to-End Connectivity - 2.8.2

The **ping** command can be used to test connectivity to another device on the network or a website on the internet.

Click Play in the figure to view a video demonstration using the **ping** command to test connectivity to a switch and to another PC.

Follow Along in Packet Tracer

Download the same PKT file that is used in the video. Practice using the **ping** command, as shown in the video.

Module Practice and Quiz - 2.9

Refer to **Packet Tracer Activity** for this chapter

Packet Tracer - Basic Switch and End Device Configuration - 2.9.1

As a recently hired LAN technician, you have been asked by your network manager to demonstrate your ability to configure a small LAN. Your tasks include configuring initial settings on two switches by using the Cisco IOS and configuring IP address parameters on host devices to provide end-to-end connectivity. You are to use two switches and two hosts on a cabled and powered network.

Refer to **Lab Activity** for this chapter

Lab - Basic Switch and End Device Configuration - 2.9.2

In this lab, you will complete the following objectives:

- Part 1: Set Up the Network Topology
- Part 2: Configure PC Hosts
- Part 3: Configure and Verify Basic Switch Settings

What did I learn in this module? - 2.9.3

All end devices and network devices require an operating system (OS). The user can interact with the shell using a command-line interface (CLI) to use a keyboard to run CLI-based network programs, use a keyboard to enter text and text-based commands, and view output on a monitor.

As a security feature, the Cisco IOS software separates management access into the following two command modes: User EXEC Mode and Privileged EXEC Mode.

Global configuration mode is accessed before other specific configuration modes. From global config mode, the user can enter different subconfiguration modes. Each of these modes allows the configuration of a particular part or function of the IOS device. Two common subconfiguration modes include: Line Configuration Mode and Interface

Configuration Mode. To move in and out of global configuration mode, use the **configure terminal** privileged EXEC mode command. To return to the privileged EXEC mode, enter the **exit** global config mode command.

Each IOS command has a specific format or syntax and can only be executed in the appropriate mode. The general syntax for a command is the command followed by any appropriate keywords and arguments. The IOS has two forms of help available: context-sensitive help and command syntax check.

The first configuration command on any device should be to give it a unique device name or hostname. Network devices should always have passwords configured to limit administrative access. Cisco IOS can be configured to use hierarchical mode passwords to allow different access privileges to a network device. Configure and encrypt all passwords. Provide a method for declaring that only authorized personnel should attempt to access the device by adding a banner to the device output.

There are two system files that store the device configuration: startup-config and running-config. Running configuration files can be altered if they have not been saved. Configuration files can also be saved and archived to a text document.

IP addresses enable devices to locate one another and establish end-to-end communication on the internet. Each end device on a network must be configured with an IP address. The structure of an IPv4 address is called dotted decimal notation and is represented by four decimal numbers between 0 and 255.

IPv4 address information can be entered into end devices manually, or automatically using Dynamic Host Configuration Protocol (DHCP). In a network, DHCP enables automatic IPv4 address configuration for every end device that is DHCP-enabled. To access the switch remotely, an IP address and a subnet mask must be configured on the SVI. To configure an SVI on a switch, use the **interface vlan 1 global configuration** command. Vlan 1 is not an actual physical interface but a virtual one.

In the same way that you use commands and utilities to verify a PC host's network configuration, you also use commands to verify the interfaces and address settings of intermediary devices like switches and routers. The **show ip interface brief** command verifies the condition of the switch interfaces. The **ping** command can be used to test connectivity to another device on the network or a website on the internet.

Go to the online course to take the quiz and exam.

Chapter Quiz - Basic Switch and End Device Configuration

Your Chapter Notes

CHAPTER 3

Protocols and Models

Introduction - 3.0

Why should I take this module? - 3.0.1

Welcome to Protocols and Models!

You know the basic components of a simple network, as well as initial configuration. But after you have configured and connected these components, how do you know they will work together? Protocols! Protocols are sets of agreed upon rules that have been created by standards organizations. But, because you cannot pick up a rule and look closely at it, how do you truly understand why there is such a rule and what it is supposed to do? Models! Models give you a way to visualize the rules and their place in your network. This module gives you an overview of network protocols and models. You are about to have a much deeper understanding of how networks actually work!

What will I learn to do in this module? - 3.0.2

Module Title: Protocols and Models

Module Objective: Explain how network protocols enable devices to access local and remote network resources.

Topic Title	Topic Objective
The Rules	Describe the types of rules that are necessary to successfully communicate.
Protocols	Explain why protocols are necessary in network communication.
Protocol Suites	Explain the purpose of adhering to a protocol suite.
Standards Organizations	Explain the role of standards organizations in establishing protocols for network interoperability.
Reference Models	Explain how the TCP/IP model and the OSI model are used to facilitate standardization in the communication process.
Data Encapsulation	Explain how data encapsulation allows data to be transported across the network.
Data Access	Explain how local hosts access local resources on a network.

Refer to
Lab Activity
for this chapter

Class Activity - Design a Communications System - 3.0.3

You have just purchased a new automobile for your personal use. After driving the car for a week or so, you find that it is not working correctly. Discussing the problem with several of your peers, you decide to take it to an automotive repair facility that they highly recommend. It is the only repair facility located in close proximity.

When you arrive at the repair facility, you find that all the mechanics speak another language. You are having difficulty explaining the automobile's performance problems, but the repairs really need to be done. You are not sure you can drive it back home to research other options.

You must find a way to work with the repair facility to ensure your automobile is fixed correctly.

How will you communicate with the mechanics? Design a communications model to ensure that the car is properly repaired.

The Rules - 3.1

Refer to **Video** in online course

Video - Devices in a Bubble - 3.1.1

Click Play in the figure to view a video explaining how a network device operates within a network.

Communications Fundamentals - 3.1.2

Networks vary in size, shape, and function. They can be as complex as devices connected across the internet, or as simple as two computers directly connected to one another with a single cable, and anything in-between. However, simply having a wired or wireless physical connection between end devices is not enough to enable communication. For communication to occur, devices must know "how" to communicate.

People exchange ideas using many different communication methods. However, all communication methods have the following three elements in common:

- **Message source (sender)** - Message sources are people, or electronic devices, that need to send a message to other individuals or devices.

- **Message Destination (receiver)** - The destination receives the message and interprets it.

- **Channel** - This consists of the media that provides the pathway over which the message travels from source to destination.

Refer to **Interactive Graphic** in online course

Communication Protocols - 3.1.3

Sending a message, whether by face-to-face communication or over a network, is governed by rules called protocols. These protocols are specific to the type of communication method being used. In our day-to-day personal communication, the rules we use to communicate over one medium, like a telephone call, are not necessarily the same as the rules for using another medium, such as sending a letter.

The process of sending a letter is similar to communication that occurs in computer networks.

Click each button for an analogy and a network example of the communication process.

Analogy

Click Play in the figure to view an animation of two people communicating face-to-face.

Prior to communicating, they must agree on how to communicate. If the communication is using voice, they must first agree on the language. Next, when they have a message to share, they must be able to format that message in a way that is understandable.

If someone uses the English language, but poor sentence structure, the message can easily be misunderstood. Each of these tasks describe protocols that are used to accomplish communication.

Network

Click Play in the figure to view an animation of two devices communicating.

As shown in the animation, this is also true for computer communication. Many different rules or protocols govern all methods of communication that exist in the world today.

Rule Establishment - 3.1.4

Before communicating with one another, individuals must use established rules or agreements to govern the conversation. Consider this message for example:

```
humans communication between govern rules. It is verydifficult
tounderstand messages that are not correctly formatted and donot
follow the established rules and protocols. A estrutura da gramatica,
da lingua, da pontuacao e do sentence faz a configuracao humana
compreensivel por muitos individuos diferentes.
```

Notice how it is difficult to read the message because it is not formatted properly. It should be written using rules (i.e., protocols) that are necessary for effective communication. The example shows the message which is now properly formatted for language and grammar.

```
Rules govern communication between humans. It is very difficult to
understand messages that are not correctly formatted and do not follow
the established rules and protocols. The structure of the grammar,
the language, the punctuation and the sentence make the configuration
humanly understandable for many different individuals.
```

Protocols must account for the following requirements to successfully deliver a message that is understood by the receiver:

- An identified sender and receiver
- Common language and grammar
- Speed and timing of delivery
- Confirmation or acknowledgment requirements

Network Protocol Requirements - 3.1.5

The protocols that are used in network communications share many of these fundamental traits. In addition to identifying the source and destination, computer and network protocols define the details of how a message is transmitted across a network. Common computer protocols include the following requirements:

- Message encoding
- Message formatting and encapsulation
- Message size
- Message timing
- Message delivery options

Refer to
Interactive Graphic
in online course

Message Encoding - 3.1.6

One of the first steps to sending a message is encoding. Encoding is the process of converting information into another acceptable form, for transmission. Decoding reverses this process to interpret the information.

Click each button for an analogy and a network example of message encoding.

Analogy

Imagine a person calls a friend to discuss the details of a beautiful sunset. Click Play in the figure to view an animation of message encoding.

To communicate the message, she converts her thoughts into an agreed upon language. She then speaks the words using the sounds and inflections of spoken language that convey the message. Her friend listens to the description and decodes the sounds to understand the message he received.

Network

Click Play in the figure to view an animation of message encoding also occurs in computer communication.

Encoding between hosts must be in an appropriate format for the medium. Messages sent across the network are first converted into bits by the sending host. Each bit is encoded into a pattern of voltages on copper wires, infrared light in optical fibers, or microwaves for wireless systems. The destination host receives and decodes the signals to interpret the message.

Refer to
Interactive Graphic
in online course

Message Formatting and Encapsulation - 3.1.7

When a message is sent from source to destination, it must use a specific format or structure. Message formats depend on the type of message and the channel that is used to deliver the message.

Click each button for an analogy and a network example of message formatting and encapsulation.

Analogy

A common example of requiring the correct format in human communications is when sending a letter. Click Play in the figure to view an animation of formatting and encapsulating a letter.

An envelope has the address of the sender and receiver, each located at the proper place on the envelope. If the destination address and formatting are not correct, the letter is not delivered.

The process of placing one message format (the letter) inside another message format (the envelope) is called encapsulation. De-encapsulation occurs when the process is reversed by the recipient and the letter is removed from the envelope.

Network

Similar to sending a letter, a message that is sent over a computer network follows specific format rules for it to be delivered and processed.

Internet Protocol (IP) is a protocol with a similar function to the envelope example. In the figure, the fields of the Internet Protocol version 6 (IPv6) packet identify the source of the packet and its destination. IP is responsible for sending a message from the message source to destination over one or more networks.

Note: The fields of the IPv6 packet are discussed in detail in another module.

Refer to
Interactive Graphic
in online course

Message Size - 3.1.8

Another rule of communication is message size.

Click each button for an analogy and a network example of message size.

Analogy

Click Play in the figure to view an animation of message size in face-to-face communications.

When people communicate with each other, the messages that they send are usually broken into smaller parts or sentences. These sentences are limited in size to what the receiving person can process at one time, as shown in the figure. It also makes it easier for the receiver to read and comprehend.

Network

Encoding also occurs in computer communication. Click Play in the figure to view an animation of message size in computer networks.

Encoding between hosts must be in an appropriate format for the medium. Messages sent across the network are first converted into bits by the sending host. Each bit is encoded into a pattern of sounds, light waves, or electrical impulses depending on the network media over which the bits are transmitted. The destination host receives and decodes the signals to interpret the message.

Refer to
Interactive Graphic
in online course

Message Timing - 3.1.9

Message timing is also very important in network communications. Message timing includes the following:

- **Flow Control** - This is the process of managing the rate of data transmission. Flow control defines how much information can be sent and the speed at which it can be delivered. For example, if one person speaks too quickly, it may be difficult for the receiver to hear and understand the message. In network communication, there are network protocols used by the source and destination devices to negotiate and manage the flow of information.

- **Response Timeout** - If a person asks a question and does not hear a response within an acceptable amount of time, the person assumes that no answer is coming and reacts accordingly. The person may repeat the question or instead, may go on with the conversation. Hosts on the network use network protocols that specify how long to wait for responses and what action to take if a response timeout occurs.

- **Access method** - This determines when someone can send a message. Click Play in the figure to see an animation of two people talking at the same time, then a "collision of information" occurs, and it is necessary for the two to back off and start again. Likewise, when a device wants to transmit on a wireless LAN, it is necessary for the WLAN network interface card (NIC) to determine whether the wireless medium is available.

Refer to
Interactive Graphic
in online course

Message Delivery Options - 3.1.10

A message can be delivered in different ways.

Click each button for an analogy and a network example of message delivery options.

Analogy

Sometimes, a person wants to communicate information to a single individual. At other times, the person may need to send information to a group of people at the same time, or even to all people in the same area.

Click the unicast, multicast, and broadcast buttons in the figure for an example of each.

Network

Network communications has similar delivery options to communicate. As shown in the figure, there three types of data communications include:

- **Unicast** - Information is being transmitted to a single end device.

- **Multicast** - Information is being transmitted to a one or more end devices.

- **Broadcast** - Information is being transmitted to all end devices.

Click the unicast, multicast, and broadcast buttons in the figure for an example of each.

Refer to
Online Course
for Illustration

A Note About the Node Icon - 3.1.11

Networking documents and topologies often represent networking and end devices using a node icon. Nodes are typically represented as a circle. The figure shows a comparison of the three different delivery options using node icons instead of computer icons.

Go to the online
course to take the
quiz and exam.

Check Your Understanding - The Rules - 3.1.12

Protocols - 3.2

Network Protocol Overview - 3.2.1

You know that for end devices to be able to communicate over a network, each device must abide by the same set of rules. These rules are called protocols and they have many functions in a network. This topic gives you a overview of network protocols.

Network protocols define a common format and set of rules for exchanging messages between devices. Protocols are implemented by end devices and intermediary devices in software, hardware, or both. Each network protocol has its own function, format, and rules for communications.

The table lists the various types of protocols that are needed to enable communications across one or more networks.

Protocol Type	Description
Network Communications Protocols	Protocols enable two or more devices to communicate over one or more networks. The Ethernet family of technologies involves a variety of protocols such as IP, Transmission Control Protocol (TCP), HyperText Transfer Protocol (HTTP), and many more.
Network Security Protocols	Protocols secure data to provide authentication, data integrity, and data encryption. Examples of secure protocols include Secure Shell (SSH), Secure Sockets Layer (SSL), and Transport Layer Security (TLS).
Routing Protocols	Protocols enable routers to exchange route information, compare path information, and then to select the best path to the destination network. Examples of routing protocols include Open Shortest Path First (OSPF) and Border Gateway Protocol (BGP).
Service Discovery Protocols	Protocols are used for the automatic detection of devices or services. Examples of service discovery protocols include Dynamic Host Configuration Protocol (DHCP) which discovers services for IP address allocation, and Domain Name System (DNS) which is used to perform name-to-IP address translation.

Refer to
Online Course
for Illustration

Network Protocol Functions - 3.2.2

Network communication protocols are responsible for a variety of functions necessary for network communications between end devices. For example, in the figure how does the computer send a message, across several network devices, to the server?

Computers and network devices use agreed-upon protocols to communicate. The table lists the functions of these protocols.

Function	Description
Addressing	This identifies the sender and the intended receiver of the message using a defined addressing scheme. Examples of protocols that provide addressing include Ethernet, IPv4, and IPv6.
Reliability	This function provides guaranteed delivery mechanisms in case messages are lost or corrupted in transit. TCP provides guaranteed delivery.
Flow control	This function ensures that data flows at an efficient rate between two communicating devices. TCP provides flow control services.
Sequencing	This function uniquely labels each transmitted segment of data. The receiving device uses the sequencing information to reassemble the information correctly. This is useful if the data segments are lost, delayed or received out-of-order. TCP provides sequencing services.
Error Detection	This function is used to determine if data became corrupted during transmission. Various protocols that provide error detection include Ethernet, IPv4, IPv6, and TCP.
Application Interface	This function contains information used for process-to-process communications between network applications. For example, when accessing a web page, HTTP or HTTPS protocols are used to communicate between the client and server web processes.

Refer to
Online Course
for Illustration

Protocol Interaction - 3.2.3

A message sent over a computer network typically requires the use of several protocols, each one with its own functions and format. The figure shows some common network protocols that are used when a device sends a request to a web server for its web page.

Go to the online
course to take the
quiz and exam.

Check Your Understanding - Protocols - 3.2.4

Protocol Suites - 3.3

Refer to
Online Course
for Illustration

Network Protocol Suites - 3.3.1

In many cases, protocols must be able to work with other protocols so that your online experience gives you everything you need for network communications. Protocol suites are designed to work with each other seamlessly.

A protocol suite is a group of inter-related protocols necessary to perform a communication function.

One of the best ways to visualize how the protocols within a suite interact is to view the interaction as a stack. A protocol stack shows how the individual protocols within a suite are implemented. The protocols are viewed in terms of layers, with each higher-level service depending on the functionality defined by the protocols shown in the lower levels. The lower layers of the stack are concerned with moving data over the network and providing services to the upper layers, which are focused on the content of the message being sent.

As illustrated in the figure, we can use layers to describe the activity occurring in face-to-face communication. At the bottom is the physical layer where we have two people with voices saying words out loud. In the middle is the rules layer that stipulates the requirements of communication including that a common language must be chosen. At the top is the content layer and this is where the content of the communication is actually spoken.

Refer to
Online Course
for Illustration

Evolution of Protocol Suites - 3.3.2

A protocol suite is a set of protocols that work together to provide comprehensive network communication services. Since the 1970s there have been several different protocol suites, some developed by a standards organization and others developed by various vendors.

During the evolution of network communications and the internet there were several competing protocol suites, as shown in the figure.

Refer to
Online Course
for Illustration

TCP/IP Protocol Example - 3.3.3

TCP/IP protocols are available for the application, transport, and internet layers. There are no TCP/IP protocols in the network access layer. The most common network access layer LAN protocols are Ethernet and WLAN (wireless LAN) protocols. Network access layer protocols are responsible for delivering the IP packet over the physical medium.

The figure shows an example of the three TCP/IP protocols used to send packets between the web browser of a host and the web server. HTTP, TCP, and IP are the TCP/IP protocols used. At the network access layer, Ethernet is used in the example. However, this could also be a wireless standard such as WLAN or cellular service.

Refer to
Online Course
for Illustration

TCP/IP Protocol Suite - 3.3.4

Today, the TCP/IP protocol suite includes many protocols and continues to evolve to support new services. Some of the more popular ones are shown in the figure.

Click each button for a brief description of protocols at each layer.

Refer to
Interactive Graphic
in online course

Application Layer

Name System

■ **DNS** - Domain Name System. Translates domain names such as cisco.com, into IP addresses.

Host Config

■ **DHCPv4** - Dynamic Host Configuration Protocol for IPv4. A DHCPv4 server dynamically assigns IPv4 addressing information to DHCPv4 clients at start-up and allows the addresses to be re-used when no longer needed.

- **DHCPv6** - Dynamic Host Configuration Protocol for IPv6. DHCPv6 is similar to DHCPv4. A DHCPv6 server dynamically assigns IPv6 addressing information to DHCPv6 clients at start-up.

- **SLAAC** - Stateless Address Autoconfiguration. A method that allows a device to obtain its IPv6 addressing information without using a DHCPv6 server.

Email

- **SMTP** - Simple Mail Transfer Protocol. Enables clients to send email to a mail server and enables servers to send email to other servers.

- **POP3** - Post Office Protocol version 3. Enables clients to retrieve email from a mail server and download the email to the client's local mail application.

- **IMAP** - Internet Message Access Protocol. Enables clients to access email stored on a mail server as well as maintaining email on the server.

File Transfer

- **FTP** - File Transfer Protocol. Sets the rules that enable a user on one host to access and transfer files to and from another host over a network. FTP is a reliable, connection-oriented, and acknowledged file delivery protocol.

- **SFTP** - SSH File Transfer Protocol. As an extension to Secure Shell (SSH) protocol, SFTP can be used to establish a secure file transfer session in which the file transfer is encrypted. SSH is a method for secure remote login that is typically used for accessing the command line of a device.

- **TFTP** - Trivial File Transfer Protocol. A simple, connectionless file transfer protocol with best-effort, unacknowledged file delivery. It uses less overhead than FTP.

Web and Web Service

- **HTTP** - Hypertext Transfer Protocol. A set of rules for exchanging text, graphic images, sound, video, and other multimedia files on the World Wide Web.

- **HTTPS** - HTTP Secure. A secure form of HTTP that encrypts the data that is exchanged over the World Wide Web.

- **REST** - Representational State Transfer. A web service that uses application programming interfaces (APIs) and HTTP requests to create web applications.

Transport layer

Connection-Oriented

- **TCP** - Transmission Control Protocol. Enables reliable communication between processes running on separate hosts and provides reliable, acknowledged transmissions that confirm successful delivery.

Connectionless

- **UDP** - User Datagram Protocol. Enables a process running on one host to send packets to a process running on another host. However, UDP does not confirm successful datagram transmission.

Internet Layer

Internet Protocol

- **IPv4** - Internet Protocol version 4. Receives message segments from the transport layer, packages messages into packets, and addresses packets for end-to-end delivery over a network. IPv4 uses a 32-bit address.

- **IPv6** - IP version 6. Similar to IPv4 but uses a 128-bit address.

- **NAT** - Network Address Translation. Translates IPv4 addresses from a private network into globally unique public IPv4 addresses.

Messaging

- **ICMPv4** - Internet Control Message Protocol for IPv4. Provides feedback from a destination host to a source host about errors in packet delivery.

- **ICMPv6** - ICMP for IPv6. Similar functionality to ICMPv4 but is used for IPv6 packets.

- **ICMPv6 ND** - ICMPv6 Neighbor Discovery. Includes four protocol messages that are used for address resolution and duplicate address detection.

Routing Protocols

- **OSPF** - Open Shortest Path First. Link-state routing protocol that uses a hierarchical design based on areas. OSPF is an open standard interior routing protocol.

- **EIGRP** - Enhanced Interior Gateway Routing Protocol. A Cisco proprietary routing protocol that uses a composite metric based on bandwidth, delay, load and reliability.

- **BGP** - Border Gateway Protocol. An open standard exterior gateway routing protocol used between Internet Service Providers (ISPs). BGP is also commonly used between ISPs and their large private clients to exchange routing information.

Network Access Layer

Address Resolution

- **ARP** - Address Resolution Protocol. Provides dynamic address mapping between an IPv4 address and a hardware address.

Data Link Protocols

- **Ethernet** - Defines the rules for wiring and signaling standards of the network access layer.

- **WLAN** - Wireless Local Area Network. Defines the rules for wireless signaling across the 2.4 GHz and 5 GHz radio frequencies.

Refer to
Interactive Graphic
in online course

TCP/IP Communication Process - 3.3.5

The animations in the figures demonstrate the complete communication process using an example of a web server transmitting data to a client.

Click the Play in the figure to view an animation of a web server encapsulating and sending a web page to a client.

Click the Play in the next figure to view an animation of the client receiving, and de-encapsulating the web page for display in the web browser.

Go to the online
course to take the
quiz and exam.

Check Your Understanding - Protocol Suites - 3.3.6

Standards Organizations - 3.4

Open Standards - 3.4.1

Refer to
Online Course
for Illustration

When buying new tires for a car, there are many manufacturers you might choose. Each of them will have at least one type of tire that fits your car. That is because the automotive industry uses standards when they make cars. It is the same with protocols. Because there are many different manufacturers of network components, they must all use the same standards. In networking, standards are developed by international standards organizations.

Open standards encourage interoperability, competition, and innovation. They also guarantee that the product of no single company can monopolize the market or have an unfair advantage over its competition.

A good example of this is when purchasing a wireless router for the home. There are many different choices available from a variety of vendors, all of which incorporate standard protocols such as IPv4, IPv6, DHCP, SLAAC, Ethernet, and 802.11 Wireless LAN. These open standards also allow a client running the Apple OS X operating system to download a web page from a web server running the Linux operating system. This is because both operating systems implement the open standard protocols, such as those in the TCP/IP protocol suite.

Standards organizations are usually vendor-neutral, non-profit organizations established to develop and promote the concept of open standards. These organizations are important in maintaining an open internet with freely accessible specifications and protocols that can be implemented by any vendor.

A standards organization may draft a set of rules entirely on its own or, in other cases, may select a proprietary protocol as the basis for the standard. If a proprietary protocol is used, it usually involves the vendor who created the protocol.

The figure shows the logo for each standards organization.

Refer to
Online Course
for Illustration

Internet Standards - 3.4.2

Various organizations have different responsibilities for promoting and creating standards for the internet and TCP/IP protocol.

The figure displays standards organizations involved with the development and support of the internet.

The next figure displays standards organizations involved with the development and support of TCP/IP and include IANA and ICANN.

Electronic and Communications Standards - 3.4.3

Other standards organizations have responsibilities for promoting and creating the electronic and communication standards used to deliver the IP packets as electronic signals over a wired or wireless medium.

These standard organizations include the following:

- **Institute of Electrical and Electronics Engineers (IEEE, pronounced "I-triple-E")** - Organization of electrical engineering and electronics dedicated to advancing technological innovation and creating standards in a wide area of industries including power and energy, healthcare, telecommunications, and networking. Important IEEE networking standards include 802.3 Ethernet and 802.11 WLAN standard. Search the internet for other IEEE network standards.

- **Electronic Industries Alliance (EIA)** - Organization is best known for its standards relating to electrical wiring, connectors, and the 19-inch racks used to mount networking equipment.

- **Telecommunications Industry Association (TIA)** - Organization responsible for developing communication standards in a variety of areas including radio equipment, cellular towers, Voice over IP (VoIP) devices, satellite communications, and more. The figure shows an example of a certified Ethernet cable which was developed cooperatively by the TIA and the EIA.

- **International Telecommunications Union-Telecommunication Standardization Sector (ITU-T)** - One of the largest and oldest communication standards organizations. The ITU-T defines standards for video compression, Internet Protocol Television (IPTV), and broadband communications, such as a digital subscriber line (DSL).

Refer to
Lab Activity
for this chapter

Lab - Research Networking Standards - 3.4.4

In this lab, you will complete the following objectives:

- Part 1: Research Networking Standards Organizations
- Part 2: Reflect on Internet and Computer Networking Experience

Go to the online course to take the quiz and exam.

Check Your Understanding - Standards Organizations

Reference Models - 3.5

Refer to **Online Course** for Illustration

The Benefits of Using a Layered Model - 3.5.1

You cannot actually watch real packets travel across a real network, the way you can watch the components of a car being put together on an assembly line. so, it helps to have a way of thinking about a network so that you can imagine what is happening. A model is useful in these situations.

Complex concepts such as how a network operates can be difficult to explain and understand. For this reason, a layered model is used to modularize the operations of a network into manageable layers.

These are the benefits of using a layered model to describe network protocols and operations:

■ Assisting in protocol design because protocols that operate at a specific layer have defined information that they act upon and a defined interface to the layers above and below

■ Fostering competition because products from different vendors can work together

■ Preventing technology or capability changes in one layer from affecting other layers above and below

■ Providing a common language to describe networking functions and capabilities

As shown in the figure, there are two layered models that are used to describe network operations:

■ Open System Interconnection (OSI) Reference Model

■ TCP/IP Reference Model

The OSI Reference Model - 3.5.2

The OSI reference model provides an extensive list of functions and services that can occur at each layer. This type of model provides consistency within all types of network protocols and services by describing what must be done at a particular layer, but not prescribing how it should be accomplished.

It also describes the interaction of each layer with the layers directly above and below. The TCP/IP protocols discussed in this course are structured around both the OSI and TCP/IP models. The table shows details about each layer of the OSI model. The functionality of each layer and the relationship between layers will become more evident throughout this course as the protocols are discussed in more detail.

OSI Model Layer	Description
7 - Application	The application layer contains protocols used for process-to-process communications.
6 - Presentation	The presentation layer provides for common representation of the data transferred between application layer services.
5 - Session	The session layer provides services to the presentation layer to organize its dialogue and to manage data exchange.
4 - Transport	The transport layer defines services to segment, transfer, and reassemble the data for individual communications between the end devices.
3 - Network	The network layer provides services to exchange the individual pieces of data over the network between identified end devices.
2 - Data Link	The data link layer protocols describe methods for exchanging data frames between devices over a common media
1 - Physical	The physical layer protocols describe the mechanical, electrical, functional, and procedural means to activate, maintain, and de-activate physical connections for a bit transmission to and from a network device.

NOTE: Whereas the TCP/IP model layers are referred to only by name, the seven OSI model layers are more often referred to by number rather than by name. For instance, the physical layer is referred to as Layer 1 of the OSI model, data link layer is Layer2, and so on.

The TCP/IP Protocol Model - 3.5.3

The TCP/IP protocol model for internetwork communications was created in the early 1970s and is sometimes referred to as the internet model. This type of model closely matches the structure of a particular protocol suite. The TCP/IP model is a protocol model because it describes the functions that occur at each layer of protocols within the TCP/IP suite. TCP/IP is also used as a reference model. The table shows details about each layer of the OSI model.

TCP/IP Model Layer	Description
4 - Application	Represents data to the user, plus encoding and dialog control.
3 - Transport	Supports communication between various devices across diverse networks.
2 - Internet	Determines the best path through the network.
1 - Network Access	Controls the hardware devices and media that make up the network.

The definitions of the standard and the TCP/IP protocols are discussed in a public forum and defined in a publicly available set of IETF RFCs. An RFC is authored by networking engineers and sent to other IETF members for comments.

Refer to
Online Course
for Illustration

OSI and TCP/IP Model Comparison - 3.5.4

The protocols that make up the TCP/IP protocol suite can also be described in terms of the OSI reference model. In the OSI model, the network access layer and the application layer of the TCP/IP model are further divided to describe discrete functions that must occur at these layers.

At the network access layer, the TCP/IP protocol suite does not specify which protocols to use when transmitting over a physical medium; it only describes the handoff from the internet layer to the physical network protocols. OSI Layers 1 and 2 discuss the necessary procedures to access the media and the physical means to send data over a network.

Refer to **Packet Tracer Activity** for this chapter

Packet Tracer - Investigate the TCP/IP and OSI Models in Action - 3.5.5

This simulation activity is intended to provide a foundation for understanding the TCP/IP protocol suite and the relationship to the OSI model. Simulation mode allows you to view the data contents being sent across the network at each layer.

As data moves through the network, it is broken down into smaller pieces and identified so that the pieces can be put back together when they arrive at the destination. Each piece is assigned a specific name and is associated with a specific layer of the TCP/IP and OSI models. The assigned name is called a protocol data unit (PDU). Using Packet Tracer simulation mode, you can view each of the layers and the associated PDU. The following steps lead the user through the process of requesting a web page from a web server by using the web browser application available on a client PC.

Even though much of the information displayed will be discussed in more detail later, this is an opportunity to explore the functionality of Packet Tracer and be able to visualize the encapsulation process.

Data Encapsulation - 3.6

Refer to **Interactive Graphic** in online course

Segmenting Messages - 3.6.1

Knowing the OSI reference model and the TCP/IP protocol model will come in handy when you learn about how data is encapsulated as it moves across a network. It is not as simple as a physical letter being sent through the mail system.

In theory, a single communication, such as a video or an email message with many large attachments, could be sent across a network from a source to a destination as one massive, uninterrupted stream of bits. However, this would create problems for other devices needing to use the same communication channels or links. These large streams of data would result in significant delays. Further, if any link in the interconnected network infrastructure failed during the transmission, the complete message would be lost and would have to be retransmitted in full.

A better approach is to divide the data into smaller, more manageable pieces to send over the network. Segmentation is the process of dividing a stream of data into smaller units for transmissions over the network. Segmentation is necessary because data networks use the TCP/IP protocol suite send data in individual IP packets. Each packet is sent separately, similar to sending a long letter as a series of individual postcards. Packets containing segments for the same destination can be sent over different paths.

This leads to segmenting messages having two primary benefits:

- **Increases speed** - Because a large data stream is segmented into packets, large amounts of data can be sent over the network without tying up a communications link. This allows many different conversations to be interleaved on the network called multiplexing.

- **Increases efficiency** - If a single segment is fails to reach its destination due to a failure in the network or network congestion, only that segment needs to be retransmitted instead of resending the entire data stream.

Click each button in the figure to view the animations of segmentation and multiplexing.

Refer to
Online Course
for Illustration

Sequencing - 3.6.2

The challenge to using segmentation and multiplexing to transmit messages across a network is the level of complexity that is added to the process. Imagine if you had to send a 100-page letter, but each envelope could only hold one page. Therefore, 100 envelopes would be required and each envelope would need to be addressed individually. It is possible that the 100-page letter in 100 different envelopes arrives out-of-order. Consequently, the information in the envelope would need to include a sequence number to ensure that the receiver could reassemble the pages in the proper order.

In network communications, each segment of the message must go through a similar process to ensure that it gets to the correct destination and can be reassembled into the content of the original message, as shown in the figure. TCP is responsible for sequencing the individual segments.

Refer to
Online Course
for Illustration

Protocol Data Units - 3.6.3

As application data is passed down the protocol stack on its way to be transmitted across the network media, various protocol information is added at each level. This is known as the encapsulation process.

Note: Although the UDP PDU is called datagram, IP packets are sometimes also referred to as IP datagrams.

The form that a piece of data takes at any layer is called a protocol data unit (PDU). During encapsulation, each succeeding layer encapsulates the PDU that it receives from the layer above in accordance with the protocol being used. At each stage of the process, a PDU has a different name to reflect its new functions. Although there is no universal naming convention for PDUs, in this course, the PDUs are named according to the protocols of the TCP/IP suite. The PDUs for each form of data are shown in the figure.

Refer to
Interactive Graphic
in online course

Encapsulation Example - 3.6.4

When messages are being sent on a network, the encapsulation process works from top to bottom. At each layer, the upper layer information is considered data within the encapsulated protocol. For example, the TCP segment is considered data within the IP packet.

You saw this animation previously in this module. This time, click Play and focus on the encapsulation process as a web server sends a web page to a web client.

Refer to
Interactive Graphic
in online course

De-encapsulation Example - 3.6.5

This process is reversed at the receiving host and is known as de-encapsulation. De-encapsulation is the process used by a receiving device to remove one or more of the protocol headers. The data is de-encapsulated as it moves up the stack toward the end-user application.

You saw this animation previously in this module. This time, click Play and focus on the de-encapsulation process.

Go to the online
course to take the
quiz and exam.

Check Your Understanding - Data Encapsulation - 3.6.6

Data Access - 3.7

Refer to
Online Course
for Illustration

Addresses - 3.7.1

As you just learned, it is necessary to segment messages in a network. But those segmented messages will not go anywhere if they are not addressed properly. This topic gives an overview of network addresses. You will also get the chance to use the Wireshark tool, which will help you to 'view' network traffic.

The network and data link layers are responsible for delivering the data from the source device to the destination device. As shown in the figure, protocols at both layers contain a source and destination address, but their addresses have different purposes:

- **Network layer source and destination addresses** - Responsible for delivering the IP packet from the original source to the final destination, which may be on the same network or a remote network.

- **Data link layer source and destination addresses** - Responsible for delivering the data link frame from one network interface card (NIC) to another NIC on the same network.

Refer to
Online Course
for Illustration

Layer 3 Logical Address - 3.7.2

An IP address is the network layer, or Layer 3, logical address used to deliver the IP packet from the original source to the final destination, as shown in the figure.

The IP packet contains two IP addresses:

- **Source IP address** - The IP address of the sending device, which is the original source of the packet.

- **Destination IP address** - The IP address of the receiving device, which is the final destination of the packet.

The IP addresses indicate the original source IP address and final destination IP address. This is true whether the source and destination are on the same IP network or different IP networks.

An IP address contains two parts:

■ **Network portion (IPv4) or Prefix (IPv6)** - The left-most part of the address that indicates the network in which the IP address is a member. All devices on the same network will have the same network portion of the address.

■ **Host portion (IPv4) or Interface ID (IPv6)** - The remaining part of the address that identifies a specific device on the network. This portion is unique for each device or interface on the network.

Note: The subnet mask (IPv4) or prefix-length (IPv6) is used to identify the network portion of an IP address from the host portion.

Refer to
Online Course
for Illustration

Devices on the Same Network - 3.7.3

In this example we have a client computer, PC1, communicating with an FTP server on the same IP network.

■ **Source IPv4 address** - The IPv4 address of the sending device, the client computer PC1: 192.168.1.110.

■ **Destination IPv4 address** - The IPv4 address of the receiving device, FTP server: 192.168.1.9.

Notice in the figure that the network portion of both the source IPv4 address and destination IPv4 address are on the same network. Notice in the figure that the network portion of the source IPv4 address and the network portion of the destination IPv4 address are the same and therefore; the source and destination are on the same network.

Refer to
Online Course
for Illustration

Role of the Data Link Layer Addresses: Same IP Network - 3.7.4

When the sender and receiver of the IP packet are on the same network, the data link frame is sent directly to the receiving device. On an Ethernet network, the data link addresses are known as Ethernet Media Access Control (MAC) addresses, as highlighted in the figure.

MAC addresses are physically embedded on the Ethernet NIC.

■ **Source MAC address** - This is the data link address, or the Ethernet MAC address, of the device that sends the data link frame with the encapsulated IP packet. The MAC address of the Ethernet NIC of PC1 is AA-AA-AA-AA-AA-AA, written in hexadecimal notation.

■ **Destination MAC address** - When the receiving device is on the same network as the sending device, this is the data link address of the receiving device. In this example, the destination MAC address is the MAC address of the FTP server: CC-CC-CC-CC-CC-CC, written in hexadecimal notation.

The frame with the encapsulated IP packet can now be transmitted from PC1 directly to the FTP server.

Devices on a Remote Network - 3.7.5

But what are the roles of the network layer address and the data link layer address when a device is communicating with a device on a remote network? In this example we have a client computer, PC1, communicating with a server, named Web Server, on a different IP network.

Refer to
Online Course
for Illustration

Role of the Network Layer Addresses - 3.7.6

When the sender of the packet is on a different network from the receiver, the source and destination IP addresses will represent hosts on different networks. This will be indicated by the network portion of the IP address of the destination host.

- **Source IPv4 address** - The IPv4 address of the sending device, the client computer PC1: 192.168.1.110.

- **Destination IPv4 address** - The IPv4 address of the receiving device, the server, Web Server: 172.16.1.99.

Notice in the figure that the network portion of the source IPv4 address and destination IPv4 address are on different networks.

Refer to
Online Course
for Illustration

Role of the Data Link Layer Addresses: Different IP Networks - 3.7.7

When the sender and receiver of the IP packet are on different networks, the Ethernet data link frame cannot be sent directly to the destination host because the host is not directly reachable in the network of the sender. The Ethernet frame must be sent to another device known as the router or default gateway. In our example, the default gateway is R1. R1 has an Ethernet data link address that is on the same network as PC1. This allows PC1 to reach the router directly.

- **Source MAC address** - The Ethernet MAC address of the sending device, PC1. The MAC address of the Ethernet interface of PC1 is AA-AA-AA-AA-AA-AA.

- **Destination MAC address** - When the receiving device, the destination IP address, is on a different network from the sending device, the sending device uses the Ethernet MAC address of the default gateway or router. In this example, the destination MAC address is the MAC address of the R1 Ethernet interface, 11-11-11-11-11-11. This is the interface that is attached to the same network as PC1, as shown in the figure.

The Ethernet frame with the encapsulated IP packet can now be transmitted to R1. R1 forwards the packet to the destination, Web Server. This may mean that R1 forwards the packet to another router or directly to Web Server if the destination is on a network connected to R1.

It is important that the IP address of the default gateway be configured on each host on the local network. All packets to a destination on remote networks are sent to the default gateway. Ethernet MAC addresses and the default gateway are discussed in more detail in other modules.

Refer to
Online Course
for Illustration

Data Link Addresses - 3.7.8

Refer to
Interactive Graphic
in online course

The data link Layer 2 physical address has a different role. The purpose of the data link address is to deliver the data link frame from one network interface to another network interface on the same network.

Before an IP packet can be sent over a wired or wireless network, it must be encapsulated in a data link frame, so it can be transmitted over the physical medium.

Click each button to view an illustration of how the data link layer addresses change at every hop from source to destination.

Host to Router

Router to Router

Router to Server

As the IP packet travels from host-to-router, router-to-router, and finally router-to-host, at each point along the way the IP packet is encapsulated in a new data link frame. Each data link frame contains the source data link address of the NIC card sending the frame, and the destination data link address of the NIC card receiving the frame.

The Layer 2, data link protocol is only used to deliver the packet from NIC-to-NIC on the same network. The router removes the Layer 2 information as it is received on one NIC and adds new data link information before forwarding out the exit NIC on its way towards the final destination.

The IP packet is encapsulated in a data link frame that contains the following data link information:

- **Source data link address** - The physical address of the NIC that is sending the data link frame.

- **Destination data link address** - The physical address of the NIC that is receiving the data link frame. This address is either the next hop router or the address of the final destination device.

Refer to
Lab Activity
for this chapter

Lab - Install Wireshark - 3.7.9

Wireshark is a software protocol analyzer, or "packet sniffer" application, used for network troubleshooting, analysis, software and protocol development, and education. Wireshark is used throughout the course to demonstrate network concepts. In this lab, you will download and install Wireshark.

Refer to
Lab Activity
for this chapter

Lab - Use Wireshark to View Network Traffic - 3.7.10

In this lab, you will use Wireshark to capture and analyze traffic.

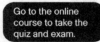
Go to the online
course to take the
quiz and exam.

Check Your Understanding - Data Access 3.7.11

Module Practice and Quiz - 3.8

What did I learn in this module? - 3.8.1

The Rules

All communication methods have three elements in common: message source (sender), message destination (receiver), and channel. Sending a message is governed by rules called *protocols*. Protocols must include: an identified sender and receiver, common language and grammar, speed and timing of delivery, and confirmation or acknowledgment requirements. Common computer protocols include these requirements: message encoding, formatting and encapsulation, size, timing, and delivery options. Encoding is the process of converting information into another acceptable form, for transmission. Decoding reverses this process to interpret the information. Message formats depend on the type of message and the channel that is used to deliver the message. Message timing includes flow control, response timeout, and access method. Message delivery options include unicast, multicast, and broadcast.

Protocols

Protocols are implemented by end-devices and intermediary devices in software, hardware, or both. A message sent over a computer network typically requires the use of several protocols, each one with its own functions and format. Each network protocol has its own function, format, and rules for communications. The Ethernet family of protocols includes IP, TCP, HTTP, and many more. Protocols secure data to provide authentication, data integrity, and data encryption: SSH, SSL, and TLS. Protocols enable routers to exchange route information, compare path information, and then to select the best path to the destination network: OSPF and BGP. Protocols are used for the automatic detection of devices or services: DHCP and DNS. Computers and network devices use agreed-upon protocols that provide the following functions: addressing, reliability, flow control, sequencing, error-detection, and application interface.

Protocol Suites

A protocol suite is a group of inter-related protocols necessary to perform a communication function. A protocol stack shows how the individual protocols within a suite are implemented. Since the 1970s there have been several different protocol suites, some developed by a standards organization and others developed by various vendors. TCP/IP protocols are available for the application, transport, and internet layers. TCP/IP is the protocol suite used by today's networks and internet. TCP/IP offers two important aspects to vendors and manufacturers: open standard protocol suite, and standards-based protocol suite. The TCP/IP protocol suite communication process enables such processes as a web server encapsulating and sending a web page to a client, as well as the client de-encapsulating the web page for display in a web browser.

Standards Organizations

Open standards encourage interoperability, competition, and innovation. Standards organizations are usually vendor-neutral, non-profit organizations established to develop and promote the concept of open standards. Various organizations have different responsibilities for promoting and creating standards for the internet including: ISOC, IAB, IETF, and IRTF. Standards organizations that develop and support TCP/IP include: ICANN and IANA. Electronic and communications standards organizations include: IEEE, EIA, TIA, and ITU-T.

Reference Models

The two reference models that are used to describe network operations are OSI and TCP/IP. The OSI model has seven layers:

7 - Application

6 - Presentation

5 - Session

4 - Transport

3 - Network

2 - Data Link

1 - Physical

The TCP/IP model has four layers:

4 - Application

3 - Transport

2 - Internet

1 - Network Access

Data Encapsulation

Segmenting messages has two primary benefits:

- By sending smaller individual pieces from source to destination, many different conversations can be interleaved on the network. This is called *multiplexing*.

- Segmentation can increase the efficiency of network communications. If part of the message fails to make it to the destination only the missing parts need to be retransmitted.

TCP is responsible for sequencing the individual segments. The form that a piece of data takes at any layer is called a *protocol data unit (PDU)*. During encapsulation, each succeeding layer encapsulates the PDU that it receives from the layer above in accordance with the protocol being used. When sending messages on a network, the encapsulation process works from top to bottom. This process is reversed at the receiving host and is known as *de-encapsulation*. De-encapsulation is the process used by a receiving device to remove one or more of the protocol headers. The data is de-encapsulated as it moves up the stack toward the end-user application.

Data Access

The network and data link layers are responsible for delivering the data from the source device to the destination device. Protocols at both layers contain a source and destination address, but their addresses have different purposes:

- **Network layer source and destination addresses** - Responsible for delivering the IP packet from the original source to the final destination, which may be on the same network or a remote network.

- **Data link layer source and destination addresses** - Responsible for delivering the data link frame from one network interface card (NIC) to another NIC on the same network.

The IP addresses indicate the original source IP address and final destination IP address. An IP address contains two parts: the network portion (IPv4) or Prefix (IPv6) and the host portion (IPv4) or Interface ID (IPv6). When the sender and receiver of the IP packet are on the same network, the data link frame is sent directly to the receiving device. On an Ethernet network, the data link addresses are known as Ethernet Media Access Control (MAC) addresses. When the sender of the packet is on a different network from the receiver, the source and destination IP addresses will represent hosts on different networks. The Ethernet frame must be sent to another device known as the router or default gateway.

Go to the online course to take the quiz and exam.

Chapter Quiz - Protocols and Models

Your Chapter Notes

CHAPTER 4

Physical Layer

Introduction - 4.0

Why should I take this module? - 4.0.1

Welcome to Physical Layer!

The physical layer of the OSI model sits at the bottom of the stack. It is part of the Network Access layer of the TCP/IP model. Without the physical layer, you would not have a network. This module explains, in detail, the three ways to connect to the physical layer. Packet Tracer activities and labs will give you the confidence you need to cable up your own network! Let's get busy!

What will I learn to do in this module? - 4.0.2

Module Title: Physical Layer

Module Objective: Explain how physical layer protocols, services, and network media support communications across data networks.

Topic Title	Topic Objective
Purpose of the Physical Layer	Describe the purpose and functions of the physical layer in the network.
Physical Layer Characteristics	Describe characteristics of the physical layer.
Copper Cabling	Identify the basic characteristics of copper cabling.
UTP Cabling	Explain how UTP cable is used in Ethernet networks.
Fiber-Optic Cabling	Describe fiber optic cabling and its main advantages over other media.
Wireless Media	Connect devices using wired and wireless media.

Purpose of the Physical Layer - 4.1

Refer to
Online Course
for Illustration

The Physical Connection - 4.1.1

Whether connecting to a local printer in the home or a website in another country, before any network communications can occur, a physical connection to a local network must be established. A physical connection can be a wired connection using a cable or a wireless connection using radio waves.

The type of physical connection used depends upon the setup of the network. For example, in many corporate offices, employees have desktop or laptop computers that are physically connected, via cable, to a shared switch. This type of setup is a wired network. Data is transmitted through a physical cable.

In addition to wired connections, many businesses also offer wireless connections for laptops, tablets, and smartphones. With wireless devices, data is transmitted using radio waves. Wireless connectivity is common as individuals and businesses alike discover its advantages. Devices on a wireless network must be connected to a wireless access point (AP) or wireless router like the one shown in the figure.

Similar to a corporate office, most homes offer both wired and wireless connectivity to the network. The figures show a home router and a laptop connecting to the local area network (LAN).

Network Interface Cards

Network interface cards (NICs) connect a device to the network. Ethernet NICs are used for a wired connection, as shown in the figure, whereas wireless local area network (WLAN) NICs are used for wireless. An end-user device may include one or both types of NICs. A network printer, for example, may only have an Ethernet NIC, and therefore, must connect to the network using an Ethernet cable. Other devices, such as tablets and smartphones, might only contain a WLAN NIC and must use a wireless connection.

Not all physical connections are equal, in terms of the performance level, when connecting to a network.

Refer to
Interactive Graphic
in online course

The Physical Layer - 4.1.2

The OSI physical layer provides the means to transport the bits that make up a data link layer frame across the network media. This layer accepts a complete frame from the data link layer and encodes it as a series of signals that are transmitted to the local media. The encoded bits that comprise a frame are received by either an end device or an intermediate device.

Click Play in the figure to see an example of the encapsulation process. The last part of this process shows the bits being sent over the physical medium. The physical layer encodes the frames and creates the electrical, optical, or radio wave signals that represent the bits in each frame. These signals are then sent over the media, one at a time.

The destination node physical layer retrieves these individual signals from the media, restores them to their bit representations, and passes the bits up to the data link layer as a complete frame.

Go to the online course to take the quiz and exam.

Check Your Understanding - Purpose of the Physical Layer - 4.1.3

Physical Layer Characteristics - 4.2

Physical Layer Standards - 4.2.1

Refer to
Online Course
for Illustration

In the previous topic, you gained a high level overview of the physical layer and its place in a network. This topic dives a bit deeper into the specifics of the physical layer. This includes the components and the media used to build a network, as well as the standards that are required so that everything works together.

The protocols and operations of the upper OSI layers are performed using software designed by software engineers and computer scientists. The services and protocols in the TCP/IP suite are defined by the Internet Engineering Task Force (IETF).

The physical layer consists of electronic circuitry, media, and connectors developed by engineers. Therefore, it is appropriate that the standards governing this hardware are defined by the relevant electrical and communications engineering organizations.

There are many different international and national organizations, regulatory government organizations, and private companies involved in establishing and maintaining physical layer standards. For instance, the physical layer hardware, media, encoding, and signaling standards are defined and governed by these standards organizations:

- International Organization for Standardization (ISO)

- Telecommunications Industry Association/Electronic Industries Association (TIA/EIA)

- International Telecommunication Union (ITU)

- American National Standards Institute (ANSI)

- Institute of Electrical and Electronics Engineers (IEEE)

- National telecommunications regulatory authorities including the Federal Communication Commission (FCC) in the USA and the European Telecommunications Standards Institute (ETSI)

In addition to these, there are often regional cabling standards groups such as CSA (Canadian Standards Association), CENELEC (European Committee for Electrotechnical Standardization), and JSA/JIS (Japanese Standards Association), which develop local specifications.

Physical Components - 4.2.2

The physical layer standards address three functional areas:

- Physical Components

- Encoding

- Signaling

Physical Components

The physical components are the electronic hardware devices, media, and other connectors that transmit the signals that represent the bits. Hardware components such as NICs, interfaces and connectors, cable materials, and cable designs are all specified in standards associated with the physical layer. The various ports and interfaces on a Cisco 1941 router are also examples of physical components with specific connectors and pinouts resulting from standards.

Refer to
Online Course
for Illustration

Encoding - 4.2.3

Encoding or line encoding is a method of converting a stream of data bits into a predefined "code". Codes are groupings of bits used to provide a predictable pattern that can be recognized by both the sender and the receiver. In other words, encoding is the method or pattern used to represent digital information. This is similar to how Morse code encodes a message using a series of dots and dashes.

For example, Manchester encoding represents a 0 bit by a high to low voltage transition, and a 1 bit is represented as a low to high voltage transition. An example of Manchester encoding is illustrated in the figure. The transition occurs at the middle of each bit period. This type of encoding is used in 10 Mbps Ethernet. Faster data rates require more complex encoding. Manchester encoding is used in older Ethernet standards such as 10BASE-T. Ethernet 100BASE-TX uses 4B/5B encoding and 1000BASE-T uses 8B/10B encoding.

Refer to
Interactive Graphic
in online course

Signaling - 4.2.4

Refer to
Online Course
for Illustration

The physical layer must generate the electrical, optical, or wireless signals that represent the "1" and "0" on the media. The way that bits are represented is called the signaling method. The physical layer standards must define what type of signal represents a "1" and what type of signal represents a "0". This can be as simple as a change in the level of an electrical signal or optical pulse. For example, a long pulse might represent a 1 whereas a short pulse might represent a 0.

This is similar to the signaling method used in Morse code, which may use a series of on-off tones, lights, or clicks to send text over telephone wires or between ships at sea.

The figures display signaling

Click each button for illustrations of signaling for copper cable, fiber-optic cable, and wireless media.

Copper Cable

Electrical Signals Over Copper Cable

Fiber Optic Cable

Light Pulses Over Fiber-Optic Cable

Wireless Media

Microwave Signals Over Wireless

Bandwidth - 4.2.5

Different physical media support the transfer of bits at different rates. Data transfer is usually discussed in terms of bandwidth. Bandwidth is the capacity at which a medium can carry data. Digital bandwidth measures the amount of data that can flow from one place to another in a given amount of time. Bandwidth is typically measured in kilobits per second (kbps), megabits per second (Mbps), or gigabits per second (Gbps). Bandwidth is sometimes thought of as the speed that bits travel, however this is not accurate. For example, in both 10Mbps and 100Mbps Ethernet, the bits are sent at the speed of electricity. The difference is the number of bits that are transmitted per second.

A combination of factors determines the practical bandwidth of a network:

- The properties of the physical media

- The technologies chosen for signaling and detecting network signals

Physical media properties, current technologies, and the laws of physics all play a role in determining the available bandwidth.

The table shows the commonly used units of measure for bandwidth.

Unit of Bandwidth	Abbreviation	Equivalence
Bits per second	bps	1 bps = fundamental unit of bandwidth
Kilobits per second	Kbps	1 Kbps = 1,000 bps = 10^3 bps
Megabits per second	Mbps	1 Mbps = 1,000,000 bps = 10^6 bps
Gigabits per second	Gbps	1 Gbps = 1,000,000,000 bps = 10^9 bps
Terabits per second	Tbps	1 Tbps = 1,000,000,000,000 bps = 10^{12} bps

Refer to **Online Course** for Illustration

Bandwidth Terminology - 4.2.6

Terms used to measure the quality of bandwidth include:

- Latency

- Throughput

- Goodput

Latency

Latency refers to the amount of time, including delays, for data to travel from one given point to another.

In an internetwork, or a network with multiple segments, throughput cannot be faster than the slowest link in the path from source to destination. Even if all, or most, of the segments have high bandwidth, it will only take one segment in the path with low throughput to create a bottleneck in the throughput of the entire network.

Throughput

Throughput is the measure of the transfer of bits across the media over a given period of time.

Due to a number of factors, throughput usually does not match the specified bandwidth in physical layer implementations. Throughput is usually lower than the bandwidth. There are many factors that influence throughput:

- The amount of traffic

- The type of traffic

- The latency created by the number of network devices encountered between source and destination

There are many online speed tests that can reveal the throughput of an internet connection. The figure provides sample results from a speed test.

Goodput

There is a third measurement to assess the transfer of usable data; it is known as goodput. Goodput is the measure of usable data transferred over a given period of time. Goodput is throughput minus traffic overhead for establishing sessions, acknowledgments, encapsulation, and retransmitted bits. Goodput is always lower than throughput, which is generally lower than the bandwidth.

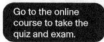

Check Your Understanding - Physical Layer Characteristics - 4.2.7

Copper Cabling - 4.3

Characteristics of Copper Cabling - 4.3.1

Copper cabling is the most common type of cabling used in networks today. In fact, copper cabling is not just one type of cable. There are three different types of copper cabling that are each used in specific situations.

Networks use copper media because it is inexpensive, easy to install, and has low resistance to electrical current. However, copper media is limited by distance and signal interference.

Data is transmitted on copper cables as electrical pulses. A detector in the network interface of a destination device must receive a signal that can be successfully decoded to match the signal sent. However, the farther the signal travels, the more it deteriorates. This is referred to as signal attenuation. For this reason, all copper media must follow strict distance limitations as specified by the guiding standards.

The timing and voltage values of the electrical pulses are also susceptible to interference from two sources:

- **Electromagnetic interference (EMI) or radio frequency interference (RFI)** - EMI and RFI signals can distort and corrupt the data signals being carried by copper media. Potential sources of EMI and RFI include radio waves and electromagnetic devices, such as fluorescent lights or electric motors.

- **Crosstalk** - Crosstalk is a disturbance caused by the electric or magnetic fields of a signal on one wire to the signal in an adjacent wire. In telephone circuits, crosstalk can result in hearing part of another voice conversation from an adjacent circuit. Specifically, when an electrical current flows through a wire, it creates a small, circular magnetic field around the wire, which can be picked up by an adjacent wire.

The figure shows how data transmission can be affected by interference.

To counter the negative effects of EMI and RFI, some types of copper cables are wrapped in metallic shielding and require proper grounding connections.

To counter the negative effects of crosstalk, some types of copper cables have opposing circuit wire pairs twisted together, which effectively cancels the crosstalk.

The susceptibility of copper cables to electronic noise can also be limited using these recommendations:

- Selecting the cable type or category most suited to a given networking environment
- Designing a cable infrastructure to avoid known and potential sources of interference in the building structure
- Using cabling techniques that include the proper handling and termination of the cables

Refer to Online Course for Illustration

Types of Copper Cabling - 4.3.2

There are three main types of copper media used in networking.

Refer to Online Course for Illustration

Unshielded twisted-pair (UTP) - 4.3.3

Unshielded twisted-pair (UTP) cabling is the most common networking media. UTP cabling, terminated with RJ-45 connectors, is used for interconnecting network hosts with intermediary networking devices, such as switches and routers.

In LANs, UTP cable consists of four pairs of color-coded wires that have been twisted together and then encased in a flexible plastic sheath that protects from minor physical damage. The twisting of wires helps protect against signal interference from other wires.

As seen in the figure, the color codes identify the individual pairs and wires and aid in cable termination.

Refer to Online Course for Illustration

Shielded twisted-pair (STP) - 4.3.4

Shielded twisted-pair (STP) provides better noise protection than UTP cabling. However, compared to UTP cable, STP cable is significantly more expensive and difficult to install. Like UTP cable, STP uses an RJ-45 connector.

STP cables combine the techniques of shielding to counter EMI and RFI, and wire twisting to counter crosstalk. To gain the full benefit of the shielding, STP cables are terminated with special shielded STP data connectors. If the cable is improperly grounded, the shield may act as an antenna and pick up unwanted signals.

The STP cable shown uses four pairs of wires, each wrapped in a foil shield, which are then wrapped in an overall metallic braid or foil.

Refer to Online Course for Illustration

Coaxial cable - 4.3.5

Coaxial cable, or coax for short, gets its name from the fact that there are two conductors that share the same axis. As shown in the figure, coaxial cable consists of the following:

- A copper conductor is used to transmit the electronic signals.
- A layer of flexible plastic insulation surrounds a copper conductor.

- The insulating material is surrounded in a woven copper braid, or metallic foil, that acts as the second wire in the circuit and as a shield for the inner conductor. This second layer, or shield, also reduces the amount of outside electromagnetic interference.

- The entire cable is covered with a cable jacket to prevent minor physical damage.

There are different types of connectors used with coax cable. The Bayonet Neill–Concelman (BNC), N type, and F type connectors are shown in the figure.

Although UTP cable has essentially replaced coaxial cable in modern Ethernet installations, the coaxial cable design is used in the following situations:

- **Wireless installations** - Coaxial cables attach antennas to wireless devices. The coaxial cable carries radio frequency (RF) energy between the antennas and the radio equipment.

- **Cable internet installations** - Cable service providers provide internet connectivity to their customers by replacing portions of the coaxial cable and supporting amplification elements with fiber-optic cable. However, the wiring inside the customer's premises is still coax cable.

Go to the online course to take the quiz and exam.

Check Your Understanding - Copper Cabling - 4.3.6

UTP Cabling - 4.4

Refer to **Online Course** for Illustration

Properties of UTP Cabling - 4.4.1

In the previous topic, you learned a bit about unshielded twisted-pair (UTP) copper cabling. Because UTP cabling is the standard for use in LANs, this topic goes into detail about its advantages and limitations, and what can be done to avoid problems.

When used as a networking medium, UTP cabling consists of four pairs of color-coded copper wires that have been twisted together and then encased in a flexible plastic sheath. Its small size can be advantageous during installation.

UTP cable does not use shielding to counter the effects of EMI and RFI. Instead, cable designers have discovered other ways that they can limit the negative effect of crosstalk:

- **Cancellation** - Designers now pair wires in a circuit. When two wires in an electrical circuit are placed close together, their magnetic fields are the exact opposite of each other. Therefore, the two magnetic fields cancel each other and also cancel out any outside EMI and RFI signals.

- **Varying the number of twists per wire pair** - To further enhance the cancellation effect of paired circuit wires, designers vary the number of twists of each wire pair in a cable. UTP cable must follow precise specifications governing how many twists or braids are permitted per meter (3.28 feet) of cable. Notice in the figure that the orange/orange white pair is twisted less than the blue/blue white pair. Each colored pair is twisted a different number of times.

UTP cable relies solely on the cancellation effect produced by the twisted wire pairs to limit signal degradation and effectively provide self-shielding for wire pairs within the network media.

Refer to **Online Course** for Illustration

UTP Cabling Standards and Connectors - 4.4.2

UTP cabling conforms to the standards established jointly by the TIA/EIA. Specifically, TIA/EIA-568 stipulates the commercial cabling standards for LAN installations and is the standard most commonly used in LAN cabling environments. Some of the elements defined are as follows:

- Cable types

- Cable lengths

- Connectors

- Cable termination

- Methods of testing cable

The electrical characteristics of copper cabling are defined by the Institute of Electrical and Electronics Engineers (IEEE). IEEE rates UTP cabling according to its performance. Cables are placed into categories based on their ability to carry higher bandwidth rates. For example, Category 5 cable is used commonly in 100BASE-TX Fast Ethernet installations. Other categories include Enhanced Category 5 cable, Category 6, and Category 6a.

Cables in higher categories are designed and constructed to support higher data rates. As new gigabit speed Ethernet technologies are being developed and adopted, Category 5e is now the minimally acceptable cable type, with Category 6 being the recommended type for new building installations.

The figure shows three categories of UTP cable:

- Category 3 was originally used for voice communication over voice lines, but later used for data transmission.

- Category 5 and 5e is used for data transmission. Category 5 supports 100Mbps and Category 5e supports 1000 Mbps

- Category 6 has an added separator between each wire pair to support higher speeds. Category 6 supports up to 10 Gbps.

- Category 7 also supports 10 Gbps.

- Category 8 supports 40 Gbps.

Some manufacturers are making cables exceeding the TIA/EIA Category 6a specifications and refer to these as Category 7.

UTP cable is usually terminated with an RJ-45 connector. The TIA/EIA-568 standard describes the wire color codes to pin assignments (pinouts) for Ethernet cables.

As shown in the figure, the RJ-45 connector is the male component, crimped at the end of the cable.

The socket, shown in the figure, is the female component of a network device, wall, cubicle partition outlet, or patch panel. When terminated improperly, each cable is a potential source of physical layer performance degradation.

This figure shows an example of a badly terminated UTP cable. This bad connector has wires that are exposed, untwisted, and not entirely covered by the sheath.

The next figure shows a properly terminated UTP cable. It is a good connector with wires that are untwisted only to the extent necessary to attach the connector.

Note: Improper cable termination can impact transmission performance.

Refer to
Online Course
for Illustration

Straight-through and Crossover UTP Cables - 4.4.3

Different situations may require UTP cables to be wired according to different wiring conventions. This means that the individual wires in the cable have to be connected in different orders to different sets of pins in the RJ-45 connectors.

The following are the main cable types that are obtained by using specific wiring conventions:

- **Ethernet Straight-through** - The most common type of networking cable. It is commonly used to interconnect a host to a switch and a switch to a router.

- **Ethernet Crossover** - A cable used to interconnect similar devices. For example, to connect a switch to a switch, a host to a host, or a router to a router. However, crossover cables are now considered legacy as NICs use medium-dependent interface crossover (auto-MDIX) to automatically detect the cable type and make the internal connection.

Note: Another type of cable is a rollover cable, which is Cisco proprietary. It is used to connect a workstation to a router or switch console port.

Using a crossover or straight-through cable incorrectly between devices may not damage the devices, but connectivity and communication between the devices will not take place. This is a common error and checking that the device connections are correct should be the first troubleshooting action if connectivity is not achieved.

The figure identifies the individual wire pairs for the T568A and T568B standards.

The table shows the UTP cable type, related standards, and typical application of these cables.

Cable Types and Standards

Cable Type	Standard	Application
Ethernet Straight-through	Both ends T568A or both ends T568B	Connects a network host to a network device such as a switch or hub
Ethernet Crossover	One end T568A, other end T568B	Connects two network hosts Connects two network intermediary devices (switch to switch or router to router)
Rollover	Cisco proprietary	Connects a workstation serial port to a router console port, using an adapter

Activity - Cable Pinouts - 4.4.4

For this activity, correctly order the wire colors to a TIA/EIA cable pinout. Select a wire case color by clicking it. Then click a wire to apply that casing to it.

Fiber-Optic Cabling - 4.5

Properties of Fiber-Optic Cabling - 4.5.1

As you have learned, fiber-optic cabling is the other type of cabling used in networks. Because it is expensive, it is not as commonly used at the various types of copper cabling. But fiber-optic cabling has certain properties that make it the best option in certain situations, which you will discover in this topic.

Optical fiber cable transmits data over longer distances and at higher bandwidths than any other networking media. Unlike copper wires, fiber-optic cable can transmit signals with less attenuation and is completely immune to EMI and RFI. Optical fiber is commonly used to interconnect network devices.

Optical fiber is a flexible, but extremely thin, transparent strand of very pure glass, not much bigger than a human hair. Bits are encoded on the fiber as light impulses. The fiber-optic cable acts as a waveguide, or "light pipe," to transmit light between the two ends with minimal loss of signal.

As an analogy, consider an empty paper towel roll with the inside coated like a mirror. It is a thousand meters in length, and a small laser pointer is used to send Morse code signals at the speed of light. Essentially that is how a fiber-optic cable operates, except that it is smaller in diameter and uses sophisticated light technologies.

Types of Fiber Media - 4.5.2

Fiber-optic cables are broadly classified into two types:

- Single-mode fiber (SMF)
- Multimode fiber (MMF)

Click each button for an illustration and explanation of each type.

Single-Mode Fiber

SMF consists of a very small core and uses expensive laser technology to send a single ray of light, as shown in the figure. SMF is popular in long-distance situations spanning hundreds of kilometers, such as those required in long haul telephony and cable TV applications.

Multimode Fiber

MMF consists of a larger core and uses LED emitters to send light pulses. Specifically, light from an LED enters the multimode fiber at different angles, as shown in the figure. Popular in LANs because they can be powered by low-cost LEDs. It provides bandwidth up to 10 Gb/s over link lengths of up to 550 meters.

One of the highlighted differences between MMF and SMF is the amount of dispersion. Dispersion refers to the spreading out of a light pulse over time. Increased dispersion means increased loss of signal strength. MMF has a greater dispersion than SMF. That is why MMF can only travel up to 500 meters before signal loss.

Fiber-Optic Cabling Usage - 4.5.3

Fiber-optic cabling is now being used in four types of industry:

- **Enterprise Networks** - Used for backbone cabling applications and interconnecting infrastructure devices

- **Fiber-to-the-Home (FTTH)** - Used to provide always-on broadband services to homes and small businesses

- **Long-Haul Networks** - Used by service providers to connect countries and cities

- **Submarine Cable Networks** - Used to provide reliable high-speed, high-capacity solutions capable of surviving in harsh undersea environments at up to transoceanic distances. Search the internet for "submarine cables telegeography map" to view various maps online.

Our focus in this course is the use of fiber within the enterprise.

Refer to
Interactive Graphic
in online course

Fiber-Optic Connectors - 4.5.4

Refer to
Online Course
for Illustration

An optical-fiber connector terminates the end of an optical fiber. A variety of optical-fiber connectors are available. The main differences among the types of connectors are dimensions and methods of coupling. Businesses decide on the types of connectors that will be used, based on their equipment.

Note: Some switches and routers have ports that support fiber-optic connectors through a small form-factor pluggable (SFP) transceiver. Search the internet for various types of SFPs.

Click each fiber-optic connector type for an image and more information.

Straight-Tip (ST) Connectors

ST connectors were one of the first connector types used. The connector locks securely with a "Twist-on/twist-off" bayonet-style mechanism.

Subscriber Connector (SC) Connectors

SC connectors are sometimes referred to as square connector or standard connector. They are a widely-adopted LAN and WAN connector that uses a push-pull mechanism to ensure positive insertion. This connector type is used with multimode and single-mode fiber.

Lucent Connector (LC) Simplex Connectors

LC simplex connectors are a smaller version of the SC connector. These are sometimes called little or local connectors and are quickly growing in popularity due to their smaller size.

Duplex Multimode LC Connectors

A duplex multimode LC connector is similar to a LC simplex connector, but uses a duplex connector.

Until recently, light could only travel in one direction over optical fiber. Two fibers were required to support the full duplex operation. Therefore, fiber-optic patch cables bundle together two optical fiber cables and terminate them with a pair of standard, single-fiber connectors. Some fiber connectors accept both the transmitting and receiving fibers in a single connector known as a duplex connector, as shown in the Duplex Multimode LC Connector in the figure. BX standards such as 100BASE-BX use different wavelengths for sending and receiving over a single fiber.

Refer to **Interactive Graphic** in online course

Refer to **Online Course** for Illustration

Fiber Patch Cords - 4.5.5

Fiber patch cords are required for interconnecting infrastructure devices. The use of color distinguishes between single-mode and multimode patch cords. A yellow jacket is for single-mode fiber cables and orange (or aqua) for multimode fiber cables.

Click each fiber patch cord for an image.

SC-SC Multimode Patch Cord

LC-LC Single-mode Patch Cord

ST-LC Multimode Patch Cord

SC-ST Single-mode Patch Cord

Note: Fiber cables should be protected with a small plastic cap when not in use.

Fiber versus Copper - 4.5.6

There are many advantages to using fiber-optic cable compared to copper cables. The table highlights some of these differences.

At present, in most enterprise environments, optical fiber is primarily used as backbone cabling for high-traffic, point-to-point connections between data distribution facilities. It is also used for the interconnection of buildings in multi-building campuses. Because fiber-optic cables do not conduct electricity and have a low signal loss, they are well suited for these uses.

UTP and Fiber-Optic Cabling Comparison

Implementation Issues	UTP Cabling	Fiber-Optic Cabling
Bandwidth supported	10 Mb/s - 10 Gb/s	10 Mb/s - 100 Gb/s
Distance	Relatively short (1 - 100 meters)	Relatively long (1 - 100,000 meters)
Immunity to EMI and RFI	Low	High (Completely immune)
Immunity to electrical hazards	Low	High (Completely immune)

Implementation Issues	UTP Cabling	Fiber-Optic Cabling
Media and connector costs	Lowest	Highest
Installation skills required	Lowest	Highest
Safety precautions	Lowest	Highest

Go to the online course to take the quiz and exam.

Check Your Understanding - Fiber-Optic Cabling - 4.5.7

Wireless Media - 4.6

Properties of Wireless Media - 4.6.1

You may be taking this course using a tablet or a smart phone. This is only possible due to wireless media, which is the third way to connect to the physical layer of a network.

Wireless media carry electromagnetic signals that represent the binary digits of data communications using radio or microwave frequencies.

Wireless media provide the greatest mobility options of all media, and the number of wireless-enabled devices continues to increase. Wireless is now the primary way users connect to home and enterprise networks.

These are some of the limitations of wireless:

- **Coverage area** - Wireless data communication technologies work well in open environments. However, certain construction materials used in buildings and structures, and the local terrain, will limit the effective coverage.

- **Interference** - Wireless is susceptible to interference and can be disrupted by such common devices as household cordless phones, some types of fluorescent lights, microwave ovens, and other wireless communications.

- **Security** - Wireless communication coverage requires no access to a physical strand of media. Therefore, devices and users, not authorized for access to the network, can gain access to the transmission. Network security is a major component of wireless network administration.

- **Shared medium** - WLANs operate in half-duplex, which means only one device can send or receive at a time. The wireless medium is shared amongst all wireless users. Many users accessing the WLAN simultaneously results in reduced bandwidth for each user.

Although wireless is increasing in popularity for desktop connectivity, copper and fiber are the most popular physical layer media for deployment of intermediary network devices, such as routers and switches.

Types of Wireless Media - 4.6.2

The IEEE and telecommunications industry standards for wireless data communications cover both the data link and physical layers. In each of these standards, physical layer specifications are applied to areas that include the following:

- Data to radio signal encoding

- Frequency and power of transmission

- Signal reception and decoding requirements

- Antenna design and construction

These are the wireless standards:

- **Wi-Fi (IEEE 802.11)** - Wireless LAN (WLAN) technology, commonly referred to as Wi-Fi. WLAN uses a contention-based protocol known as carrier sense multiple access/collision avoidance (CSMA/CA). The wireless NIC must first listen before transmitting to determine if the radio channel is clear. If another wireless device is transmitting, then the NIC must wait until the channel is clear. Wi-Fi is a trademark of the Wi-Fi Alliance. Wi-Fi is used with certified WLAN devices based on the IEEE 802.11 standards.

- **Bluetooth (IEEE 802.15)** - This is a wireless personal area network (WPAN) standard, commonly known as "Bluetooth." It uses a device pairing process to communicate over distances from 1 to 100 meters.

- **WiMAX (IEEE 802:16)** - Commonly known as Worldwide Interoperability for Microware Access (WiMAX), this wireless standard uses a point-to-multipoint topology to provide wireless broadband access.

- **Zigbee (IEEE 802.15.4)** - Zigbee is a specification used for low-data rate, low-power communications. It is intended for applications that require short-range, low data-rates and long battery life. Zigbee is typically used for industrial and Internet of Things (IoT) environments such as wireless light switches and medical device data collection.

Note: Other wireless technologies such as cellular and satellite communications can also provide data network connectivity. However, these wireless technologies are out of scope for this module.

Refer to
Online Course
for Illustration

Wireless LAN - 4.6.3

A common wireless data implementation is enabling devices to connect wirelessly via a LAN. In general, a WLAN requires the following network devices:

- **Wireless Access Point (AP)** - These concentrate the wireless signals from users and connect to the existing copper-based network infrastructure, such as Ethernet. Home and small business wireless routers integrate the functions of a router, switch, and access point into one device, as shown in the figure.

- **Wireless NIC adapters** - These provide wireless communication capability to network hosts.

As the technology has developed, a number of WLAN Ethernet-based standards have emerged. When purchasing wireless devices, ensure compatibility and interoperability.

The benefits of wireless data communications technologies are evident, especially the savings on costly premises wiring and the convenience of host mobility. Network administrators must develop and apply stringent security policies and processes to protect WLANs from unauthorized access and damage.

Go to the online course to take the quiz and exam.

Check Your Understanding - Wireless Media - 4.6.4

Refer to Packet Tracer Activity for this chapter

Packet Tracer - Connect a Wired and Wireless LAN - 4.6.5

When working in Packet Tracer, a lab environment, or a corporate setting, you should know how to select the appropriate cable and how to properly connect devices. This activity will examine device configurations in Packet Tracer, selecting the proper cable based on the configuration, and connecting the devices. This activity will also explore the physical view of the network in Packet Tracer.

Refer to Lab Activity for this chapter

Lab - View Wired and Wireless NIC Information - 4.6.6

In this lab, you will complete the following objectives:

- Part 1: Identify and Work with PC NICs
- Part 2: Identify and Use the System Tray Network Icons

Module Practice and Quiz - 4.7

Refer to Packet Tracer Activity for this chapter

Packet Tracer - Connect the Physical Layer - 4.7.1

In this activity, you will explore the different options available on internetworking devices. You will also be required to determine which options provide the necessary connectivity when connecting multiple devices. Finally, you will add the correct modules and connect the devices.

What did I learn in this module? - 4.7.2

Purpose of the Physical Layer

Before any network communications can occur, a physical connection to a local network must be established. A physical connection can be a wired connection using a cable or a wireless connection using radio waves. Network Interface Cards (NICs) connect a device to the network. Ethernet NICs are used for a wired connection, whereas WLAN (Wireless Local Area Network) NICs are used for wireless. The OSI physical layer provides the means to transport the bits that make up a data link layer frame across the network media. This layer accepts a complete frame from the data link layer and encodes it as a series of signals that are transmitted onto the local media. The encoded bits that comprise a frame are received by either an end device or an intermediary device.

Physical Layer Characteristics

The physical layer consists of electronic circuitry, media, and connectors developed by engineers. The physical layer standards address three functional areas: physical components, encoding, and signaling. Bandwidth is the capacity at which a medium can carry data. Digital bandwidth measures the amount of data that can flow from one place to another in a given amount of time. Throughput is the measure of the transfer of bits across the media over a given period of time and is usually lower than bandwidth. Latency refers to the amount of time, including delays, for data to travel from one given point to another. Goodput is the measure of usable data transferred over a given period of time. The physical layer produces the representation and groupings of bits for each type of media as follows:

- Copper cable - The signals are patterns of electrical pulses.

- Fiber-optic cable - The signals are patterns of light.

- Wireless - The signals are patterns of microwave transmissions.

Copper Cabling

Networks use copper media because it is inexpensive, easy to install, and has low resistance to electrical current. However, copper media is limited by distance and signal interference. The timing and voltage values of the electrical pulses are also susceptible to interference from two sources: EMI and crosstalk. Three types of copper cabling are: UTP, STP, and coaxial cable (coax). UTP has an outer jacket to protect the copper wires from physical damage, twisted pairs to protect the signal from interference, and color-coded plastic insulation that electrically isolates wires from each other and identifies each pair. The STP cable uses four pairs of wires, each wrapped in a foil shield, which are then wrapped in an overall metallic braid or foil. Coaxial cable, or coax for short, gets its name from the fact that there are two conductors that share the same axis. Coax is used to attach antennas to wireless devices. Cable internet providers use coax inside their customers' premises.

UTP Cabling

UTP cabling consists of four pairs of color-coded copper wires that have been twisted together and then encased in a flexible plastic sheath. UTP cable does not use shielding to counter the effects of EMI and RFI. Instead, cable designers have discovered other ways that they can limit the negative effect of crosstalk: cancellation and varying the number of twists per wire pair. UTP cabling conforms to the standards established jointly by the TIA/EIA. The electrical characteristics of copper cabling are defined by the Institute of Electrical and Electronics Engineers (IEEE). UTP cable is usually terminated with an RJ-45 connector. The main cable types that are obtained by using specific wiring conventions are Ethernet Straight-through and Ethernet Crossover. Cisco has a proprietary UTP cable called a rollover that connects a workstation to a router console port.

Fiber-Optic Cabling

Optical fiber cable transmits data over longer distances and at higher bandwidths than any other networking media. Fiber-optic cable can transmit signals with less attenuation than copper wire and is completely immune to EMI and RFI. Optical fiber is a flexible, but extremely thin, transparent strand of very pure glass, not much bigger than a human hair. Bits are encoded on the fiber as light impulses. Fiber-optic cabling is now being used in four types of industry: enterprise networks, FTTH, long-haul networks, and submarine cable networks. There are four types of fiber-optic connectors: ST, SC, LC, and duplex multimode LC. Fiber-optic patch cords include SC-SC multimode, LC-LC single-mode, ST-LC multimode, and SC-ST single-mode. In most enterprise environments, optical fiber is primarily used as backbone cabling for high-traffic point-to-point connections between data distribution facilities and for the interconnection of buildings in multi-building campuses.

Wireless Media

Wireless media carry electromagnetic signals that represent the binary digits of data communications using radio or microwave frequencies. Wireless does have some limitations, including: coverage area, interference, security, and the problems that occur with any shared medium. Wireless standards include the following: Wi-Fi (IEEE 802.11), Bluetooth (IEEE 802.15), WiMAX (IEEE 802.16), and Zigbee (IEEE 802.15.4). Wireless LAN (WLAN) requires a wireless AP and wireless NIC adapters.

Go to the online
course to take the
quiz and exam.

Chapter Quiz - Physical Layer

Your Chapter Notes

CHAPTER 5

Number Systems

Introduction - 5.0

Why should I take this module? - 5.0.1

Welcome to Number Systems!

Guess what? This is a 32-bit IPv4 address of a computer in a network: 11000000.10101000. 00001010.00001010. It is shown in binary. This is the IPv4 address for the same computer in dotted decimal: 192.168.10.10. Which one would you rather work with? IPv6 addresses are 128 bits! To make these addresses more manageable, IPv6 uses a hexadecimal system of 0-9 and the letters A-F.

As a network administrator you must know how to convert binary addresses into dotted decimal and dotted decimal addresses into binary. You will also need to know how to convert dotted decimal into hexadecimal and vice versa. (Hint: You still need your binary conversion skills to make this work.)

Surprisingly, it is not that hard when you learn a few tricks. This module contains an activity called the Binary Game which will really help you get started. So, why wait?

What will I learn to do in this module? - 5.0.2

Module Title: Number Systems

Module Objective: Calculate numbers between decimal, binary, and hexadecimal systems.

Topic Title	Topic Objective
Binary Number System	Calculate numbers between decimal and binary systems.
Hexadecimal Number System	Calculate numbers between decimal and hexadecimal systems.

Binary Number System - 5.1

Binary and IPv4 Addresses - 5.1.1

Refer to
Online Course
for Illustration

IPv4 addresses begin as binary, a series of only 1s and 0s. These are difficult to manage, so network administrators must convert them to decimal. This topic shows you a few ways to do this.

Binary is a numbering system that consists of the digits 0 and 1 called bits. In contrast, the decimal numbering system consists of 10 digits consisting of the digits 0 – 9.

Binary is important for us to understand because hosts, servers, and network devices use binary addressing. Specifically, they use binary IPv4 addresses, as shown in the figure, to identify each other.

Each address consists of a string of 32 bits, divided into four sections called octets. Each octet contains 8 bits (or 1 byte) separated with a dot. For example, PC1 in the figure is assigned IPv4 address 11000000.10101000.00001010.00001010. Its default gateway address would be that of R1 Gigabit Ethernet interface 11000000.10101000.00001010. 00000001.

Binary works well with hosts and network devices. However, it is very challenging for humans to work with.

For ease of use by people, IPv4 addresses are commonly expressed in dotted decimal notation. PC1 is assigned the IPv4 address 192.168.10.10, and its default gateway address is 192.168.10.1, as shown in the figure.

For a solid understanding of network addressing, it is necessary to know binary addressing and gain practical skills converting between binary and dotted decimal IPv4 addresses. This section will cover how to convert between base two (binary) and base 10 (decimal) numbering systems.

Refer to **Video** in online course

Video - Converting Between Binary and Decimal Numbering Systems - 5.1.2

Click Play in the figure for a video demonstrating how to convert between binary and decimal numbering systems.

Binary Positional Notation - 5.1.3

Learning to convert binary to decimal requires an understanding of positional notation. Positional notation means that a digit represents different values depending on the "position" the digit occupies in the sequence of numbers. You already know the most common numbering system, the decimal (base 10) notation system.

The decimal positional notation system operates as described in the table.

Radix	10	10	10	10
Position in Number	3	2	1	0
Calculate	(10^3)	(10^2)	(10^1)	(10^0)
Position value	1000	100	10	1

The following bullets describe each row of the table.

- Row 1, Radix is the number base. Decimal notation is based on 10, therefore the radix is 10.

- Row 2, Position in number considers the position of the decimal number starting with, from right to left, 0 (1st position), 1 (2nd position), 2 (3rd position), 3 (4th position). These numbers also represent the exponential value use to calculate the positional value in the 4th row.

- Row 3 calculates the positional value by taking the radix and raising it by the exponential value of its position in row 2.

Note: n^0 is = 1.

- Row 4 positional value represents units of thousands, hundreds, tens, and ones.

To use the positional system, match a given number to its positional value. The example in the table illustrates how positional notation is used with the decimal number 1234.

	Thousands	Hundreds	Tens	Ones
Positional Value	1000	100	10	1
Decimal Number (1234)	1	2	3	4
Calculate	1 x 1000	2 x 100	3 x 10	4 x 1
Add them up...	1000	+ 200	+ 30	+ 4
Result	1,234			

In contrast, the binary positional notation operates as described in the table.

Radix	2	2	2	2	2	2	2	2
Position in Number	7	6	5	4	3	2	1	0
Calculate	(2^7)	(2^6)	(2^5)	(2^4)	(2^3)	(2^2)	(2^1)	(2^0)
Position value	128	64	32	16	8	4	2	1

The following bullets describe each row of the table.

- Row 1, Radix is the number base. Binary notation is based on 2, therefore the radix is 2.

- Row 2, Position in number considers the position of the binary number starting with, from right to left, 0 (1st position), 1 (2nd position), 2 (3rd position), 3 (4th position). These numbers also represent the exponential value use to calculate the positional value in the 4th row.

- Row 3 calculates the positional value by taking the radix and raising it by the exponential value of its position in row 2.

Note: n^0 is = 1.

- Row 4 positional value represents units of ones, twos, fours, eights, etc.

The example in the table illustrates how a binary number 11000000 corresponds to the number 192. If the binary number had been 10101000, then the corresponding decimal number would be 168.

Positional Value	128	64	32	16	8	4	2	1
Binary Number (11000000)	1	1	0	0	0	0	0	0
Calculate	1 x 128	1 x 64	0 x 32	0 x 16	0 x 8	0 x 4	0 x 2	0 x 1
Add Them Up..	128	+ 64	+ 0	+ 0	+ 0	+ 0	+ 0	+ 0
Result	192							

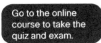
Go to the online course to take the quiz and exam.

Check Your Understanding - Binary Number System - 5.1.4

Convert Binary to Decimal - 5.1.5

To convert a binary IPv4 address to its dotted decimal equivalent, divide the IPv4 address into four 8-bit octets. Next apply the binary positional value to the first octet binary number and calculate accordingly.

For example, consider that 11000000.10101000.00001011.00001010 is the binary IPv4 address of a host. To convert the binary address to decimal, start with the first octet, as shown in the table. Enter the 8-bit binary number under the positional value of row 1 and then calculate to produce the decimal number 192. This number goes into the first octet of the dotted decimal notation.

Positional Value	128	64	32	16	8	4	2	1
Binary Number (11000000)	1	1	0	0	0	0	0	0
Calculate	128	64	32	16	8	4	2	1
Add Them Up...	128	+ 64	+ 0	+ 0	+ 0	+ 0	+ 0	+ 0
Result	192							

Next convert the second octet of 10101000 as shown in the table. The resulting decimal value is 168, and it goes into the second octet.

Positional Value	128	64	32	16	8	4	2	1
Binary Number (10101000)	1	0	1	0	1	0	0	0
Calculate	128	64	32	16	8	4	2	1
Add Them Up...	128	+ 0	+ 32	+ 0	+ 8	+ 0	+ 0	+ 0
Result	168							

Convert the third octet of 00001011 as shown in the table.

Positional Value	128	64	32	16	8	4	2	1
Binary Number (00001011)	0	0	0	0	1	0	1	1
Calculate	128	64	32	16	8	4	2	1
Add Them Up...	0	+ 0	+ 0	+ 0	+ 8	+ 0	+ 2	+ 1
Result	11							

Convert the fourth octet of 00001010 as shown in the table. This completes the IP address and produces **192.168.11.10**.

Positional Value	128	64	32	16	8	4	2	1
Binary Number (00001010)	0	0	0	0	1	0	1	0
Calculate	128	64	32	16	8	4	2	1
Add Them Up...	0	+ 0	+ 0	+ 0	+ 8	+ 0	+ 2	+ 0
Result	10							

Refer to
Lab Activity
for this chapter

Activity - Binary to Decimal Conversions - 5.1.6

This activity allows you to practice 8-bit binary to decimal conversion as much as necessary. We recommend that you work with this tool until you are able to do the conversion without error. Convery the binary number shown in the octet to its decimal value.

Refer to
Interactive Graphic
in online course

Refer to
Online Course
for Illustration

Decimal to Binary Conversion - 5.1.7

It is also necessary to understand how to convert a dotted decimal IPv4 address to binary. A useful tool is the binary positional value table.

Click each position starting at 128 and work your way from left to right to the 1 position.

128

Is the decimal number of the octet (n) equal to or greater than the most-significant bit (128)?

- If no, then enter binary 0 in the 128 positional value.
- If yes, then add a binary 1 in the 128 positional value and subtract 128 from the decimal number.

64

Is the decimal number of the octet (n) equal to or greater than the next most-significant bit (64)?

- If no, then enter binary 0 in the 64 positional value.
- If yes, then add a binary 1 in the 64 positional value and subtract 64 from the decimal number.

32

Is the decimal number of the octet (n) equal to or greater than the next most-significant bit (32)?

- If no, then enter binary 0 in the 32 positional value.
- If yes, then add a binary 1 in the 32 positional value and subtract 32 from the decimal number.

16

Is the decimal number of the octet (n) equal to or greater than the next most-significant bit (16)?

- If no, then enter binary 0 in the 16 positional value.
- If yes, then add a binary 1 in the 16 positional value and subtract 16 from the decimal number.

8

Is the decimal number of the octet (n) equal to or greater than the next most-significant bit (8)?

- If no, then enter binary 0 in the 8 positional value.
- If yes, then add a binary 1 in the 8 positional value and subtract 8 from the decimal number.

4

Is the decimal number of the octet (n) equal to or greater than the next most-significant bit (**4**)?

- If no, then enter binary **0** in the **4** positional value.

- If yes, then add a binary **1** in the **4** positional value and subtract **4** from the decimal number.

2

Is the decimal number of the octet (n) equal to or greater than the next most-significant bit (**2**)?

- If no, then enter binary **0** in the **2** positional value.

- If yes, then add a binary **1** in the **2** positional value and subtract **2** from the decimal number.

1

Is the decimal number of the octet (n) equal to or greater than the last most-significant bit (**1**)?

- If no, then enter binary **0** in the **1** positional value.

- If yes, then add a binary **1** in the **1** positional value and subtract **1** from the last decimal number.

Refer to
Interactive Graphic
in online course

Refer to
Online Course
for Illustration

Decimal to Binary Conversion Example - 5.1.8

To help understand the process, consider the IP address 192.168.11.10.

The first octet number 192 is converted to binary using the previously explained positional notation process.

It is possible to bypass the process of subtraction with easier or smaller decimal numbers. For instance, notice that it is fairly easy to calculate the third octet converted to a binary number without actually going through the subtraction process (8 + 2 = 10). The binary value of the third octet is 00001010.

The fourth octet is 11 (8 + 2 + 1). The binary value of the fourth octet is 00001011.

Converting between binary and decimal may seem challenging at first, but with practice it should become easier over time.

Click each step to see the conversion of the IP address of 192.168.10.11 into binary.

Step 1

Is the first octet number 192 equal to or greater than the high-order bit 128?

- Yes it is, therefore add a 1 to the high-order positional value to a represent 128.

- Subtract 128 from 192 to produce a remainder of 64.

Step 2

Is the remainder 64 equal to or greater than the next high-order bit 64?

- It is equal, therefore add a 1 to next high-order positional value.

Step 3

Since there is no remainder, enter binary **0** in the remaining positional values.

- The binary value of the first octet is **11000000**.

Step 4

Is the second octet number **168** equal to or greater than the high-order bit **128**?

- Yes it is, therefore add a **1** to the high-order positional value to represent **128**.
- Subtract **128** from **168** to produce a remainder of **40**.

Step 5

Is the remainder **40** equal to or greater than the next high-order bit **64**?

- No it is not, therefore, enter a binary **0** in the positional value.

Step 6

Is the remainder **40** equal to or greater than the next high-order bit **32**?

- Yes it is, therefore add a **1** to the high-order positional value to represent **32**.
- Subtract **32** from **40** to produce a remainder of **8**.

Step 7

Is the remainder **8** equal to or greater than the next high-order bit **16**?

- No it is not, therefore, enter a binary 0 in the positional value.

Step 8

Is the remainder **8** equal to or greater than the next high-order bit **8**?

- It is equal, therefore add a **1** to next high-order positional value.

Step 9

Since there is no remainder, enter binary **0** in the remaining positional values.

- The binary value of the second octet is **10101000**.

Step 10

The binary value of the third octet is **00001010**.

Step 11

The binary value of the fourth octet is **00001011**.

Refer to
Lab Activity
for this chapter

Activity - Decimal to Binary Conversions - 5.1.9

This activity allows you to practice decimal conversion to 8-bit binary values. We recommend that you work with this tool until you are able to do the conversion without error. Convert the decimal number shown in the Decimal Value row to its binary bits.

Activity - Binary Game - 5.1.10

This is a fun way to learn binary numbers for networking.

Game Link: https://learningnetwork.cisco.com/docs/DOC-1803

You will need to log in to cisco.com to use this link. It will be necessary to create an account if you do not already have one.

Mobile Download: https://learningnetwork.cisco.com/docs/DOC-11119

Refer to
Interactive Graphic
in online course

Refer to
Online Course
for Illustration

IPv4 Addresses - 5.1.11

As mentioned in the beginning of this topic, routers and computers only understand binary, while humans work in decimal. It is important for you to gain a thorough understanding of these two numbering systems and how they are used in networking.

Click each button to contrast the dotted decimal address and the 32-bit address.

Dotted Decimal Address

192.168.10.10 is an IP address that is assigned to a computer.

Octets

This address is made up of four different octets.

32-bit Address

The computer stores the address as the entire 32-bit data stream.

Hexadecimal Number System - 5.2

Refer to
Online Course
for Illustration

Hexadecimal and IPv6 Addresses - 5.2.1

Now you know how to convert binary to decimal and decimal to binary. You need that skill to understand IPv4 addressing in your network. But you are just as likely to be using IPv6 addresses in your network. To understand IPv6 addresses, you must be able to convert hexadecimal to decimal and vice versa.

Just as decimal is a base ten number system, hexadecimal is a base sixteen system. The base sixteen number system uses the digits 0 to 9 and the letters A to F. The figure shows the equivalent decimal and hexadecimal values for binary 0000 to 1111.

Binary and hexadecimal work well together because it is easier to express a value as a single hexadecimal digit than as four binary bits.

The hexadecimal numbering system is used in networking to represent IP Version 6 addresses and Ethernet MAC addresses.

IPv6 addresses are 128 bits in length and every 4 bits is represented by a single hexadecimal digit; for a total of 32 hexadecimal values. IPv6 addresses are not case-sensitive and can be written in either lowercase or uppercase.

As shown in the figure, the preferred format for writing an IPv6 address is x:x:x:x:x:x:x:x, with each "x" consisting of four hexadecimal values. When referring to 8 bits of an IPv4 address we use the term octet. In IPv6, a *hextet* is the unofficial term used to refer to a segment of 16 bits or four hexadecimal values. Each "x" is a single hextet, 16 bits, or four hexadecimal digits.

The sample topology in the figure displays IPv6 hexadecimal addresses.

Refer to **Video** in online course

Video - Converting Between Hexadecimal and Decimal Numbering Systems - 5.2.2

Click Play in the video to see how to convert between hexadecimal and decimal numbering systems.

Decimal to Hexadecimal Conversions - 5.2.3

Converting decimal numbers to hexadecimal values is straightforward. Follow the steps listed:

1. Convert the decimal number to 8-bit binary strings.

2. Divide the binary strings in groups of four starting from the rightmost position.

3. Convert each four binary numbers into their equivalent hexadecimal digit.

The example provides the steps for converting 168 to hexadecimal.

For example, 168 converted into hex using the three-step process.

1. 168 in binary is 10101000.

2. 10101000 in two groups of four binary digits is 1010 and 1000.

3. 1010 is hex A and 1000 is hex 8.

Answer: 168 is A8 in hexadecimal.

Hexadecimal to Decimal Conversion - 5.2.4

Converting hexadecimal numbers to decimal values is also straightforward. Follow the steps listed:

1. Convert the hexadecimal number to 4-bit binary strings.

2. Create 8-bit binary grouping starting from the rightmost position.

3. Convert each 8-bit binary grouping into their equivalent decimal digit.

This example provides the steps for converting D2 to decimal.

1. D2 in 4-bit binary strings is 1101 and 0010.

2. 1101 and 0010 is 11010010 in an 8-bit grouping.

3. 11010010 in binary is equivalent to 210 in decimal.

Answer: D2 in hexadecimal is 210 in decimal.

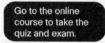

Go to the online
course to take the
quiz and exam.

Check Your Understanding - Hexadecimal Number System - 5.2.5

Module Practice and Quiz

What did I learn in this module? - 5.3.1

Binary Number System

Binary is a numbering system that consists of the numbers 0 and 1 called bits. In contrast, the decimal numbering system consists of 10 digits consisting of the numbers 0 – 9. Binary is important for us to understand because hosts, servers, and network devices use binary addressing, specifically, binary IPv4 addresses, to identify each other. You must know binary addressing and how to convert between binary and dotted decimal IPv4 addresses. This topic presented a few ways to convert decimal to binary and binary to decimal.

Hexadecimal Number System

Just as decimal is a base ten number system, hexadecimal is a base sixteen system. The base sixteen number system uses the numbers 0 to 9 and the letters A to F. The hexadecimal numbering system is used in networking to represent IPv6 addresses and Ethernet MAC addresses. IPv6 addresses are 128 bits in length and every 4 bits is represented by a single hexadecimal digit; for a total of 32 hexadecimal values. To convert hexadecimal to decimal, you must first convert the hexadecimal to binary, then convert the binary to decimal. To convert decimal to hexadecimal, you must also first convert the decimal to binary.

Go to the online course to take the quiz and exam.

Chapter Quiz - Number Systems

Your Chapter Notes

CHAPTER 6

Data Link Layer

Introduction - 6.0

Why should I take this module? - 6.0.1

Welcome to Data Link Layer!

Every network has physical components and media connecting the components. Different types of media need different information about the data in order to accept it and move it across the physical network. Think of it this way: A well-hit golf ball moves through the air fast and far. It can also move through water but not as fast or as far unless it is helped by a more forceful hit. This is because the golf ball is traveling through a different medium; water instead of air.

Data must have help to move it across different media. The data link layer provides this help. As you might have guessed, this help differs based on a number of factors. This module gives you an overview of these factors, how they affect data, and the protocols designed to ensure successful delivery. Let's get started!

What will I learn to do in this module? - 6.0.2

Module Title: Data Link Layer

Module Objective: Explain how media access control in the data link layer supports communication across networks.

Topic Title	Topic Objective
Purpose of the Data Link Layer	Describe the purpose and function of the data link layer in preparing communication for transmission on specific media.
Topologies	Compare the characteristics of media access control methods on WAN and LAN topologies.
Data Link Frame	Describe the characteristics and functions of the data link frame.

Purpose of the Data Link Layer - 6.1

The Data Link Layer - 6.1.1

Refer to Online Course for Illustration

The data link layer of the OSI model (Layer 2), as shown in the figure, prepares network data for the physical network. The data link layer is responsible for network interface card (NIC) to network interface card communications. The data link layer does the following:

- Enables upper layers to access the media. The upper layer protocol is completely unaware of the type of media that is used to forward the data.

- Accepts data, usually Layer 3 packets (i.e., IPv4 or IPv6), and encapsulates them into Layer 2 frames.

- Controls how data is placed and received on the media.

- Exchanges frames between endpoints over the network media.

- Receives encapsulated data, usually Layer 3 packets, and directs them to the proper upper-layer protocol.

- Performs error detection and rejects any corrupt frame.

In computer networks, a node is a device that can receive, create, store, or forward data along a communications path. A node can be either an end device such as a laptop or mobile phone, or an intermediary device such as an Ethernet switch.

Without the data link layer, network layer protocols such as IP, would have to make provisions for connecting to every type of media that could exist along a delivery path. Additionally, every time a new network technology or medium was developed IP, would have to adapt.

The figure displays an example of how the data link layer adds Layer 2 Ethernet destination and source NIC information to a Layer 3 packet. It would then convert this information to a format supported by the physical layer (i.e., Layer 1).

Refer to
Online Course
for Illustration

IEEE 802 LAN/MAN Data Link Sublayers - 6.1.2

IEEE 802 LAN/MAN standards are specific to Ethernet LANs, wireless LANs (WLAN), wireless personal area networks (WPAN) and other types of local and metropolitan area networks. The IEEE 802 LAN/MAN data link layer consists of the following two sublayers:

- **Logical Link Control (LLC)** - This IEEE 802.2 sublayer communicates between the networking software at the upper layers and the device hardware at the lower layers. It places information in the frame that identifies which network layer protocol is being used for the frame. This information allows multiple Layer 3 protocols, such as IPv4 and IPv6, to use the same network interface and media.

- **Media Access Control (MAC)** – Implements this sublayer (IEEE 802.3, 802.11, or 802.15) in hardware. It is responsible for data encapsulation and media access control. It provides data link layer addressing and it is integrated with various physical layer technologies.

The figure shows the two sublayers (LLC and MAC) of the data link layer.

The LLC sublayer takes the network protocol data, which is typically an IPv4 or IPv6 packet, and adds Layer 2 control information to help deliver the packet to the destination node.

The MAC sublayer controls the NIC and other hardware that is responsible for sending and receiving data on the wired or wireless LAN/MAN medium.

The MAC sublayer provides data encapsulation:

- **Frame delimiting** - The framing process provides important delimiters to identify fields within a frame. These delimiting bits provide synchronization between the transmitting and receiving nodes.

- **Addressing** - Provides source and destination addressing for transporting the Layer 2 frame between devices on the same shared medium.

- **Error detection** - Includes a trailer used to detect transmission errors.

The MAC sublayer also provides media access control, allowing multiple devices to communicate over a shared (half-duplex) medium. Full-duplex communications do not require access control.

Refer to
Interactive Graphic
in online course

Providing Access to Media - 6.1.3

Each network environment that packets encounter as they travel from a local host to a remote host can have different characteristics. For example, an Ethernet LAN usually consists of many hosts contending for access on the network medium. The MAC sublayer resolves this. With serial links the access method may only consist of a direct connection between only two devices, usually two routers. Therefore, they do not require the techniques employed by the IEEE 802 MAC sublayer.

Router interfaces encapsulate the packet into the appropriate frame. A suitable media access control method is used to access each link. In any given exchange of network layer packets, there may be numerous data link layers and media transitions.

At each hop along the path, a router performs the following Layer 2 functions:

1. Accepts a frame from a medium

2. De-encapsulates the frame

3. Re-encapsulates the packet into a new frame

4. Forwards the new frame appropriate to the medium of that segment of the physical network

Press play to view the animation. The router in the figure has an Ethernet interface to connect to the LAN and a serial interface to connect to the WAN. As the router processes frames, it will use data link layer services to receive the frame from one medium, de-encapsulate it to the Layer 3 PDU, re-encapsulate the PDU into a new frame, and place the frame on the medium of the next link of the network.

Refer to
Online Course
for Illustration

Data Link Layer Standards - 6.1.4

Data link layer protocols are generally not defined by Request for Comments (RFCs), unlike the protocols of the upper layers of the TCP/IP suite. The Internet Engineering Task Force (IETF) maintains the functional protocols and services for the TCP/IP protocol suite in the upper layers, but they do not define the functions and operation of the TCP/IP network access layer.

Engineering organizations that define open standards and protocols that apply to the network access layer (i.e., the OSI physical and data link layers) include the following:

■ Institute of Electrical and Electronics Engineers (IEEE)

■ International Telecommunication Union (ITU)

■ International Organization for Standardization (ISO)

■ American National Standards Institute (ANSI)

The logos for these organizations are shown in the figure.

Go to the online course to take the quiz and exam.

Check Your Understanding - Purpose of the Data Link Layer - 6.1.5

Topologies - 6.2

Refer to
Online Course
for Illustration

Physical and Logical Topologies - 6.2.1

As you learned in the previous topic, the data link layer prepares network data for the physical network. It must know the logical topology of a network in order to be able to determine what is needed to transfer frames from one device to another. This topic explains the ways in which the data link layer works with different logical network topologies.

The topology of a network is the arrangement, or the relationship, of the network devices and the interconnections between them.

There are two types of topologies used when describing LAN and WAN networks:

- **Physical topology** – Identifies the physical connections and how end devices and intermediary devices (i.e, routers, switches, and wireless access points) are interconnected. The topology may also include specific device location such as room number and location on the equipment rack. Physical topologies are usually point-to-point or star.

- **Logical topology** - Refers to the way a network transfers frames from one node to the next. This topology identifies virtual connections using device interfaces and Layer 3 IP addressing schemes.

The data link layer "sees" the logical topology of a network when controlling data access to the media. It is the logical topology that influences the type of network framing and media access control used.

The figure displays a sample **physical** topology for a small sample network.

The next figure displays a sample **logical** topology for the same network.

Refer to
Interactive Graphic
in online course

WAN Topologies - 6.2.2

The figures illustrate how WANs are commonly interconnected using three common physical WAN topologies.

Click each button for more information.

Refer to
Online Course
for Illustration

Point-to-Point

This is the simplest and most common WAN topology. It consists of a permanent link between two endpoints.

Hub and Spoke

This is a WAN version of the star topology in which a central site interconnects branch sites through the use of point-to-point links. Branch sites cannot exchange data with other branch sites without going through the central site.

Mesh

This topology provides high availability but requires that every end system is interconnected to every other system. Therefore, the administrative and physical costs can be significant. Each link is essentially a point-to-point link to the other node.

A hybrid is a variation or combination of any topologies. For example, a partial mesh is a hybrid topology in which some, but not all, end devices are interconnected.

Refer to **Online Course** for Illustration

Point-to-Point WAN Topology - 6.2.3

Physical point-to-point topologies directly connect two nodes, as shown in the figure. In this arrangement, two nodes do not have to share the media with other hosts. Additionally, when using a serial communications protocol such as Point-to-Point Protocol (PPP), a node does not have to make any determination about whether an incoming frame is destined for it or another node. Therefore, the logical data link protocols can be very simple, as all frames on the media can only travel to or from the two nodes. The node places the frames on the media at one end and those frames are taken from the media by the node at the other end of the point-to-point circuit.

Note: A point-to-point connection over Ethernet requires the device to determine if the incoming frame is destined for this node.

A source and destination node may be indirectly connected to each other over some geographical distance using multiple intermediary devices. However, the use of physical devices in the network does not affect the logical topology, as illustrated in the figure. In the figure, adding intermediary physical connections may not change the logical topology. The logical point-to-point connection is the same.

Refer to **Online Course** for Illustration

LAN Topologies - 6.2.4

In multiaccess LANs, end devices (i.e., nodes) are interconnected using star or extended star topologies, as shown in the figure. In this type of topology, end devices are connected to a central intermediary device, in this case, an Ethernet switch. An **extended star** extends this topology by interconnecting multiple Ethernet switches. The star and extended topologies are easy to install, very scalable (easy to add and remove end devices), and easy to troubleshoot. Early star topologies interconnected end devices using Ethernet hubs.

At times there may be only two devices connected on the Ethernet LAN. An example is two interconnected routers. This would be an example of Ethernet used on a point-to-point topology.

Legacy LAN Topologies

Early Ethernet and legacy Token Ring LAN technologies included two other types of topologies:

- **Bus** - All end systems are chained to each other and terminated in some form on each end. Infrastructure devices such as switches are not required to interconnect the end devices. Legacy Ethernet networks were often bus topologies using coax cables because it was inexpensive and easy to set up.

- **Ring** - End systems are connected to their respective neighbor forming a ring. The ring does not need to be terminated, unlike in the bus topology. Legacy Fiber Distributed Data Interface (FDDI) and Token Ring networks used ring topologies.

The figures illustrate how end devices are interconnected on LANs. It is common for a straight line in networking graphics to represent an Ethernet LAN including a simple star and an extended star.

Refer to
Interactive Graphic
in online course

Half and Full Duplex Communication - 6.2.5

Understanding duplex communication is important when discussing LAN topologies because it refers to the direction of data transmission between two devices. There are two common modes of duplex.

Half-duplex communication

Both devices can transmit and receive on the media but cannot do so simultaneously. WLANs and legacy bus topologies with Ethernet hubs use the half-duplex mode. Half-duplex allows only one device to send or receive at a time on the shared medium. Click play in the figure to see the animation showing half-duplex communication.

Full-duplex communication

Both devices can simultaneously transmit and receive on the shared media. The data link layer assumes that the media is available for transmission for both nodes at any time. Ethernet switches operate in full-duplex mode by default, but they can operate in half-duplex if connecting to a device such as an Ethernet hub. Click play in the figure to see the animation showing full-duplex communication.

In summary, half-duplex communications restrict the exchange of data to one direction at a time. Full-duplex allows the sending and receiving of data to happen simultaneously.

It is important that two interconnected interfaces, such as a host NIC and an interface on an Ethernet switch, operate using the same duplex mode. Otherwise, there will be a duplex mismatch creating inefficiency and latency on the link.

Refer to
Online Course
for Illustration

Access Control Methods - 6.2.6

Ethernet LANs and WLANs are examples of multiaccess networks. A multiaccess network is a network that can have two or more end devices attempting to access the network simultaneously.

Some multiaccess networks require rules to govern how devices share the physical media. There are two basic access control methods for shared media:

- Contention-based access
- Controlled access

Contention-based access

In contention-based multiaccess networks, all nodes are operating in half-duplex, competing for the use of the medium. However, only one device can send at a time. Therefore, there is a process if more than one device transmits at the same time. Examples of contention-based access methods include the following:

- Carrier sense multiple access with collision detection (CSMA/CD) used on legacy bus-topology Ethernet LANs

- Carrier sense multiple access with collision avoidance (CSMA/CA) used on Wireless LANs

Controlled access

In a controlled-based multiaccess network, each node has its own time to use the medium. These deterministic types of legacy networks are inefficient because a device must wait its turn to access the medium. Examples of multiaccess networks that use controlled access include the following:

- Legacy Token Ring

- Legacy ARCNET

Note: Today, Ethernet networks operate in full-duplex and do not require an access method.

Refer to
Interactive Graphic
in online course

Refer to
Online Course
for Illustration

Contention-Based Access - CSMA/CD - 6.2.7

Examples of contention-based access networks include the following:

- Wireless LAN (uses CSMA/CA)

- Legacy bus-topology Ethernet LAN (uses CSMA/CD)

- Legacy Ethernet LAN using a hub (uses CSMA/CD)

These networks operate in half-duplex mode, meaning only one device can send or receive at a time. This requires a process to govern when a device can send and what happens when multiple devices send at the same time.

If two devices transmit at the same time, a collision will occur. For legacy Ethernet LANs, both devices will detect the collision on the network. This is the collision detection (CD) portion of CSMA/CD. The NIC compares data transmitted with data received, or by recognizing that the signal amplitude is higher than normal on the media. The data sent by both devices will be corrupted and will need to be resent.

Click each button for an image and description of the CSMA/CD process in legacy Ethernet LANs that use a hub.

PC1 Sends a Frame

PC1 has an Ethernet frame to send to PC3. The PC1 NIC needs to determine if any device is transmitting on the medium. If it does not detect a carrier signal (in other words, it is not receiving transmissions from another device), it will assume the network is available to send.

The PC1 NIC sends the Ethernet Frame when the medium is available, as shown in the figure.

The Hub Receives the Frame

The Ethernet hub receives and sends the frame. An Ethernet hub is also known as a multi-port repeater. Any bits received on an incoming port are regenerated and sent out all other ports, as shown in the figure.

If another device, such as PC2, wants to transmit, but is currently receiving a frame, it must wait until the channel is clear, as shown in the figure.

The Hub Sends the Frame

All devices attached to the hub will receive the frame. However, because the frame has a destination data link address for PC3, only that device will accept and copy in the entire frame. All other device NICs will ignore the frame, as shown in the figure.

Refer to
Online Course
for Illustration

Contention-Based Access - CSMA/CA - 6.2.8

Another form of CSMA used by IEEE 802.11 WLANs is carrier sense multiple access/collision avoidance (CSMA/CA).

CMSA/CA uses a method similar to CSMA/CD to detect if the media is clear. CMSA/CA uses additional techniques. In wireless environments it may not be possible for a device to detect a collision. CMSA/CA does not detect collisions but attempts to avoid them by waiting before transmitting. Each device that transmits includes the time duration that it needs for the transmission. All other wireless devices receive this information and know how long the medium will be unavailable.

In the figure, if host A is receiving a wireless frame from the access point, hosts B, and C will also see the frame and how long the medium will be unavailable.

After a wireless device sends an 802.11 frame, the receiver returns an acknowledgment so that the sender knows the frame arrived.

Whether it is an Ethernet LAN using hubs, or a WLAN, contention-based systems do not scale well under heavy media use.

Note: Ethernet LANs using switches do not use a contention-based system because the switch and the host NIC operate in full-duplex mode.

Go to the online
course to take the
quiz and exam.

Check Your Understanding - Topologies - 6.2.9

Data Link Frame - 6.3

Refer to
Online Course
for Illustration

The Frame - 6.3.1

This topic discusses in detail what happens to the data link frame as it moves through a network. The information appended to a frame is determined by the protocol being used.

The data link layer prepares the encapsulated data (usually an IPv4 or IPv6 packet) for transport across the local media by encapsulating it with a header and a trailer to create a frame.

The data link protocol is responsible for NIC-to-NIC communications within the same network. Although there are many different data link layer protocols that describe data link layer frames, each frame type has three basic parts:

- ■ Header
- ■ Data
- ■ Trailer

Unlike other encapsulation protocols, the data link layer appends information in the form of a trailer at the end of the frame.

All data link layer protocols encapsulate the data within the data field of the frame. However, the structure of the frame and the fields contained in the header and trailer vary according to the protocol.

There is no one frame structure that meets the needs of all data transportation across all types of media. Depending on the environment, the amount of control information needed in the frame varies to match the access control requirements of the media and logical topology. For example, a WLAN frame must include procedures for collision avoidance and therefore requires additional control information when compared to an Ethernet frame.

As shown in the figure, in a fragile environment, more controls are needed to ensure delivery. The header and trailer fields are larger as more control information is needed.

Refer to **Online Course** for Illustration

Frame Fields - 6.3.2

Framing breaks the stream into decipherable groupings, with control information inserted in the header and trailer as values in different fields. This format gives the physical signals a structure that are by recognized by nodes and decoded into packets at the destination.

The generic frame fields are shown in the figure. Not all protocols include all these fields. The standards for a specific data link protocol define the actual frame format.

Data link layer protocols add a trailer to the end of each frame. In a process called error detection, the trailer determines if the frame arrived without error. It places a logical or mathematical summary of the bits that comprise the frame in the trailer. The data link layer adds error detection because the signals on the media could be subject to interference, distortion, or loss that would substantially change the bit values that those signals represent.

A transmitting node creates a logical summary of the contents of the frame, known as the cyclic redundancy check (CRC) value. This value is placed in the frame check sequence (FCS) field to represent the contents of the frame. In the Ethernet trailer, the FCS provides a method for the receiving node to determine whether the frame experienced transmission errors.

Refer to
Interactive Graphic
in online course

Refer to
Online Course
for Illustration

Layer 2 Addresses - 6.3.3

The data link layer provides the addressing used in transporting a frame across a shared local media. Device addresses at this layer are referred to as physical addresses. Data link layer addressing is contained within the frame header and specifies the frame destination node on the local network. It is typically at the beginning of the frame, so the NIC can quickly determine if it matches its own Layer 2 address before accepting the rest of the frame. The frame header may also contain the source address of the frame.

Unlike Layer 3 logical addresses, which are hierarchical, physical addresses do not indicate on what network the device is located. Rather, the physical address is unique to the specific device. A device will still function with the same Layer 2 physical address even if the device moves to another network or subnet. Therefore, Layer 2 addresses are only used to connect devices within the same shared media, on the same IP network.

The figures illustrate the function of the Layer 2 and Layer 3 addresses. As the IP packet travels from host-to-router, router-to-router, and finally router-to-host, at each point along the way the IP packet is encapsulated in a new data link frame. Each data link frame contains the source data link address of the NIC sending the frame, and the destination data link address of the NIC receiving the frame.

Click each button for more information.

Host-to-Router

The source host encapsulates the Layer 3 IP packet in a Layer 2 frame. In the frame header, the host adds its Layer 2 address as the source and the Layer 2 address for R1 as the destination.

Router-to-Router

R1 encapsulates the Layer 3 IP packet in a new Layer 2 frame. In the frame header, R1 adds its Layer 2 address as the source and the Layer 2 address for R2 as the destination.

Router-to-Host

R2 encapsulates the Layer 3 IP packet in a new Layer 2 frame. In the frame header, R2 adds its Layer 2 address as the source and the Layer 2 address for the server as the destination.

The data link layer address is only used for local delivery. Addresses at this layer have no meaning beyond the local network. Compare this to Layer 3, where addresses in the packet header are carried from the source host to the destination host, regardless of the number of network hops along the route.

If the data must pass onto another network segment, an intermediary device, such as a router, is necessary. The router must accept the frame based on the physical address and de-encapsulate the frame in order to examine the hierarchical address, which is the IP address. Using the IP address, the router can determine the network location of the destination device and the best path to reach it. When it knows where to forward the packet, the router then creates a new frame for the packet, and the new frame is sent on to the next network segment toward its final destination.

Refer to
Interactive Graphic
in online course

LAN and WAN Frames - 6.3.4

Ethernet protocols are used by wired LANs. Wireless communications fall under WLAN (IEEE 802.11) protocols. These protocols were designed for multiaccess networks.

WANs traditionally used other types of protocols for various types of point-to-point, hub-spoke, and full-mesh topologies. Some of the common WAN protocols over the years have included:

- Point-to-Point Protocol (PPP)

- High-Level Data Link Control (HDLC)

- Frame Relay

- Asynchronous Transfer Mode (ATM)

- X.25

These Layer 2 protocols are now being replaced in the WAN by Ethernet.

In a TCP/IP network, all OSI Layer 2 protocols work with IP at OSI Layer 3. However, the Layer 2 protocol used depends on the logical topology and the physical media.

Each protocol performs media access control for specified Layer 2 logical topologies. This means that a number of different network devices can act as nodes that operate at the data link layer when implementing these protocols. These devices include the NICs on computers as well as the interfaces on routers and Layer 2 switches.

The Layer 2 protocol that is used for a particular network topology is determined by the technology used to implement that topology. The technology used is determined by the size of the network, in terms of the number of hosts and the geographic scope, and the services to be provided over the network.

A LAN typically uses a high bandwidth technology capable of supporting large numbers of hosts. The relatively small geographic area of a LAN (a single building or a multi-building campus) and its high density of users make this technology cost-effective.

However, using a high bandwidth technology is usually not cost-effective for WANs that cover large geographic areas (cities or multiple cities, for example). The cost of the long-distance physical links and the technology used to carry the signals over those distances typically results in lower bandwidth capacity.

The difference in bandwidth normally results in the use of different protocols for LANs and WANs.

Data link layer protocols include:

- Ethernet

- 802.11 Wireless

- Point-to-Point Protocol (PPP)

- High-Level Data Link Control (HDLC)

- Frame Relay

Click Play to see an animation of examples of Layer 2 protocols.

Go to the online
course to take the
quiz and exam.

Check Your Understanding - Data Link Frame - 6.3.5

Module Practice and Quiz - 6.4

What did I learn in this module? - 6.4.1

Purpose of the Data Link Layer

The data link layer of the OSI model (Layer 2) prepares network data for the physical network. The data link layer is responsible for network interface card (NIC) to network interface card communications. Without the data link layer, network layer protocols such as IP, would have to make provisions for connecting to every type of media that could exist along a delivery path. The IEEE 802 LAN/MAN data link layer consists of the following two sublayers: LLC and MAC. The MAC sublayer provides data encapsulation through frame delimiting, addressing, and error detection. Router interfaces encapsulate the packet into the appropriate frame. A suitable media access control method is used to access each link. Engineering organizations that define open standards and protocols that apply to the network access layer include: IEEE, ITU, ISO, and ANSI.

Topologies

The two types of topologies used in LAN and WAN networks are physical and logical. The data link layer "sees" the logical topology of a network when controlling data access to the media. The logical topology influences the type of network framing and media access control used. Three common types of physical WAN topologies are: point-to-point, hub and spoke, and mesh. Physical point-to-point topologies directly connect two end devices (nodes). Adding intermediate physical connections may not change the logical topology. In multi-access LANs, nodes are interconnected using star or extended star topologies. In this type of topology, nodes are connected to a central intermediary device. Physical LAN topologies include: star, extended star, bus, and ring. Half-duplex communications exchange data in one direction at a time. Full-duplex sends and receives data simultaneously. Two interconnected interfaces must use the same duplex mode or there will be a duplex mismatch creating inefficiency and latency on the link. Ethernet LANs and WLANs are examples of multi-access networks. A multi-access network is a network that can have multiple nodes accessing the network simultaneously. Some multi-access networks require rules to govern how devices share the physical media. There are two basic access control methods for shared media: contention-based access and controlled access. In contention-based multi-access networks, all nodes are operating in half-duplex. There is a process if more than one device transmits at the same time. Examples of contention-based access methods include: CSMA/CD for bus-topology Ethernet LANs and CSMA/CA for WLANs.

Data Link Frame

The data link layer prepares the encapsulated data (usually an IPv4 or IPv6 packet) for transport across the local media by encapsulating it with a header and a trailer to create a frame. The data link protocol is responsible for NIC-to-NIC communications within the same network. There are many different data link layer protocols that describe data link layer frames, each frame type has three basic parts: header, data, and trailer. Unlike other encapsulation protocols, the data link layer appends information in the trailer. There is no one frame structure that meets the needs of all data transportation across all types of media. Depending on the environment, the amount of control information needed in the frame varies to match the access control requirements of the media and logical topology. Frame fields include: frame start and stop indicator flags, addressing, type, control, data, and error detection. The data link layer provides addressing used to transport a frame across shared local media. Device addresses at this layer are physical addresses. Data link layer addressing is contained within the frame header and specifies the frame destination node on the local network. The data link layer address is only used for local delivery. In a TCP/IP network, all OSI Layer 2 protocols work with IP at OSI Layer 3. However, the Layer 2 protocol used depends on the logical topology and the physical media. Each protocol performs media access control for specified Layer 2 logical topologies. The Layer 2 protocol that is used for a particular network topology is determined by the technology used to implement that topology. Data link layer protocols include: Ethernet, 802.11 Wireless, PPP, HDLC, and Frame Relay.

Go to the online course to take the quiz and exam.

Chapter Quiz - Data Link Layer

Your Chapter Notes

CHAPTER 7

Ethernet Switching

Introduction - 7.0

Why should I take this module? - 7.0.1

Welcome to Ethernet Switching!

If you are planning to become a network administrator or a network architect, you will definitely need to know about Ethernet and Ethernet switching. The two most prominent LAN technologies in use today are Ethernet and WLAN. Ethernet supports bandwidths of up to 100 Gbps, which explains its popularity. This module contains a lab using Wireshark in which you can look at Ethernet frames and another lab where you view network device MAC addresses. There are also some instructional videos to help you better understand Ethernet. By the time you have finished this module, you too could create a switched network that uses Ethernet!

What will I learn to do in this module? - 7.0.2

Module Title: Ethernet Switching

Module Objective: Explain how Ethernet operates in a switched network.

Topic Title	Topic Objective
Ethernet Frame	Explain how the Ethernet sublayers are related to the frame fields.
Ethernet MAC Address	Describe the Ethernet MAC address.
The MAC Address Table	Explain how a switch builds its MAC address table and forwards frames.
Switch Speeds and Forwarding Methods	Describe switch forwarding methods and port settings available on Layer 2 switch ports.

Ethernet Frames - 7.1

Refer to
Online Course
for Illustration

Ethernet Encapsulation - 7.1.1

This module starts with a discussion of Ethernet technology including an explanation of MAC sublayer and the Ethernet frame fields.

Ethernet is one of two LAN technologies used today, with the other being wireless LANs (WLANs). Ethernet uses wired communications, including twisted pair, fiber-optic links, and coaxial cables.

Ethernet operates in the data link layer and the physical layer. It is a family of networking technologies defined in the IEEE 802.2 and 802.3 standards. Ethernet supports data bandwidths of the following:

- 10 Mbps
- 100 Mbps
- 1000 Mbps (1 Gbps)
- 10,000 Mbps (10 Gbps)
- 40,000 Mbps (40 Gbps)
- 100,000 Mbps (100 Gbps)

As shown in the figure, Ethernet standards define both the Layer 2 protocols and the Layer 1 technologies.

Data Link Sublayers - 7.1.2

Refer to
Online Course
for Illustration

IEEE 802 LAN/MAN protocols, including Ethernet, use the following two separate sublayers of the data link layer to operate. They are the Logical Link Control (LLC) and the Media Access Control (MAC), as shown in the figure.

Recall that LLC and MAC have the following roles in the data link layer:

- **LLC Sublayer** - This IEEE 802.2 sublayer communicates between the networking software at the upper layers and the device hardware at the lower layers. It places information in the frame that identifies which network layer protocol is being used for the frame. This information allows multiple Layer 3 protocols, such as IPv4 and IPv6, to use the same network interface and media.

- **MAC Sublayer** - This sublayer (IEEE 802.3, 802.11, or 802.15 for example) is implemented in hardware and is responsible for data encapsulation and media access control. It provides data link layer addressing and is integrated with various physical layer technologies.

MAC Sublayer - 7.1.3

Refer to
Online Course
for Illustration

The MAC sublayer is responsible for data encapsulation and accessing the media.

Data Encapsulation

IEEE 802.3 data encapsulation includes the following:

- **Ethernet frame** - This is the internal structure of the Ethernet frame.

- **Ethernet Addressing** - The Ethernet frame includes both a source and destination MAC address to deliver the Ethernet frame from Ethernet NIC to Ethernet NIC on the same LAN.

- **Ethernet Error detection** - The Ethernet frame includes a frame check sequence (FCS) trailer used for error detection.

Accessing the Media

As shown in the figure, the IEEE 802.3 MAC sublayer includes the specifications for different Ethernet communications standards over various types of media including copper and fiber.

Recall that legacy Ethernet using a bus topology or hubs, is a shared, half-duplex medium. Ethernet over a half-duplex medium uses a contention-based access method, carrier sense multiple access/collision detection (CSMA/CD) This ensures that only one device is transmitting at a time. CSMA/CD allows multiple devices to share the same half-duplex medium, detecting a collision when more than one device attempts to transmit simultaneously. It also provides a back-off algorithm for retransmission.

Ethernet LANs of today use switches that operate in full-duplex. Full-duplex communications with Ethernet switches do not require access control through CSMA/CD.

Refer to **Online Course** for Illustration

Ethernet Frame Fields - 7.1.4

The minimum Ethernet frame size is 64 bytes and the maximum is 1518 bytes. This includes all bytes from the destination MAC address field through the frame check sequence (FCS) field. The preamble field is not included when describing the size of the frame.

Any frame less than 64 bytes in length is considered a "collision fragment" or "runt frame" and is automatically discarded by receiving stations. Frames with more than 1500 bytes of data are considered "jumbo" or "baby giant frames".

If the size of a transmitted frame is less than the minimum, or greater than the maximum, the receiving device drops the frame. Dropped frames are likely to be the result of collisions or other unwanted signals. They are considered invalid. Jumbo frames are usually supported by most Fast Ethernet and Gigabit Ethernet switches and NICs.

The figure shows each field in the Ethernet frame. Refer to the table for more information about the function of each field.

Ethernet Frame Fields Detail

Field	Description
Preamble and Start Frame Delimiter Fields	The Preamble (7 bytes) and Start Frame Delimiter (SFD), also called the Start of Frame (1 byte), fields are used for synchronization between the sending and receiving devices. These first eight bytes of the frame are used to get the attention of the receiving nodes. Essentially, the first few bytes tell the receivers to get ready to receive a new frame.
Destination MAC Address Field	This 6-byte field is the identifier for the intended recipient. As you will recall, this address is used by Layer 2 to assist devices in determining if a frame is addressed to them. The address in the frame is compared to the MAC address in the device. If there is a match, the device accepts the frame. Can be a unicast, multicast or broadcast address.
Source MAC Address Field	This 6-byte field identifies the originating NIC or interface of the frame.
Type / Length	This 2-byte field identifies the upper layer protocol encapsulated in the Ethernet frame. Common values are, in hexadecimal, 0x800 for IPv4, 0x86DD for IPv6 and 0x806 for ARP. **Note:** You may also see this field referred to as EtherType, Type, or Length.

Field	Description
Data Field	This field (46 - 1500 bytes) contains the encapsulated data from a higher layer, which is a generic Layer 3 PDU, or more commonly, an IPv4 packet. All frames must be at least 64 bytes long. If a small packet is encapsulated, additional bits called a pad are used to increase the size of the frame to this minimum size.
Frame Check Sequence Field	The Frame Check Sequence (FCS) field (4 bytes) is used to detect errors in a frame. It uses a cyclic redundancy check (CRC). The sending device includes the results of a CRC in the FCS field of the frame. The receiving device receives the frame and generates a CRC to look for errors. If the calculations match, no error occurred. Calculations that do not match are an indication that the data has changed; therefore, the frame is dropped. A change in the data could be the result of a disruption of the electrical signals that represent the bits.

Go to the online course to take the quiz and exam.

Check Your Understanding - Ethernet Switching - 7.1.5

Refer to **Lab Activity** for this chapter

Lab - Use Wireshark to Examine Ethernet Frames - 7.1.6

In this lab, you will complete the following objectives:

- Part 1: Examine the Header Fields in an Ethernet II Frame
- Part 2: Use Wireshark to Capture and Analyze Ethernet Frames

Ethernet MAC Address - 7.2

Refer to **Online Course** for Illustration

MAC Address and Hexadecimal - 7.2.1

In networking, IPv4 addresses are represented using the decimal base ten number system and the binary base 2 number system. IPv6 addresses and Ethernet addresses are represented using the hexadecimal base sixteen number system. To understand hexadecimal, you must first be very familiar with binary and decimal.

The hexadecimal numbering system uses the numbers 0 to 9 and the letters A to F.

An Ethernet MAC address consists of a 48-bit binary value. Hexadecimal is used to identify an Ethernet address because a single hexadecimal digit represents four binary bits. Therefore, a 48-bit Ethernet MAC address can be expressed using only 12 hexadecimal values.

The figure compares the equivalent decimal and hexadecimal values for binary 0000 to 1111.

Given that 8 bits (one byte) is a common binary grouping, binary 00000000 to 11111111 can be represented in hexadecimal as the range 00 to FF, as shown in the next figure.

When using hexadecimal, leading zeroes are always displayed to complete the 8-bit representation. For example, in the table, the binary value 0000 1010 is shown in hexadecimal as 0A.

Hexadecimal numbers are often represented by the value preceded by **0x** (e.g., 0x73) to distinguish between decimal and hexadecimal values in documentation.

Hexadecimal may also be represented by a subscript 16, or the hex number followed by an H (e.g., 73H).

You may have to convert between decimal and hexadecimal values. If such conversions are required, convert the decimal or hexadecimal value to binary, and then to convert the binary value to either decimal or hexadecimal as appropriate.

Refer to **Online Course** for Illustration

Ethernet MAC Address - 7.2.2

In an Ethernet LAN, every network device is connected to the same, shared media. The MAC address is used to identify the physical source and destination devices (NICs) on the local network segment. MAC addressing provides a method for device identification at the data link layer of the OSI model.

An Ethernet MAC address is a 48-bit address expressed using 12 hexadecimal digits, as shown in the figure. Because a byte equals 8 bits, we can also say that a MAC address is 6 bytes in length.

All MAC addresses must be unique to the Ethernet device or Ethernet interface. To ensure this, all vendors that sell Ethernet devices must register with the IEEE to obtain a unique 6 hexadecimal (i.e., 24-bit or 3-byte) code called the organizationally unique identifier (OUI).

When a vendor assigns a MAC address to a device or Ethernet interface, the vendor must do as follows:

- Use its assigned OUI as the first 6 hexadecimal digits.
- Assign a unique value in the last 6 hexadecimal digits.

Therefore, an Ethernet MAC address consists of a 6 hexadecimal vendor OUI code followed by a 6 hexadecimal vendor-assigned value, as shown in the figure.

For example, assume that Cisco needs to assign a unique MAC address to a new device. The IEEE has assigned Cisco a OUI of **00-60-2F**. Cisco would then configure the device with a unique vendor code such as **3A-07-BC**. Therefore, the Ethernet MAC address of that device would be **00-60-2F-3A-07-BC**.

It is the responsibility of the vendor to ensure that none of its devices be assigned the same MAC address. However, it is possible for duplicate MAC addresses to exist because of mistakes made during manufacturing, mistakes made in some virtual machine implementation methods, or modifications made using one of several software tools. In any case, it will be necessary to modify the MAC address with a new NIC or make modifications via software.

Refer to **Interactive Graphic** in online course

Frame Processing - 7.2.3

Sometimes the MAC address is referred to as a burned-in address (BIA) because the address is hard coded into read-only memory (ROM) on the NIC. This means that the address is encoded into the ROM chip permanently.

Note: On modern PC operating systems and NICs, it is possible to change the MAC address in software. This is useful when attempting to gain access to a network that filters based on BIA. Consequently, filtering or controlling traffic based on the MAC address is no longer as secure.

When the computer boots up, the NIC copies its MAC address from ROM into RAM. When a device is forwarding a message to an Ethernet network, the Ethernet header includes these:

- **Source MAC address** - This is the MAC address of the source device NIC.
- **Destination MAC address** - This is the MAC address of the destination device NIC.

Click Play in the animation to view the frame forwarding process.

When a NIC receives an Ethernet frame, it examines the destination MAC address to see if it matches the physical MAC address that is stored in RAM. If there is no match, the device discards the frame. If there is a match, it passes the frame up the OSI layers, where the de-encapsulation process takes place.

Note: Ethernet NICs will also accept frames if the destination MAC address is a broadcast or a multicast group of which the host is a member.

Any device that is the source or destination of an Ethernet frame, will have an Ethernet NIC and therefore, a MAC address. This includes workstations, servers, printers, mobile devices, and routers.

Refer to
Interactive Graphic
in online course

Unicast MAC Address - 7.2.4

In Ethernet, different MAC addresses are used for Layer 2 unicast, broadcast, and multicast communications.

A unicast MAC address is the unique address that is used when a frame is sent from a single transmitting device to a single destination device.

Click Play in the animation to view how a unicast frame is processed. In this example the destination MAC address and the destination IP address are both unicast.

In the example shown in the animation, a host with IPv4 address 192.168.1.5 (source) requests a web page from the server at IPv4 unicast address 192.168.1.200. For a unicast packet to be sent and received, a destination IP address must be in the IP packet header. A corresponding destination MAC address must also be present in the Ethernet frame header. The IP address and MAC address combine to deliver data to one specific destination host.

The process that a source host uses to determine the destination MAC address associated with an IPv4 address is known as Address Resolution Protocol (ARP). The process that a source host uses to determine the destination MAC address associated with an IPv6 address is known as Neighbor Discovery (ND).

Note: The source MAC address must always be a unicast.

Refer to
Interactive Graphic
in online course

Broadcast MAC Address - 7.2.5

An Ethernet broadcast frame is received and processed by every device on the Ethernet LAN. The features of an Ethernet broadcast are as follows:

- It has a destination MAC address of FF-FF-FF-FF-FF-FF in hexadecimal (48 ones in binary).

- It is flooded out all Ethernet switch ports except the incoming port.

- It is not forwarded by a router.

If the encapsulated data is an IPv4 broadcast packet, this means the packet contains a destination IPv4 address that has all ones (1s) in the host portion. This numbering in the address means that all hosts on that local network (broadcast domain) will receive and process the packet.

Click Play in the animation to view how a broadcast frame is processed. In this example the destination MAC address and destination IP address are both broadcasts.

As shown in the animation, the source host sends an IPv4 broadcast packet to all devices on its network. The IPv4 destination address is a broadcast address, 192.168.1.255. When the IPv4 broadcast packet is encapsulated in the Ethernet frame, the destination MAC address is the broadcast MAC address of FF-FF-FF-FF-FF-FF in hexadecimal (48 ones in binary).

DHCP for IPv4 is an example of a protocol that uses Ethernet and IPv4 broadcast addresses.

However, not all Ethernet broadcasts carry an IPv4 broadcast packet. For example, ARP Requests do not use IPv4, but the ARP message is sent as an Ethernet broadcast.

Refer to **Interactive Graphic** in online course

Multicast MAC Address - 7.2.6

An Ethernet multicast frame is received and processed by a group of devices on the Ethernet LAN that belong to the same multicast group. The features of an Ethernet multicast are as follows:

- There is a destination MAC address of 01-00-5E when the encapsulated data is an IPv4 multicast packet and a destination MAC address of 33-33 when the encapsulated data is an IPv6 multicast packet.

- There are other reserved multicast destination MAC addresses for when the encapsulated data is not IP, such as Spanning Tree Protocol (STP) and Link Layer Discovery Protocol (LLDP).

- It is flooded out all Ethernet switch ports except the incoming port, unless the switch is configured for multicast snooping.

- It is not forwarded by a router, unless the router is configured to route multicast packets.

If the encapsulated data is an IP multicast packet, the devices that belong to a multicast group are assigned a multicast group IP address. The range of IPv4 multicast addresses is 224.0.0.0 to 239.257.257.257. The range of IPv6 multicast addresses begins with ff00::/8. Because multicast addresses represent a group of addresses (sometimes called a host group), they can only be used as the destination of a packet. The source will always be a unicast address.

As with the unicast and broadcast addresses, the multicast IP address requires a corresponding multicast MAC address to deliver frames on a local network. The multicast MAC address is associated with, and uses addressing information from, the IPv4 or IPv6 multicast address.

Click Play in the animation to view how a multicast frame is processed. In this example, the destination MAC address and destination IP address are both multicasts.

Routing protocols and other network protocols use multicast addressing. Applications such as video and imaging software may also use multicast addressing, although multicast applications are not as common.

Refer to
Lab Activity
for this chapter

Lab - View Network Device MAC Addresses - 7.2.7

In this lab, you will complete the following objectives:

- Part 1: Set Up the Topology and Initialize Devices
- Part 2: Configure Devices and Verify Connectivity
- Part 3: Display, Describe, and Analyze Ethernet MAC Addresses

(cam table) # The MAC Address Table - 7.3

Refer to
Online Course
for Illustration

Switch Fundamentals - 7.3.1

Now that you know all about Ethernet MAC addresses, it is time to talk about how a switch uses these addresses to forward (or discard) frames to other devices on a network. If a switch just forwarded every frame it received out all ports, your network would be so congested that it would probably come to a complete halt.

A Layer 2 Ethernet switch uses Layer 2 MAC addresses to make forwarding decisions. It is completely unaware of the data (protocol) being carried in the data portion of the frame, such as an IPv4 packet, an ARP message, or an IPv6 ND packet. The switch makes its forwarding decisions based solely on the Layer 2 Ethernet MAC addresses.

An Ethernet switch examines its MAC address table to make a forwarding decision for each frame, unlike legacy Ethernet hubs that repeat bits out all ports except the incoming port. In the figure, the four-port switch was just powered on. The table shows the MAC Address Table which has not yet learned the MAC addresses for the four attached PCs.

Note: MAC addresses are shortened throughout this topic for demonstration purposes.

Note: The MAC address table is sometimes referred to as a content addressable memory (CAM) table. While the term CAM table is fairly common, for the purposes of this course, we will refer to it as a MAC address table.

Refer to
Interactive Graphic
in online course

Refer to
Online Course
for Illustration

Switch Learning and Forwarding - 7.3.2

The switch dynamically builds the MAC address table by examining the source MAC address of the frames received on a port. The switch forwards frames by searching for a match between the destination MAC address in the frame and an entry in the MAC address table.

Click the Learn and Forward buttons for an illustration and explanation of this process.

Learn

Examine the Source MAC Address

Every frame that enters a switch is checked for new information to learn. It does this by examining the source MAC address of the frame and the port number where the frame entered the switch. If the source MAC address does not exist, it is added to the table along with the incoming port number. If the source MAC address does exist, the switch updates the refresh timer for that entry. By default, most Ethernet switches keep an entry in the table for 5 minutes.

In the figure for example, PC-A is sending an Ethernet frame to PC-D. The table shows the switch adds the MAC address for PC-A to the MAC Address Table.

Note: If the source MAC address does exist in the table but on a different port, the switch treats this as a new entry. The entry is replaced using the same MAC address but with the more current port number.

Forward

Find the Destination MAC Address

If the destination MAC address is a unicast address, the switch will look for a match between the destination MAC address of the frame and an entry in its MAC address table. If the destination MAC address is in the table, it will forward the frame out the specified port. If the destination MAC address is not in the table, the switch will forward the frame out all ports except the incoming port. This is called an unknown unicast.

As shown in the figure, the switch does not have the destination MAC address in its table for PC-D, so it sends the frame out all ports except port 1.

Note: If the destination MAC address is a broadcast or a multicast, the frame is also flooded out all ports except the incoming port.

Refer to
Interactive Graphic
in online course

Refer to
Online Course
for Illustration

Filtering Frames - 7.3.3

As a switch receives frames from different devices, it is able to populate its MAC address table by examining the source MAC address of every frame. When the MAC address table of the switch contains the destination MAC address, it is able to filter the frame and forward out a single port.

Click each button for an illustration and explanation of how a switch filters frames.

PC-D to Switch

In the figure, PC-D is replying back to PC-A. The switch sees the MAC address of PC-D in the incoming frame on port 4. The switch then puts the MAC address of PC-D into the MAC Address Table associated with port 4.

Switch to PC-A

Next, because the switch has destination MAC address for PC-A in the MAC Address Table, it will send the frame only out port 1, as shown in the figure.

PC-A to Switch to PC-D

Next, PC-A sends another frame to PC-D as shown in the figure. The MAC address table already contains the MAC address for PC-A; therefore, the five-minute refresh timer for that entry is reset. Next, because the switch table contains the destination MAC address for PC-D, it sends the frame only out port 4.

Refer to **Video**
in online course

Video - MAC Address Tables on Connected Switches - 7.3.4

A switch can have multiple MAC addresses associated with a single port. This is common when the switch is connected to another switch. The switch will have a separate MAC address table entry for each frame received with a different source MAC address.

Click Play in the figure to view a demonstration of how two connected switches build MAC address tables.

Refer to **Video**
in online course

Video - Sending the Frame to the Default Gateway - 7.3.5

When a device has an IP address that is on a remote network, the Ethernet frame cannot be sent directly to the destination device. Instead, the Ethernet frame is sent to the MAC address of the default gateway, the router.

Click Play in the figure to view a demonstration of how PC-A communicates with its default gateway.

Note: In the video, the IP packet that is sent from PC-A to a destination on a remote network has a source IP address of PC-A and a destination IP address of the remote host. The returning IP packet will have the source IP address of remote host and the destination IP address will be that of PC-A.

Refer to
Lab Activity
for this chapter

Activity - Switch It! - 7.3.6

Determine how the switch forwards a frame based on the source MAC address, the destination MAC address, and information in the switch MAC table. Answer the questions using the information provided.

Refer to
Lab Activity
for this chapter

Lab - View the Switch MAC Address Table - 7.3.7

Determine how the switch forwards a frame based on the source MAC address, the destination MAC address, and information in the switch MAC table. Answer the questions using the information provided.

Switch Speeds and Forwarding Methods - 7.4

Refer to
Interactive Graphic
in online course

Frame Forwarding Methods on Cisco Switches - 7.4.1

As you learned in the previous topic, switches use their MAC address tables to determine which port to use to forward frames. With Cisco switches, there are actually two frame forwarding methods and there are good reasons to use one instead of the other, depending on the situation.

Switches use one of the following forwarding methods for switching data between network ports:

- **Store-and-forward switching** - This frame forwarding method receives the entire frame and computes the CRC. CRC uses a mathematical formula, based on the number of bits (1s) in the frame, to determine whether the received frame has an error. If the CRC is valid, the switch looks up the destination address, which determines the outgoing interface. Then the frame is forwarded out of the correct port.

- **Cut-through switching** - This frame forwarding method forwards the frame before it is entirely received. At a minimum, the destination address of the frame must be read before the frame can be forwarded.

A big advantage of store-and-forward switching is that it determines if a frame has errors before propagating the frame. When an error is detected in a frame, the switch discards the frame. Discarding frames with errors reduces the amount of bandwidth consumed by corrupt data. Store-and-forward switching is required for quality of service (QoS) analysis on converged networks where frame classification for traffic prioritization is necessary. For example, voice over IP (VoIP) data streams need to have priority over web-browsing traffic.

Click Play in the animation for a demonstration of the store-and-forward process.

Refer to
Interactive Graphic
in online course

Cut-Through Switching - 7.4.2

In cut-through switching, the switch acts upon the data as soon as it is received, even if the transmission is not complete. The switch buffers just enough of the frame to read the destination MAC address so that it can determine to which port it should forward out the data. The destination MAC address is located in the first 6 bytes of the frame following the preamble. The switch looks up the destination MAC address in its switching table, determines the outgoing interface port, and forwards the frame onto its destination through the designated switch port. The switch does not perform any error checking on the frame.

Click Play in the animation for a demonstration of the cut-through switching process.

There are two variants of cut-through switching:

- **Fast-forward switching** - Fast-forward switching offers the lowest level of latency. Fast-forward switching immediately forwards a packet after reading the destination address. Because fast-forward switching starts forwarding before the entire packet has been received, there may be times when packets are relayed with errors. This occurs infrequently, and the destination NIC discards the faulty packet upon receipt. In fast-forward mode, latency is measured from the first bit received to the first bit transmitted. Fast-forward switching is the typical cut-through method of switching.

■ **Fragment-free switching** - In fragment-free switching, the switch stores the first 64 bytes of the frame before forwarding. Fragment-free switching can be viewed as a compromise between store-and-forward switching and fast-forward switching. The reason fragment-free switching stores only the first 64 bytes of the frame is that most network errors and collisions occur during the first 64 bytes. Fragment-free switching tries to enhance fast-forward switching by performing a small error check on the first 64 bytes of the frame to ensure that a collision has not occurred before forwarding the frame. Fragment-free switching is a compromise between the high latency and high integrity of store-and-forward switching, and the low latency and reduced integrity of fast-forward switching.

Some switches are configured to perform cut-through switching on a per-port basis until a user-defined error threshold is reached, and then they automatically change to store-and-forward. When the error rate falls below the threshold, the port automatically changes back to cut-through switching.

Memory Buffering on Switches - 7.4.3

An Ethernet switch may use a buffering technique to store frames before forwarding them. Buffering may also be used when the destination port is busy because of congestion. The switch stores the frame until it can be transmitted.

As shown in the table, there are two methods of memory buffering:

Memory Buffering Methods

Method	Description
Port-based memory	• Frames are stored in queues that are linked to specific incoming and outgoing ports.
	• A frame is transmitted to the outgoing port only when all the frames ahead in the queue have been successfully transmitted.
	• It is possible for a single frame to delay the transmission of all the frames in memory because of a busy destination port.
	• This delay occurs even if the other frames could be transmitted to open destination ports.
Shared memory	• Deposits all frames into a common memory buffer shared by all switch ports and the amount of buffer memory required by a port is dynamically allocated.
	• The frames in the buffer are dynamically linked to the destination port enabling a packet to be received on one port and then transmitted on another port, without moving it to a different queue.

Shared memory buffering also results in the ability to store larger frames with potentially fewer dropped frames. This is important with asymmetric switching which allows for different data rates on different ports such as when connecting a server to a 10 Gbps switch port and PCs to 1 Gbps ports.

Duplex and Speed Settings - 7.4.4

Two of the most basic settings on a switch are the bandwidth (sometimes referred to as "speed") and duplex settings for each individual switch port. It is critical that the duplex and bandwidth settings match between the switch port and the connected devices, such as a computer or another switch.

There are two types of duplex settings used for communications on an Ethernet network:

- **Full-duplex** - Both ends of the connection can send and receive simultaneously.
- **Half-duplex** - Only one end of the connection can send at a time.

Autonegotiation is an optional function found on most Ethernet switches and NICs. It enables two devices to automatically negotiate the best speed and duplex capabilities. Full-duplex is chosen if both devices have the capability along with their highest common bandwidth.

In the figure, the Ethernet NIC for PC-A can operate in full-duplex or half-duplex, and in 10 Mbps or 100 Mbps.

Note: Most Cisco switches and Ethernet NICs default to autonegotiation for speed and duplex. Gigabit Ethernet ports only operate in full-duplex.

Duplex mismatch is one of the most common causes of performance issues on 10/100 Mbps Ethernet links. It occurs when one port on the link operates at half-duplex while the other port operates at full-duplex, as shown in the figure.

Duplex mismatch occurs when one or both ports on a link are reset, and the autonegotiation process does not result in both link partners having the same configuration. It also can occur when users reconfigure one side of a link and forget to reconfigure the other. Both sides of a link should have autonegotiation on, or both sides should have it off. Best practice is to configure both Ethernet switch ports as full-duplex.

Auto-MDIX - 7.4.5

Connections between devices once required the use of either a crossover or straight-through cable. The type of cable required depended on the type of interconnecting devices.

For example, the figure identifies the correct cable type required to interconnect switch-to-switch, switch-to-router, switch-to-host, or router-to-host devices. A crossover cable is used when connecting like devices, and a straight-through cable is used for connecting unlike devices.

Note: A direct connection between a router and a host requires a cross-over connection.

Most switch devices now support the automatic medium-dependent interface crossover (auto-MDIX) feature. When enabled, the switch automatically detects the type of cable attached to the port and configures the interfaces accordingly. Therefore, you can use either a crossover or a straight-through cable for connections to a copper 10/100/1000 port on the switch, regardless of the type of device on the other end of the connection.

The auto-MDIX feature is enabled by default on switches running Cisco IOS Release 12.2(18)SE or later. However, the feature could be disabled. For this reason, you should always use the correct cable type and not rely on the auto-MDIX feature. Auto-MDIX can be re-enabled using the **mdix auto** interface configuration command.

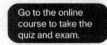

Go to the online course to take the quiz and exam.

Check Your Understanding - Switch Speeds and Forwarding Methods - 7.4.6

Module Practice and Quiz - 7.5

What did I learn in this module? - 7.5.1

Ethernet Frame

Ethernet operates in the data link layer and the physical layer. Ethernet standards define both the Layer 2 protocols and the Layer 1 technologies. Ethernet uses the LLC and MAC sublayers of the data link layer to operate. Data encapsulation includes the following: Ethernet frame, Ethernet addressing, and Ethernet error detection. Ethernet LANs use switches that operate in full-duplex. The Ethernet frame fields are: preamble and start frame delimiter, destination MAC address, source MAC address, EtherType, data, and FCS.

Ethernet MAC Address

Binary number system uses the digits 0 and 1. Decimal uses 0 through 9. Hexadecimal uses 0 through 9 and the letters A through F. The MAC address is used to identify the physical source and destination devices (NICs) on the local network segment. MAC addressing provides a method for device identification at the data link layer of the OSI model. An Ethernet MAC address is a 48-bit address expressed using 12 hexadecimal digits, or 6 bytes. An Ethernet MAC address consists of a 6 hexadecimal vendor OUI code followed by a 6 hexadecimal vendor assigned value. When a device is forwarding a message to an Ethernet network, the Ethernet header includes the source and destination MAC addresses. In Ethernet, different MAC addresses are used for Layer 2 unicast, broadcast, and multicast communications.

The MAC Address Table

A Layer 2 Ethernet switch makes its forwarding decisions based solely on the Layer 2 Ethernet MAC addresses. The switch dynamically builds the MAC address table by examining the source MAC address of the frames received on a port. The switch forwards frames by searching for a match between the destination MAC address in the frame and an entry in the MAC address table. As a switch receives frames from different devices, it is able to populate its MAC address table by examining the source MAC address of every frame. When the MAC address table of the switch contains the destination MAC address, it is able to filter the frame and forward out a single port.

Switch Speeds and Forwarding Methods

Switches use one of the following forwarding methods for switching data between network ports: store-and-forward switching or cut-through switching. Two variants of cut-through switching are fast-forward and fragment-free. Two methods of memory buffering are port-based memory and shared memory. There are two types of duplex settings used for communications on an Ethernet network: full-duplex and half-duplex. Autonegotiation is an optional function found on most Ethernet switches and NICs. It enables two devices to automatically negotiate the best speed and duplex capabilities. Full-duplex is chosen if both devices have the capability along with their highest common bandwidth. Most switch devices now support the automatic medium-dependent interface crossover (auto-MDIX) feature. When enabled, the switch automatically detects the type of cable attached to the port and configures the interfaces accordingly.

Go to the online course to take the quiz and exam.

Chapter Quiz - Ethernet Switching

Your Chapter Notes

CHAPTER 8

Network Layer

Introduction - 8.0

Why should I take this module? - 8.0.1

Welcome to Network Layer!

By now you may have noticed that the modules in this course are progressing from the bottom up through the OSI model layers. At the network layer of the OSI model, we introduce you to communication protocols and routing protocols. Say you want to send an email to a friend who lives in another city, or even another country. This person is not on the same network as you. A simple switched network cannot get your message any further than the end of your own network. You need some help to keep this message moving along the path to your friend's end device. To send an email (a video, or a file, etc.) to anyone who is not on your local network, you must have access to routers. To access routers, you must use network layer protocols. To help you visualize these processes, this module contains two Wireshark activities. Enjoy!

What will I learn to do in this module? - 8.0.2

Module Title: Network Layer

Module Objective: Explain how routers use network layer protocols and services to enable end-to-end connectivity.

Topic Title	Topic Objective
Network Layer Characteristics	Explain how the network layer uses IP protocols for reliable communications.
IPv4 Packet	Explain the role of the major header fields in the IPv4 packet.
IPv6 Packet	Explain the role of the major header fields in the IPv6 packet.
How a Host Routes	Explain how network devices use routing tables to direct packets to a destination network.
Router Routing Tables	Explain the function of fields in the routing table of a router.

Network Layer Characteristics - 8.1

The Network Layer - 8.1.1

Refer to
Online Course
for Illustration

Refer to
Interactive Graphic
in online course

The network layer, or OSI Layer 3, provides services to allow end devices to exchange data across networks. As shown in the figure, IP version 4 (IPv4) and IP version 6 (IPv6) are the principle network layer communication protocols. Other network layer protocols include routing protocols such as Open Shortest Path First (OSPF) and messaging protocols such as Internet Control Message Protocol (ICMP).

To accomplish end-to-end communications across network boundaries, network layer protocols perform four basic operations:

- **Addressing end devices** - End devices must be configured with a unique IP address for identification on the network.

- **Encapsulation** - The network layer encapsulates the protocol data unit (PDU) from the transport layer into a packet. The encapsulation process adds IP header information, such as the IP address of the source (sending) and destination (receiving) hosts. The encapsulation process is performed by the source of the IP packet.

- **Routing** - The network layer provides services to direct the packets to a destination host on another network. To travel to other networks, the packet must be processed by a router. The role of the router is to select the best path and direct packets toward the destination host in a process known as routing. A packet may cross many routers before reaching the destination host. Each router a packet crosses to reach the destination host is called a hop.

- **De-encapsulation** - When the packet arrives at the network layer of the destination host, the host checks the IP header of the packet. If the destination IP address within the header matches its own IP address, the IP header is removed from the packet. After the packet is de-encapsulated by the network layer, the resulting Layer 4 PDU is passed up to the appropriate service at the transport layer. The de-encapsulation process is performed by the destination host of the IP packet.

Unlike the transport layer (OSI Layer 4), which manages the data transport between the processes running on each host, network layer communication protocols (i.e., IPv4 and IPv6) specify the packet structure and processing used to carry the data from one host to another host. Operating without regard to the data carried in each packet allows the network layer to carry packets for multiple types of communications between multiple hosts.

Click Play in the figure to view an animation that demonstrates the exchange of data.

IP Encapsulation - 8.1.2

Refer to **Online Course** for Illustration

IP encapsulates the transport layer (the layer just above the network layer) segment or other data by adding an IP header. The IP header is used to deliver the packet to the destination host.

The figure illustrates how the transport layer PDU is encapsulated by the network layer PDU to create an IP packet.

The process of encapsulating data layer by layer enables the services at the different layers to develop and scale without affecting the other layers. This means the transport layer segments can be readily packaged by IPv4 or IPv6 or by any new protocol that might be developed in the future.

The IP header is examined by Layer 3 devices (i.e., routers and Layer 3 switches) as it travels across a network to its destination. It is important to note, that the IP addressing information remains the same from the time the packet leaves the source host until it arrives at the destination host, except when translated by the device performing Network Address Translation (NAT) for IPv4.

Note: NAT is discussed in later modules.

Routers implement routing protocols to route packets between networks. The routing performed by these intermediary devices examines the network layer addressing in the packet header. In all cases, the data portion of the packet, that is, the encapsulated transport layer PDU or other data, remains unchanged during the network layer processes.

Characteristics of IP - 8.1.3

IP was designed as a protocol with low overhead. It provides only the functions that are necessary to deliver a packet from a source to a destination over an interconnected system of networks. The protocol was not designed to track and manage the flow of packets. These functions, if required, are performed by other protocols at other layers, primarily TCP at Layer 4.

These are the basic characteristics of IP:

- **Connectionless** - There is no connection with the destination established before sending data packets.

- **Best Effort** - IP is inherently unreliable because packet delivery is not guaranteed.

- **Media Independent** - Operation is independent of the medium (i.e., copper, fiber-optic, or wireless) carrying the data.

Refer to
Online Course
for Illustration

Connectionless - 8.1.4

IP is connectionless, meaning that no dedicated end-to-end connection is created by IP before data is sent. Connectionless communication is conceptually similar to sending a letter to someone without notifying the recipient in advance. The figure summarizes this key point.

Connectionless data communications work on the same principle. As shown in the figure, IP requires no initial exchange of control information to establish an end-to-end connection before packets are forwarded.

Refer to
Online Course
for Illustration

Best Effort - 8.1.5

IP also does not require additional fields in the header to maintain an established connection. This process greatly reduces the overhead of IP. However, with no pre-established end-to-end connection, senders are unaware whether destination devices are present and functional when sending packets, nor are they aware if the destination receives the packet, or if the destination device is able to access and read the packet.

The IP protocol does not guarantee that all packets that are delivered are, in fact, received. The figure illustrates the unreliable or best-effort delivery characteristic of the IP protocol.

Refer to
Online Course
for Illustration

Media Independent - 8.1.6

Unreliable means that IP does not have the capability to manage and recover from undelivered or corrupt packets. This is because while IP packets are sent with information about the location of delivery, they do not contain information that can be processed to inform the sender whether delivery was successful. Packets may arrive at the destination corrupted, out of sequence, or not at all. IP provides no capability for packet retransmissions if errors occur.

If out-of-order packets are delivered, or packets are missing, then applications using the data, or upper layer services, must resolve these issues. This allows IP to function very efficiently. In the TCP/IP protocol suite, reliability is the role of the TCP protocol at the transport layer.

IP operates independently of the media that carry the data at lower layers of the protocol stack. As shown in the figure, IP packets can be communicated as electronic signals over copper cable, as optical signals over fiber, or wirelessly as radio signals.

The OSI data link layer is responsible for taking an IP packet and preparing it for transmission over the communications medium. This means that the delivery of IP packets is not limited to any particular medium.

There is, however, one major characteristic of the media that the network layer considers: the maximum size of the PDU that each medium can transport. This characteristic is referred to as the maximum transmission unit (MTU). Part of the control communication between the data link layer and the network layer is the establishment of a maximum size for the packet. The data link layer passes the MTU value up to the network layer. The network layer then determines how large packets can be.

In some cases, an intermediate device, usually a router, must split up an IPv4 packet when forwarding it from one medium to another medium with a smaller MTU. This process is called fragmenting the packet, or fragmentation. Fragmentation causes latency. IPv6 packets cannot be fragmented by the router.

Go to the online course to take the quiz and exam.

Check Your Understanding - IP Characteristics - 8.1.7

IPv4 Packet - 8.2

IPv4 Packet Header - 8.2.1

IPv4 is one of the primary network layer communication protocols. The IPv4 packet header is used to ensure that this packet is delivered to its next stop on the way to its destination end device.

An IPv4 packet header consists of fields containing important information about the packet. These fields contain binary numbers which are examined by the Layer 3 process.

Refer to Online Course for Illustration

IPv4 Packet Header Fields - 8.2.2

The binary values of each field identify various settings of the IP packet. Protocol header diagrams, which are read left to right, and top down, provide a visual to refer to when discussing protocol fields. The IP protocol header diagram in the figure identifies the fields of an IPv4 packet.

The two most commonly referenced fields are the source and destination IP addresses. These fields identify where the packet is coming from and where it is going. Typically, these addresses do not change while travelling from the source to the destination.

The Internet Header Length (IHL), Total Length, and Header Checksum fields are used to identify and validate the packet.

Other fields are used to reorder a fragmented packet. Specifically, the IPv4 packet uses Identification, Flags, and Fragment Offset fields to keep track of the fragments. A router may have to fragment an IPv4 packet when forwarding it from one medium to another with a smaller MTU.

The Options and Padding fields are rarely used and are beyond the scope of this module.

Refer to **Video** in online course

Video - Sample IPv4 Headers in Wireshark - 8.2.3

Click Play in the figure to view a demonstration of examining IPv4 headers in a Wireshark capture.

Go to the online course to take the quiz and exam.

Check Your Understanding - IPv4 Packet - 8.2.4

IPv6 Packet - 8.3

Limitations of IPv4 - 8.3.1

IPv4 is still in use today. This topic is about IPv6, which will eventually replace IPv4. To better understand why you need to know the IPv6 protocol, it helps to know the limitations of IPv4 and the advantages of IPv6.

Through the years, additional protocols and processes have been developed to address new challenges. However, even with changes, IPv4 still has three major issues:

- **IPv4 address depletion** - IPv4 has a limited number of unique public addresses available. Although there are approximately 4 billion IPv4 addresses, the increasing number of new IP-enabled devices, always-on connections, and the potential growth of less-developed regions have increased the need for more addresses.

- **Lack of end-to-end connectivity** - Network Address Translation (NAT) is a technology commonly implemented within IPv4 networks. NAT provides a way for multiple devices to share a single public IPv4 address. However, because the public IPv4 address is shared, the IPv4 address of an internal network host is hidden. This can be problematic for technologies that require end-to-end connectivity.

- **Increased network complexity** - While NAT has extended the lifespan of IPv4 it was only meant as a transition mechanism to IPv6. NAT in its various implementation creates additional complexity in the network, creating latency and making troubleshooting more difficult.

Refer to **Online Course** for Illustration

IPv6 Overview - 8.3.2

In the early 1990s, the Internet Engineering Task Force (IETF) grew concerned about the issues with IPv4 and began to look for a replacement. This activity led to the development of IP version 6 (IPv6). IPv6 overcomes the limitations of IPv4 and is a powerful enhancement with features that better suit current and foreseeable network demands.

Improvements that IPv6 provides include the following:

- **Increased address space** - IPv6 addresses are based on 128-bit hierarchical addressing as opposed to IPv4 with 32 bits.

- **Improved packet handling** - The IPv6 header has been simplified with fewer fields.

- **Eliminates the need for NAT** - With such a large number of public IPv6 addresses, NAT between a private IPv4 address and a public IPv4 is not needed. This avoids some of the NAT-induced problems experienced by applications that require end-to-end connectivity.

The 32-bit IPv4 address space provides approximately 4,294,967,296 unique addresses. IPv6 address space provides 340,282,366,920,938,463,463,374,607,431,768,211,456, or 340 undecillion addresses. This is roughly equivalent to every grain of sand on Earth.

The figure provides a visual to compare the IPv4 and IPv6 address space.

Refer to
Online Course
for Illustration

IPv4 Packet Header Fields in the IPv6 Packet Header - 8.3.3

One of the major design improvements of IPv6 over IPv4 is the simplified IPv6 header.

For example, the IPv4 header consists of a variable length header of 20 octets (up to 60 bytes if the Options field is used) and 12 basic header fields, not including the Options field and Padding field.

For IPv6, some fields have remained the same, some fields have changed names and positions, and some IPv4 fields are no longer required, as highlighted in the figure.

In contrast, the simplified IPv6 header shown the next figure consists of a fixed length header of 40 octets (largely due to the length of the source and destination IPv6 addresses).

The IPv6 simplified header allows for more efficient processing of IPv6 headers.

Refer to
Online Course
for Illustration

IPv6 Packet Header - 8.3.4

The IP protocol header diagram in the figure identifies the fields of an IPv6 packet.

An IPv6 packet may also contain extension headers (EH), which provide optional network layer information. Extension headers are optional and are placed between the IPv6 header and the payload. EHs are used for fragmentation, security, to support mobility and more.

Unlike IPv4, routers do not fragment routed IPv6 packets.

Refer to **Video**
in online course

Video - Sample IPv6 Headers in Wireshark - 8.3.5

Click Play in the figure to view a demonstration of examining IPv6 headers in a Wireshark capture.

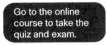
Go to the online
course to take the
quiz and exam.

Check Your Understanding - IPv6 Packet - 8.3.6

How a Host Routes - 8.4

Refer to
Online Course
for Illustration

Host Forwarding Decision - 8.4.1

With both IPv4 and IPv6, packets are always created at the source host. The source host must be able to direct the packet to the destination host. To do this, host end devices create their own routing table. This topic discusses how end devices use routing tables.

Another role of the network layer is to direct packets between hosts. A host can send a packet to the following:

- **Itself** - A host can ping itself by sending a packet to a special IPv4 address of 127.0.0.1 or an IPv6 address ::/1, which is referred to as the loopback interface. Pinging the loopback interface tests the TCP/IP protocol stack on the host.

- **Local host** - This is a destination host that is on the same local network as the sending host. The source and destination hosts share the same network address.

- **Remote host** - This is a destination host on a remote network. The source and destination hosts do not share the same network address.

The figure illustrates PC1 connecting to a local host on the same network, and to a remote host located on another network.

Whether a packet is destined for a local host or a remote host is determined by the source end device. The source end device determines whether the destination IP address is on the same network that the source device itself is on. The method of determination varies by IP version:

- **In IPv4** - The source device uses its own subnet mask along with its own IPv4 address and the destination IPv4 address to make this determination.

- **In IPv6** - The local router advertises the local network address (prefix) to all devices on the network.

In a home or business network, you may have several wired and wireless devices interconnected together using an intermediary device, such as a LAN switch or a wireless access point (WAP). This intermediary device provides interconnections between local hosts on the local network. Local hosts can reach each other and share information without the need for any additional devices. If a host is sending a packet to a device that is configured with the same IP network as the host device, the packet is simply forwarded out of the host interface, through the intermediary device, and to the destination device directly.

Of course, in most situations we want our devices to be able to connect beyond the local network segment, such as out to other homes, businesses, and the internet. Devices that are beyond the local network segment are known as remote hosts. When a source device sends a packet to a remote destination device, then the help of routers and routing is needed. Routing is the process of identifying the best path to a destination. The router connected to the local network segment is referred to as the default gateway.

Default Gateway - 8.4.2

The default gateway is the network device (i.e., router or Layer 3 switch) that can route traffic to other networks. If you use the analogy that a network is like a room, then the default gateway is like a doorway. If you want to get to another room or network you need to find the doorway.

On a network, a default gateway is usually a router with these features:

■ It has a local IP address in the same address range as other hosts on the local network.

■ It can accept data into the local network and forward data out of the local network.

■ It routes traffic to other networks.

A default gateway is required to send traffic outside of the local network. Traffic cannot be forwarded outside the local network if there is no default gateway, the default gateway address is not configured, or the default gateway is down.

Refer to Online Course for Illustration

A Host Routes to the Default Gateway - 8.4.3

A host routing table will typically include a default gateway. In IPv4, the host receives the IPv4 address of the default gateway either dynamically from Dynamic Host Configuration Protocol (DHCP) or configured manually. In IPv6, the router advertises the default gateway address or the host can be configured manually.

In the figure, PC1 and PC2 are configured with the IPv4 address of 192.168.10.1 as the default gateway.

Having a default gateway configured creates a default route in the routing table of the PC. A default route is the route or pathway your computer will take when it tries to contact a remote network.

Both PC1 and PC2 will have a default route to send all traffic destined to remote networks to R1.

Refer to Online Course for Illustration

Host Routing Tables - 8.4.4

On a Windows host, the **route print** or **netstat -r** command can be used to display the host routing table. Both commands generate the same output. The output may seem overwhelming at first, but is fairly simple to understand.

The figure displays a sample topology and the output generated by the **netstat −r** command.

IPv4 Routing Table for PC1

```
C:\Users\PC1> netstat -r

IPv4 Route Table

===========================================================================

Active Routes:

Network Destination        Netmask          Gateway       Interface   Metric
          0.0.0.0          0.0.0.0    192.168.10.1  192.168.10.10       25
```

127.0.0.0	255.0.0.0	On-link	127.0.0.1	306
127.0.0.1	255.255.255.255	On-link	127.0.0.1	306
127.255.255.255	255.255.255.255	On-link	127.0.0.1	306
192.168.10.0	255.255.255.0	On-link	192.168.10.10	281
192.168.10.10	255.255.255.255	On-link	192.168.10.10	281
192.168.10.255	255.255.255.255	On-link	192.168.10.10	281
224.0.0.0	240.0.0.0	On-link	127.0.0.1	306
224.0.0.0	240.0.0.0	On-link	192.168.10.10	281
255.255.255.255	255.255.255.255	On-link	127.0.0.1	306
255.255.255.255	255.255.255.255	On-link	192.168.10.10	281

Note: The output only displays the IPv4 route table.

Entering the **netstat -r** command or the equivalent **route print** command displays three sections related to the current TCP/IP network connections:

- **Interface List** - Lists the Media Access Control (MAC) address and assigned interface number of every network-capable interface on the host, including Ethernet, Wi-Fi, and Bluetooth adapters.

- **IPv4 Route Table** - Lists all known IPv4 routes, including direct connections, local network, and local default routes.

- **IPv6 Route Table** - Lists all known IPv6 routes, including direct connections, local network, and local default routes.

Go to the online course to take the quiz and exam.

Check Your Understanding - How a Host Routes - 8.4.5

Introduction to Routing - 8.5

Refer to **Online Course** for Illustration

Router Packet Forwarding Decision - 8.5.1

The previous topic discussed host routing tables. Most networks also contain routers, which are intermediary devices. Routers also contain routing tables. This topic covers router operations at the network layer. When a host sends a packet to another host, it consults its routing table to determine where to send the packet. If the destination host is on a remote network, the packet is forwarded to the default gateway, which is usually the local router.

What happens when a packet arrives on a router interface?

The router examines the destination IP address of the packet and searches its routing table to determine where to forward the packet. The routing table contains a list of all known network addresses (prefixes) and where to forward the packet. These entries are known as route entries or routes. The router will forward the packet using the best (longest) matching route entry.

The following table shows the pertinent information from the R1 routing table.

R1 Routing Table

Route	Next Hop or Exit Interface
192.168.10.0 /24	G0/0/0
209.165.200.224/30	G0/0/1
10.1.1.0/24	**via R2**
Default Route 0.0.0.0/0	via R2

Refer to **Online Course** for Illustration

IP Router Routing Table - 8.5.2

The routing table of the router contains network route entries listing all the possible known network destinations.

The routing table stores three types of route entries:

- **Directly-connected networks** - These network route entries are active router interfaces. Routers add a directly connected route when an interface is configured with an IP address and is activated. Each router interface is connected to a different network segment. In the figure, the directly-connected networks in the R1 IPv4 routing table would be 192.168.10.0/24 and 209.165.200.224/30.

- **Remote networks** - These network route entries are connected to other routers. Routers learn about remote networks either by being explicitly configured by an administrator or by exchanging route information using a dynamic routing protocol. In the figure, the remote network in the R1 IPv4 routing table would be 10.1.1.0/24.

- **Default route** - Like a host, most routers also include a default route entry, a gateway of last resort. The default route is used when there is no better (longer) match in the IP routing table. In the figure, the R1 IPv4 routing table would most likely include a default route to forward all packets to router R2.

The figure identifies the directly connected and remote networks of router R1.

A router can learn about remote networks in one of two ways:

- **Manually** - Remote networks are manually entered into the route table using static routes.

- **Dynamically** - Remote routes are automatically learned using a dynamic routing protocol.

Refer to **Online Course** for Illustration

Static Routing - 8.5.3

Static routes are route entries that are manually configured. The figure shows an example of a static route that was manually configured on router R1. The static route includes the remote network address and the IP address of the next hop router.

If there is a change in the network topology, the static route is not automatically updated and must be manually reconfigured. For example, in the figure R1 has a static route to reach the 10.1.1.0/24 network via R2. If that path is no longer available, R1 would need to be reconfigured with a new static route to the 10.1.1.0/24 network via R3. Router R3 would therefore need to have a route entry in its routing table to send packets destined for 10.1.1.0/24 to R2.

Static routing has the following characteristics:

- A static route must be configured manually.

- The administrator needs to reconfigure a static route if there is a change in the topology and the static route is no longer viable.

- A static route is appropriate for a small network and when there are few or no redundant links.

- A static route is commonly used with a dynamic routing protocol for configuring a default route.

Refer to **Online Course** for Illustration

Dynamic Routing - 8.5.4

A dynamic routing protocol allows the routers to automatically learn about remote networks, including a default route, from other routers. Routers that use dynamic routing protocols automatically share routing information with other routers and compensate for any topology changes without involving the network administrator. If there is a change in the network topology, routers share this information using the dynamic routing protocol and automatically update their routing tables.

Dynamic routing protocols include OSPF and Enhanced Interior Gateway Routing Protocol (EIGRP). The figure shows an example of routers R1 and R2 automatically sharing network information using the routing protocol OSPF.

Basic configuration only requires the network administrator to enable the directly connected networks within the dynamic routing protocol. The dynamic routing protocol will automatically do as follows:

- Discover remote networks

- Maintain up-to-date routing information

- Choose the best path to destination networks

- Attempt to find a new best path if the current path is no longer available

When a router is manually configured with a static route or learns about a remote network dynamically using a dynamic routing protocol, the remote network address and next hop address are entered into the IP routing table. As shown in the figure, if there is a change in the network topology, the routers will automatically adjust and attempt to find a new best path.

Note: It is common for some routers to use a combination of both static routes and a dynamic routing protocol.

Refer to **Video**
in online course

Video- IPv4 Router Routing Tables - 8.5.5

Unlike a host computer routing table, there are no column headings identifying the information contained in the routing table of a router. It is important to learn the meaning of the different items included in each entry of the routing table.

Click Play in the figure to view an introduction to the IPv4 routing table.

Refer to
Online Course
for Illustration

Introduction to an IPv4 Routing Table - 8.5.6

Notice in the figure that R2 is connected to the internet. Therefore, the administrator configured R1 with a default static route sending packets to R2 when there is no specific entry in the routing table that matches the destination IP address. R1 and R2 are also using OSPF routing to advertise directly connected networks.

```
R1# show ip route

Codes: L - local, C - connected, S - static, R - RIP, M - mobile,
       B - BGP

       D - EIGRP, EX - EIGRP external, O - OSPF, IA - OSPF inter area

       N1 - OSPF NSSA external type 1, N2 - OSPF NSSA external type 2

       E1 - OSPF external type 1, E2 - OSPF external type 2

       i - IS-IS, su - IS-IS summary, L1 - IS-IS level-1, L2 - IS-IS
          level-2

       ia - IS-IS inter area, * - candidate default, U - per-user static
          route

       o - ODR, P - periodic downloaded static route, H - NHRP,
          l - LISP

       a - application route

       + - replicated route, % - next hop override, p - overrides from
          PfR

Gateway of last resort is 209.165.200.226 to network 0.0.0.0

S*     0.0.0.0/0 [1/0] via 209.165.200.226, GigabitEthernet0/0/1

       10.0.0.0/24 is subnetted, 1 subnets

O      10.1.1.0 [110/2] via 209.165.200.226, 00:02:45,
          GigabitEthernet0/0/1

       192.168.10.0/24 is variably subnetted, 2 subnets, 2 masks

C      192.168.10.0/24 is directly connected, GigabitEthernet0/0/0

L      192.168.10.1/32 is directly connected, GigabitEthernet0/0/0

       209.165.200.0/24 is variably subnetted, 2 subnets, 2 masks

C      209.165.200.224/30 is directly connected, GigabitEthernet0/0/1

L      209.165.200.225/32 is directly connected, GigabitEthernet0/0/1

R1#
```

The **show ip route** privileged EXEC mode command is used to view the IPv4 routing table on a Cisco IOS router. The example shows the IPv4 routing table of router R1. At the beginning of each routing table entry is a code that is used to identify the type of route or how the route was learned. Common route sources (codes) include these:

- L - Directly connected local interface IP address
- C - Directly connected network
- S - Static route was manually configured by an administrator
- O - OSPF
- D - EIGRP

The routing table displays all of the known IPv4 destination routes for R1.

A directly connected route is automatically created when a router interface is configured with IP address information and is activated. The router adds two route entries with the codes C (i.e., the connected network) and L (i.e., the local interface IP address of the connected network). The route entries also identify the exit interface to use to reach the network. The two directly connected networks in this example are 192.168.10.0/24 and 209.165.200.224/30.

Routers R1 and R2 are also using the OSPF dynamic routing protocol to exchange router information. In the example routing table, R1 has a route entry for the 10.1.1.0/24 network that it learned dynamically from router R2 via the OSPF routing protocol.

A default route has a network address of all zeroes. For example, the IPv4 network address is 0.0.0.0. A static route entry in the routing table begins with a code of S*, as highlighted in the example.

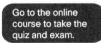
Go to the online course to take the quiz and exam.

Check Your Understanding - Introduction to Routing - 8.5.7

Module Practice and Quiz - 8.6

What did I learn in this module? - 8.6.1

Network Layer Characteristics

The network layer (OSI Layer 3) provides services to allow end devices to exchange data across networks. IPv4 and IPv6 are the principle network layer communication protocols. The network layer also includes the routing protocol OSPF and messaging protocols such as ICMP. Network layer protocols perform four basic operations: addressing end devices, encapsulation, routing, and de-encapsulation. IPv4 and IPv6 specify the packet structure and processing used to carry the data from one host to another host. IP encapsulates the transport layer segment by adding an IP header, which is used to deliver the packet to the destination host. The IP header is examined by Layer 3 devices (i.e., routers) as it travels across a network to its destination. The characteristics of IP are that it is connection-less, best effort, and media independent. IP is connectionless, meaning that no dedicated end-to-end connection is created by IP before data is sent. The IP protocol does not guarantee that all packets that are delivered are, in fact, received. This is the definition of the unreliable, or best effort characteristic. IP operates independently of the media that carry the data at lower layers of the protocol stack.

IPv4 Packet

An IPv4 packet header consists of fields containing information about the packet. These fields contain binary numbers which are examined by the Layer 3 process. The binary values of each field identify various settings of the IP packet. Significant fields in the IPv6 header include: version, DS, header checksum, TTL, protocol, and the source and destination IPv4 addresses.

IPv6 Packet

IPv6 is designed to overcome the limitations of IPv4 including: IPv4 address depletion, lack of end-to-end connectivity, and increased network complexity. IPv6 increases the available address space, improves packet handling, and eliminates the need for NAT. The fields in the IPv6 packet header include: version, traffic class, flow label, payload length, next header, hop limit, and the source and destination IPv6 addresses.

How a Host Routes

A host can send a packet to itself, another local host, and a remote host. In IPv4, the source device uses its own subnet mask along with its own IPv4 address and the destination IPv4 address to determine whether the destination host is on the same network. In IPv6, the local router advertises the local network address (prefix) to all devices on the network, to make this determination. The default gateway is the network device (i.e., router) that can route traffic to other networks. On a network, a default gateway is usually a router that has a local IP address in the same address range as other hosts on the local network, can accept data into the local network and forward data out of the local network, and route traffic to other networks. A host routing table will typically include a default gateway. In IPv4, the host receives the IPv4 address of the default gateway either dynamically via DHCP or it is configured manually. In IPv6, the router advertises the default gateway address, or the host can be configured manually. On a Windows host, the **route print** or **netstat -r** command can be used to display the host routing table.

Introduction to Routing

When a host sends a packet to another host, it consults its routing table to determine where to send the packet. If the destination host is on a remote network, the packet is forwarded to the default gateway which is usually the local router. What happens when a packet arrives on a router interface? The router examines the packet's destination IP address and searches its routing table to determine where to forward the packet. The routing table contains a list of all known network addresses (prefixes) and where to forward the packet. These entries are known as route entries or routes. The router will forward the packet using the best (longest) matching route entry. The routing table of a router stores three types of route entries: directly connected networks, remote networks, and a default route. Routers learn about remote networks manually, or dynamically using a dynamic routing protocol. Static routes are route entries that are manually configured. Static routes include the remote network address and the IP address of the next hop router. OSPF and EIGRP are two dynamic routing protocols. The **show ip route** privileged EXEC mode command is used to view the IPv4 routing table on a Cisco IOS router. At the beginning of an IPv4 routing table is a code that is used to identify the type of route or how the route was learned. Common route sources (codes) include:

L - Directly connected local interface IP address

C - Directly connected network

S - Static route was manually configured by an administrator

O - Open Shortest Path First (OSPF)

D - Enhanced Interior Gateway Routing Protocol (EIGRP)

Go to the online
course to take the
quiz and exam.

Chapter Quiz - Network Layer

Your Chapter Notes

CHAPTER 9

Address Resolution

Introduction - 9.0

Why should I take this module? - 9.0.1

Welcome to Address Resolution!

Hosts and routers both create routing tables to ensure that they can send and receive data across networks. So how does this information get created in a routing table? As a network administrator, you could enter these MAC and IP addresses manually. But that would take a lot of time and the likelihood of making a few mistakes is great. Are you thinking that there must be some way that this could be done automatically, by the hosts and routers themselves? Of course, you are correct! And even though it is automatic, you must still understand how this works, because you may have to troubleshoot a problem, or worse, your network could be attacked by a threat actor. Are you ready to learn about address resolution? This module has several very good videos to help explain the concepts, as well as three Packet Tracer activities to cement your understanding. Why wait?

What will I learn to do in this module? - 9.0.2

Module Title: Address Resolution

Module Objective: Explain how ARP and ND enable communication on a network.

Topic Title	Topic Objective
MAC and IP	Compare the roles of the MAC address and the IP address.
ARP	Describe the purpose of ARP.
Neighbor Discovery	Describe the operation of IPv6 neighbor discovery.

MAC and IP - 9.1

Destination on Same Network - 9.1.1

Refer to Online Course for Illustration

Sometimes a host must send a message, but it only knows the IP address of the destination device. The host needs to know the MAC address of that device, but how can it be discovered? That is where address resolution becomes critical.

There are two primary addresses assigned to a device on an Ethernet LAN:

- **Physical address (the MAC address)** - Used for NIC to NIC communications on the same Ethernet network.

- **Logical address (the IP address)** - Used to send the packet from the source device to the destination device. The destination IP address may be on the same IP network as the source or it may be on a remote network.

Layer 2 physical addresses (i.e., Ethernet MAC addresses) are used to deliver the data link frame with the encapsulated IP packet from one NIC to another NIC that is on the same network. If the destination IP address is on the same network, the destination MAC address will be that of the destination device.

Consider the following example using simplified MAC address representations.

In this example, PC1 wants to send a packet to PC2. The figure displays the Layer 2 destination and source MAC addresses and the Layer 3 IPv4 addressing that would be included in the packet sent from PC1.

The Layer 2 Ethernet frame contains the following:

- **Destination MAC address** - This is the simplified MAC address of PC2, 55-55-55.

- **Source MAC address** - This is the simplified MAC address of the Ethernet NIC on PC1, aa-aa-aa.

The Layer 3 IP packet contains the following:

- **Source IPv4 address** - This is the IPv4 address of PC1, 192.168.10.10.

- **Destination IPv4 address** - This is the IPv4 address of PC2, 192.168.10.11.

Refer to **Online Course** for Illustration

Destination on Remote Network - 9.1.2

When the destination IP address (IPv4 or IPv6) is on a remote network, the destination MAC address will be the address of the host default gateway (i.e., the router interface).

Consider the following example using a simplified MAC address representation.

In this example, PC1 wants to send a packet to PC2. PC2 is located on remote network. Because the destination IPv4 address is not on the same local network as PC1, the destination MAC address is that of the local default gateway on the router.

Routers examine the destination IPv4 address to determine the best path to forward the IPv4 packet. When the router receives the Ethernet frame, it de-encapsulates the Layer 2 information. Using the destination IPv4 address, it determines the next-hop device, and then encapsulates the IPv4 packet in a new data link frame for the outgoing interface.

In our example, R1 would now encapsulate the packet with new Layer 2 address information as shown in the figure.

The new destination MAC address would be that of the R2 G0/0/1 interface and the new source MAC address would be that of the R1 G0/0/1 interface.

Along each link in a path, an IP packet is encapsulated in a frame. The frame is specific to the data link technology that is associated with that link, such as Ethernet. If the next-hop device is the final destination, the destination MAC address will be that of the device Ethernet NIC, as shown in the figure.

How are the IP addresses of the IP packets in a data flow associated with the MAC addresses on each link along the path to the destination? For IPv4 packets, this is done through a process called Address Resolution Protocol (ARP). For IPv6 packets, the process is ICMPv6 Neighbor Discovery (ND).

Refer to **Packet Tracer Activity** for this chapter

Packet Tracer - Identify MAC and IP Addresses - 9.1.3

In this Packet Tracer, activity you will complete the following objectives:

- Gather PDU Information for Local Network Communication
- Gather PDU Information for Remote Network Communication

This activity is optimized for viewing PDUs. The devices are already configured. You will gather PDU information in simulation mode and answer a series of questions about the data you collect.

Go to the online course to take the quiz and exam.

Check Your Understanding - MAC and IP - 9.1.4

ARP - 9.2

Refer to **Online Course** for Illustration

ARP Overview - 9.2.1

If your network is using the IPv4 communications protocol, the Address Resolution Protocol, or ARP, is what you need to map IPv4 addresses to MAC addresses. This topic explains how ARP works.

Every IP device on an Ethernet network has a unique Ethernet MAC address. When a device sends an Ethernet Layer 2 frame, it contains these two addresses:

- **Destination MAC address** - The Ethernet MAC address of the destination device on the same local network segment. If the destination host is on another network, then the destination address in the frame would be that of the default gateway (i.e., router).
- **Source MAC address** - The MAC address of the Ethernet NIC on the source host.

The figure illustrates the problem when sending a frame to another host on the same segment on an IPv4 network.

To send a packet to another host on the same local IPv4 network, a host must know the IPv4 address and the MAC address of the destination device. Device destination IPv4 addresses are either known or resolved by device name. However, MAC addresses must be discovered.

A device uses Address Resolution Protocol (ARP) to determine the destination MAC address of a local device when it knows its IPv4 address.

ARP provides two basic functions:

- Resolving IPv4 addresses to MAC addresses
- Maintaining a table of IPv4 to MAC address mappings

Refer to **Interactive Graphic** in online course

ARP Functions - 9.2.2

When a packet is sent to the data link layer to be encapsulated into an Ethernet frame, the device refers to a table in its memory to find the MAC address that is mapped to the IPv4 address. This table is stored temporarily in RAM memory and called the ARP table or the ARP cache.

The sending device will search its ARP table for a destination IPv4 address and a corresponding MAC address.

- If the packet's destination IPv4 address is on the same network as the source IPv4 address, the device will search the ARP table for the destination IPv4 address.

- If the destination IPv4 address is on a different network than the source IPv4 address, the device will search the ARP table for the IPv4 address of the default gateway.

In both cases, the search is for an IPv4 address and a corresponding MAC address for the device.

Each entry, or row, of the ARP table binds an IPv4 address with a MAC address. We call the relationship between the two values a map. This simply means that you can locate an IPv4 address in the table and discover the corresponding MAC address. The ARP table temporarily saves (caches) the mapping for the devices on the LAN.

If the device locates the IPv4 address, its corresponding MAC address is used as the destination MAC address in the frame. If there is no entry is found, then the device sends an ARP request.

Click Play in the figure to see an animation of the ARP function.

Refer to Video in online course

Video - ARP Request - 9.2.3

An ARP request is sent when a device needs to determine the MAC address that is associated with an IPv4 address, and it does not have an entry for the IPv4 address in its ARP table.

ARP messages are encapsulated directly within an Ethernet frame. There is no IPv4 header. The ARP request is encapsulated in an Ethernet frame using the following header information:

- **Destination MAC address** - This is a broadcast address FF-FF-FF-FF-FF-FF requiring all Ethernet NICs on the LAN to accept and process the ARP request.

- **Source MAC address** - This is MAC address of the sender of the ARP request.

- **Type** - ARP messages have a type field of 0x806. This informs the receiving NIC that the data portion of the frame needs to be passed to the ARP process.

Because ARP requests are broadcasts, they are flooded out all ports by the switch, except the receiving port. All Ethernet NICs on the LAN process broadcasts and must deliver the ARP request to its operating system for processing. Every device must process the ARP request to see if the target IPv4 address matches its own. A router will not forward broadcasts out other interfaces.

Only one device on the LAN will have an IPv4 address that matches the target IPv4 address in the ARP request. All other devices will not reply.

Click Play in the figure to view a demonstration of an ARP request for a destination IPv4 address that is on the local network.

Refer to **Video**
in online course

Video - ARP Operation - ARP Reply - 9.2.4

Only the device with the target IPv4 address associated with the ARP request will respond with an ARP reply. The ARP reply is encapsulated in an Ethernet frame using the following header information:

- **Destination MAC address** - This is the MAC address of the sender of the ARP request.

- **Source MAC address** - This is the MAC address of the sender of the ARP reply.

- **Type** - ARP messages have a type field of 0x806. This informs the receiving NIC that the data portion of the frame needs to be passed to the ARP process.

Only the device that originally sent the ARP request will receive the unicast ARP reply. After the ARP reply is received, the device will add the IPv4 address and the corresponding MAC address to its ARP table. Packets destined for that IPv4 address can now be encapsulated in frames using its corresponding MAC address.

If no device responds to the ARP request, the packet is dropped because a frame cannot be created.

Entries in the ARP table are time stamped. If a device does not receive a frame from a particular device before the timestamp expires, the entry for this device is removed from the ARP table.

Additionally, static map entries can be entered in an ARP table, but this is rarely done. Static ARP table entries do not expire over time and must be manually removed.

Note: IPv6 uses a similar process to ARP for IPv4, known as ICMPv6 Neighbor Discovery (ND). IPv6 uses neighbor solicitation and neighbor advertisement messages, similar to IPv4 ARP requests and ARP replies.

Click Play in the figure to view a demonstration of an ARP reply.

Refer to **Video**
in online course

Video - ARP Role in Remote Communications - 9.2.5

When the destination IPv4 address is not on the same network as the source IPv4 address, the source device needs to send the frame to its default gateway. This is the interface of the local router. Whenever a source device has a packet with an IPv4 address on another network, it will encapsulate that packet in a frame using the destination MAC address of the router.

The IPv4 address of the default gateway is stored in the IPv4 configuration of the hosts. When a host creates a packet for a destination, it compares the destination IPv4 address and its own IPv4 address to determine if the two IPv4 addresses are located on the same Layer 3 network. If the destination host is not on its same network, the source checks its ARP table for an entry with the IPv4 address of the default gateway. If there is not an entry, it uses the ARP process to determine a MAC address of the default gateway.

Click Play to view a demonstration of an ARP request and ARP reply associated with the default gateway.

Refer to
Online Course
for Illustration

Removing Entries from an ARP Table - 9.2.6

For each device, an ARP cache timer removes ARP entries that have not been used for a specified period of time. The times differ depending on the operating system of the device. For example, newer Windows operating systems store ARP table entries between 15 and 45 seconds, as illustrated in the figure.

Commands may also be used to manually remove some or all of the entries in the ARP table. After an entry has been removed, the process for sending an ARP request and receiving an ARP reply must occur again to enter the map in the ARP table.

ARP Tables on Networking Devices - 9.2.7

On a Cisco router, the **show ip arp** command is used to display the ARP table, as shown in the figure.

```
R1# show ip arp

Protocol  Address         Age (min)  Hardware Addr   Type   Interface

Internet  192.168.10.1         -     a0e0.af0d.e140  ARPA   GigabitEthernet0/0/0

Internet  209.165.200.225      -     a0e0.af0d.e141  ARPA   GigabitEthernet0/0/1

Internet  209.165.200.226      1     a03d.6fe1.9d91  ARPA   GigabitEthernet0/0/1

R1#
```

On a Windows 10 PC, the **arp –a** command is used to display the ARP table, as shown in the figure.

```
C:\Users\PC> arp -a

Interface: 192.168.1.124 --- 0x10

  Internet Address      Physical Address      Type
  192.168.1.1           c8-d7-19-cc-a0-86     dynamic
  192.168.1.101         08-3e-0c-f5-f7-77     dynamic
  192.168.1.110         08-3e-0c-f5-f7-56     dynamic
  192.168.1.112         ac-b3-13-4a-bd-d0     dynamic
  192.168.1.117         08-3e-0c-f5-f7-5c     dynamic
  192.168.1.126         24-77-03-45-5d-c4     dynamic
  192.168.1.146         94-57-a5-0c-5b-02     dynamic
  192.168.1.255         ff-ff-ff-ff-ff-ff     static
  224.0.0.22            01-00-5e-00-00-16     static
  224.0.0.251           01-00-5e-00-00-fb     static
  239.255.255.250       01-00-5e-7f-ff-fa     static
  255.255.255.255       ff-ff-ff-ff-ff-ff     static

C:\Users\PC>
```

Refer to
Online Course
for Illustration

ARP Issues - ARP Broadcasts and ARP Spoofing - 9.2.8

As a broadcast frame, an ARP request is received and processed by every device on the local network. On a typical business network, these broadcasts would probably have minimal impact on network performance. However, if a large number of devices were to be powered up and all start accessing network services at the same time, there could be some reduction in performance for a short period of time, as shown in the figure. After the devices send out the initial ARP broadcasts and have learned the necessary MAC addresses, any impact on the network will be minimized.

In some cases, the use of ARP can lead to a potential security risk. A threat actor can use ARP spoofing to perform an ARP poisoning attack. This is a technique used by a threat actor to reply to an ARP request for an IPv4 address belonging to another device, such as the default gateway, as shown in the figure. The threat actor sends an ARP reply with its own MAC address. The receiver of the ARP reply will add the wrong MAC address to its ARP table and send these packets to the threat actor.

Enterprise level switches include mitigation techniques known as dynamic ARP inspection (DAI). DAI is beyond the scope of this course.

Refer to **Packet
Tracer Activity**
for this chapter

Packet Tracer - Examine the ARP Table - 9.2.9

In this Packet Tracer, activity you will complete the following objectives:

- Examine an ARP Request
- Examine a Switch MAC Address Table
- Examine the ARP Process in Remote Communications

This activity is optimized for viewing PDUs. The devices are already configured. You will gather PDU information in simulation mode and answer a series of questions about the data you collect.

Go to the online
course to take the
quiz and exam.

Check Your Understanding - ARP - 9.2.10

IPv6 Neighbor Discovery - 9.3

Refer to **Video**
in online course

Video - IPv6 Neighbor Discovery - 9.3.1

If your network is using the IPv6 communications protocol, the Neighbor Discovery protocol, or ND, is what you need to match IPv6 addresses to MAC addresses. This topic explains how ND works.

Click Play in the figure to view a demonstration of IPv6 Neighbor Discovery.

Refer to
Online Course
for Illustration

IPv6 Neighbor Discovery Messages - 9.3.2

IPv6 Neighbor Discovery protocol is sometimes referred to as ND or NDP. In this course, we will refer to it as ND. ND provides address resolution, router discovery, and redirection services for IPv6 using ICMPv6. ICMPv6 ND uses five ICMPv6 messages to perform these services:

- Neighbor Solicitation messages
- Neighbor Advertisement messages
- Router Solicitation messages
- Router Advertisement messages
- Redirect Message

Neighbor Solicitation and Neighbor Advertisement messages are used for device-to-device messaging such as address resolution (similar to ARP for IPv4). Devices include both host computers and routers.

Router Solicitation and Router Advertisement messages are for messaging between devices and routers. Typically router discovery is used for dynamic address allocation and stateless address autoconfiguration (SLAAC).

Note: The fifth ICMPv6 ND message is a redirect message which is used for better next-hop selection. This is beyond the scope of this course.

IPv6 ND is defined in the IETF RFC 4861.

Refer to
Online Course
for Illustration

IPv6 Neighbor Discovery - Address Resolution - 9.3.3

Much like ARP for IPv4, IPv6 devices use IPv6 ND to determine the MAC address of a device that has a known IPv6 address.

ICMPv6 Neighbor Solicitation and Neighbor Advertisement messages are used for MAC address resolution. This is similar to ARP Requests and ARP Replies used by ARP for IPv4. For example, assume PC1 wants to ping PC2 at IPv6 address 2001:db8:acad::11. To determine the MAC address for the known IPv6 address, PC1 sends an ICMPv6 Neighbor Solicitation message as illustrated in the figure.

ICMPv6 Neighbor Solicitation messages are sent using special Ethernet and IPv6 multicast addresses. This allows the Ethernet NIC of the receiving device to determine whether the Neighbor Solicitation message is for itself without having to send it to the operating system for processing.

PC2 replies to the request with an ICMPv6 Neighbor Advertisement message which includes its MAC address.

Refer to **Packet Tracer Activity** for this chapter

Packet Tracer - IPv6 Neighbor Discovery - 9.3.4

In order for a device to communicate with another device, the MAC address of the destination device must be known. With IPv6, a process called Neighbor Discovery is responsible for determining the destination MAC address. You will gather PDU information in simulation mode to better understand the process. There is no Packet Tracer scoring for this activity.

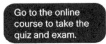
Go to the online course to take the quiz and exam.

Check Your Understanding - Neighbor Discovery - 9.3.5

Module Practice and Quiz - 9.4

What did I learn in this module? - 9.4.1

MAC and IP

Layer 2 physical addresses (i.e., Ethernet MAC addresses) are used to deliver the data link frame with the encapsulated IP packet from one NIC to another NIC on the same network. If the destination IP address is on the same network, the destination MAC address will be that of the destination device. When the destination IP address (IPv4 or IPv6) is on a remote network, the destination MAC address will be the address of the host default gateway (i.e., the router interface). Along each link in a path, an IP packet is encapsulated in a frame. The frame is specific to the data link technology associated that is associated with that link, such as Ethernet. If the next-hop device is the final destination, the destination MAC address will be that of the device Ethernet NIC. How are the IP addresses of the IP packets in a data flow associated with the MAC addresses on each link along the path to the destination? For IPv4 packets, this is done through a process called ARP. For IPv6 packets, the process is ICMPv6 ND.

ARP

Every IP device on an Ethernet network has a unique Ethernet MAC address. When a device sends an Ethernet Layer 2 frame, it contains these two addresses: destination MAC address and source MAC address. A device uses ARP to determine the destination MAC address of a local device when it knows its IPv4 address. ARP provides two basic functions: resolving IPv4 addresses to MAC addresses and maintaining a table of IPv4 to MAC address mappings. The ARP request is encapsulated in an Ethernet frame using this header information: source and destination MAC addresses and type. Only one device on the LAN will have an IPv4 address that matches the target IPv4 address in the ARP request. All other devices will not reply. The ARP reply contains the same header fields as the request. Only the device that originally sent the ARP request will receive the unicast ARP reply. After the ARP reply is received, the device will add the IPv4 address and the corresponding MAC address to its ARP table. When the destination IPv4 address is not on the same network as the source IPv4 address, the source device needs to send the frame to its default gateway. This is the interface of the local router. For each device, an ARP cache timer removes ARP entries that have not been used for a specified period of time. Commands may also be used to manually remove some or all of the entries in the ARP table. As a broadcast frame, an ARP request is received and processed by every device on the local network, which could cause the network to slow down. A threat actor can use ARP spoofing to perform an ARP poisoning attack.

Neighbor Discovery

IPv6 does not use ARP, it uses the ND protocol to resolve MAC addresses. ND provides address resolution, router discovery, and redirection services for IPv6 using ICMPv6. ICMPv6 ND uses five ICMPv6 messages to perform these services: neighbor solicitation, neighbor advertisement, router solicitation, router advertisement, and redirect. Much like ARP for IPv4, IPv6 devices use IPv6 ND to resolve the MAC address of a device to a known IPv6 address.

Go to the online course to take the quiz and exam.

Chapter Quiz - Address Resolution

Your Chapter Notes

CHAPTER 10

Basic Router Configuration

Introduction - 10.0

Why should I take this module? - 10.0.1

Welcome to Basic Router Configuration!

Have you ever run a relay? The first person runs the first leg of the race and hands off the baton to the next runner, who continues forward in the second leg of the race and hands off the baton to the third runner, and on it goes. Routing packets is very similar to a relay. But if the first runner does not know where to find the second runner, or drops the baton in the first leg, then that relay team will most certainly lose the race.

Routing packets is very similar to a relay. As you know, routing tables are created and used by routers to forward packets from their local networks on to other networks. But a router cannot create a routing table or forward any packets until it has been configured. If you plan to become a network administrator you definitely must know how to do this. The good news? It is easy! This module has Syntax Checker activities so that you can practice your configuration commands and see the output. There are also some Packet Tracer activities to get you started. Let's go!

What will I learn in this module? - 10.0.2

Module Title: Basic Router Configuration

Module Objective: Implement initial settings on a router and end devices.

Topic Title	Topic Objective
Configure Initial Router Settings	Configure initial settings on an IOS Cisco router.
Configure Interfaces	Configure two active interfaces on a Cisco IOS router.
Configure the Default Gateway	Configure devices to use the default gateway.

Configure Initial Router Settings - 10.1

Basic Router Configuration Steps - 10.1.1

The following tasks should be completed when configuring initial settings on a router.

1. Configure the device name.

```
Router(config)# hostname
```

2. Secure privileged EXEC mode.

```
Router(config)# enable secret password
```

3. Secure user EXEC mode.

```
Router(config)# line console 0
Router(config-line)# password password
Router(config-line)# login
```

4. Secure remote Telnet / SSH access.

```
Router(config-line)# line vty 0 4
Router(config-line)# password password
Router(config-line)# login
Router(config-line)# transport input {ssh | telnet}
```

5. Secure all passwords in the config file.

```
Router(config-line)# exit
Router(config)# service password-encryption
```

6. Provide legal notification.

```
Router(config)# banner motd delimiter message delimiter
```

7. Save the configuration.

```
Router(config)# end
Router# copy running-config startup-config
```

Refer to
Online Course
for Illustration

Basic Router Configuration Example - 10.1.2

In this example, router R1 in the topology diagram will be configured with initial settings. To configure the device name for R1, use the following commands.

```
Router> enable
Router# configure terminal
Enter configuration commands, one per line.
End with CNTL/Z.
Router(config)# hostname R1
R1(config)#
```

Note: Notice how the router prompt now displays the router hostname.

All router access should be secured. Privileged EXEC mode provides the user with complete access to the device and its configuration. Therefore, it is the most important mode to secure.

The following commands secure privileged EXEC mode and user EXEC mode, enable Telnet and SSH remote access, and encrypt all plaintext (i.e., user EXEC and VTY line) passwords.

```
R1(config)# enable secret class

R1(config)#

R1(config)# line console 0

R1(config-line)# password cisco

R1(config-line)# login

R1(config-line)# exit

R1(config)#

R1(config)# line vty 0 4

R1(config-line)# password cisco

R1(config-line)# login

R1(config-line)# transport input ssh telnet

R1(config-line)# exit

R1(config)#

R1(config)# service password-encryption

R1(config)#
```

The legal notification warns users that the device should only be accessed by permitted users. Legal notification is configured as follows.

```
R1(config)# banner motd #

Enter TEXT message. End with a new line and the #

************************************************

WARNING: Unauthorized access is prohibited!

************************************************

#

R1(config)#
```

If the previous commands were configured and the router accidently lost power, all configured commands would be lost. For this reason, it is important to save the configuration when changes are implemented. The following command saves the configuration to NVRAM.

```
R1# copy running-config startup-config

Destination filename [startup-config]?

Building configuration...

[OK]

R1#
```

Refer to
Interactive Graphic
in online course

Syntax Checker - Configure Initial Router Settings - 10.1.3

Use this syntax checker to practice configuring the initial settings on a router.

- Configure the device name.

- Secure the privileged EXEC mode.

- Secure and enable remote SSH and Telnet access.

- Secure all plaintext passwords.

- Provide legal notification.

Refer to Packet
Tracer Activity
for this chapter

Packet Tracer - Configure Initial Router Settings - 10.1.4

In this activity, you will perform basic router configurations. You will secure access to the CLI and console port using encrypted and plaintext passwords. You will also configure messages for users logging into the router. These banners also warn unauthorized users that access is prohibited. Finally, you will verify and save your running configuration.

Configure Interfaces - 10.2

Configure Router Interfaces - 10.2.1

At this point, your routers have their basic configurations. The next step is to configure their interfaces. This is because routers are not reachable by end devices until the interfaces are configured. There are many different types of interfaces available on Cisco routers. For example, the Cisco ISR 4321 router is equipped with two Gigabit Ethernet interfaces:

- GigabitEthernet 0/0/0 (G0/0/0)

- GigabitEthernet 0/0/1 (G0/0/1)

The task to configure a router interface is very similar to a management SVI on a switch. Specifically, it includes issuing the following commands:

```
Router(config)# interface type-and-number
Router(config-if)# description description-text
Router(config-if)# ip address ipv4-address subnet-mask
Router(config-if)# ipv6 address ipv6-address/prefix-length
Router(config-if)# no shutdown
```

Note: When a router interface is enabled, information messages should be displayed confirming the enabled link.

Although the **description** command is not required to enable an interface, it is good practice to use it. It can be helpful in troubleshooting on production networks by providing information about the type of network connected. For example, if the interface connects to an ISP or service carrier, the **description** command would be helpful to enter the third-party connection and contact information.

Note: The *description-text* is limited to 240 characters.

Using the **no shutdown** command activates the interface and is similar to powering on the interface. The interface must also be connected to another device, such as a switch or a router, for the physical layer to be active.

Note: On inter-router connections where there is no Ethernet switch, both interconnecting interfaces must be configured and enabled.

Refer to
Online Course
for Illustration

Configure Router Interfaces Example - 10.2.2

In this example, the directly connected interfaces of R1 in the topology diagram will be enabled.

To configure the interfaces on R1, use the following commands.

```
R1> enable

R1# configure terminal

Enter configuration commands, one per line.

End with CNTL/Z.

R1(config)# interface gigabitEthernet 0/0/0

R1(config-if)# description Link to LAN

R1(config-if)# ip address 192.168.10.1 255.255.255.0

R1(config-if)# ipv6 address 2001:db8:acad:10::1/64

R1(config-if)# no shutdown

R1(config-if)# exit

R1(config)#

*Aug  1 01:43:53.435: %LINK-3-UPDOWN: Interface GigabitEthernet0/0/0,
changed state to down

*Aug  1 01:43:56.447: %LINK-3-UPDOWN: Interface GigabitEthernet0/0/0,
changed state to up

*Aug  1 01:43:57.447: %LINEPROTO-5-UPDOWN: Line protocol on Interface
GigabitEthernet0/0/0, changed state to up

R1(config)#

R1(config)#
```

```
R1(config)# interface gigabitEthernet 0/0/1

R1(config-if)# description Link to R2

R1(config-if)# ip address 209.165.200.225 255.255.255.252

R1(config-if)# ipv6 address 2001:db8:feed:224::1/64

R1(config-if)# no shutdown

R1(config-if)# exit

R1(config)#

*Aug  1 01:46:29.170: %LINK-3-UPDOWN: Interface GigabitEthernet0/0/1,
changed state to down

*Aug  1 01:46:32.171: %LINK-3-UPDOWN: Interface GigabitEthernet0/0/1,
changed state to up

*Aug  1 01:46:33.171: %LINEPROTO-5-UPDOWN: Line protocol on Interface
GigabitEthernet0/0/1, changed state to up

R1(config)#
```

Note: Notice the informational messages informing us that G0/0/0 and G0/0/1 are enabled.

Verify Interface Configuration - 10.2.3

There are several commands that can be used to verify interface configuration. The most useful of these is the **show ip interface brief** and **show ipv6 interface brief** commands, as shown in the example.

```
R1#  show ip interface brief

Interface            IP-Address       OK? Method Status           Protocol

GigabitEthernet0/0/0 192.168.10.1     YES manual up               up

GigabitEthernet0/0/1 209.165.200.225 YES manual up               up

Vlan1                unassigned       YES unset  administratively down
down

R1#  show ipv6 interface brief

GigabitEthernet0/0/0          [up/up]

    FE80::201:C9FF:FE89:4501

    2001:DB8:ACAD:10::1

GigabitEthernet0/0/1          [up/up]

    FE80::201:C9FF:FE89:4502

    2001:DB8:FEED:224::1

Vlan1                         [administratively down/down]

    unassigned

R1#
```

Refer to
Interactive Graphic
in online course

Configuration Verification Commands - 10.2.4

The table summarizes the more popular **show** commands used to verify interface configuration.

Commands	Description

`show ip interface brief`
 	
`show ipv6 interface brief`
	The output displays all interfaces, their IP addresses, and their current status. The configured and connected interfaces should display a Status of "up" and Protocol of "up". Anything else would indicate a problem with either the configuration or the cabling.

`show ip route`
 	
`show ipv6 route`
	Displays the contents of the IP routing tables stored in RAM.

`show interfaces`	Displays statistics for all interfaces on the device. However, this command will only display the IPv4 addressing information.
`show ip interfaces`	Displays the IPv4 statistics for all interfaces on a router.
`show ipv6 interface`	Displays the IPv6 statistics for all interfaces on a router.

Click each button to see the command output for each configuration verification command.

show ip interface brief

```
R1# show ip interface brief

Interface            IP-Address       OK? Method Status                 Protocol

GigabitEthernet0/0/0 192.168.10.1     YES manual up                     up

GigabitEthernet0/0/1 209.165.200.225  YES manual up                     up

Vlan1                unassigned       YES unset  administratively down
down

R1#
```

show ipv6 interface brief

```
R1# show ipv6 interface brief

GigabitEthernet0/0/0          [up/up]

    FE80::201:C9FF:FE89:4501

    2001:DB8:ACAD:10::1

GigabitEthernet0/0/1          [up/up]

    FE80::201:C9FF:FE89:4502

    2001:DB8:FEED:224::1

Vlan1                         [administratively down/down]

    unassigned

R1#
```

show ip route

```
R1# show ip route
Codes: L - local, C - connected, S - static, R - RIP, M - mobile,
       B - BGP

       D - EIGRP, EX - EIGRP external, O - OSPF, IA - OSPF inter area

       N1 - OSPF NSSA external type 1, N2 - OSPF NSSA external type 2

       E1 - OSPF external type 1, E2 - OSPF external type 2

       i - IS-IS, su - IS-IS summary, L1 - IS-IS level-1, L2 - IS-IS
       level-2

       ia - IS-IS inter area, * - candidate default, U - per-user static
        route

       o - ODR, P - periodic downloaded static route, H - NHRP, l - LISP

       a - application route

       + - replicated route, % - next hop override, p - overrides from
        PfR

Gateway of last resort is not set

      192.168.10.0/24 is variably subnetted, 2 subnets, 2 masks
C        192.168.10.0/24 is directly connected, GigabitEthernet0/0/0
L        192.168.10.1/32 is directly connected, GigabitEthernet0/0/0
      209.165.200.0/24 is variably subnetted, 2 subnets, 2 masks
C        209.165.200.224/30 is directly connected, GigabitEthernet0/0/1
L        209.165.200.225/32 is directly connected, GigabitEthernet0/0/1
R1#
```

show ipv6 route

```
R1# show ipv6 route
IPv6 Routing Table - default - 5 entries
Codes: C - Connected, L - Local, S - Static, U - Per-user Static route
       B - BGP, R - RIP, H - NHRP, I1 - ISIS L1

       I2 - ISIS L2, IA - ISIS interarea, IS - ISIS summary, D - EIGRP

       EX - EIGRP external, ND - ND Default, NDp - ND Prefix,
          DCE - Destination

       NDr - Redirect, RL - RPL, O - OSPF Intra, OI - OSPF Inter

       OE1 - OSPF ext 1, OE2 - OSPF ext 2, ON1 - OSPF NSSA ext 1

       ON2 - OSPF NSSA ext 2, a - Application
C   2001:DB8:ACAD:10::/64 [0/0]
       via GigabitEthernet0/0/0, directly connected
```

```
L    2001:DB8:ACAD:10::1/128 [0/0]
        via GigabitEthernet0/0/0, receive
C    2001:DB8:FEED:224::/64 [0/0]
        via GigabitEthernet0/0/1, directly connected
L    2001:DB8:FEED:224::1/128 [0/0]
        via GigabitEthernet0/0/1, receive
L    FF00::/8 [0/0]
        via Null0, receive
R1#
```

show interfaces

```
R1# show interfaces gig0/0/0
GigabitEthernet0/0/0 is up, line protocol is up
  Hardware is ISR4321-2x1GE, address is a0e0.af0d.e140 (bia
  a0e0.af0d.e140)
  Description: Link to LAN
  Internet address is 192.168.10.1/24
  MTU 1500 bytes, BW 100000 Kbit/sec, DLY 100 usec,
      reliability 255/255, txload 1/255, rxload 1/255
  Encapsulation ARPA, loopback not set
  Keepalive not supported
  Full Duplex, 100Mbps, link type is auto, media type is RJ45
  output flow-control is off, input flow-control is off
  ARP type: ARPA, ARP Timeout 04:00:00
  Last input 00:00:01, output 00:00:35, output hang never
  Last clearing of "show interface" counters never
  Input queue: 0/375/0/0 (size/max/drops/flushes); Total output drops: 0
  Queueing strategy: fifo
  Output queue: 0/40 (size/max)
  5 minute input rate 0 bits/sec, 0 packets/sec
  5 minute output rate 0 bits/sec, 0 packets/sec
      1180 packets input, 109486 bytes, 0 no buffer
      Received 84 broadcasts (0 IP multicasts)
      0 runts, 0 giants, 0 throttles
      0 input errors, 0 CRC, 0 frame, 0 overrun, 0 ignored
      0 watchdog, 1096 multicast, 0 pause input
      65 packets output, 22292 bytes, 0 underruns
```

```
       0 output errors, 0 collisions, 2 interface resets

       11 unknown protocol drops

       0 babbles, 0 late collision, 0 deferred

       1 lost carrier, 0 no carrier, 0 pause output

       0 output buffer failures, 0 output buffers swapped out
R1#
```

show ip interface

```
R1# show ip interface g0/0/0
GigabitEthernet0/0/0 is up, line protocol is up
  Internet address is 192.168.10.1/24
  Broadcast address is 255.255.255.255
  Address determined by setup command
  MTU is 1500 bytes
  Helper address is not set
  Directed broadcast forwarding is disabled
  Outgoing Common access list is not set
  Outgoing access list is not set
  Inbound Common access list is not set
  Inbound  access list is not set
  Proxy ARP is enabled
  Local Proxy ARP is disabled
  Security level is default
  Split horizon is enabled
  ICMP redirects are always sent
  ICMP unreachables are always sent
  ICMP mask replies are never sent
  IP fast switching is enabled
  IP Flow switching is disabled
  IP CEF switching is enabled
  IP CEF switching turbo vector
  IP Null turbo vector
  Associated unicast routing topologies:
        Topology "base", operation state is UP
  IP multicast fast switching is enabled
  IP multicast distributed fast switching is disabled
```

```
    IP route-cache flags are Fast, CEF
    Router Discovery is disabled
    IP output packet accounting is disabled
    IP access violation accounting is disabled
    TCP/IP header compression is disabled
    RTP/IP header compression is disabled
    Probe proxy name replies are disabled
    Policy routing is disabled
    Network address translation is disabled
    BGP Policy Mapping is disabled
    Input features: MCI Check
    IPv4 WCCP Redirect outbound is disabled
    IPv4 WCCP Redirect inbound is disabled
    IPv4 WCCP Redirect exclude is disabled
R1#
```

show ipv6 interface

```
R1# show ipv6 interface g0/0/0
GigabitEthernet0/0/0 is up, line protocol is up
    IPv6 is enabled, link-local address is FE80::868A:8DFF:FE44:49B0
    No Virtual link-local address(es):
    Description: Link to LAN
    Global unicast address(es):
        2001:DB8:ACAD:10::1, subnet is 2001:DB8:ACAD:10::/64
    Joined group address(es):
        FF02::1
        FF02::1:FF00:1
        FF02::1:FF44:49B0
    MTU is 1500 bytes
    ICMP error messages limited to one every 100 milliseconds
    ICMP redirects are enabled
    ICMP unreachables are sent
    ND DAD is enabled, number of DAD attempts: 1
    ND reachable time is 30000 milliseconds (using 30000)
    ND NS retransmit interval is 1000 milliseconds
R1#
```

Refer to
Interactive Graphic
in online course

Syntax Checker - Configure Interfaces - 10.2.5

Use this syntax checker to practice configuring the GigabitEthernet 0/0 interface on a router.

- Describe the link as 'Link to LAN'.
- Configure the IPv4 address as 192.168.10.1 with the subnet mask 255.255.255.0.
- Configure the IPv6 address as 2001:db8:acad:10::1 with the /64 prefix length.
- Activate the interface.

Configure the Default Gateway - 10.3

Refer to
Online Course
for Illustration

Default Gateway on a Host - 10.3.1

If your local network has only one router, it will be the gateway router and all hosts and switches on your network must be configured with this information. If your local network has multiple routers, you must select one of them to be the default gateway router. This topic explains how to configure the default gateway on hosts and switches.

For an end device to communicate over the network, it must be configured with the correct IP address information, including the default gateway address. The default gateway is only used when the host wants to send a packet to a device on another network. The default gateway address is generally the router interface address attached to the local network of the host. The IP address of the host device and the router interface address must be in the same network.

For example, assume an IPv4 network topology consisting of a router interconnecting two separate LANs. G0/0/0 is connected to network 192.168.10.0, while G0/0/1 is connected to network 192.168.11.0. Each host device is configured with the appropriate default gateway address.

In this example, if PC1 sends a packet to PC2, then the default gateway is not used. Instead, PC1 addresses the packet with the IPv4 address of PC2 and forwards the packet directly to PC2 through the switch.

What if PC1 sent a packet to PC3? PC1 would address the packet with the IPv4 address of PC3, but would forward the packet to its default gateway, which is the G0/0/0 interface of R1. The router accepts the packet and accesses its routing table to determine that G0/0/1 is the appropriate exit interface based on the destination address. R1 then forwards the packet out of the appropriate interface to reach PC3.

The same process would occur on an IPv6 network, although this is not shown in the topology. Devices would use the IPv6 address of the local router as their default gateway.

Refer to
Online Course
for Illustration

Default Gateway on a Switch - 10.3.2

A switch that interconnects client computers is typically a Layer 2 device. As such, a Layer 2 switch does not require an IP address to function properly. However, an IP configuration can be configured on a switch to give an administrator remote access to the switch.

To connect to and manage a switch over a local IP network, it must have a switch virtual interface (SVI) configured. The SVI is configured with an IPv4 address and subnet mask on the local LAN. The switch must also have a default gateway address configured to remotely manage the switch from another network.

The default gateway address is typically configured on all devices that will communicate beyond their local network.

To configure an IPv4 default gateway on a switch, use the **ip default-gateway** *ip-address* global configuration command. The *ip-address* that is configured is the IPv4 address of the local router interface connected to the switch.

The figure shows an administrator establishing a remote connection to switch S1 on another network.

In this example, the administrator host would use its default gateway to send the packet to the G0/0/1 interface of R1. R1 would forward the packet to S1 out of its G0/0/0 interface. Because the packet source IPv4 address came from another network, S1 would require a default gateway to forward the packet to the G0/0/0 interface of R1. Therefore, S1 must be configured with a default gateway to be able to reply and establish an SSH connection with the administrative host.

Note: Packets originating from host computers connected to the switch must already have the default gateway address configured on their host computer operating systems.

A workgroup switch can also be configured with an IPv6 address on an SVI. However, the switch does not require the IPv6 address of the default gateway to be configured manually. The switch will automatically receive its default gateway from the ICMPv6 Router Advertisement message from the router.

Refer to
Interactive Graphic
in online course

Syntax Checker - Configure the Default Gateway - 10.3.3

Use this syntax checker to practice configuring the default gateway of a Layer 2 switch.

Refer to **Packet
Tracer Activity**
for this chapter

Packet Tracer - Connect a Router to a LAN - 10.3.4

In this activity, you will use various **show** commands to display the current state of the router. You will then use the Addressing Table to configure router Ethernet interfaces. Finally, you will use commands to verify and test your configurations.

Refer to **Packet
Tracer Activity**
for this chapter

Packet Tracer - Troubleshoot Default Gateway Issues - 10.3.5

For a device to communicate across multiple networks, it must be configured with an IP address, subnet mask, and a default gateway. The default gateway is used when the host wants to send a packet to a device on another network. The default gateway address is generally the router interface address attached to the local network to which the host is connected. In this activity, you will finish documenting the network. You will then verify the network documentation by testing end-to-end connectivity and troubleshooting issues. The troubleshooting method you will use consists of the following steps:

1. Verify the network documentation and use tests to isolate problems.

2. Determine an appropriate solution for a given problem.

3. Implement the solution.

4. Test to verify the problem is resolved.

5. Document the solution.

Module Practice and Quiz - 10.4

Refer to **Video** in online course

Video - Network Device Differences: Part 1 - 10.4.1

Click Play in the figure to view Part 1 of a video explaining the different router and switch devices you may experience during your Packet Tracer and Lab practices.

Refer to **Video** in online course

Video - Network Device Differences: Part 2 - 10.4.2

Click Play in the figure to view Part 2 of a video explaining the different router and switch devices you may experience during your Packet Tracer and Lab practices.

Refer to **Packet Tracer Activity** for this chapter

Packet Tracer - Basic Device Configuration - 10.4.3

Your network manager is impressed with your performance in your job as a LAN technician. She would like you to now demonstrate your ability to configure a router connecting two LANs. Your tasks include configuring basic settings on a router and a switch using the Cisco IOS. You will then verify your configurations, as well as configurations on existing devices by testing end-to-end connectivity.

Refer to **Lab Activity** for this chapter

Lab - Build a Switch and Router Network - 10.4.4

In this lab, you will complete the following objectives:

■ Part 1: Set up the topology and initialize devices.

■ Part 2: Configure devices and verify connectivity.

■ Part 3: Display device information.

What did I learn in this module? - 10.4.5

Configure Initial Router Settings

The following tasks should be completed when configuring initial settings on a router.

1. Configure the device name.

2. Secure privileged EXEC mode.

3. Secure user EXEC mode.

4. Secure remote Telnet / SSH access.

5. Secure all passwords in the config file.

6. Provide legal notification.

7. Save the configuration.

Configure Interfaces

For routers to be reachable, the router interfaces must be configured. The Cisco ISR 4321 router is equipped with two Gigabit Ethernet interfaces: GigabitEthernet 0/0/0 (G0/0/0) and GigabitEthernet 0/0/1 (G0/0/1). The tasks to configure a router interface are very similar to a management SVI on a switch. Using the **no shutdown** command activates the interface. The interface must also be connected to another device, such as a switch or a router, for the physical layer to be active. There are several commands that can be used to verify interface configuration including the **show ip interface brief** and **show ipv6 interface brief**, the **show ip route** and **show ipv6 route**, as well as **show interfaces, show ip interface** and **show ipv6 interface**.

Configure the Default Gateway

For an end device to communicate over the network, it must be configured with the correct IP address information, including the default gateway address. The default gateway address is generally the router interface address for the router that is attached to the local network of the host. The IP address of the host device and the router interface address must be in the same network. To connect to and manage a switch over a local IP network, it must have a switch virtual interface (SVI) configured. The SVI is configured with an IPv4 address and subnet mask on the local LAN. The switch must also have a default gateway address configured to remotely manage the switch from another network. To configure an IPv4 default gateway on a switch, use the **ip default-gateway ip-address** global configuration command. Use the IPv4 address of the local router interface that is connected to the switch.

Go to the online course to take the quiz and exam.

Chapter Quiz - Basic Router Configuration

Your Chapter Notes

CHAPTER 11

IPv4 Addressing

Introduction - 11.0

Why should I take this module? - 11.0.1

Welcome to IPv4 Addressing!

Currently, there are still plenty of networks using IPv4 addressing, even as the organizations which use them are making the transition to IPv6. So it is still very important for network administrators to know everything they can about IPv4 addressing. This module covers the fundamental aspects of IPv4 addressing in detail. It includes how to segment a network into subnets and how to create a variable-length subnet mask (VLSM) as part of an overall IPv4 addressing scheme. Subnetting is like cutting a pie into smaller and smaller pieces. Subnetting may seem overwhelming at first, but we show you some tricks to help you along the way. This module includes several videos, activities to help you practice subnetting, Packet Tracers and a lab. Once you get the hang of it, you'll be on your way to network administration!

What will I learn to do in this module? - 11.0.2

Module Title: IPv4 Addressing

Module Objective: Calculate an IPv4 subnetting scheme to efficiently segment your network.

Topic Title	Topic Objective
IPv4 Address Structure	Describe the structure of an IPv4 address including the network portion, the host portion, and the subnet mask.
IPv4 Unicast, Broadcast, and Multicast	Compare the characteristics and uses of the unicast, broadcast and multicast IPv4 addresses.
Types of IPv4 Addresses	Explain public, private, and reserved IPv4 addresses.
Network Segmentation	Explain how subnetting segments a network to enable better communication.
Subnet an IPv4 Network	Calculate IPv4 subnets for a /24 prefix.
Subnet a /16 and a /8 Prefix	Calculate IPv4 subnets for a /16 and /8 prefix.
Subnet To Meet Requirements	Given a set of requirements for subnetting, implement an IPv4 addressing scheme.
Variable Length Subnet Masking	Explain how to create a flexible addressing scheme using variable length subnet masking (VLSM).
Structured Design	Implement a VLSM addressing scheme.

IPv4 Address Structure - 11.1

Refer to
Online Course
for Illustration

Network and Host Portions - 11.1.1

An IPv4 address is a 32-bit hierarchical address that is made up of a network portion and a host portion. When determining the network portion versus the host portion, you must look at the 32-bit stream, as shown in the figure.

The bits within the network portion of the address must be identical for all devices that reside in the same network. The bits within the host portion of the address must be unique to identify a specific host within a network. If two hosts have the same bit-pattern in the specified network portion of the 32-bit stream, those two hosts will reside in the same network.

But how do hosts know which portion of the 32-bits identifies the network and which identifies the host? That is the role of the subnet mask.

Refer to
Online Course
for Illustration

The Subnet Mask - 11.1.2

As shown in the figure, assigning an IPv4 address to a host requires the following:

- **IPv4 address** - This is the unique IPv4 address of the host.

- **Subnet mask**- This is used to identify the network/host portion of the IPv4 address.

Note: A default gateway IPv4 address is required to reach remote networks and DNS server IPv4 addresses are required to translate domain names to IPv4 addresses.

The IPv4 subnet mask is used to differentiate the network portion from the host portion of an IPv4 address. When an IPv4 address is assigned to a device, the subnet mask is used to determine the network address of the device. The network address represents all the devices on the same network.

The next figure displays the 32-bit subnet mask in dotted decimal and binary formats.

Notice how the subnet mask is a consecutive sequence of 1 bits followed by a consecutive sequence of 0 bits.

To identify the network and host portions of an IPv4 address, the subnet mask is compared to the IPv4 address bit for bit, from left to right as shown in the figure.

Note that the subnet mask does not actually contain the network or host portion of an IPv4 address, it just tells the computer where to look for the part of the IPv4 address that is the network portion and which part is the host portion.

The actual process used to identify the network portion and host portion is called ANDing.

The Prefix Length - 11.1.3

Expressing network addresses and host addresses with the dotted decimal subnet mask address can become cumbersome. Fortunately, there is an alternative method of identifying a subnet mask, a method called the prefix length.

The prefix length is the number of bits set to 1 in the subnet mask. It is written in "slash notation", which is noted by a forward slash (/) followed by the number of bits set to 1. Therefore, count the number of bits in the subnet mask and prepend it with a slash.

Refer to the table for examples. The first column lists various subnet masks that can be used with a host address. The second column displays the converted 32-bit binary address. The last column displays the resulting prefix length.

Comparing the Subnet Mask and Prefix Length

Subnet Mask	32-bit Address	Prefix Length
255.0.0.0	11111111.00000000.00000000.00000000	/8
255.255.0.0	11111111.11111111.00000000.00000000	/16
255.255.255.0	11111111.11111111.11111111.00000000	/24
255.255.255.128	11111111.11111111.11111111.10000000	/25
255.255.255.192	11111111.11111111.11111111.11000000	/26
255.255.255.224	11111111.11111111.11111111.11100000	/27
255.255.255.240	11111111.11111111.11111111.11110000	/28
255.255.255.248	11111111.11111111.11111111.11111000	/29
255.255.255.252	11111111.11111111.11111111.11111100	/30

Note: A network address is also referred to as a prefix or network prefix. Therefore, the prefix length is the number of 1 bits in the subnet mask.

When representing an IPv4 address using a prefix length, the IPv4 address is written followed by the prefix length with no spaces. For example, 192.168.10.10 255.255.255.0 would be written as 192.168.10.10/24. Using various types of prefix lengths will be discussed later. For now, the focus will be on the /24 (i.e. 255.255.255.0) prefix.

Refer to
Online Course
for Illustration

Determining the Network: Logical AND - 11.1.4

A logical AND is one of three Boolean operations used in Boolean or digital logic. The other two are OR and NOT. The AND operation is used in determining the network address.

Logical AND is the comparison of two bits that produce the results shown below. Note how only a 1 AND 1 produces a 1. Any other combination results in a 0.

- 1 AND 1 = 1
- 0 AND 1 = 0
- 1 AND 0 = 0
- 0 AND 0 = 0

Note: In digital logic, 1 represents True and 0 represents False. When using an AND operation, both input values must be True (1) for the result to be True (1).

To identify the network address of an IPv4 host, the IPv4 address is logically ANDed, bit by bit, with the subnet mask. ANDing between the address and the subnet mask yields the network address.

To illustrate how AND is used to discover a network address, consider a host with IPv4 address 192.168.10.10 and subnet mask of 255.255.255.0, as shown in the figure:

- **IPv4 host address (192.168.10.10)** - The IPv4 address of the host in dotted decimal and binary formats.

- **Subnet mask (255.255.255.0)** - The subnet mask of the host in dotted decimal and binary formats.

- **Network address (192.168.10.0)** - The logical AND operation between the IPv4 address and subnet mask results in an IPv4 network address shown in dotted decimal and binary formats.

Using the first sequence of bits as an example, notice the AND operation is performed on the 1-bit of the host address with the 1-bit of the subnet mask. This results in a 1 bit for the network address. 1 AND 1 = 1.

The AND operation between an IPv4 host address and subnet mask results in the IPv4 network address for this host. In this example, the AND operation between the host address of 192.168.10.10 and the subnet mask 255.255.255.0 (/24), results in the IPv4 network address of 192.168.10.0/24. This is an important IPv4 operation, as it tells the host what network it belongs to.

Refer to **Video** in online course

Video - Network, Host and Broadcast Addresses - 11.1.5

Click Play to view a demonstration of how the network, host, and broadcast addresses are determined for a given IPv4 address and subnet mask.

Refer to **Online Course** for Illustration

Network, Host, and Broadcast Addresses - 11.1.6

Within each network are three types of IP addresses:

- Network address
- Host addresses
- Broadcast address

Using the topology in the figure, these three types of addresses will be examined.

Network address

A network address is an address that represents a specific network. A device belongs to this network if it meets three criteria:

- It has the same subnet mask as the network address.

- It has the same network bits as the network address, as indicated by the subnet mask.

- It is located on the same broadcast domain as other hosts with the same network address.

A host determines its network address by performing an AND operation between its IPv4 address and its subnet mask.

As shown in the table, the network address has all 0 bits in the host portion, as determined by the subnet mask. In this example, the network address is 192.168.10.0/24. A network address cannot be assigned to a device.

Network, Host, and Broadcast Addresses

	Network Portion			Host Portion	Host Bits
Subnet mask 255.255.255.0 or /24	255 11111111	255 11111111	255 11111111	0 00000000	
Network address 192.168.10.0 or /24	192 11000000	168 10100000	10 00001010	0 00000000	All 0s
First address 192.168.10.1 or /24	192 11000000	168 10100000	10 00001010	1 00000001	All 0s and a 1
Last address 192.168.10.254 or /24	192 11000000	168 10100000	10 00001010	254 11111110	All 1s and a 0
Broadcast address 192.168.10.255 or /24	192 11000000	168 10100000	10 00001010	255 11111111	All 1s

Host addresses

Host addresses are addresses that can be assigned to a device such as a host computer, laptop, smart phone, web camera, printer, router, etc. The host portion of the address is the bits indicated by 0 bits in the subnet mask. Host addresses can have any combination of bits in the host portion except for all 0 bits (this would be a network address) or all 1 bits (this would be a broadcast address).

All devices within the same network, must have the same subnet mask and the same network bits. Only the host bits will differ and must be unique.

Notice that in the table, there is a first and last host address:

- **First host address** - This first host within a network has all 0 bits with the last (right-most) bit as a 1 bit. In this example it is 192.168.10.1/24.

- **Last host address** - This last host within a network has all 1 bits with the last (right-most) bit as a 0 bit. In this example it is 192.168.10.254/24.

Any addresses between and including, 192.168.10.1/24 through 192.168.10.254/24 can be assigned to a device on the network.

Broadcast address

A broadcast address is an address that is used when it is required to reach all devices on the IPv4 network. As shown in the table, the network broadcast address has all 1 bits in the host portion, as determined by the subnet mask. In this example, the network address is 192.168.10.255/24. A broadcast address cannot be assigned to a device.

Refer to
Lab Activity
for this chapter

Activity - ANDing to Determine the Network Address - 11.1.7

Use the ANDing process to determine the network address (in binary and decimal formats).

Go to the online
course to take the
quiz and exam.

Check Your Understanding - IPv4 Address Structure - 11.1.8

IPv4 Unicast, Broadcast, and Multicast - 11.2

Refer to
Interactive Graphic
in online course

Unicast - 11.2.1

In the previous topic you learned about the structure of an IPv4 address; each has a network portion and a host portion. There are different ways to send a packet from a source device, and these different transmissions affect the destination IPv4 addresses.

Unicast transmission refers to one device sending a message to one other device in one-to-one communications.

A unicast packet has a destination IP address that is a unicast address which goes to a single recipient. A source IP address can only be a unicast address, because the packet can only originate from a single source. This is regardless of whether the destination IP address is a unicast, broadcast or multicast.

Play the animation to see an example of unicast transmission.

Note: In this course, all communication between devices is unicast unless otherwise noted.

IPv4 unicast host addresses are in the address range of 1.1.1.1 to 223.255.255.255. However, within this range are many addresses that are reserved for special purposes. These special purpose addresses will be discussed later in this module.

Refer to
Interactive Graphic
in online course

Broadcast - 11.2.2

Broadcast transmission refers to a device sending a message to all the devices on a network in one-to-all communications.

A broadcast packet has a destination IP address with all ones (1s) in the host portion, or 32 one (1) bits.

Note: IPv4 uses broadcast packets. However, there are no broadcast packets with IPv6.

A broadcast packet must be processed by all devices in the same broadcast domain. A broadcast domain identifies all hosts on the same network segment. A broadcast may be directed or limited. A directed broadcast is sent to all hosts on a specific network. For example, a host on the 172.16.4.0/24 network sends a packet to 172.16.4.255. A limited broadcast is sent to 255.255.255.255. By default, routers do not forward broadcasts.

Play the animation to see an example of a limited broadcast transmission.

Broadcast packets use resources on the network and make every receiving host on the network process the packet. Therefore, broadcast traffic should be limited so that it does not adversely affect the performance of the network or devices. Because routers separate broadcast domains, subdividing networks can improve network performance by eliminating excessive broadcast traffic.

IP Directed Broadcasts

In addition to the 255.255.255.255 broadcast address, there is a broadcast IPv4 address for each network. Called a directed broadcast, this address uses the highest address in the network, which is the address where all the host bits are 1s. For example, the directed broadcast address for 192.168.1.0/24 is 192.168.1.255. This address allows communication to all the hosts in that network. To send data to all the hosts in a network, a host can send a single packet that is addressed to the broadcast address of the network.

A device that is not directly connected to the destination network forwards an IP directed broadcast in the same way it would forward unicast IP packets destined to a host on that network. When a directed broadcast packet reaches a router that is directly connected to the destination network, that packet is broadcast on the destination network.

Note: Because of security concerns and prior abuse from malicious users, directed broadcasts are turned off by default starting with Cisco IOS Release 12.0 with the global configuration command **no ip directed-broadcasts**.

Refer to
Interactive Graphic
in online course

Multicast - 11.2.3

Multicast transmission reduces traffic by allowing a host to send a single packet to a selected set of hosts that subscribe to a multicast group.

A multicast packet is a packet with a destination IP address that is a multicast address. IPv4 has reserved the 224.0.0.0 to 239.255.255.255 addresses as a multicast range.

Hosts that receive particular multicast packets are called multicast clients. The multicast clients use services requested by a client program to subscribe to the multicast group.

Each multicast group is represented by a single IPv4 multicast destination address. When an IPv4 host subscribes to a multicast group, the host processes packets addressed to this multicast address, and packets addressed to its uniquely allocated unicast address.

Routing protocols such as OSPF use multicast transmissions. For example, routers enabled with OSPF communicate with each other using the reserved OSPF multicast address 224.0.0.5. Only devices enabled with OSPF will process these packets with 224.0.0.5 as the destination IPv4 address. All other devices will ignore these packets.

The animation demonstrates clients accepting multicast packets.

Refer to
Lab Activity
for this chapter

Activity - Unicast, Broadcast, or Multicast - 11.2.4

Click **New Problem** to view the destination IP address. Next, click the host or hosts which will receive a packet based on the address type (unicast, broadcast or multicast). Click **Check** to verify your answer. Click **New Problem** to get a new problem.

Types of IPv4 Addresses - 11.3

Public and Private IPv4 Addresses - 11.3.1

Just as there are different ways to transmit an IPv4 packet, there are also different types of IPv4 addresses. Some IPv4 addresses cannot be used to go out to the internet, and others are specifically allocated for routing to the internet. Some are used to verify a connection and others are self-assigned. As a network administrator, you will eventually become very familiar with the types of IPv4 addresses, but for now, you should at least know what they are and when to use them.

Public IPv4 addresses are addresses which are globally routed between internet service provider (ISP) routers. However, not all available IPv4 addresses can be used on the internet. There are blocks of addresses called private addresses that are used by most organizations to assign IPv4 addresses to internal hosts.

In the mid-1990s, with the introduction of the World Wide Web (WWW), private IPv4 addresses were introduced because of the depletion of IPv4 address space. Private IPv4 addresses are not unique and can be used internally within any network.

Note: The long-term solution to IPv4 address depletion was IPv6.

The Private Address Blocks

Network Address and Prefix	RFC 1918 Private Address Range
Class A 10.0.0.0/8	10.0.0.0 - 10.255.255.255
Class B 172.16.0.0/12	172.16.0.0 - 172.31.255.255
Class C 192.168.0.0/16	192.168.0.0 - 192.168.255.255

Note: Private addresses are defined in RFC 1918 and sometimes referred to as RFC 1918 address space.

Routing to the Internet - 11.3.2

Refer to
Online Course
for Illustration

Most internal networks, from large enterprises to home networks, use private IPv4 addresses for addressing all internal devices (intranet) including hosts and routers. However, private addresses are not globally routable.

In the figure, customer networks 1, 2, and 3 are sending packets outside their internal networks. These packets have a source IPv4 address that is a private address and a destination IPv4 address that is public (globally routable). Packets with a private address must be filtered (discarded) or translated to a public address before forwarding the packet to an ISP.

Before the ISP can forward this packet, it must translate the source IPv4 address, which is a private address, to a public IPv4 address using Network Address Translation (NAT). NAT is used to translate between private IPv4 and public IPv4 addresses. This is usually done on the router that connects the internal network to the ISP network. Private IPv4 addresses in the organization's intranet will be translated to public IPv4 addresses before routing to the internet.

Note: Although, a device with a private IPv4 address is not directly accessible from another device across the internet, the IETF does not consider private IPv4 addresses or NAT as effective security measures.

Organizations that have resources available to the internet, such as a web server, will also have devices that have public IPv4 addresses. As shown in the figure, this part of the network is known as the DMZ (demilitarized zone). The router in the figure not only performs routing, it also performs NAT and acts as a firewall for security.

Note: Private IPv4 addresses are commonly used for educational purposes instead of using a public IPv4 address that most likely belongs to an organization.

Refer to
Lab Activity
for this chapter

Activity - Pass or Block IPv4 Addresses - 11.3.3

Decide to Pass or Block each IP address depending on whether it is Public (the Internet) or Private (small local network). Click Start to begin and click on either Pass or Block.

Special Use IPv4 Addresses - 11.3.4

There are certain addresses, such as the network address and broadcast address, that cannot be assigned to hosts. There are also special addresses that can be assigned to hosts, but with restrictions on how those hosts can interact within the network.

Loopback addresses

Loopback addresses (127.0.0.0 /8 or 127.0.0.1 to 127.255.255.254) are more commonly identified as only 127.0.0.1, these are special addresses used by a host to direct traffic to itself. For example, it can be used on a host to test if the TCP/IP configuration is operational, as shown in the figure. Notice how the 127.0.0.1 loopback address replies to the **ping** command. Also note how any address within this block will loop back to the local host, which is shown with the second **ping** in the figure.

Pinging the Loopback Interface

```
C:\Users\NetAcad> ping 127.0.0.1

Pinging 127.0.0.1 with 32 bytes of data:

Reply from 127.0.0.1: bytes=32 time<1ms TTL=128

Reply from 127.0.0.1: bytes=32 time<1ms TTL=128

Reply from 127.0.0.1: bytes=32 time<1ms TTL=128
```

```
Reply from 127.0.0.1: bytes=32 time<1ms TTL=128

Ping statistics for 127.0.0.1:
    Packets: Sent = 4, Received = 4, Lost = 0 (0% loss),
Approximate round trip times in milli-seconds:
    Minimum = 0ms, Maximum = 0ms, Average = 0ms
C:\Users\NetAcad> ping 127.1.1.1

Pinging 127.1.1.1 with 32 bytes of data:

Reply from 127.1.1.1: bytes=32 time<1ms TTL=128

Reply from 127.1.1.1: bytes=32 time<1ms TTL=128

Reply from 127.1.1.1: bytes=32 time<1ms TTL=128

Reply from 127.1.1.1: bytes=32 time<1ms TTL=128

Ping statistics for 127.1.1.1:
    Packets: Sent = 4, Received = 4, Lost = 0 (0% loss),
Approximate round trip times in milli-seconds:
    Minimum = 0ms, Maximum = 0ms, Average = 0ms
C:\Users\NetAcad>
```

Link-Local addresses

Link-local addresses (169.254.0.0 /16 or 169.254.0.1 to 169.254.255.254) are more commonly known as the Automatic Private IP Addressing (APIPA) addresses or self-assigned addresses. They are used by a Windows DHCP client to self-configure in the event that there are no DHCP servers available. Link-local addresses can be used in a peer-to-peer connection but are not commonly used for this purpose.

Refer to
Online Course
for Illustration

Legacy Classful Addressing - 11.3.5

In 1981, IPv4 addresses were assigned using classful addressing as defined in RFC 790 (https://tools.ietf.org/html/rfc790), Assigned Numbers. Customers were allocated a network address based on one of three classes, A, B, or C. The RFC divided the unicast ranges into specific classes as follows:

- **Class A (0.0.0.0/8 to 127.0.0.0/8)** - Designed to support extremely large networks with more than 16 million host addresses. Class A used a fixed /8 prefix with the first octet to indicate the network address and the remaining three octets for host addresses (more than 16 million host addresses per network).

- **Class B (128.0.0.0 /16 - 191.255.0.0 /16)** - Designed to support the needs of moderate to large size networks with up to approximately 65,000 host addresses. Class B used a fixed /16 prefix with the two high-order octets to indicate the network address and the remaining two octets for host addresses (more than 65,000 host addresses per network).

- **Class C (192.0.0.0 /24 - 223.255.255.0 /24)** - Designed to support small networks with a maximum of 254 hosts. Class C used a fixed /24 prefix with the first three octets to indicate the network and the remaining octet for the host addresses (only 254 host addresses per network).

Note: There is also a Class D multicast block consisting of 224.0.0.0 to 239.0.0.0 and a Class E experimental address block consisting of 240.0.0.0 - 255.0.0.0.

At the time, with a limited number of computers using the internet, classful addressing was an effective means to allocate addresses. As shown in the figure, Class A and B networks have a very large number of host addresses and Class C has very few. Class A networks accounted for 50% of the IPv4 networks. This caused most of the available IPv4 addresses to go unused.

In the mid-1990s, with the introduction of the World Wide Web (WWW), classful addressing was deprecated to more efficiently allocate the limited IPv4 address space. Classful address allocation was replaced with classless addressing, which is used today. Classless addressing ignores the rules of classes (A, B, C). Public IPv4 network addresses (network addresses and subnet masks) are allocated based on the number of addresses that can be justified.

Refer to Online Course for Illustration

Assignment of IP Addresses - 11.3.6

Public IPv4 addresses are addresses which are globally routed over the internet. Public IPv4 addresses must be unique.

Both IPv4 and IPv6 addresses are managed by the Internet Assigned Numbers Authority (IANA). The IANA manages and allocates blocks of IP addresses to the Regional Internet Registries (RIRs). The five RIRs are shown in the figure.

RIRs are responsible for allocating IP addresses to ISPs who provide IPv4 address blocks to organizations and smaller ISPs. Organizations can also get their addresses directly from an RIR (subject to the policies of that RIR).

Refer to Lab Activity for this chapter

Activity - Public or Private IPv4 Address - 11.3.7

Click the drop down arrow for each address to choose the correct network type "Public" or "Private" for each address.

Go to the online course to take the quiz and exam.

Check Your Understanding - Types of IPv4 Addresses - 11.3.8

Network Segmentation - 11.4

Refer to Online Course for Illustration

Broadcast Domains and Segmentation - 11.4.1

Have you ever received an email that was addressed to every person at your work or school? This was a broadcast email. Hopefully, it contained information that each of you needed to know. But often a broadcast is not really pertinent to everyone in the mailing list. Sometimes, only a segment of the population needs to read that information.

In an Ethernet LAN, devices use broadcasts and the Address Resolution Protocol (ARP) to locate other devices.. ARP sends Layer 2 broadcasts to a known IPv4 address on the local network to discover the associated MAC address. Devices on Ethernet LANs also locate other devices using services. A host typically acquires its IPv4 address configuration using the Dynamic Host Configuration Protocol (DHCP) which sends broadcasts on the local network to locate a DHCP server.

Switches propagate broadcasts out all interfaces except the interface on which it was received. For example, if a switch in the figure were to receive a broadcast, it would forward it to the other switches and other users connected in the network.

Routers do not propagate broadcasts. When a router receives a broadcast, it does not forward it out other interfaces. For instance, when R1 receives a broadcast on its Gigabit Ethernet 0/0 interface, it does not forward out another interface.

Therefore, each router interface connects to a broadcast domain and broadcasts are only propagated within that specific broadcast domain.

Refer to
Online Course
for Illustration

Problems with Large Broadcast Domains - 11.4.2

A large broadcast domain is a network that connects many hosts. A problem with a large broadcast domain is that these hosts can generate excessive broadcasts and negatively affect the network. In the figure, LAN 1 connects 400 users that could generate an excess amount of broadcast traffic. This results in slow network operations due to the significant amount of traffic it can cause, and slow device operations because a device must accept and process each broadcast packet.

The solution is to reduce the size of the network to create smaller broadcast domains in a process called subnetting. These smaller network spaces are called subnets.

In the figure, the 400 users in LAN 1 with network address 172.16.0.0 /16 have been divided into two subnets of 200 users each: 172.16.0.0 /24 and 172.16.1.0 /24. Broadcasts are only propagated within the smaller broadcast domains. Therefore, a broadcast in LAN 1 would not propagate to LAN 2.

Notice how the prefix length has changed from a single /16 network to two /24 networks. This is the basis of subnetting: using host bits to create additional subnets.

Note: The terms subnet and network are often used interchangeably. Most networks are a subnet of some larger address block.

Refer to
Interactive Graphic
in online course

Refer to
Online Course
for Illustration

Reasons for Segmenting Networks - 11.4.3

Subnetting reduces overall network traffic and improves network performance. It also enables an administrator to implement security policies such as which subnets are allowed or not allowed to communicate together. Another reason is that it reduces the number of devices affected by abnormal broadcast traffic due to misconfigurations, hardware/software problems, or malicious intent.

There are various ways of using subnets to help manage network devices.

Click each image for an illustration of how network administrators can group devices and services into subnets.

Location
Subnetting by Location

Group or Function
Subnetting by Group or Function

Device Type
Subnetting by Device Type

Network administrators can create subnets using any other division that makes sense for the network. Notice in each figure, the subnets use longer prefix lengths to identify networks.

Understanding how to subnet networks is a fundamental skill that all network administrators must develop. Various methods have been created to help understand this process. Although a little overwhelming at first, pay close attention to the detail and, with practice, subnetting will become easier.

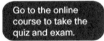
Go to the online course to take the quiz and exam.

Check Your Understanding - Network Segmentation - 11.4.4

Subnet an IPv4 Network - 11.5

Subnet on an Octet Boundary - 11.5.1

In the previous topic you learned several good reasons for segmenting a network. You also learned that segmenting a network is called subnetting. Subnetting is a critical skill to have when administering an IPv4 network. It is a bit daunting at first, but it gets much easier with practice.

IPv4 subnets are created by using one or more of the host bits as network bits. This is done by extending the subnet mask to borrow some of the bits from the host portion of the address to create additional network bits. The more host bits that are borrowed, the more subnets that can be defined. The more bits that are borrowed to increase the number of subnets reduces the number of hosts per subnet.

Networks are most easily subnetted at the octet boundary of /8, /16, and /24. The table identifies these prefix lengths. Notice that using longer prefix lengths decreases the number of hosts per subnet.

Subnet Masks on Octet Boundaries

Prefix Length	Subnet Mask	Subnet Mask in Binary (n = network, h = host)	# of hosts
/8	255.0.0.0	nnnnnnnn.hhhhhhhh.hhhhhhhh.hhhhhhhh 11111111.00000000.00000000.00000000	16,777,214
/16	255.255.0.0	nnnnnnnn.nnnnnnnn.hhhhhhhh.hhhhhhhh 11111111.11111111.00000000.00000000	65,534
/24	255.255.255.0	nnnnnnnn.nnnnnnnn.nnnnnnnn.hhhhhhhh 11111111.11111111.11111111.00000000	254

To understand how subnetting on the octet boundary can be useful, consider the following example. Assume an enterprise has chosen the private address 10.0.0.0/8 as its internal network address. That network address can connect 16,777,214 hosts in one broadcast domain. Obviously, having more than 16 million hosts on a single subnet is not ideal.

The enterprise could further subnet the 10.0.0.0/8 address at the octet boundary of /16 as shown in the table. This would provide the enterprise the ability to define up to 256 subnets (i.e., 10.0.0.0/16 - 10.255.0.0/16) with each subnet capable of connecting 65,534 hosts. Notice how the first two octets identify the network portion of the address whereas the last two octets are for host IP addresses.

Subnetting Network 10.0.0.0/8 using a /16

Subnet Address (256 Possible Subnets)	Host Range (65,534 possible hosts per subnet)	Broadcast
10.0.0.0/16	10.0.0.1 - 10.0.255.254	10.0.255.255
10.1.0.0/16	10.1.0.1 - 10.1.255.254	10.1.255.255
10.2.0.0/16	10.2.0.1 - 10.2.255.254	10.2.255.255
10.3.0.0/16	10.3.0.1 - 10.3.255.254	10.3.255.255
10.4.0.0/16	10.4.0.1 - 10.4.255.254	10.4.255.255
10.5.0.0/16	10.5.0.1 - 10.5.255.254	10.5.255.255
10.6.0.0/16	10.6.0.1 - 10.6.255.254	10.6.255.255
10.7.0.0/16	10.7.0.1 - 10.7.255.254	10.7.255.255
...	...	...
10.255.0.0/16	10.255.0.1 - 10.255.255.254	10.255.255.255

Alternatively, the enterprise could choose to subnet the 10.0.0.0/8 network at the /24 octet boundary, as shown in the table. This would enable the enterprise to define 65,536 subnets each capable of connecting 254 hosts. The /24 boundary is very popular in subnetting because it accommodates a reasonable number of hosts and conveniently subnets at the octet boundary.

Subnetting Network 10.0.0.0/8 using a /24 Prefix

$\leftarrow 2^8 - 24$

Subnet Address (65,536 Possible Subnets)	Host Range (254 possible hosts per subnet)	Broadcast
10.0.0.0/24	10.0.0.1 - 10.0.0.254	10.0.0.255
10.0.1.0/24	10.0.1.1 - 10.0.1.254	10.0.1.255
10.0.2.0/24	10.0.2.1 - 10.0.2.254	10.0.2.255
...	...	...
10.0.255.0/24	10.0.255.1 - 10.0.255.254	10.0.255.255
10.1.0.0/24	10.1.0.1 - 10.1.0.254	10.1.0.255
10.1.1.0/24	10.1.1.1 - 10.1.1.254	10.1.1.255
10.1.2.0/24	10.1.2.1 - 10.1.2.254	10.1.2.255
...	...	...
10.100.0.0/24	10.100.0.1 - 10.100.0.254	10.100.0.255
...	...	...
10.255.255.0/24	10.255.255.1 - 10.2255.255.254	10.255.255.255

Subnet within an Octet Boundary - 11.5.2

The examples shown thus far borrowed host bits from the common /8, /16, and /24 network prefixes. However, subnets can borrow bits from any host bit position to create other masks.

For instance, a /24 network address is commonly subnetted using longer prefix lengths by borrowing bits from the fourth octet. This provides the administrator with additional flexibility when assigning network addresses to a smaller number of end devices.

Refer to the table to see six ways to subnet a /24 network.

Subnet a /24 Network

Prefix Length	Subnet Mask	Subnet Mask in Binary (n = network, h = host)	# of subnets	# of hosts
/25	255.255.255.128	nnnnnnnn.nnnnnnnn.nnnnnnnn.**n**hhhhhhh 11111111.11111111.11111111.**1**0000000	2	126
/26	255.255.255.192	nnnnnnnn.nnnnnnnn.nnnnnnnn.**nn**hhhhhh 11111111.11111111.11111111.**11**000000	4	62
/27	255.255.255.224	nnnnnnnn.nnnnnnnn.nnnnnnnn.**nnn**hhhhh 11111111.11111111.11111111.**111**00000	8	30
/28	255.255.255.240	nnnnnnnn.nnnnnnnn.nnnnnnnn.**nnnn**hhhh 11111111.11111111.11111111.**1111**0000	16	14
/29	255.255.255.248	nnnnnnnn.nnnnnnnn.nnnnnnnn.**nnnnn**hhh 11111111.11111111.11111111.**11111**000	32	6
/30	255.255.255.252	nnnnnnnn.nnnnnnnn.nnnnnnnn.**nnnnnn**hh 11111111.11111111.11111111.**111111**00	64	2

For each bit borrowed in the fourth octet, the number of subnetworks available is doubled, while reducing the number of host addresses per subnet:

- **/25 row** - Borrowing 1 bit from the fourth octet creates 2 subnets supporting 126 hosts each.

- **/26 row** - Borrowing 2 bits creates 4 subnets supporting 62 hosts each.

- **/27 row** - Borrowing 3 bits creates 8 subnets supporting 30 hosts each.

- **/28 row** - Borrowing 4 bits creates 16 subnets supporting 14 hosts each.

- **/29 row** - Borrowing 5 bits creates 32 subnets supporting 6 hosts each.

- **/30 row** - Borrowing 6 bits creates 64 subnets supporting 2 hosts each.

Refer to **Video** in online course

Video - The Subnet Mask - 11.5.3

Click Play to view an explanation of the subnet mask.

Refer to **Video** in online course

Video - Subnet with the Magic Number - 11.5.4

Click Play to view an explanation of the magic number.

Refer to **Packet Tracer Activity** for this chapter

Packet Tracer - Subnet an IPv4 Network - 11.5.5

In this activity, starting from a single network address and network mask, you will subnet the Customer network into multiple subnets. The subnet scheme should be based on the number of host computers required in each subnet, as well as other network considerations, like future network host expansion.

After you have created a subnetting scheme and completed the table by filling in the missing host and interface IP addresses, you will configure the host PCs, switches and router interfaces.

After the network devices and host PCs have been configured, you will use the **ping** command to test for network connectivity.

Subnet a Slash 16 and a Slash 8 Prefix - 11.6

Create Subnets with a Slash 16 prefix - 11.6.1

Some subnetting is easier than other subnetting. This topic explains how to create subnets that each have the same number of hosts.

In a situation requiring a larger number of subnets, an IPv4 network is required that has more hosts bits available to borrow. For example, the network address 172.16.0.0 has a default mask of 255.255.0.0, or /16. This address has 16 bits in the network portion and 16 bits in the host portion. The 16 bits in the host portion are available to borrow for creating subnets. The table highlights all the possible scenarios for subnetting a /16 prefix.

Subnet a /16 Network

Prefix Length	Subnet Mask	Network Address (n = network,h = host)	# of subnets	# of hosts
/17	255.255.128.0	nnnnnnnn.nnnnnnnn.nhhhhhhh.hhhhhhhh 11111111.11111111.10000000.00000000	2	32766
/18	255.255.192.0	nnnnnnnn.nnnnnnnn.nnhhhhhh.hhhhhhhh 11111111.11111111.11000000.00000000	4	16382
/19	255.255.224.0	nnnnnnnn.nnnnnnnn.nnnhhhhh.hhhhhhhh 11111111.11111111.11100000.00000000	8	8190
/20	255.255.240.0	nnnnnnnn.nnnnnnnn.nnnnhhhh.hhhhhhhh 11111111.11111111.11110000.00000000	16	4094
/21	255.255.248.0	nnnnnnnn.nnnnnnnn.nnnnnhhh.hhhhhhhh 11111111.11111111.11111000.00000000	32	2046
/22	255.255.252.0	nnnnnnnn.nnnnnnnn.nnnnnnhh.hhhhhhhh 11111111.11111111.11111100.00000000	64	1022
/23	255.255.254.0	nnnnnnnn.nnnnnnnn.nnnnnnnh.hhhhhhhh 11111111.11111111.11111110.00000000	128	510
/24	255.255.255.0	nnnnnnnn.nnnnnnnn.nnnnnnnn.hhhhhhhh 11111111.11111111.11111111.00000000	256	254
/25	255.255.255.128	nnnnnnnn.nnnnnnnn.nnnnnnnn.nhhhhhhh 11111111.11111111.11111111.10000000	512	126
/26	255.255.255.192	nnnnnnnn.nnnnnnnn.nnnnnnnn.nnhhhhhh 11111111.11111111.11111111.11000000	1024	62
/27	255.255.255.224	nnnnnnnn.nnnnnnnn.nnnnnnnn.nnnhhhhh 11111111.11111111.11111111.11100000	2048	30
/28	255.255.255.240	nnnnnnnn.nnnnnnnn.nnnnnnnn.nnnnhhhh 11111111.11111111.11111111.11110000	4096	14
/29	255.255.255.248	nnnnnnnn.nnnnnnnn.nnnnnnnn.nnnnnhhh 11111111.11111111.11111111.11111000	8192	6
/30	255.255.255.252	nnnnnnnn.nnnnnnnn.nnnnnnnn.nnnnnnhh 11111111.11111111.11111111.11111100	16384	2

Although you do not need to memorize this table, you still need a good understanding of how each value in the table is generated. Do not let the size of the table intimidate you. The reason it is big is that it has 8 additional bits that can be borrowed, and, therefore, the numbers of subnets and hosts are simply larger.

Refer to
Online Course
for Illustration

Create 100 Subnets with a Slash 16 prefix - 11.6.2

Consider a large enterprise that requires at least 100 subnets and has chosen the private address 172.16.0.0/16 as its internal network address.

When borrowing bits from a /16 address, start borrowing bits in the third octet, going from left to right. Borrow a single bit at a time until the number of bits necessary to create 100 subnets is reached.

The figure displays the number of subnets that can be created when borrowing bits from the third octet and the fourth octet. Notice there are now up to 14 host bits that can be borrowed.

To satisfy the requirement of 100 subnets for the enterprise, 7 bits (i.e., 2^7 = 128 subnets) would need to be borrowed (for a total of 128 subnets), as shown in the figure.

Recall that the subnet mask must change to reflect the borrowed bits. In this example, when 7 bits are borrowed, the mask is extended 7 bits into the third octet. In decimal, the mask is represented as 255.255.254.0, or a /23 prefix, because the third octet is 11111110 in binary and the fourth octet is 00000000 in binary.

The figure displays the resulting subnets from 172.16.0.0 /23 up to 172.16.254.0 /23.

After borrowing 7 bits for the subnet, there is one host bit remaining in the third octet, and 8 host bits remaining in the fourth octet, for a total of 9 bits that were not borrowed. 29 results in 512 total host addresses. The first address is reserved for the network address and the last address is reserved for the broadcast address, so subtracting for these two addresses (29 - 2) equals 510 available host addresses for each /23 subnet.

As shown in the figure, the first host address for the first subnet is 172.16.0.1, and the last host address is 172.16.1.254.

Create 1000 Subnets with a Slash 8 prefix - 11.6.3

Refer to **Online Course** for Illustration

Some organizations, such as small service providers or large enterprises, may need even more subnets. For example, take a small ISP that requires 1000 subnets for its clients. Each client will need plenty of space in the host portion to create its own subnets.

The ISP has a network address 10.0.0.0 255.0.0.0 or 10.0.0.0/8. This means there are 8 bits in the network portion and 24 host bits available to borrow toward subnetting. Therefore, the small ISP will subnet the 10.0.0.0/8 network.

To create subnets, you must borrow bits from the host portion of the IPv4 address of the existing internetwork. Starting from the left to right with the first available host bit, borrow a single bit at a time until you reach the number of bits necessary to create 1000 subnets. As shown in the figure, you need to borrow 10 bits to create 1024 subnets (2^{10} = 1024). This includes 8 bits in the second octet and 2 additional bits from the third octet.

This figure displays the network address and the resulting subnet mask, which converts to 255.255.192.0 or 10.0.0.0/18.

This figure displays the subnets resulting from borrowing 10 bits, creating subnets from 10.0.0.0/18 to 10.255.128.0/18.

Borrowing 10 bits to create the subnets, leaves 14 host bits for each subnet. Subtracting two hosts per subnet (one for the network address and one for the broadcast address) equates to 214 - 2 = 16382 hosts per subnet. This means that each of the 1000 subnets can support up to 16,382 hosts.

This figure displays the specifics of the first subnet.

Video - Subnet Across Multiple Octets - 11.6.4

Refer to **Video** in online course

Click Play to view an explanation of how to use the magic number across octet boundaries.

Refer to
Lab Activity
for this chapter

Activity - Calculate the Subnet Mask - 11.6.5

In this activity, you are given a subnet mask in decimal format. Enter the binary representation of the subnet mask in the octet fields provided. Additionally, convert the mask to prefix notation format in the Prefix Notation field.

Refer to
Lab Activity
for this chapter

Lab - Calculate IPv4 Subnets - 11.6.6

In this lab, you will complete the following objectives:

- Part 1: Determine IPv4 Address Subnetting
- Part 2: Calculate IPv4 Address Subnetting

Subnet to Meet Requirements - 11.7

Refer to
Online Course
for Illustration

Subnet Private versus Public IPv4 Address Space - 11.7.1

While it is nice to quickly segment a network into subnets, your organization's network may use both public and private IPv4 addresses. This affects how you will subnet your network.

The figure shows a typical enterprise network:

- **Intranet** - This is the internal part of a company's network, accessible only within the organization. Devices in the intranet use private IPv4 addresses.

- **DMZ** - This is part of the company's network containing resources available to the internet such as a web server. Devices in the DMZ use public IPv4 addresses.

Both the intranet and the DMZ have their own subnetting requirements and challenges.

The intranet uses private IPv4 addressing space. This allows an organization to use any of the private IPv4 network addresses including the 10.0.0.0/8 prefix with 24 host bits and over 16 million hosts. Using a network address with 24 host bits makes subnetting easier and more flexible. This includes subnetting on an octet boundary using a /16 or /24.

For example, the private IPv4 network address 10.0.0.0/8 can be subnetted using a /16 mask. As shown in the table, this results in 256 subnets, with 65,534 hosts per subnet. If an organization has a need for fewer than 200 subnets, allowing for some growth, this gives each subnet more than enough host addresses.

Subnetting Network 10.0.0.0/8 using a /16

Subnet Address (256 Possible Subnets)	Host Range (65,534 possible hosts per subnet)	Broadcast
10.0.0.0/16	10.0.0.1 - 10.0.255.254	10.0.255.255
10.1.0.0/16	10.1.0.1 - 10.1.255.254	10.1.255.255
10.2.0.0/16	10.2.0.1 - 10.2.255.254	10.2.255.255

Subnet Address (256 Possible Subnets)	Host Range (65,534 possible hosts per subnet)	Broadcast
10.3.0.0/16	10.3.0.1 - 10.3.255.254	10.3.255.255
10.4.0.0/16	10.4.0.1 - 10.4.255.254	10.4.255.255
10.5.0.0/16	10.5.0.1 - 10.5.255.254	10.5.255.255
10.6.0.0/16	10.6.0.1 - 10.6.255.254	10.6.255.255
10.7.0.0/16	10.7.0.1 - 10.7.255.254	10.7.255.255
...	...	...
10.255.0.0/16	10.255.0.1 - 10.255.255.254	10.255.255.255

Another option using the 10.0.0.0/8 private IPv4 network address is to subnet using a /24 mask. As shown in the table, this results in 65,536 subnets, with 254 hosts per subnet. If an organization needs more than 256 subnets, then using a /24 can be used with 254 hosts per subnet.

Subnetting Network 10.0.0.0/8 using a /24

Subnet Address (65,536 Possible Subnets)	Host Range (254 possible hosts per subnet)	Broadcast
10.0.0.0/24	10.0.0.1 - 10.0.0.254	10.0.0.255
10.0.1.0/24	10.0.1.1 - 10.0.1.254	10.0.1.255
10.0.2.0/24	10.0.2.1 - 10.0.2.254	10.0.2.255
...	...	...
10.0.255.0/24	10.0.255.1 - 10.0.255.254	10.0.255.255
10.1.0.0/24	10.1.0.1 - 10.1.0.254	10.1.0.255
10.1.1.0/24	10.1.1.1 - 10.1.1.254	10.1.1.255
10.1.2.0/24	10.1.2.1 - 10.1.2.254	10.1.2.255
...	...	...
10.100.0.0/24	10.100.0.1 - 10.100.0.254	10.100.0.255
...	...	...
10.255.255.0/24	10.255.255.1 - 10.2255.255.254	10.255.255.255

The 10.0.0.0/8 can also be subnetted using any other number of prefix lengths, such as /12, /18, /20, etc. This would give the network administrator a wide variety of options. Using a 10.0.0.0/8 private IPv4 network address makes subnet planning and implementation easy.

What about the DMZ?

Because these devices need to be publicly accessible from the internet, the devices in the DMZ require public IPv4 addresses. The depletion of public IPv4 address space became an issue beginning in the mid-1990s. Since 2011, IANA and four out of five RIRs have run out of IPv4 address space. Although organizations are making the transition to IPv6, the remaining IPv4 address space remains severely limited. This means an organization must maximize its own limited number of public IPv4 addresses. This requires the network administrator to subnet their public address space into subnets with different subnet masks, in order to minimize the number of unused host addresses per subnet. This is known as Variable Subnet Length Masking (VLSM).

Minimize Unused Host IPv4 Addresses and Maximize Subnets - 11.7.2

To minimize the number of unused host IPv4 addresses and maximize the number of available subnets, there are two considerations when planning subnets: the number of host addresses required for each network and the number of individual subnets needed.

The table displays the specifics for subnetting a /24 network. Notice how there is an inverse relationship between the number of subnets and the number of hosts. The more bits that are borrowed to create subnets, the fewer host bits remain available. If more host addresses are needed, more host bits are required, resulting in fewer subnets.

The number of host addresses required in the largest subnet will determine how many bits must be left in the host portion. Recall that two of the addresses cannot be used, so the usable number of addresses can be calculated as 2n-2.

Subnetting a /24 Network

Prefix Length	Subnet Mask	Subnet Mask in Binary (n = network, h = host)	# of subnets	# of hosts per subnet
/25	255.255.255.128	nnnnnnnn.nnnnnnnn.nnnnnnnn.**n**hhhhhhh 11111111.11111111.11111111.**1**0000000	2	126
/26	255.255.255.192	nnnnnnnn.nnnnnnnn.nnnnnnnn.**nn**hhhhhh 11111111.11111111.11111111.**11**000000	4	62
/27	255.255.255.224	nnnnnnnn.nnnnnnnn.nnnnnnnn.**nnn**hhhhh 11111111.11111111.11111111.**111**00000	8	30
/28	255.255.255.240	nnnnnnnn.nnnnnnnn.nnnnnnnn.**nnnn**hhhh 11111111.11111111.11111111.**1111**0000	16	14
/29	255.255.255.248	nnnnnnnn.nnnnnnnn.nnnnnnnn.**nnnnn**hhh 11111111.11111111.11111111.**11111**000	32	6
/30	255.255.255.252	nnnnnnnn.nnnnnnnn.nnnnnnnn.**nnnnnn**hh 11111111.11111111.11111111.**111111**00	64	2

Network administrators must devise the network addressing scheme to accommodate the maximum number of hosts for each network and the number of subnets. The addressing scheme should allow for growth in both the number of host addresses per subnet and the total number of subnets.

Refer to
Online Course
for Illustration

Example: Efficient IPv4 Subnetting - 11.7.3

In this example, corporate headquarters has been allocated a public network address of 172.16.0.0/22 (10 host bits) by its ISP. As shown in the figure, this will provide 1,022 host addresses.

Note: 172.16.0.0/22 is part of the IPv4 private address space. We are using this address instead of an actual public IPv4 address.

The corporate headquarters has a DMZ and four branch offices, each needing its own public IPv4 address space. Corporate headquarters needs to make best use of its limited IPv4 address space.

The topology shown in the figure consists of five sites; a corporate office and four branch sites. Each site requires internet connectivity and therefore, five internet connections. This means that the organization requires 10 subnets from the company's 172.16.0.0/22 public address. The largest subnet requires 40 addresses.

The 172.16.0.0/22 network address has 10 host bits, as shown in the figure. Because the largest subnet requires 40 hosts, a minimum of 6 host bits are needed to provide addressing for 40 hosts. This is determined by using this formula: $2^6 - 2 = 62$ hosts.

Using the formula for determining subnets results in 16 subnets: $2^4 = 16$. Because the example internetwork requires 10 subnets, this will meet the requirement and allow for some additional growth.

Therefore, the first 4 host bits can be used to allocate subnets. This means two bits from the 3rd octet and two bits from the 4th octet will be borrowed. When 4 bits are borrowed from the 172.16.0.0/22 network, the new prefix length is /26 with a subnet mask of 255.255.255.192.

As shown in this figure, the subnets can be assigned to each location and router-to-ISP connections.

Refer to
Lab Activity
for this chapter

Activity - Determine the Number of Bits to Borrow - 11.7.4

In this activity, you are given the number of hosts that are needed. Determine the subnet mask that would support the number of hosts as specified. Enter your answers in binary, decimal, and prefix notation format in the fields provided.

Refer to **Packet
Tracer Activity**
for this chapter

Packet Tracer - Subnetting Scenario - 11.7.5

In this activity, you are given the network address of 192.168.100.0/24 to subnet and provide the IP addressing for the network shown in the topology. Each LAN in the network requires enough space for at least 25 addresses, which includes end devices as well as the switch and the router. The connection between R1 to R2 will require an IP address for each end of the link.

VLSM - 11.8 *"Subnetting a subnet"*

Refer to **Video** in online course

Video - VLSM Basics - 11.8.1

As mentioned in the previous topic, public and private addresses affect the way you would subnet your network. There are also other issues that affect subnetting schemes. A standard /16 subnetting scheme creates subnets that each have the same number of hosts. Not every subnet you create will need this many hosts, leaving many IPv4 addresses unused. Perhaps you will need one subnet that contains many more hosts. This is why the variable-length subnet mask (VLSM) was developed.

Click Play to view a demonstration of basic VLSM techniques.

Refer to **Video** in online course

Video - VLSM Example - 11.8.2

Click Play to view a demonstration of VLSM subnetting.

Refer to **Online Course** for Illustration

IPv4 Address Conservation - 11.8.3

Because of the depletion of public IPv4 address space, making the most out of the available host addresses is a primary concern when subnetting IPv4 networks.

Note: The larger IPv6 address allows for much easier address planning and allocation than IPv4 allows. Conserving IPv6 addresses is not an issue. This is one of the driving forces for transitioning to IPv6.

Using traditional subnetting, the same number of addresses is allocated for each subnet. If all the subnets have the same requirements for the number of hosts, or if conserving IPv4 address space is not an issue, these fixed-size address blocks would be efficient. Typically, with public IPv4 addresses, that is not the case.

For example, the topology shown in the figure requires seven subnets, one for each of the four LANs, and one for each of the three connections between the routers.

Using traditional subnetting with the given address of 192.168.20.0/24, three bits can be borrowed from the host portion in the last octet to meet the subnet requirement of seven subnets. As shown in the figure, borrowing 3 bits creates 8 subnets and leaves 5 host bits with 30 usable hosts per subnet. This scheme creates the needed subnets and meets the host requirement of the largest LAN.

These seven subnets could be assigned to the LAN and WAN networks, as shown in the figure.

Although this traditional subnetting meets the needs of the largest LAN and divides the address space into an adequate number of subnets, it results in significant waste of unused addresses.

For example, only two addresses are needed in each subnet for the three WAN links. Because each subnet has 30 usable addresses, there are 28 unused addresses in each of these subnets. As shown in the figure, this results in 84 unused addresses (28x3).

Further, this limits future growth by reducing the total number of subnets available. This inefficient use of addresses is characteristic of traditional subnetting. Applying a traditional subnetting scheme to this scenario is not very efficient and is wasteful.

The variable-length subnet mask (VLSM) was developed to avoid wasting addresses by enabling us to subnet a subnet.

Refer to **Online Course** for Illustration

VLSM - 11.8.4

In all of the previous subnetting examples, the same subnet mask was applied for all the subnets. This means that each subnet has the same number of available host addresses. As illustrated in the left side of the figure, traditional subnetting creates subnets of equal size. Each subnet in a traditional scheme uses the same subnet mask. As shown in the right side of the figure, VLSM allows a network space to be divided into unequal parts. With VLSM, the subnet mask will vary depending on how many bits have been borrowed for a particular subnet, thus the "variable" part of the VLSM.

VLSM is just subnetting a subnet. The same topology used previously is shown in the figure. Again, we will use the 192.168.20.0/24 network and subnet it for seven subnets, one for each of the four LANs, and one for each of the three connections between the routers.

The figure shows how network 192.168.20.0/24 subnetted into eight equal-sized subnets with 30 usable host addresses per subnet. Four subnets are used for the LANs and three subnets could be used for the connections between the routers.

However, the connections between the routers require only two host addresses per subnet (one host address for each router interface). Currently all subnets have 30 usable host addresses per subnet. To avoid wasting 28 addresses per subnet, VLSM can be used to create smaller subnets for the inter-router connections.

To create smaller subnets for the inter-router links, one of the subnets will be divided. In this example, the last subnet, 192.168.20.224/27, will be further subnetted. The figure shows the last subnet has been subnetted further by using the subnet mask 255.255.255.252 or /30.

Why /30? Recall that when the number of needed host addresses is known, the formula 2n-2 (where n equals the number of host bits remaining) can be used. To provide two usable addresses, two host bits must be left in the host portion.

Because there are five host bits in the subnetted 192.168.20.224/27 address space, three more bits can be borrowed, leaving two bits in the host portion. The calculations at this point are exactly the same as those used for traditional subnetting. The bits are borrowed, and the subnet ranges are determined. The figure shows how the four /27 subnets have been assigned to the LANs and three of the /30 subnets have been assigned to the inter-router links.

This VLSM subnetting scheme reduces the number of addresses per subnet to a size appropriate for the networks that require fewer subnets. Subnetting subnet 7 for inter-router links, allows subnets 4, 5, and 6 to be available for future networks, as well as five additional subnets available for inter-router connections.

Note: When using VLSM, always begin by satisfying the host requirements of the largest subnet. Continue subnetting until the host requirements of the smallest subnet are satisfied.

Refer to
Online Course
for Illustration

VLSM Topology Address Assignment - 11.8.5

Using the VLSM subnets, the LAN and inter-router networks can be addressed without unnecessary waste.

The figure shows the network address assignments and the IPv4 addresses assigned to each router interface.

Using a common addressing scheme, the first host IPv4 address for each subnet is assigned to the LAN interface of the router. Hosts on each subnet will have a host IPv4 address from the range of host addresses for that subnet and an appropriate mask. Hosts will use the address of the attached router LAN interface as the default gateway address.

The table shows the network addresses and range of host addresses for each network. The default gateway address is displayed for the four LANs.

	Network Address	Range of Host Addresses	Default Gateway Address
Building A	192.168.20.0/27	192.168.20.1/27 to 192.168.20.30/27	192.168.20.1/27
Building B	192.168.20.32/27	192.168.20.33/27 to 192.168.20.62/27	192.168.20.33/27
Building C	192.168.20.64/27	192.168.20.65/27 to 192.168.20.94/27	192.168.20.65/27
Building D	192.168.20.96/27	192.168.20.97/27 to 192.168.20.126/27	192.168.20.97/27
R1-R2	192.168.20.224/30	192.168.20.225/30 to 192.168.20.226/30	
R2-R3	192.168.20.228/30	192.168.20.229/30 to 192.168.20.230/30	
R3-R4	192.168.20.232/30	192.168.20.233/30 to 192.168.20.234/30	

Refer to
Lab Activity
for this chapter

Activity - VLSM Practice - 11.8.6

Structured Design - 11.9

IPv4 Network Address Planning - 11.9.1

Before you start subnetting, you should develop an IPv4 addressing scheme for your entire network. You will need to know how many subnets you need, how many hosts a particular subnet requires, what devices are part of the subnet, which parts of your network use private addresses, and which use public, and many other determining factors. A good addressing scheme allows for growth. A good addressing scheme is also the sign of a good network administrator.

Planning IPv4 network subnets requires you to examine both the needs of an organization's network usage, and how the subnets will be structured. Performing a network requirement study is the starting point. This means looking at the entire network, both the intranet and the DMZ, and determining how each area will be segmented. The address plan includes determining where address conservation is needed (usually within the DMZ), and where there is more flexibility (usually within the intranet).

Where address conservation is required, the plan should determine how many subnets are needed and how many hosts per subnet. As discussed earlier, this is usually required for public IPv4 address space within the DMZ. This will most likely include using VLSM.

Within the corporate intranet, address conservation is usually less of an issue This is largely due to using private IPv4 addressing, including 10.0.0.0/8, with over 16 million host IPv4 addresses.

For most organizations, private IPv4 addresses allow for more than enough internal (intranet) addresses. For many larger organizations and ISPs, even private IPv4 address space is not large enough to accommodate their internal needs. This is another reason why organizations are transitioning to IPv6.

For intranets that use private IPv4 addresses and DMZs that use public IPv4 addresses, address planning and assignment is important.

Where required, the address plan includes determining the needs of each subnet in terms of size. How many hosts there will be per subnet? The address plan also needs to include how host addresses will be assigned, which hosts will require static IPv4 addresses, and which hosts can use DHCP for obtaining their addressing information. This will also help prevent the duplication of addresses, while allowing for monitoring and managing of addresses for performance and security reasons.

Knowing your IPv4 address requirements will determine the range, or ranges, of host addresses that you implement and help ensure that there are enough addresses to cover your network needs.

Device Address Assignment - 11.9.2

Within a network, there are different types of devices that require addresses:

- **End user clients** - Most networks allocate IPv4 addresses to client devices dynamically, using Dynamic Host Configuration Protocol (DHCP). This reduces the burden on network support staff and virtually eliminates entry errors. With DHCP, addresses are only leased for a period of time, and can be reused when the lease expires. This is an important feature for networks that support transient users and wireless devices. Changing the subnetting scheme means that the DHCP server needs to be reconfigured, and the clients must renew their IPv4 addresses. IPv6 clients can obtain address information using DHCPv6 or SLAAC.

- **Servers and peripherals** - These should have a predictable static IP address. Use a consistent numbering system for these devices.

- **Servers that are accessible from the internet** - Servers that need to be publicly available on the internet must have a public IPv4 address, most often accessed using NAT. In some organizations, internal servers (not publicly available) must be made available to the remote users. In most cases, these servers are assigned private addresses internally, and the user is required to create a virtual private network (VPN) connection to access the server. This has the same effect as if the user is accessing the server from a host within the intranet.

- **Intermediary devices** - These devices are assigned addresses for network management, monitoring, and security. Because we must know how to communicate with intermediary devices, they should have predictable, statically assigned addresses.

- **Gateway** - Routers and firewall devices have an IP address assigned to each interface which serves as the gateway for the hosts in that network. Typically, the router interface uses either the lowest or highest address in the network.

When developing an IP addressing scheme, it is generally recommended that you have a set pattern of how addresses are allocated to each type of device. This benefits administrators when adding and removing devices, filtering traffic based on IP, as well as simplifying documentation.

Refer to **Packet Tracer Activity** for this chapter

Packet Tracer - VLSM Design and Implementation Practice - 11.9.3

In this activity, you are given a /24 network address to use to design a VLSM addressing scheme. Based on a set of requirements, you will assign subnets and addressing, configure devices, and verify connectivity.

Module Practice and Quiz - 11.10

Refer to **Packet Tracer Activity** for this chapter

Packet Tracer - Design and Implement a VLSM Addressing Scheme - 11.10.1

In this lab you will design a VLSM addressing scheme given a network address and host requirements. You will configure addressing on routers, switches, and network hosts.

- Design a VLSM IP addressing scheme given requirements.
- Configure addressing on network devices and hosts.
- Verify IP connectivity.
- Troubleshoot connectivity issues as required.

Refer to **Lab Activity** for this chapter

Lab - Design and Implement a VLSM Addressing Scheme - 11.10.2

In this lab, use the 192.168.33.128/25 network address to develop an addressing scheme for the network displayed in the topology diagram. VLSM is used to meet the IPv4 addressing requirements. After you have designed the VLSM address scheme, you will configure the interfaces on the routers with the appropriate IP address information. The future LANs at BR2 need to have addresses allocated, but no interfaces will be configured at this time.

What did I learn in this module? - 11.10.3

IPv4 Addressing Structure

An IPv4 address is a 32-bit hierarchical address that is made up of a network portion and a host portion. The bits within the network portion of the address must be identical for all devices that reside in the same network. The bits within the host portion of the address must be unique to identify a specific host within a network. A host requires a unique IPv4 address and a subnet mask to show the network/host portions of the address. The prefix length is the number of bits set to 1 in the subnet mask. It is written in "slash notation", which is a "/" followed by the number of bits set to 1. Logical AND is the comparison of two bits. Only a 1 AND 1 produces a 1 and all other combination results in a 0. Any other combination results in a 0. Within each network there are network addresses, host addresses, and a broadcast address.

IPv4 Unicast, Broadcast, and Multicast

Unicast transmission refers to a device sending a message to one other device in one-to-one communications. A unicast packet is a packet with a destination IP address that is a unicast address which is the address of a single recipient. Broadcast transmission refers to a device sending a message to all the devices on a network in one-to-all communications. A broadcast packet has a destination IP address with all ones (1s) in the host portion, or 32 one (1) bits. Multicast transmission reduces traffic by allowing a host to send a single packet to a selected set of hosts that subscribe to a multicast group. A multicast packet is a packet with a destination IP address that is a multicast address. IPv4 has reserved the 224.0.0.0 to 239.255.255.255 addresses as a multicast range.

Types of IPv4 Addresses

Public IPv4 addresses are globally routed between ISP routers. Not all available IPv4 addresses can be used on the internet. There are blocks of addresses called private addresses that are used by most organizations to assign IPv4 addresses to internal hosts. Most internal networks use private IPv4 addresses for addressing all internal devices (intranet); however, these private addresses are not globally routable. Loopback addresses used by a host to direct traffic back to itself. Link-local addresses are more commonly known as APIPA addresses, or self-assigned addresses. In 1981, IPv4 addresses were assigned using classful addressing: A, B, or C. Public IPv4 addresses must be unique, and are globally routed over the internet. Both IPv4 and IPv6 addresses are managed by the IANA, which allocates blocks of IP addresses to the RIRs.

Network Segmentation

In an Ethernet LAN, devices broadcast to locate other devices using ARP. Switches propagate broadcasts out all interfaces except the interface on which it was received. Routers do not propagate broadcasts, instead each router interface connects a broadcast domain and broadcasts are only propagated within that specific domain. A large broadcast domain is a network that connects many hosts. A problem with a large broadcast domain is that these hosts can generate excessive broadcasts and negatively affect the network. The solution is to reduce the size of the network to create smaller broadcast domains in a process called subnetting. These smaller network spaces are called subnets. Subnetting reduces overall network traffic and improves network performance. An administrator may subnet by location, between networks, or by device type.

Subnet an IPv4 Network

IPv4 subnets are created by using one or more of the host bits as network bits. This is done by extending the subnet mask to borrow some of the bits from the host portion of the address to create additional network bits. The more host bits that are borrowed, the more subnets that can be defined. The more bits that are borrowed to increase the number of subnets also reduces the number of hosts per subnet. Networks are most easily subnetted at the octet boundary of /8, /16, and /24. Subnets can borrow bits from any host bit position to create other masks.

Subnet a /16 and a /8 Prefix

In a situation requiring a larger number of subnets, an IPv4 network is required that has more hosts bits available to borrow. To create subnets, you must borrow bits from the host portion of the IPv4 address of the existing internetwork. Starting from the left to the right with the first available host bit, borrow a single bit at a time until you reach the number of bits necessary to create the number of subnets required. When borrowing bits from a /16 address, start borrowing bits in the third octet, going from left to right. The first address is reserved for the network address and the last address is reserved for the broadcast address.

Subnet to Meet Requirements

A typical enterprise network contains an intranet and a DMZ. Both have subnetting requirements and challenges. The intranet uses private IPv4 addressing space. The 10.0.0.0/8 can also be subnetted using any other number of prefix lengths, such as /12, /18, /20, etc., giving the network administrator many options. Because these devices need to be publicly accessible from the internet, the devices in the DMZ require public IPv4 addresses. Organizations must maximize their own limited number of public IPv4 addresses. To reduce the number of unused host addresses per subnet, the network administrator must subnet their public address space into subnets with different subnet masks. This is known as Variable Subnet Length Masking (VLSM). Administrators must consider how many host addresses are required for each network, and how many subnets are needed.

Variable Length Subnet Masking

Traditional subnetting might meet an organization's needs for its largest LAN and divide the address space into an adequate number of subnets. But it likely also results in significant waste of unused addresses. VLSM allows a network space to be divided into unequal parts. With VLSM, the subnet mask will vary depending on how many bits have been borrowed for a particular subnet (this is the "variable" part of the VLSM). VLSM is just subnetting a subnet. When using VLSM, always begin by satisfying the host requirements of the largest subnet. Continue subnetting until the host requirements of the smallest subnet are satisfied. Subnets always need to be started on an appropriate bit boundary.

Structured Design

A network administrator should study the network requirements to better plan how the IPv4 network subnets will be structured. This means looking at the entire network, both the intranet and the DMZ, and determining how each area will be segmented. The address plan includes determining where address conservation is needed (usually within the DMZ), and where there is more flexibility (usually within the intranet). Where address conservation is required the plan should determine how many subnets are needed and how many hosts per subnet. This is usually required for public IPv4 address space within the DMZ. This will most likely include using VLSM. The address plan includes how host addresses will be assigned, which hosts will require static IPv4 addresses, and which hosts can use DHCP for obtaining their addressing information. Within a network, there are different types of devices that require addresses: end user clients, servers and peripherals, servers that are accessible from the internet, intermediary devices, and gateways. When developing an IP addressing scheme, have a set pattern of how addresses are allocated to each type of device. This helps when adding and removing devices, filtering traffic based on IP, as well as simplifying documentation.

Go to the online
course to take the
quiz and exam.

Chapter Quiz - IPv4 Addressing

Your Chapter Notes

CHAPTER 12

IPv6 Addressing

Introduction - 12.0

Why should I take this module? - 12.0.1

Welcome to IPv6 Addressing!

It is a great time to be (or become) a network administrator! Why? Because in many networks, you will find both IPv4 and IPv6 working together. After the hard work of learning to subnet an IPv4 network, you may find that subnetting an IPv6 network is much easier. You probably didn't expect that, did you? A Packet Tracer at the end of this module will give you the opportunity to subnet an IPv6 network. Go ahead, jump in!

What will I learn in this module? - 12.0.2

Module Title: IPv6 Addressing

Module Objective: Implement an IPv6 addressing scheme.

Topic Title	Topic Objective
IPv4 Issues	Explain the need for IPv6 addressing.
IPv6 Address Representation	Explain how IPv6 addresses are represented.
IPv6 Address Types	Compare types of IPv6 network addresses.
GUA and LLA Static Configuration	Explain how to Configure static global unicast and link-local IPv6 network addresses.
Dynamic Addressing for IPv6 GUAs	Explain how to configure global unicast addresses dynamically.
Dynamic Addressing for IPv6 LLAs	Configure link-local addresses dynamically.
IPv6 Multicast Addresses	Identify IPv6 addresses.
Subnet an IPv6 Network	Implement a subnetted IPv6 addressing scheme.

IPv4 Issues - 12.1

Need for IPv6 - 12.1.1

Refer to
Online Course
for Illustration

You already know that IPv4 is running out of addresses. That is why you need to learn about IPv6.

IPv6 is designed to be the successor to IPv4. IPv6 has a larger 128-bit address space, providing 340 undecillion (i.e., 340 followed by 36 zeroes) possible addresses. However, IPv6 is more than just larger addresses.

When the IETF began its development of a successor to IPv4, it used this opportunity to fix the limitations of IPv4 and include enhancements. One example is Internet Control Message Protocol version 6 (ICMPv6), which includes address resolution and address autoconfiguration not found in ICMP for IPv4 (ICMPv4).

The depletion of IPv4 address space has been the motivating factor for moving to IPv6. As Africa, Asia and other areas of the world become more connected to the internet, there are not enough IPv4 addresses to accommodate this growth. As shown in the figure, four out of the five RIRs have run out of IPv4 addresses.

IPv4 has a theoretical maximum of 4.3 billion addresses. Private addresses in combination with Network Address Translation (NAT) have been instrumental in slowing the depletion of IPv4 address space. However, NAT is problematic for many applications, creates latency, and has limitations that severely impede peer-to-peer communications.

With the ever-increasing number of mobile devices, mobile providers have been leading the way with the transition to IPv6. The top two mobile providers in the United States report that over 90% of their traffic is over IPv6.

Most top ISPs and content providers such as YouTube, Facebook, and NetFlix, have also made the transition. Many companies like Microsoft, Facebook, and LinkedIn are transitioning to IPv6-only internally. In 2018, broadband ISP Comcast reported a deployment of over 65% and British Sky Broadcasting over 86%.

Internet of Things

The internet of today is significantly different than the internet of past decades. The internet of today is more than email, web pages, and file transfers between computers. The evolving internet is becoming an Internet of Things (IoT). No longer will the only devices accessing the internet be computers, tablets, and smartphones. The sensor-equipped, internet-ready devices of tomorrow will include everything from automobiles and biomedical devices, to household appliances and natural ecosystems.

With an increasing internet population, a limited IPv4 address space, issues with NAT and the IoT, the time has come to begin the transition to IPv6.

Refer to Interactive Graphic in online course

Refer to Online Course for Illustration

IPv4 and IPv6 Coexistence - 12.1.2

There is no specific date to move to IPv6. Both IPv4 and IPv6 will coexist in the near future and the transition will take several years. The IETF has created various protocols and tools to help network administrators migrate their networks to IPv6. The migration techniques can be divided into three categories:

Click each button for more information.

Dual Stack

Dual stack allows IPv4 and IPv6 to coexist on the same network segment. Dual stack devices run both IPv4 and IPv6 protocol stacks simultaneously. Known as native IPv6, this means the customer network has an IPv6 connection to their ISP and is able to access content found on the internet over IPv6.

Tunneling

Tunneling is a method of transporting an IPv6 packet over an IPv4 network. The IPv6 packet is encapsulated inside an IPv4 packet, similar to other types of data.

Translation

Network Address Translation 64 (NAT64) allows IPv6-enabled devices to communicate with IPv4-enabled devices using a translation technique similar to NAT for IPv4. An IPv6 packet is translated to an IPv4 packet and an IPv4 packet is translated to an IPv6 packet.

Note: Tunneling and translation are for transitioning to native IPv6 and should only be used where needed. The goal should be native IPv6 communications from source to destination.

Go to the online course to take the quiz and exam.

Check Your Understanding - IPv4 Issues - 12.1.3

IPv6 Address Representation - 12.2

Refer to **Online Course** for Illustration

IPv6 Addressing Formats - 12.2.1

The first step to learning about IPv6 in networks is to understand the way an IPv6 address is written and formatted. IPv6 addresses are much larger than IPv4 addresses, which is why we are unlikely to run out of them.

IPv6 addresses are 128 bits in length and written as a string of hexadecimal values. Every four bits is represented by a single hexadecimal digit; for a total of 32 hexadecimal values, as shown in the figure. IPv6 addresses are not case-sensitive and can be written in either lowercase or uppercase.

Preferred Format

The previous figure also shows that the preferred format for writing an IPv6 address is x:x:x:x:x:x:x:x, with each "x" consisting of four hexadecimal values. The term octet refers to the eight bits of an IPv4 address. In IPv6, a hextet is the unofficial term used to refer to a segment of 16 bits, or four hexadecimal values. Each "x" is a single hextet which is 16 bits or four hexadecimal digits.

Preferred format means that you write IPv6 address using all 32 hexadecimal digits. It does not necessarily mean that it is the ideal method for representing the IPv6 address. In this module, you will see two rules that help to reduce the number of digits needed to represent an IPv6 address.

These are examples of IPv6 addresses in the preferred format.

```
2001 : 0db8 : 0000 : 1111 : 0000 : 0000 : 0000: 0200  hextect

2001 : 0db8 : 0000 : 00a3 : abcd : 0000 : 0000: 1234

2001 : 0db8 : 000a : 0001 : c012 : 9aff : fe9a: 19ac

2001 : 0db8 : aaaa : 0001 : 0000 : 0000 : 0000: 0000

fe80 : 0000 : 0000 : 0000 : 0123 : 4567 : 89ab: cdef

fe80 : 0000 : 0000 : 0000 : 0000 : 0000 : 0000: 0001

fe80 : 0000 : 0000 : 0000 : c012 : 9aff : fe9a: 19ac
```

```
fe80 : 0000 : 0000 : 0000 : 0123 : 4567 : 89ab: cdef

0000 : 0000 : 0000 : 0000 : 0000 : 0000 : 0000: 0001

0000 : 0000 : 0000 : 0000 : 0000 : 0000 : 0000: 0000
```

Rule 1 - Omit Leading Zeros - 12.2.2

The first rule to help reduce the notation of IPv6 addresses is to omit any leading 0s (zeros) in any hextet. Here are four examples of ways to omit leading zeros:

- 01ab can be represented as 1ab

- 09f0 can be represented as 9f0

- 0a00 can be represented as a00

- 00ab can be represented as ab

This rule only applies to leading 0s, NOT to trailing 0s, otherwise the address would be ambiguous. For example, the hextet "abc" could be either "0abc" or "abc0", but these do not represent the same value.

Omitting Leading 0s

Type	Format							
Preferred	2001 :	0db8 :	0000 :	1111 :	0000 :	0000 :	0000 :	0200
No leading 0s	2001 :	db8 :	0 :	1111 :	0 :	0 :	0 :	200
Preferred	2001 :	0db8 :	0000 :	00a3 :	ab00 :	0ab0 :	00ab :	1234
No leading 0s	2001 :	db8 :	0 :	a3 :	ab00 :	ab0 :	ab :	1234
Preferred	2001 :	0db8 :	000a :	0001 :	c012 :	90ff :	fe90 :	0001
No leading 0s	2001 :	db8 :	a :	1 :	c012 :	90ff :	fe90 :	1
Preferred	2001 :	0db8 :	aaaa :	0001 :	0000 :	0000 :	0000 :	0000
No leading 0s	2001 :	db8 :	aaaa :	1 :	0 :	0 :	0 :	0
Preferred	fe80 :	0000 :	0000 :	0000 :	0123 :	4567 :	89ab :	cdef
No leading 0s	fe80 :	0 :	0 :	0 :	123 :	4567 :	89ab :	cdef

Type	Format							
Preferred	fe80 :	0000 :	0000 :	0000 :	0000 :	0000 :	0000 :	0001
No leading 0s	fe80 :	0 :	0 :	0 :	0 :	0 :	0 :	1
Preferred	0000 :	0000 :	0000 :	0000 :	0000 :	0000 :	0000 :	0001
No leading 0s	0 :	0 :	0 :	0 :	0 :	0 :	0 :	1
Preferred	0000 :	0000 :	0000 :	0000 :	0000 :	0000 :	0000 :	0000
No leading 0s	0 :	0 :	0 :	0 :	0 :	0 :	0 :	0

Rule 2 - Double Colon - 12.2.3

The second rule to help reduce the notation of IPv6 addresses is that a double colon (::) can replace any single, contiguous string of one or more 16-bit hextets consisting of all zeros. For example, 2001:db8:cafe:1:0:0:0:1 (leading 0s omitted) could be represented as 2001:db8:cafe:1::1. The double colon (::) is used in place of the three all-0 hextets (0:0:0).

The double colon (::) can only be used once within an address, otherwise there would be more than one possible resulting address. When used with the omitting leading 0s technique, the notation of IPv6 address can often be greatly reduced. This is commonly known as the compressed format.

Here is an example of the incorrect use of the double colon: 2001:db8::abcd::1234.

The double colon is used twice in the example above. Here are the possible expansions of this incorrect compressed format address:

- 2001:db8::abcd:0000:0000:1234
- 2001:db8::abcd:0000:0000:0000:1234
- 2001:db8:0000:abcd::1234
- 2001:db8:0000:0000:abcd::1234

If an address has more than one contiguous string of all-0 hextets, best practice is to use the double colon (::) on the longest string. If the strings are equal, the first string should use the double colon (::).

Omitting Leading 0s and All 0 Segments

Type	Format							
Preferred	2001 :	0db8 :	0000 :	1111 :	0000 :	0000 :	0000 :	0200
Compressed/spaces	2001 :	db8 :	0 :	1111 :			:	200
Compressed	2001:db8:0:1111::200							

Type	Format
Preferred	2001 : 0db8 : 0000 : 0000 : ab00 : 0000 : 0000 : 0000
Compressed/spaces	2001 : db8 : 0 : 0 : ab00 ::
Compressed	2001:db8:0:0:ab00::
Preferred	2001 : 0db8 : aaaa : 0001 : 0000 : 0000 : 0000 : 0000
Compressed/spaces	2001 : db8 : aaaa : 1 ::
Compressed	2001:db8:aaaa:1::
Preferred	fe80 : 0000 : 0000 : 0000 : 0123 : 4567 : 89ab : cdef
Compressed/spaces	fe80 : : 123 : 4567 : 89ab : cdef
Compressed	fe80::123:4567:89ab:cdef
Preferred	fe80 : 0000 : 0000 : 0000 : 0000 : 0000 : 0000 : 0001
Compressed/spaces	fe80 : : 1
Compressed	fe80::0
Preferred	0000 : 0000 : 0000 : 0000 : 0000 : 0000 : 0000 : 0001
Compressed/spaces	:: 1
Compressed	::1
Preferred	0000 : 0000 : 0000 : 0000 : 0000 : 0000 : 0000 : 0000
Compressed/spaces	::
Compressed	::

Refer to Lab Activity for this chapter

Activity - IPv6 Address Representation - 12.2.4

Convert the IPv6 addresses into short (omit the leading zeroes) and compressed forms. Enter letters in lowercase. Click Next to advance the activity to the next address.

IPv6 Address Types - 12.3

Unicast, Multicast, Anycast - 12.3.1

As with IPv4, there are different types of IPv6 addresses. In fact, there are three broad categories of IPv6 addresses:

- **Unicast** - An IPv6 unicast address uniquely identifies an interface on an IPv6-enabled device.

- **Multicast** - An IPv6 multicast address is used to send a single IPv6 packet to multiple destinations.

- **Anycast** - An IPv6 anycast address is any IPv6 unicast address that can be assigned to multiple devices. A packet sent to an anycast address is routed to the nearest device having that address. Anycast addresses are beyond the scope of this course.

Unlike IPv4, IPv6 does not have a broadcast address. However, there is an IPv6 all-nodes multicast address that essentially gives the same result.

Refer to **Online Course** for Illustration

IPv6 Prefix Length - 12.3.2

The prefix, or network portion, of an IPv4 address can be identified by a dotted-decimal subnet mask or prefix length (slash notation). For example, an IPv4 address of 192.168.1.10 with dotted-decimal subnet mask 255.255.255.0 is equivalent to 192.168.1.10/24.

In IPv4 the /24 is called the prefix. In IPv6 it is called the prefix length. IPv6 does not use the dotted-decimal subnet mask notation. Like IPv4, the prefix length is represented in slash notation and is used to indicate the network portion of an IPv6 address.

The prefix length can range from 0 to 128. The recommended IPv6 prefix length for LANs and most other types of networks is /64, as shown in the figure.

It is strongly recommended to use a 64-bit Interface ID for most networks. This is because stateless address autoconfiguration (SLAAC) uses 64 bits for the Interface ID. It also makes subnetting easier to create and manage.

Refer to **Online Course** for Illustration

Types of IPv6 Unicast Addresses - 12.3.3

An IPv6 unicast address uniquely identifies an interface on an IPv6-enabled device. A packet sent to a unicast address is received by the interface which is assigned that address. Similar to IPv4, a source IPv6 address must be a unicast address. The destination IPv6 address can be either a unicast or a multicast address. The figure shows the different types of IPv6 unicast addresses.

Unlike IPv4 devices that have only a single address, IPv6 addresses typically have two unicast addresses:

- **Global Unicast Address (GUA)** - This is similar to a public IPv4 address. These are globally unique, internet-routable addresses. GUAs can be configured statically or assigned dynamically.

- **Link-local Address (LLA)** - This is required for every IPv6-enabled device. LLAs are used to communicate with other devices on the same local link. With IPv6, the term link refers to a subnet. LLAs are confined to a single link. Their uniqueness must only be confirmed on that link because they are not routable beyond the link. In other words, routers will not forward packets with a link-local source or destination address.

A Note About the Unique Local Address - 12.3.4

Unique local addresses (range fc00::/7 to fdff::/7) are not yet commonly implemented. Therefore, this module only covers GUA and LLA configuration. However, unique local addresses may eventually be used to address devices that should not be accessible from the outside, such as internal servers and printers.

The IPv6 unique local addresses have some similarity to RFC 1918 private addresses for IPv4, but there are significant differences:

- Unique local addresses are used for local addressing within a site or between a limited number of sites.

- Unique local addresses can be used for devices that will never need to access another network.

- Unique local addresses are not globally routed or translated to a global IPv6 address.

Note: Many sites also use the private nature of RFC 1918 addresses to attempt to secure or hide their network from potential security risks. However, this was never the intended use of these technologies, and the IETF has always recommended that sites take the proper security precautions on their internet-facing router.

Refer to **Online Course** for Illustration

IPv6 GUA - 12.3.5

IPv6 global unicast addresses (GUAs) are globally unique and routable on the IPv6 internet. These addresses are equivalent to public IPv4 addresses. The Internet Committee for Assigned Names and Numbers (ICANN), the operator for IANA, allocates IPv6 address blocks to the five RIRs. Currently, only GUAs with the first three bits of 001 or 2000::/3 are being assigned, as shown in the figure.

The figure shows the range of values for the first hextet where the first hexadecimal digit for currently available GUAs begins with a 2 or a 3. This is only 1/8th of the total available IPv6 address space, excluding only a very small portion for other types of unicast and multicast addresses.

Note: The 2001:db8::/32 address has been reserved for documentation purposes, including use in examples.

The next figure shows the structure and range of a GUA.

IPv6 GUA Structure - 12.3.6

Global Routing Prefix

The global routing prefix is the prefix, or network, portion of the address that is assigned by the provider, such as an ISP, to a customer or site. For example, it is common for ISPs to assign a /48 global routing prefix to its customers. The global routing prefix will usually vary depending on the policies of the ISP.

The previous figure shows a GUA using a /48 global routing prefix. /48 prefixes are a common global routing prefix that is assigned and will be used in most of the examples throughout this course.

For example, the IPv6 address 2001:db8:acad::/48 has a global routing prefix that indicates that the first 48 bits (3 hextets) (2001:db8:acad) is how the ISP knows of this prefix (network). The double colon (::) following the /48 prefix length means the rest of the address contains all 0s. The size of the global routing prefix determines the size of the subnet ID.

Subnet ID

The Subnet ID field is the area between the Global Routing Prefix and the Interface ID. Unlike IPv4 where you must borrow bits from the host portion to create subnets, IPv6 was designed with subnetting in mind. The Subnet ID is used by an organization to identify subnets within its site. The larger the subnet ID, the more subnets available.

Note: Many organizations are receiving a /32 global routing prefix. Using the recommended /64 prefix in order to create a 64-bit Interface ID, leaves a 32 bit Subnet ID. This means an organization with a /32 global routing prefix and a 32-bit Subnet ID will have 4.3 billion subnets, each with 18 quintillion devices per subnet. That is as many subnets as there are public IPv4 addresses!

The IPv6 address in the previous figure has a /48 Global Routing Prefix, which is common among many enterprise networks. This makes it especially easy to examine the different parts of the address. Using a typical /64 prefix length, the first four hextets are for the network portion of the address, with the fourth hextet indicating the Subnet ID. The remaining four hextets are for the Interface ID.

Interface ID

The IPv6 interface ID is equivalent to the host portion of an IPv4 address. The term Interface ID is used because a single host may have multiple interfaces, each having one or more IPv6 addresses. The figure shows an example of the structure of an IPv6 GUA. It is strongly recommended that in most cases /64 subnets should be used, which creates a 64-bit interface ID. A 64-bit interface ID allows for 18 quintillion devices or hosts per subnet.

A /64 subnet or prefix (Global Routing Prefix + Subnet ID) leaves 64 bits for the interface ID. This is recommended to allow SLAAC-enabled devices to create their own 64-bit interface ID. It also makes developing an IPv6 addressing plan simple and effective.

Note: Unlike IPv4, in IPv6, the all-0s and all-1s host addresses can be assigned to a device. The all-1s address can be used because broadcast addresses are not used within IPv6. The all-0s address can also be used, but is reserved as a Subnet-Router anycast address, and should be assigned only to routers.

Refer to
Online Course
for Illustration

IPv6 LLA - 12.3.7

An IPv6 link-local address (LLA) enables a device to communicate with other IPv6-enabled devices on the same link and only on that link (subnet). Packets with a source or destination LLA cannot be routed beyond the link from which the packet originated.

The GUA is not a requirement. However, every IPv6-enabled network interface must have an LLA.

If an LLA is not configured manually on an interface, the device will automatically create its own without communicating with a DHCP server. IPv6-enabled hosts create an IPv6 LLA even if the device has not been assigned a global unicast IPv6 address. This allows IPv6-enabled devices to communicate with other IPv6-enabled devices on the same subnet. This includes communication with the default gateway (router).

IPv6 LLAs are in the fe80::/10 range. The /10 indicates that the first 10 bits are 1111 1110 10xx xxxx. The first hextet has a range of 1111 1110 10**00 0000** (fe80) to 1111 1110 10**11 1111** (febf).

The figure shows an example of communication using IPv6 LLAs. The PC is able to communicate directly with the printer using the LLAs.

The next figure shows some of the uses for IPv6 LLAs.

Note: Typically, it is the LLA of the router, and not the GUA, that is used as the default gateway for other devices on the link.

There are two ways that a device can obtain an LLA:

- **Statically** - This means the device has been manually configured.

- **Dynamically** - This means the device creates its own interface ID by using randomly generated values or using the Extended Unique Identifier (EUI) method, which uses the client MAC address along with additional bits.

Go to the online course to take the quiz and exam.

Check Your Understanding - IPv6 Address Types - 12.3.8

GUA and LLA Static Configuration - 12.4

Refer to **Online Course** for Illustration

Static GUA Configuration on a Router - 12.4.1

As you learned in the previous topic, IPv6 GUAs are the same as public IPv4 addresses. They are globally unique and routable on the IPv6 internet. An IPv6 LLA lets two IPv6-enabled devices communicate with each other on the same link (subnet). It is easy to statically configure IPv6 GUAs and LLAs on routers to help you create an IPv6 network. This topic teaches you how to do just that!

Most IPv6 configuration and verification commands in the Cisco IOS are similar to their IPv4 counterparts. In many cases, the only difference is the use of **ipv6** in place of **ip** within the commands.

For example, the Cisco IOS command to configure an IPv4 address on an interface is **ip address** *ip-address subnet-mask*. In contrast, the command to configure an IPv6 GUA on an interface is **ipv6 address** *ipv6-address/prefix-length*.

Notice that there is no space between *ipv6-address* and *prefix-length*.

The example configuration uses the topology shown in the figure and these IPv6 subnets:

- 2001:db8:acad:1:/64

- 2001:db8:acad:2:/64

- 2001:db8:acad:3:/64

The example shows the commands required to configure the IPv6 GUA on GigabitEthernet 0/0/0, GigabitEthernet 0/0/1, and the Serial 0/1/0 interface of R1.

IPv6 GUA Configuration on Router R1

```
R1(config)# interface gigabitethernet 0/0/0

R1(config-if)# ipv6 address 2001:db8:acad:1::1/64

R1(config-if)# no shutdown

R1(config-if)# exit

R1(config)# interface gigabitethernet 0/0/1

R1(config-if)# ipv6 address 2001:db8:acad:2::1/64

R1(config-if)# no shutdown

R1(config-if)# exit

R1(config)# interface serial 0/1/0

R1(config-if)# ipv6 address 2001:db8:acad:3::1/64

R1(config-if)# no shutdown
```

Static GUA Configuration on a Windows Host - 12.4.2

Refer to Online Course for Illustration

Manually configuring the IPv6 address on a host is similar to configuring an IPv4 address.

As shown in the figure, the default gateway address configured for PC1 is 2001:db8:acad:1::1. This is the GUA of the R1 GigabitEthernet interface on the same network. Alternatively, the default gateway address can be configured to match the LLA of the GigabitEthernet interface. Using the LLA of the router as the default gateway address is considered best practice. Either configuration will work.

Just as with IPv4, configuring static addresses on clients does not scale to larger environments. For this reason, most network administrators in an IPv6 network will enable dynamic assignment of IPv6 addresses.

There are two ways in which a device can obtain an IPv6 GUA automatically:

- Stateless Address Autoconfiguration (SLAAC)
- Stateful DHCPv6

SLAAC and DHCPv6 are covered in the next topic.

Note: When DHCPv6 or SLAAC is used, the LLA of the router will automatically be specified as the default gateway address.

Static Configuration of a Link-Local Unicast Address - 12.4.3

Refer to Online Course for Illustration

Configuring the LLA manually lets you create an address that is recognizable and easier to remember. Typically, it is only necessary to create recognizable LLAs on routers. This is beneficial because router LLAs are used as default gateway addresses and in routing advertisement messages.

LLAs can be configured manually using the **ipv6 address** *ipv6-link-local-address* **link-local** command. When an address begins with this hextet within the range of fe80 to febf, the **link-local** parameter must follow the address.

The figure shows an example topology with LLAs on each interface.

The example shows the configuration of an LLA on router R1.

```
R1(config)# interface gigabitethernet 0/0/0
R1(config-if)# ipv6 address fe80::1:1 link-local
R1(config-if)# exit
R1(config)# interface gigabitethernet 0/0/1
R1(config-if)# ipv6 address fe80::1:2 link-local
R1(config-if)# exit
R1(config)# interface serial 0/1/0
R1(config-if)# ipv6 address fe80::1:3 link-local
R1(config-if)# exit
```

Statically configured LLAs are used to make them more easily recognizable as belonging to router R1. In this example, all the interfaces of router R1 have been configured with an LLA that begins with **fe80::1:***n* and a unique right-most digit "n". The "1" represents router R1.

Following the same syntax as router R1, if the topology included router R2, it would have its three interfaces configured with the LLAs fe80::2:1, fe80::2:2, and fe80::2:3.

Note: The exact same LLA could be configured on each link as long as it is unique on that link. This is because LLAs only have to be unique on that link. However, common practice is to create a different LLA on each interface of the router to make it easy to identify the router and the specific interface.

Refer to
Interactive Graphic
in online course

Syntax Checker - GUA and LLA Static Configuration - 12.4.4

Assign IPv6 GUAs and LLAs to the specified interfaces on router R1.

Dynamic Addressing for IPv6 GUAs - 12.5

Refer to
Online Course
for Illustration

RS and RA Messages - 12.5.1

If you do not want to statically configure IPv6 GUAs, no need to worry. Most devices obtain their IPv6 GUAs dynamically. This topic explains how this process works using Router Advertisement (RA) and Router Solicitation (RS) messages. This topic gets rather technical, but when you understand the difference between the three methods that a router advertisement can use, as well as how the EUI-64 process for creating an interface ID differs from a randomly generated process, you will have made a huge leap in your IPv6 expertise!

For the GUA, a device obtains the address dynamically through Internet Control Message Protocol version 6 (ICMPv6) messages. IPv6 routers periodically send out ICMPv6 RA messages, every 200 seconds, to all IPv6-enabled devices on the network. An RA message will also be sent in response to a host sending an ICMPv6 RS message, which is a request for an RA message. Both messages are shown in the figure.

RA messages are on IPv6 router Ethernet interfaces. The router must be enabled for IPv6 routing, which is not enabled by default. To enable a router as an IPv6 router, the **ipv6 unicast-routing** global configuration command must be used.

The ICMPv6 RA message is a suggestion to a device on how to obtain an IPv6 GUA. The ultimate decision is up to the device operating system. The ICMPv6 RA message includes the following:

- **Network prefix and prefix length** - This tells the device which network it belongs to.
- **Default gateway address** - This is an IPv6 LLA, the source IPv6 address of the RA message.
- **DNS addresses and domain name** - These are the addresses of DNS servers and a domain name.

There are three methods for RA messages:

- **Method 1: SLAAC** - "I have everything you need including the prefix, prefix length, and default gateway address."
- **Method 2: SLAAC with a stateless DHCPv6 server** - "Here is my information but you need to get other information such as DNS addresses from a stateless DHCPv6 server."
- **Method 3: Stateful DHCPv6 (no SLAAC)** - "I can give you your default gateway address. You need to ask a stateful DHCPv6 server for all your other information."

Refer to **Online Course** for Illustration

Method 1: SLAAC - 12.5.2

SLAAC is a method that allows a device to create its own GUA without the services of DHCPv6. Using SLAAC, devices rely on the ICMPv6 RA messages of the local router to obtain the necessary information.

By default, the RA message suggests that the receiving device use the information in the RA message to create its own IPv6 GUA and all other necessary information. The services of a DHCPv6 server are not required.

SLAAC is stateless, which means there is no central server (for example, a stateful DHCPv6 server) allocating GUAs and keeping a list of devices and their addresses. With SLAAC, the client device uses the information in the RA message to create its own GUA. As shown in the figure, the two parts of the address are created as follows:

- **Prefix** - This is advertised in the RA message.
- **Interface ID** - This uses the EUI-64 process or by generating a random 64-bit number, depending on the device operating system.

Refer to
Online Course
for Illustration

Method 2: SLAAC and Stateless DHCPv6 - 12.5.3

A router interface can be configured to send a router advertisement using SLAAC and stateless DHCPv6.

As shown in the figure, with this method, the RA message suggests devices use the following:

- SLAAC to create its own IPv6 GUA
- The router LLA, which is the RA source IPv6 address, as the default gateway address
- A stateless DHCPv6 server to obtain other information such as a DNS server address and a domain name

Note: A stateless DHCPv6 server distributes DNS server addresses and domain names. It does not allocate GUAs.

Refer to
Online Course
for Illustration

Method 3: Stateful DHCPv6 - 12.5.4

A router interface can be configured to send an RA using stateful DHCPv6 only.

Stateful DHCPv6 is similar to DHCP for IPv4. A device can automatically receive its addressing information including a GUA, prefix length, and the addresses of DNS servers from a stateful DHCPv6 server.

As shown in the figure, with this method, the RA message suggests devices use the following:

- The router LLA, which is the RA source IPv6 address, for the default gateway address.
- A stateful DHCPv6 server to obtain a GUA, DNS server address, domain name and other necessary information.

A stateful DHCPv6 server allocates and maintains a list of which device receives which IPv6 address. DHCP for IPv4 is stateful.

Note: The default gateway address can only be obtained dynamically from the RA message. The stateless or stateful DHCPv6 server does not provide the default gateway address.

Refer to
Online Course
for Illustration

EUI-64 Process vs. Randomly Generated - 12.5.5

When the RA message is either SLAAC or SLAAC with stateless DHCPv6, the client must generate its own interface ID. The client knows the prefix portion of the address from the RA message, but must create its own interface ID. The interface ID can be created using the EUI-64 process or a randomly generated 64-bit number, as shown in the figure.

Refer to
Online Course
for Illustration

EUI-64 Process - 12.5.6

IEEE defined the Extended Unique Identifier (EUI) or modified EUI-64 process. This process uses the 48-bit Ethernet MAC address of a client, and inserts another 16 bits in the middle of the 48-bit MAC address to create a 64-bit interface ID.

Ethernet MAC addresses are usually represented in hexadecimal and are made up of two parts:

- **Organizationally Unique Identifier (OUI)** - The OUI is a 24-bit (6 hexadecimal digits) vendor code assigned by IEEE.

- **Device Identifier** - The device identifier is a unique 24-bit (6 hexadecimal digits) value within a common OUI.

An EUI-64 Interface ID is represented in binary and is made up of three parts:

- 24-bit OUI from the client MAC address, but the 7th bit (the Universally/Locally (U/L) bit) is reversed. This means that if the 7th bit is a 0, it becomes a 1, and vice versa.

- The inserted 16-bit value fffe (in hexadecimal).

- 24-bit Device Identifier from the client MAC address.

The EUI-64 process is illustrated in the figure, using the R1 GigabitEthernet MAC address of fc99:4775:cee0.

The example output for the **ipconfig** command shows the IPv6 GUA being dynamically created using SLAAC and the EUI-64 process. An easy way to identify that an address was probably created using EUI-64 is the **fffe** located in the middle of the interface ID.

The advantage of EUI-64 is that the Ethernet MAC address can be used to determine the interface ID. It also allows network administrators to easily track an IPv6 address to an end-device using the unique MAC address. However, this has caused privacy concerns among many users who worried that their packets could be traced to the actual physical computer. Due to these concerns, a randomly generated interface ID may be used instead.

EUI-64 Generated Interface ID

```
C:\> ipconfig

Windows IP Configuration

Ethernet adapter Local Area Connection:

    Connection-specific DNS Suffix  . :

    IPv6 Address. . . . . . . . . . . : 2001:db8:acad:1:fc99:47ff:fe75:
                                        cee0

    Link-local IPv6 Address . . . . . : fe80::fc99:47ff:fe75:cee0

    Default Gateway . . . . . . . . . : fe80::1
C:\>
```

Randomly Generated Interface IDs - 12.5.7

Depending upon the operating system, a device may use a randomly generated interface ID instead of using the MAC address and the EUI-64 process. Beginning with Windows Vista, Windows uses a randomly generated interface ID instead of one created with EUI-64. Windows XP and previous Windows operating systems used EUI-64.

After the interface ID is established, either through the EUI-64 process or through random generation, it can be combined with an IPv6 prefix in the RA message to create a GUA, as shown in the figure.

Random 64-bit Generated Interface ID

```
C:\> ipconfig

Windows IP Configuration

Ethernet adapter Local Area Connection:

   Connection-specific DNS Suffix   . :

   IPv6 Address. . . . . . . . . . . : 2001:db8:acad:1:50a5:8a35:a5bb:
                                       66e1

   Link-local IPv6 Address . . . . . : fe80::50a5:8a35:a5bb:66e1

   Default Gateway . . . . . . . . . : fe80::1

C:\>
```

Note: To ensure the uniqueness of any IPv6 unicast address, the client may use a process known as Duplicate Address Detection (DAD). This is similar to an ARP request for its own address. If there is no reply, then the address is unique.

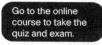
Go to the online course to take the quiz and exam.

Check Your Understanding - Dynamic Addressing for IPv6 GUAs - 12.5.8

Dynamic Addressing for IPv6 LLAs - 12.6

Refer to
Online Course
for Illustration

Dynamic LLAs - 12.6.1

All IPv6 devices must have an IPv6 LLA. Like IPv6 GUAs, you can also create LLAs dynamically. Regardless of how you create your LLAs (and your GUAs), it is important that you verify all IPv6 address configuration. This topic explains dynamically generated LLAs and IPv6 configuration verification.

The figure shows the LLA is dynamically created using the fe80::/10 prefix and the interface ID using the EUI-64 process, or a randomly generated 64-bit number.

Dynamic LLAs on Windows - 12.6.2

Operating systems, such as Windows, will typically use the same method for both a SLAAC-created GUA and a dynamically assigned LLA. See the highlighted areas in the following examples that were shown previously.

EUI-64 Generated Interface ID

```
C:\> ipconfig

Windows IP Configuration

Ethernet adapter Local Area Connection:
```

```
Connection-specific DNS Suffix . :

IPv6 Address. . . . . . . . . . : 2001:db8:acad:1:fc99:47ff:fe75:cee0

Link-local IPv6 Address . . . . : fe80::fc99:47ff:fe75:cee0

Default Gateway . . . . . . . . : fe80::1

C:\>
```

Random 64-bit Generated Interface ID

```
C:\> ipconfig

Windows IP Configuration

Ethernet adapter Local Area Connection:

   Connection-specific DNS Suffix  . :

   IPv6 Address. . . . . . . . . . : 2001:db8:acad:1:50a5:8a35:a5bb:
                                      66e1

   Link-local IPv6 Address . . . . . : fe80::50a5:8a35:a5bb:66e1

   Default Gateway . . . . . . . . : fe80::1

C:\>
```

Dynamic LLAs on Cisco Routers - 12.6.3

Cisco routers automatically create an IPv6 LLA whenever a GUA is assigned to the interface. By default, Cisco IOS routers use EUI-64 to generate the interface ID for all LLAs on IPv6 interfaces. For serial interfaces, the router will use the MAC address of an Ethernet interface. Recall that an LLA must be unique only on that link or network. However, a drawback to using the dynamically assigned LLA is its long interface ID, which makes it challenging to identify and remember assigned addresses. The example displays the MAC address on the GigabitEthernet 0/0/0 interface of router R1. This address is used to dynamically create the LLA on the same interface, and also for the Serial 0/1/0 interface.

To make it easier to recognize and remember these addresses on routers, it is common to statically configure IPv6 LLAs on routers.

IPv6 LLA Using EUI-64 on Router R1

```
R1# show interface gigabitEthernet 0/0/0

GigabitEthernet0/0/0 is up, line protocol is up

  Hardware is ISR4221-2x1GE, address is 7079.b392.3640 (bia 7079.
  b392.3640)

(Output omitted)

R1# show ipv6 interface brief

GigabitEthernet0/0/0   [up/up]

    FE80::7279:B3FF:FE92:3640

    2001:DB8:ACAD:1::1
```

```
GigabitEthernet0/0/1    [up/up]

    FE80::7279:B3FF:FE92:3641

    2001:DB8:ACAD:2::1

Serial0/1/0             [up/up]

    FE80::7279:B3FF:FE92:3640

    2001:DB8:ACAD:3::1

Serial0/1/1             [down/down]

    unassigned

R1#
```

Refer to
Interactive Graphic
in online course

Refer to
Online Course
for Illustration

Verify IPv6 Address Configuration - 12.6.4

The figure shows the example topology.

Click each button for the output and a description of the command.

show ipv6 interface brief

The **show ipv6 interface brief** command displays the MAC address of the Ethernet interfaces. EUI-64 uses this MAC address to generate the interface ID for the LLA. Additionally, the **show ipv6 interface brief** command displays abbreviated output for each of the interfaces. The [up/up] output on the same line as the interface indicates the Layer 1/Layer 2 interface state. This is the same as the Status and Protocol columns in the equivalent IPv4 command.

Notice that each interface has two IPv6 addresses. The second address for each interface is the GUA that was configured. The first address, the one that begins with fe80, is the link-local unicast address for the interface. Recall that the LLA is automatically added to the interface when a GUA is assigned.

Also, notice that the R1 Serial 0/1/0 LLA is the same as its GigabitEthernet 0/0/0 interface. Serial interfaces do not have Ethernet MAC addresses, so Cisco IOS uses the MAC address of the first available Ethernet interface. This is possible because link-local interfaces only have to be unique on that link.

The show ipv6 interface brief Command on R1

```
R1# show ipv6 interface brief

GigabitEthernet0/0/0    [up/up]

    FE80::1:1

    2001:DB8:ACAD:1::1

GigabitEthernet0/0/1    [up/up]

    FE80::1:2

    2001:DB8:ACAD:2::1

Serial0/1/0             [up/up]

    FE80::1:3
```

```
      2001:DB8:ACAD:3::1
Serial0/1/1               [down/down]
      unassigned
R1#
```

show ipv6 route

As shown in the example, the **show ipv6 route** command can be used to verify that IPv6 networks and specific IPv6 interface addresses have been installed in the IPv6 routing table. The **show ipv6 route** command will only display IPv6 networks, not IPv4 networks.

Within the route table, a **C** next to a route indicates that this is a directly connected network. When the router interface is configured with a GUA and is in the "up/up" state, the IPv6 prefix and prefix length is added to the IPv6 routing table as a connected route.

Note: The L indicates a Local route, the specific IPv6 address assigned to the interface. This is not an LLA. LLAs are not included in the routing table of the router because they are not routable addresses.

The IPv6 GUA configured on the interface is also installed in the routing table as a local route. The local route has a /128 prefix. Local routes are used by the routing table to efficiently process packets with a destination address of the router interface address.

The show ipv6 route Command on R1

```
R1# show ipv6 route
IPv6 Routing Table - default - 7 entries
Codes: C - Connected, L - Local, S - Static, U - Per-user Static route


C    2001:DB8:ACAD:1::/64 [0/0]
       via GigabitEthernet0/0/0, directly connected
L    2001:DB8:ACAD:1::1/128 [0/0]
       via GigabitEthernet0/0/0, receive
C    2001:DB8:ACAD:2::/64 [0/0]
       via GigabitEthernet0/0/1, directly connected
L    2001:DB8:ACAD:2::1/128 [0/0]
       via GigabitEthernet0/0/1, receive
C    2001:DB8:ACAD:3::/64 [0/0]
       via Serial0/1/0, directly connected
L    2001:DB8:ACAD:3::1/128 [0/0]
       via Serial0/1/0, receive
L    FF00::/8 [0/0]
       via Null0, receive
R1#
```

ping

The **ping** command for IPv6 is identical to the command used with IPv4, except that an IPv6 address is used. As shown in the example, the command is used to verify Layer 3 connectivity between R1 and PC1. When pinging an LLA from a router, Cisco IOS will prompt the user for the exit interface. Because the destination LLA can be on one or more of its links or networks, the router needs to know which interface to send the ping to.

The ping Command on R1

```
R1# ping 2001:db8:acad:1::10

Type escape sequence to abort.

Sending 5, 100-byte ICMP Echos to 2001:DB8:ACAD:1::10, timeout is
2 seconds:

!!!!!

Success rate is 100 percent (5/5), round-trip min/avg/max = 1/1/1 ms
R1#
```

Refer to
Interactive Graphic
in online course

Syntax Checker - Verify IPv6 Address Configuration - 12.6.5

Use **show** commands to verify IPv6 address configuration on router R1 interfaces.

Refer to **Packet Tracer Activity**
for this chapter

Packet Tracer - Configure IPv6 Addressing - 12.6.6

In this activity, you will practice configuring IPv6 addresses on a router, servers, and clients. You will also practice verifying your IPv6 addressing implementation.

IPv6 Multicast Addresses - 12.7

Assigned IPv6 Multicast Addresses - 12.7.1

Earlier in this module, you learned that there are three broad categories of IPv6 addresses: unicast, anycast, and multicast. This topic goes into more detail about multicast addresses.

IPv6 multicast addresses are similar to IPv4 multicast addresses. Recall that a multicast address is used to send a single packet to one or more destinations (multicast group). IPv6 multicast addresses have the prefix ff00::/8.

Note: Multicast addresses can only be destination addresses and not source addresses.

There are two types of IPv6 multicast addresses:

- Well-known multicast addresses
- Solicited node multicast addresses

Refer to
Online Course
for Illustration

Well-Known IPv6 Multicast Addresses - 12.7.2

Well-known IPv6 multicast addresses are assigned. Assigned multicast addresses are reserved multicast addresses for predefined groups of devices. An assigned multicast address is a single address used to reach a group of devices running a common protocol or service. Assigned multicast addresses are used in context with specific protocols such as DHCPv6.

These are two common IPv6 assigned multicast groups:

- **ff02::1 All-nodes multicast group** - This is a multicast group that all IPv6-enabled devices join. A packet sent to this group is received and processed by all IPv6 interfaces on the link or network. This has the same effect as a broadcast address in IPv4. The figure shows an example of communication using the all-nodes multicast address. An IPv6 router sends ICMPv6 RA messages to the all-node multicast group.

- **ff02::2 All-routers multicast group** - This is a multicast group that all IPv6 routers join. A router becomes a member of this group when it is enabled as an IPv6 router with the **ipv6 unicast-routing** global configuration command. A packet sent to this group is received and processed by all IPv6 routers on the link or network.

Refer to
Online Course
for Illustration

Solicited-Node IPv6 Multicast Addresses - 12.7.3

A solicited-node multicast address is similar to the all-nodes multicast address. The advantage of a solicited-node multicast address is that it is mapped to a special Ethernet multicast address. This allows the Ethernet NIC to filter the frame by examining the destination MAC address without sending it to the IPv6 process to see if the device is the intended target of the IPv6 packet.

Refer to
Lab Activity
for this chapter

Lab - Identify IPv6 Addresses - 12.7.4

In this lab, you will complete the following objectives:

- Part 1: Identify the Different Types of IPv6 Addresses
- Part 2: Examine a Host IPv6 Network Interface and Address
- Part 3: Practice IPv6 Address Abbreviation

Subnet an IPv6 Network - 12.8

Refer to
Online Course
for Illustration

Subnet Using the Subnet ID - 12.8.1

The introduction to this module mentioned subnetting an IPv6 network. It also said that you might discover that it is a bit easier than subnetting an IPv4 network. You are about to find out!

Recall that with IPv4, we must borrow bits from the host portion to create subnets. This is because subnetting was an afterthought with IPv4. However, IPv6 was designed with subnetting in mind. A separate subnet ID field in the IPv6 GUA is used to create subnets. As shown in the figure, the subnet ID field is the area between the Global Routing Prefix and the interface ID.

The benefit of a 128-bit address is that it can support more than enough subnets and hosts per subnet, for each network. Address conservation is not an issue. For example, if the global routing prefix is a /48, and using a typical 64 bits for the interface ID, this will create a 16-bit subnet ID:

- **16-bit subnet ID** - Creates up to 65,536 subnets.

- **64-bit interface ID** - Supports up to 18 quintillion host IPv6 addresses per subnet (i.e., 18,000,000,000,000,000,000).

Note: Subnetting into the 64-bit interface ID (or host portion) is also possible but it is rarely required.

IPv6 subnetting is also easier to implement than IPv4, because there is no conversion to binary required. To determine the next available subnet, just count up in hexadecimal.

<table>
<tr><td>Refer to
Online Course
for Illustration</td></tr>
</table>

IPv6 Subnetting Example - 12.8.2

For example, assume an organization has been assigned the 2001:db8:acad::/48 global routing prefix with a 16 bit subnet ID. This would allow the organization to create 65,536 /64 subnets, as shown in the figure. Notice how the global routing prefix is the same for all subnets. Only the subnet ID hextet is incremented in hexadecimal for each subnet.

<table>
<tr><td>Refer to
Online Course
for Illustration</td></tr>
</table>

IPv6 Subnet Allocation - 12.8.3

With over 65,536 subnets to choose from, the task of the network administrator becomes one of designing a logical scheme to address the network.

As shown in the figure, the example topology requires five subnets, one for each LAN as well as for the serial link between R1 and R2. Unlike the example for IPv4, with IPv6 the serial link subnet will have the same prefix length as the LANs. Although this may seem to "waste" addresses, address conservation is not a concern when using IPv6.

As shown in the next figure, the five IPv6 subnets were allocated, with the subnet ID field 0001 through 0005 used for this example. Each /64 subnet will provide more addresses than will ever be needed.

Router Configured with IPv6 Subnets - 12.8.4

Similar to configuring IPv4, the example shows that each of the router interfaces has been configured to be on a different IPv6 subnet.

IPv6 Address Configuration on Router R1

```
R1(config)# interface gigabitethernet 0/0/0
R1(config-if)# ipv6 address 2001:db8:acad:1::1/64
R1(config-if)# no shutdown
R1(config-if)# exit
R1(config)# interface gigabitethernet 0/0/1
R1(config-if)# ipv6 address 2001:db8:acad:2::1/64
```

```
R1(config-if)# no shutdown
R1(config-if)# exit
R1(config)# interface serial 0/1/0
R1(config-if)# ipv6 address 2001:db8:acad:3::1/64
R1(config-if)# no shutdown
```

Go to the online course to take the quiz and exam.

Check Your Understanding - Subnet an IPv6 Network - 12.8.5

Module Practice and Quiz - 12.9

Refer to Packet Tracer Activity for this chapter

Packet Tracer - Implement a Subnetted IPv6 Addressing Scheme - 12.9.1

Your network administrator wants you to assign five /64 IPv6 subnets to the network shown in the topology. Your job is to determine the IPv6 subnets, assign IPv6 addresses to the routers, and set the PCs to automatically receive IPv6 addressing. Your final step is to verify connectivity between IPv6 hosts.

Refer to Lab Activity for this chapter

Lab - Configure IPv6 Addresses on Network Devices - 12.9.2

In this lab, you will complete the following objectives:

■ Part 1: Set Up Topology and Configure Basic Router and Switch Settings

■ Part 2: Configure IPv6 Addresses Manually

■ Part 3: Verify End-to-End Connectivity

What did I learn in this module? - 12.9.3

IPv4 Issues

IPv4 has a theoretical maximum of 4.3 billion addresses. Private addresses in combination with NAT have helped to slow the depletion of IPv4 address space. With an increasing internet population, a limited IPv4 address space, issues with NAT and the IoT, the time has come to begin the transition to IPv6. Both IPv4 and IPv6 will coexist in the near future and the transition will take several years. The IETF has created various protocols and tools to help network administrators migrate their networks to IPv6. The migration techniques can be divided into three categories: dual stack, tunneling, and translation.

IPv6 Address Representation

IPv6 addresses are 128 bits in length and written as a string of hexadecimal values. Every 4 bits is represented by a single hexadecimal digit; for a total of 32 hexadecimal values. The preferred format for writing an IPv6 address is x:x:x:x:x:x:x:x, with each "x" consisting of four hexadecimal values. For example: 2001:0db8:0000:1111:0000:0000:0000:0200. Two rules that help to reduce the number of digits needed to represent an IPv6 address. The first rule to help reduce the notation of IPv6 addresses is to omit any leading 0s (zeros) in any hextet. For example: 2001:db8:0:1111:0:0:0:200. The second rule to help reduce the notation of IPv6 addresses is that a double colon (::) can replace any single, contiguous string of one or more 16-bit hextets consisting of all zeros. For example: 2001:db8:0:1111::200.

IPv6 Address Types

There are three types of IPv6 addresses: unicast, multicast, and anycast. IPv6 does not use the dotted-decimal subnet mask notation. Like IPv4, the prefix length is represented in slash notation and is used to indicate the network portion of an IPv6 address. An IPv6 unicast address uniquely identifies an interface on an IPv6-enabled device. IPv6 addresses typically have two unicast addresses: GUA and LLA. IPv6 unique local addresses have the following uses: they are used for local addressing within a site or between a limited number of sites, they can be used for devices that will never need to access another network, and they are not globally routed or translated to a global IPv6 address. IPv6 global unicast addresses (GUAs) are globally unique and routable on the IPv6 internet. These addresses are equivalent to public IPv4 addresses. A GUA has three parts: a global routing prefix, a subnet ID, and an interface ID. An IPv6 link-local address (LLA) enables a device to communicate with other IPv6-enabled devices on the same link and only on that link (subnet). Devices can obtain an LLA either statically or dynamically.

GUA and LLA Static Configuration

The Cisco IOS command to configure an IPv4 address on an interface is **ip address** *ip-address subnet-mask*. In contrast, the command to configure an IPv6 GUA on an interface is **ipv6 address** *ipv6-address/prefix-length*. Just as with IPv4, configuring static addresses on clients does not scale to larger environments. For this reason, most network administrators in an IPv6 network will enable dynamic assignment of IPv6 addresses. Configuring the LLA manually lets you create an address that is recognizable and easier to remember. Typically, it is only necessary to create recognizable LLAs on routers. LLAs can be configured manually using the **ipv6 address** *ipv6-link-local-address* **link-local** command.

Dynamic Addressing for IPv6 GUAs

A device obtains a GUA dynamically through ICMPv6 messages. IPv6 routers periodically send out ICMPv6 RA messages, every 200 seconds, to all IPv6-enabled devices on the network. An RA message will also be sent in response to a host sending an ICMPv6 RS message, which is a request for an RA message. The ICMPv6 RA message includes: network prefix and prefix length, default gateway address, and the DNS addresses and domain name. RA messages have three methods: SLAAC, SLAAC with a stateless DHCPv6 server, and stateful DHCPv6 (no SLAAC). With SLAAC, the client device uses the information in the RA message to create its own GUA because the message contains the prefix and the interface ID. With SLAAC with stateless DHCPv6 the RA message suggests devices use SLAAC to create their own IPv6 GUA, use the router LLA as the default gateway address, and use a stateless DHCPv6 server to obtain other necessary information. With stateful DHCPv6 the RA suggests that devices use the router LLA as the default gateway address, and the stateful DHCPv6 server to obtain a GUA, a DNS server address, domain name and all other necessary information. The interface ID can be created using the EUI-64 process or a randomly generated 64-bit number. The EUIs process uses the 48-bit Ethernet MAC address of the client and inserts another 16 bits in the middle of MAC address to create a 64-bit interface ID. Depending upon the operating system, a device may use a randomly generated interface ID.

Dynamic Addressing for IPv6 LLAs

All IPv6 devices must have an IPv6 LLA. An LLA can be configured manually or created dynamically. Operating systems, such as Windows, will typically use the same method for both a SLAAC-created GUA and a dynamically assigned LLA. Cisco routers automatically create an IPv6 LLA whenever a GUA is assigned to the interface. By default, Cisco IOS routers use EUI-64 to generate the Interface ID for all LLAs on IPv6 interfaces. For serial interfaces, the router will use the MAC address of an Ethernet interface. To make it easier to recognize and remember these addresses on routers, it is common to statically configure IPv6 LLAs on routers. To verify IPv6 address configuration use the following three commands: **show ipv6 interface brief**, **show ipv6 route**, and **ping**.

IPv6 Multicast Addresses

There are two types of IPv6 multicast addresses: well-known multicast addresses and solicited node multicast addresses. Assigned multicast addresses are reserved multicast addresses for predefined groups of devices. Well-known multicast addresses are assigned. Two commonIPv6 assigned multicast groups are: ff02::1 All-nodes multicast group and ff02::2 All-routers multicast group. A solicited-node multicast address is similar to the all-nodes multicast address. The advantage of a solicited-node multicast address is that it is mapped to a special Ethernet multicast address.

Subnet an IPv6 Network

IPv6 was designed with subnetting in mind. A separate subnet ID field in the IPv6 GUA is used to create subnets. The subnet ID field is the area between the Global Routing Prefix and the interface ID. The benefit of a 128-bit address is that it can support more than enough subnets and hosts per subnet for each network. Address conservation is not an issue. For example, if the global routing prefix is a /48, and using a typical 64 bits for the interface ID, this will create a 16-bit subnet ID:

- 16-bit subnet ID - Creates up to 65,536 subnets.

- 64-bit interface ID - Supports up to 18 quintillion host IPv6 addresses per subnet (i.e., 18,000,000,000,000,000,000).

With over 65,536 subnets to choose from, the task of the network administrator becomes one of designing a logical scheme to address the network. Address conservation is not a concern when using IPv6. Similar to configuring IPv4, each router interface can be configured to be on a different IPv6 subnet.

Go to the online course to take the quiz and exam.

Chapter Quiz - IPv6 Addressing

Your Chapter Notes

CHAPTER 13

ICMP

Introduction - 13.0

Why should I take this module? - 13.0.1

Welcome to ICMP!

Imagine that you have an intricate model train set. Your tracks and trains are all connected and powered up and ready to go. You throw the switch. The train goes halfway around the track and stops. You know right away that the problem is most likely located where the train has stopped, so you look there first. It is not as easy to visualize this with a network. Fortunately, there are tools to help you locate problem areas in your network, AND they work with both IPv4 and IPv6 networks! You will be happy to know that this module has a couple Packet Tracer activities to help you practice using these tools, so let's get testing!

What will I learn in this module? - 13.0.2

Module Title: ICMP

Module Objective: Use various tools to test network connectivity.

Topic Title	Topic Objective
ICMP Messages	Explain how ICMP is used to test network connectivity.
Ping and Traceroute Testing	Use ping and traceroute utilities to test network connectivity.

ICMP Messages - 13.1

ICMPv4 and ICMPv6 Messages - 13.1.1

In this topic, you will learn about the different types of Internet Control Message Protocols (ICMPs), and the tools that are used to send them.

Although IP is only a best-effort protocol, the TCP/IP suite does provide for error messages and informational messages when communicating with another IP device. These messages are sent using the services of ICMP. The purpose of these messages is to provide feedback about issues related to the processing of IP packets under certain conditions, not to make IP reliable. ICMP messages are not required and are often not allowed within a network for security reasons.

ICMP is available for both IPv4 and IPv6. ICMPv4 is the messaging protocol for IPv4. ICMPv6 provides these same services for IPv6 but includes additional functionality. In this course, the term ICMP will be used when referring to both ICMPv4 and ICMPv6.

The types of ICMP messages, and the reasons why they are sent, are extensive. The ICMP messages common to both ICMPv4 and ICMPv6 and discussed in this module include:

- Host reachability

- Destination or Service Unreachable

- Time exceeded

Refer to
Interactive Graphic
in online course

Host Reachability - 13.1.2

An ICMP Echo Message can be used to test the reachability of a host on an IP network. The local host sends an ICMP Echo Request to a host. If the host is available, the destination host responds with an Echo Reply. In the figure, click the Play button to see an animation of the ICMP Echo Request/Echo Reply. This use of the ICMP Echo messages is the basis of the **ping** utility.

Destination or Service Unreachable - 13.1.3

When a host or gateway receives a packet that it cannot deliver, it can use an ICMP Destination Unreachable message to notify the source that the destination or service is unreachable. The message will include a code that indicates why the packet could not be delivered.

Some of the Destination Unreachable codes for ICMPv4 are as follows:

- 0 - Net unreachable

- 1 - Host unreachable

- 2 - Protocol unreachable

- 3 - Port unreachable

Some of the Destination Unreachable codes for ICMPv6 are as follows:

- 0 - No route to destination

- 1 - Communication with the destination is administratively prohibited (e.g., firewall)

- 2 - Beyond scope of the source address

- 3 - Address unreachable

- 4 - Port unreachable

Note: ICMPv6 has similar but slightly different codes for Destination Unreachable messages.

Time Exceeded - 13.1.4

An ICMPv4 Time Exceeded message is used by a router to indicate that a packet cannot be forwarded because the Time to Live (TTL) field of the packet was decremented to 0. If a router receives a packet and decrements the TTL field in the IPv4 packet to zero, it discards the packet and sends a Time Exceeded message to the source host.

ICMPv6 also sends a Time Exceeded message if the router cannot forward an IPv6 packet because the packet has expired. Instead of the IPv4 TTL field, ICMPv6 uses the IPv6 Hop Limit field to determine if the packet has expired.

Note: Time Exceeded messages are used by the **traceroute** tool.

Refer to
Interactive Graphic
in online course

Refer to
Online Course
for Illustration

ICMPv6 Messages - 13.1.5

The informational and error messages found in ICMPv6 are very similar to the control and error messages implemented by ICMPv4. However, ICMPv6 has new features and improved functionality not found in ICMPv4. ICMPv6 messages are encapsulated in IPv6.

ICMPv6 includes four new protocols as part of the Neighbor Discovery Protocol (ND or NDP).

Messaging between an IPv6 router and an IPv6 device, including dynamic address allocation are as follows:

- Router Solicitation (RS) message
- Router Advertisement (RA) message

Messaging between IPv6 devices, including duplicate address detection and address resolution are as follows:

- Neighbor Solicitation (NS) message
- Neighbor Advertisement (NA) message

Note: ICMPv6 ND also includes the redirect message, which has a similar function to the redirect message used in ICMPv4.

Click each for an illustration and explanation of ICMPv6 messages.

RA Message

RA messages are sent by IPv6-enabled routers every 200 seconds to provide addressing information to IPv6-enabled hosts. The RA message can include addressing information for the host such as the prefix, prefix length, DNS address, and domain name. A host using Stateless Address Autoconfiguration (SLAAC) will set its default gateway to the link-local address of the router that sent the RA.

RS Message

An IPv6-enabled router will also send out an RA message in response to an RS message. In the figure, PC1 sends a RS message to determine how to receive its IPv6 address information dynamically.

NS Message

When a device is assigned a global IPv6 unicast or link-local unicast address, it may perform duplicate address detection (DAD) to ensure that the IPv6 address is unique. To check the uniqueness of an address, the device will send an NS message with its own IPv6 address as the targeted IPv6 address, as shown in the figure.

If another device on the network has this address, it will respond with an NA message. This NA message will notify the sending device that the address is in use. If a corresponding NA message is not returned within a certain amount of time, the unicast address is unique and acceptable for use.

Note: DAD is not required, but RFC 4861 recommends that DAD is performed on unicast addresses.

NA Message

Address resolution is used when a device on the LAN knows the IPv6 unicast address of a destination but does not know its Ethernet MAC address. To determine the MAC address for the destination, the device will send an NS message to the solicited node address. The message will include the known (targeted) IPv6 address. The device that has the targeted IPv6 address will respond with an NA message containing its Ethernet MAC address.

In the figure, R1 sends a NS message to 2001:db8:acad:1::10 asking for its MAC address.

Go to the online course to take the quiz and exam.

Check Your Understanding - ICMP Messages - 13.1.6

Ping and Traceroute Tests - 13.2

Ping - Test Connectivity - 13.2.1

In the previous topic, you were introduced to the **ping** and traceroute (**tracert**) tools. In this topic, you will learn about the situations in which each tool is used, and how to use them. Ping is an IPv4 and IPv6 testing utility that uses ICMP echo request and echo reply messages to test connectivity between hosts.

To test connectivity to another host on a network, an echo request is sent to the host address using the **ping** command. If the host at the specified address receives the echo request, it responds with an echo reply. As each echo reply is received, **ping** provides feedback on the time between when the request was sent and when the reply was received. This can be a measure of network performance.

Ping has a timeout value for the reply. If a reply is not received within the timeout, ping provides a message indicating that a response was not received. This may indicate that there is a problem, but could also indicate that security features blocking ping messages have been enabled on the network. It is common for the first ping to timeout if address resolution (ARP or ND) needs to be performed before sending the ICMP Echo Request.

After all the requests are sent, the **ping** utility provides a summary that includes the success rate and average round-trip time to the destination.

Type of connectivity tests performed with **ping** include the following:

- Pinging the local loopback
- Pinging the default gateway
- Pinging the remote host

Refer to
Online Course
for Illustration

Ping the Loopback - 13.2.2

Ping can be used to test the internal configuration of IPv4 or IPv6 on the local host. To perform this test, **ping** the local loopback address of 127.0.0.1 for IPv4 (::1 for IPv6).

A response from 127.0.0.1 for IPv4, or ::1 for IPv6, indicates that IP is properly installed on the host. This response comes from the network layer. This response is not, however, an indication that the addresses, masks, or gateways are properly configured. Nor does it indicate anything about the status of the lower layer of the network stack. This simply tests IP down through the network layer of IP. An error message indicates that TCP/IP is not operational on the host.

Refer to
Online Course
for Illustration

Ping the Default Gateway - 13.2.3

You can also use **ping** to test the ability of a host to communicate on the local network. This is generally done by pinging the IP address of the default gateway of the host. A successful **ping** to the default gateway indicates that the host and the router interface serving as the default gateway are both operational on the local network.

For this test, the default gateway address is most often used because the router is normally always operational. If the default gateway address does not respond, a **ping** can be sent to the IP address of another host on the local network that is known to be operational.

If either the default gateway or another host responds, then the local host can successfully communicate over the local network. If the default gateway does not respond but another host does, this could indicate a problem with the router interface serving as the default gateway.

One possibility is that the wrong default gateway address has been configured on the host. Another possibility is that the router interface may be fully operational but have security applied to it that prevents it from processing or responding to ping requests.

Refer to
Interactive Graphic
in online course

Ping a Remote Host - 13.2.4

Ping can also be used to test the ability of a local host to communicate across an internetwork. The local host can ping an operational IPv4 host of a remote network, as shown in the figure. The router uses its IP routing table to forward the packets.

If this ping is successful, the operation of a large piece of the internetwork can be verified. A successful **ping** across the internetwork confirms communication on the local network, the operation of the router serving as the default gateway, and the operation of all other routers that might be in the path between the local network and the network of the remote host.

Additionally, the functionality of the remote host can be verified. If the remote host could not communicate outside of its local network, it would not have responded.

Note: Many network administrators limit or prohibit the entry of ICMP messages into the corporate network; therefore, the lack of a **ping** response could be due to security restrictions.

Refer to
Interactive Graphic
in online course

Traceroute - Test the Path - 13.2.5

Ping is used to test connectivity between two hosts but does not provide information about the details of devices between the hosts. Traceroute (**tracert**) is a utility that generates a list of hops that were successfully reached along the path. This list can provide important verification and troubleshooting information. If the data reaches the destination, then the trace lists the interface of every router in the path between the hosts. If the data fails at some hop along the way, the address of the last router that responded to the trace can provide an indication of where the problem or security restrictions are found.

Round Trip Time (RTT)

Using traceroute provides round-trip time for each hop along the path and indicates if a hop fails to respond. The round-trip time is the time a packet takes to reach the remote host and for the response from the host to return. An asterisk (*) is used to indicate a lost or unreplied packet.

This information can be used to locate a problematic router in the path or may indicate that the router is configured not to reply. If the display shows high response times or data losses from a particular hop, this is an indication that the resources of the router or its connections may be stressed.

IPv4 TTL and IPv6 Hop Limit

Traceroute makes use of a function of the TTL field in IPv4 and the Hop Limit field in IPv6 in the Layer 3 headers, along with the ICMP Time Exceeded message.

Play the animation in the figure to see how traceroute takes advantage of TTL.

The first sequence of messages sent from traceroute will have a TTL field value of 1. This causes the TTL to time out the IPv4 packet at the first router. This router then responds with an ICMPv4 Time Exceeded message. Traceroute now has the address of the first hop.

Traceroute then progressively increments the TTL field (2, 3, 4...) for each sequence of messages. This provides the trace with the address of each hop as the packets time out further down the path. The TTL field continues to be increased until the destination is reached, or it is incremented to a predefined maximum.

After the final destination is reached, the host responds with either an ICMP Port Unreachable message or an ICMP Echo Reply message instead of the ICMP Time Exceeded message.

Refer to **Packet Tracer Activity** for this chapter

Packet Tracer - Verify IPv4 and IPv6 Addressing - 13.2.6

IPv4 and IPv6 can coexist on the same network. From the command prompt of a PC, there are some differences in the way commands are issued and in the way output is displayed.

Refer to **Packet Tracer Activity** for this chapter

Packet Tracer - Use Ping and Traceroute to Test Network Connectivity - 13.2.7

There are connectivity issues in this activity. In addition to gathering and documenting information about the network, you will locate the problems and implement acceptable solutions to restore connectivity.

Module Practice and Quiz - 13.3

Refer to **Packet Tracer Activity** for this chapter

Packet Tracer - Use ICMP to Test and Correct Network Connectivity - 13.3.1

In this lab you will use ICMP to test network connectivity and locate network problems. You will also correct simple configuration issues and restore connectivity to the network.

Use ICMP to locate connectivity issues.

Configure network devices to correct connectivity issues.

Refer to **Lab Activity** for this chapter

Lab - Use Ping and Traceroute to Test Network Connectivity - 13.3.2

In this lab, you will complete the following objectives:

- Part 1: Build and Configure the Network
- Part 2: Use Ping Command for Basic Network Testing
- Part 3: Use Tracert and Traceroute Commands for Basic Network Testing
- Part 4: Troubleshoot the Topology

What did I learn in this module? - 13.3.3

ICMP Messages

The TCP/IP suite provides for error messages and informational messages when communicating with another IP device. These messages are sent using ICMP. The purpose of these messages is to provide feedback about issues related to the processing of IP packets under certain conditions. The ICMP messages common to both ICMPv4 and ICMPv6 are: Host reachability, Destination or Service Unreachable, and Time exceeded. An ICMP Echo Message tests the reachability of a host on an IP network. The local host sends an ICMP Echo Request to a host. If the host is available, the destination host responds with an Echo Reply. This is the basis of the **ping** utility. When a host or gateway receives a packet that it cannot deliver, it can use an ICMP Destination Unreachable message to notify the source. The message will include a code that indicates why the packet could not be delivered. An ICMPv4 Time Exceeded message is used by a router to indicate that a packet cannot be forwarded because the Time to Live (TTL) field of the packet was decremented to zero. If a router receives a packet and decrements the TTL field to zero, it discards the packet and sends a Time Exceeded message to the source host. ICMPv6 also sends a Time Exceeded in this situation. ICMPv6 uses the IPv6 hop limit field to determine if the packet has expired. Time Exceeded messages are used by the **traceroute** tool. The messages between an IPv6 router and an IPv6 device including dynamic address allocation include RS and RA. The messages between IPv6 devices include the redirect (similar to IPv4), NS and NA.

Ping and Traceroute Testing

Ping (used by IPv4 and IPv6) uses ICMP echo request and echo reply messages to test connectivity between hosts. To test connectivity to another host on a network, an echo request is sent to the host address using the ping command. If the host at the specified address receives the echo request, it responds with an echo reply. As each echo reply is received, ping provides feedback on the time between when the request was sent and when the reply was received. After all the requests are sent, the ping utility provides a summary that includes the success rate and average round-trip time to the destination. Ping can be used to test the internal configuration of IPv4 or IPv6 on the local host. Ping the local loopback address of 127.0.0.1 for IPv4 (::1 for IPv6). Use **ping** to test the ability of a host to communicate on the local network, by pinging the IP address of the default gateway of the host. A successful ping to the default gateway indicates that the host and the router interface serving as the default gateway are both operational on the local network. Ping can also be used to test the ability of a local host to communicate across an internetwork. The local host can **ping** an operational IPv4 host of a remote network. Traceroute (tracert) generates a list of hops that were successfully reached along the path. This list provides verification and troubleshooting information. If the data reaches the destination, then the trace lists the interface of every router in the path between the hosts. If the data fails at some hop along the way, the address of the last router that responded to the trace can provide an indication of where the problem or security restrictions are found. The round-trip time is the time a packet takes to reach the remote host and for the response from the host to return. Traceroute makes use of a function of the TTL field in IPv4 and the Hop Limit field in IPv6 in the Layer 3 headers, along with the ICMP time exceeded message.

Go to the online
course to take the
quiz and exam.

Chapter Quiz - ICMP

Your Chapter Notes

CHAPTER 14

Transport Layer

Introduction - 14.0

Why should I take this module? - 14.0.1

Welcome to Transport Layer!

The transport layer is where, as the name implies, data is transported from one host to another. This is where your network really gets moving! The transport layer uses two protocols: TCP and UDP. Think of TCP as getting a registered letter in the mail. You have to sign for it before the mail carrier will let you have it. This slows down the process a bit, but the sender knows for certain that you received the letter and when you received it. UDP is more like a regular, stamped letter. It arrives in your mailbox and, if it does, it is probably intended for you, but it might actually be for someone else who does not live there. Also, it may not arrive in your mailbox at all. The sender cannot be sure you received it. Nevertheless, there are times when UDP, like a stamped letter, is the protocol that is needed. This topic dives into how TCP and UDP work in the transport layer. Later in this module there are several videos to help you understand these processes.

What will I learn to do in this module? - 14.0.2

Module Title: Transport Layer

Module Objective: Compare the operations of transport layer protocols in supporting end-to-end communication.

Topic Title	Topic Objective
Transportation of Data	Explain the purpose of the transport layer in managing the transportation of data in end-to-end communication.
TCP Overview	Explain characteristics of TCP.
UDP Overview	Explain characteristics of UDP.
Port Numbers	Explain how TCP and UDP use port numbers.
TCP Communication Process	Explain how TCP session establishment and termination processes facilitate reliable communication.
Reliability and Flow Control	Explain how TCP protocol data units are transmitted and acknowledged to guarantee delivery.
UDP Communication	Compare the operations of transport layer protocols in supporting end-to-end communication.

Transportation of Data - 14.1

Refer to
Online Course
for Illustration

Role of the Transport Layer - 14.1.1

Application layer programs generate data that must be exchanged between source and destination hosts. The transport layer is responsible for logical communications between applications running on different hosts. This may include services such as establishing a temporary session between two hosts and the reliable transmission of information for an application.

As shown in the figure, the transport layer is the link between the application layer and the lower layers that are responsible for network transmission.

The transport layer has no knowledge of the destination host type, the type of media over which the data must travel, the path taken by the data, the congestion on a link, or the size of the network.

The transport layer includes two protocols:

- Transmission Control Protocol (TCP)

- User Datagram Protocol (UDP)

Refer to
Interactive Graphic
in online course

Transport Layer Responsibilities - 14.1.2

The transport layer has many responsibilities.

Click each button for more information.

Refer to
Online Course
for Illustration

Tracking Individual Conversations

At the transport layer, each set of data flowing between a source application and a destination application is known as a conversation and is tracked separately. It is the responsibility of the transport layer to maintain and track these multiple conversations.

As illustrated in the figure, a host may have multiple applications that are communicating across the network simultaneously.

Most networks have a limitation on the amount of data that can be included in a single packet. Therefore, data must be divided into manageable pieces.

Segmenting Data and Reassembling Segments

It is the transport layer responsibility to divide the application data into appropriately sized blocks. Depending on the transport layer protocol used, the transport layer blocks are called either segments or datagrams. The figure illustrates the transport layer using different blocks for each conversation.

The transport layer divides the data into smaller blocks (i.e., segments or datagrams) that are easier to manage and transport.

Add Header Information

The transport layer protocol also adds header information containing binary data organized into several fields to each block of data. It is the values in these fields that enable various transport layer protocols to perform different functions in managing data communication.

For instance, the header information is used by the receiving host to reassemble the blocks of data into a complete data stream for the receiving application layer program.

The transport layer ensures that even with multiple application running on a device, all applications receive the correct data.

Identifying the Applications

The transport layer must be able to separate and manage multiple communications with different transport requirement needs. To pass data streams to the proper applications, the transport layer identifies the target application using an identifier called a port number. As illustrated in the figure, each software process that needs to access the network is assigned a port number unique to that host.

Conversation Multiplexing

Sending some types of data (e.g., a streaming video) across a network, as one complete communication stream, can consume all the available bandwidth. This would prevent other communication conversations from occurring at the same time. It would also make error recovery and retransmission of damaged data difficult.

As shown in the figure, the transport layer uses segmentation and multiplexing to enable different communication conversations to be interleaved on the same network.

Error checking can be performed on the data in the segment, to determine if the segment was altered during transmission.

Refer to
Online Course
for Illustration

Transport Layer Protocols - 14.1.3

IP is concerned only with the structure, addressing, and routing of packets. IP does not specify how the delivery or transportation of the packets takes place.

Transport layer protocols specify how to transfer messages between hosts, and are responsible for managing reliability requirements of a conversation. The transport layer includes the TCP and UDP protocols.

Different applications have different transport reliability requirements. Therefore, TCP/IP provides two transport layer protocols, as shown in the figure.

Refer to
Interactive Graphic
in online course

Transmission Control Protocol (TCP) - 14.1.4

IP is concerned only with the structure, addressing, and routing of packets, from original sender to final destination. IP is not responsible for guaranteeing delivery or determining whether a connection between the sender and receiver needs to be established.

TCP is considered a reliable, full-featured transport layer protocol, which ensures that all of the data arrives at the destination. TCP includes fields which ensure the delivery of the application data. These fields require additional processing by the sending and receiving hosts.

Note: TCP divides data into segments.

TCP transport is analogous to sending packages that are tracked from source to destination. If a shipping order is broken up into several packages, a customer can check online to see the order of the delivery.

TCP provides reliability and flow control using these basic operations:

- Number and track data segments transmitted to a specific host from a specific application

- Acknowledge received data

- Retransmit any unacknowledged data after a certain amount of time

- Sequence data that might arrive in wrong order

- Send data at an efficient rate that is acceptable by the receiver

In order to maintain the state of a conversation and track the information, TCP must first establish a connection between the sender and the receiver. This is why TCP is known as a connection-oriented protocol.

Click Play in the figure to see how TCP segments and acknowledgments are transmitted between sender and receiver.

Refer to
Interactive Graphic
in online course

User Datagram Protocol (UDP) - 14.1.5

UDP is a simpler transport layer protocol than TCP. It does not provide reliability and flow control, which means it requires fewer header fields. Because the sender and the receiver UDP processes do not have to manage reliability and flow control, this means UDP datagrams can be processed faster than TCP segments. UDP provides the basic functions for delivering datagrams between the appropriate applications, with very little overhead and data checking.

Note: UDP divides data into datagrams that are also referred to as segments.

UDP is a connectionless protocol. Because UDP does not provide reliability or flow control, it does not require an established connection. Because UDP does not track information sent or received between the client and server, UDP is also known as a stateless protocol.

UDP is also known as a best-effort delivery protocol because there is no acknowledgment that the data is received at the destination. With UDP, there are no transport layer processes that inform the sender of a successful delivery.

UDP is like placing a regular, nonregistered, letter in the mail. The sender of the letter is not aware of the availability of the receiver to receive the letter. Nor is the post office responsible for tracking the letter or informing the sender if the letter does not arrive at the final destination.

Click Play in the figure to see an animation of UDP datagrams being transmitted from sender to receiver.

Refer to
Online Course
for Illustration

The Right Transport Layer Protocol for the Right Application - 14.1.6

Some applications can tolerate some data loss during transmission over the network, but delays in transmission are unacceptable. For these applications, UDP is the better choice because it requires less network overhead. UDP is preferable for applications such as Voice over IP (VoIP). Acknowledgments and retransmission would slow down delivery and make the voice conversation unacceptable.

UDP is also used by request-and-reply applications where the data is minimal, and retransmission can be done quickly. For example, domain name service (DNS) uses UDP for this type of transaction. The client requests IPv4 and IPv6 addresses for a known domain name from a DNS server. If the client does not receive a response in a predetermined amount of time, it simply sends the request again.

For example, if one or two segments of a live video stream fail to arrive, it creates a momentary disruption in the stream. This may appear as distortion in the image or sound, but may not be noticeable to the user. If the destination device had to account for lost data, the stream could be delayed while waiting for retransmissions, therefore causing the image or sound to be greatly degraded. In this case, it is better to render the best media possible with the segments received, and forego reliability.

For other applications it is important that all the data arrives and that it can be processed in its proper sequence. For these types of applications, TCP is used as the transport protocol. For example, applications such as databases, web browsers, and email clients, require that all data that is sent arrives at the destination in its original condition. Any missing data could corrupt a communication, making it either incomplete or unreadable. For example, it is important when accessing banking information over the web to make sure all the information is sent and received correctly.

Application developers must choose which transport protocol type is appropriate based on the requirements of the applications. Video may be sent over TCP or UDP. Applications that stream stored audio and video typically use TCP. The application uses TCP to perform buffering, bandwidth probing, and congestion control, in order to better control the user experience.

Real-time video and voice usually use UDP, but may also use TCP, or both UDP and TCP. A video conferencing application may use UDP by default, but because many firewalls block UDP, the application can also be sent over TCP.

Applications that stream stored audio and video use TCP. For example, if your network suddenly cannot support the bandwidth needed to watch an on-demand movie, the application pauses the playback. During the pause, you might see a "buffering..." message while TCP works to re-establish the stream. When all the segments are in order and a minimum level of bandwidth is restored, your TCP session resumes, and the movie resumes playing.

The figure summarizes differences between UDP and TCP.

Go to the online course to take the quiz and exam.

Check Your Understanding - Transportation of Data - 14.1.7

TCP Overview - 14.2

TCP Features - 14.2.1

In the previous topic, you learned that TCP and UDP are the two transport layer protocols. This topic gives more details about what TCP does and when it is a good idea to use it instead of UDP.

To understand the differences between TCP and UDP, it is important to understand how each protocol implements specific reliability features and how each protocol tracks conversations.

In addition to supporting the basic functions of data segmentation and reassembly, TCP also provides the following services:

- **Establishes a Session** - TCP is a connection-oriented protocol that negotiates and establishes a permanent connection (or session) between source and destination devices prior to forwarding any traffic. Through session establishment, the devices negotiate the amount of traffic that can be forwarded at a given time, and the communication data between the two can be closely managed.

- **Ensures Reliable Delivery** - For many reasons, it is possible for a segment to become corrupted or lost completely, as it is transmitted over the network. TCP ensures that each segment that is sent by the source arrives at the destination.

- **Provides Same-Order Delivery** - Because networks may provide multiple routes that can have different transmission rates, data can arrive in the wrong order. By numbering and sequencing the segments, TCP ensures segments are reassembled into the proper order.

- **Supports Flow Control** - Network hosts have limited resources (i.e., memory and processing power). When TCP is aware that these resources are overtaxed, it can request that the sending application reduce the rate of data flow. This is done by TCP regulating the amount of data the source transmits. Flow control can prevent the need for retransmission of the data when the resources of the receiving host are overwhelmed.

For more information on TCP, search the internet for the RFC 793.

TCP Header - 14.2.2

Refer to Online Course for Illustration

TCP is a stateful protocol which means it keeps track of the state of the communication session. To track the state of a session, TCP records which information it has sent and which information has been acknowledged. The stateful session begins with the session establishment and ends with the session termination.

A TCP segment adds 20 bytes (i.e., 160 bits) of overhead when encapsulating the application layer data. The figure shows the fields in a TCP header.

TCP Header Fields - 14.2.3

The table identifies and describes the ten fields in a TCP header.

TCP Header Field	Description
Source Port	A 16-bit field used to identify the source application by port number.
Destination Port	A 16-bit field used to identify the destination application by port number.
Sequence Number	A 32-bit field used for data reassembly purposes.
Acknowledgment Number	A 32-bit field used to indicate that data has been received and the next byte expected from the source.
Header Length	A 4-bit field known as Đdata offsetĐ that indicates the length of the TCP segment header.
Reserved	A 6-bit field that is reserved for future use.
Control bits	A 6-bit field used that includes bit codes, or flags, which indicate the purpose and function of the TCP segment.
Window size	A 16-bit field used to indicate the number of bytes that can be accepted at one time.
Checksum	A 16-bit field used for error checking of the segment header and data.
Urgent	A 16-bit field used to indicate if the contained data is urgent.

Refer to **Online Course** for Illustration

Applications that use TCP - 14.2.4

TCP is a good example of how the different layers of the TCP/IP protocol suite have specific roles. TCP handles all tasks associated with dividing the data stream into segments, providing reliability, controlling data flow, and reordering segments. TCP frees the application from having to manage any of these tasks. Applications, like those shown in the figure, can simply send the data stream to the transport layer and use the services of TCP.

Go to the online course to take the quiz and exam.

Check Your Understanding - TCP Overview - 14.2.5

UDP Overview - 14.3

UDP Features - 14.3.1

This topic will cover UDP, what it does, and when it is a good idea to use it instead of TCP. UDP is a best-effort transport protocol. UDP is a lightweight transport protocol that offers the same data segmentation and reassembly as TCP, but without TCP reliability and flow control.

UDP is such a simple protocol that it is usually described in terms of what it does not do compared to TCP.

UDP features include the following:

- Data is reconstructed in the order that it is received.

- Any segments that are lost are not resent.

- There is no session establishment.

- The sending is not informed about resource availability.

For more information on UDP, search the internet for the RFC.

Refer to
Online Course
for Illustration

UDP Header - 14.3.2

UDP is a stateless protocol, meaning neither the client, nor the server, tracks the state of the communication session. If reliability is required when using UDP as the transport protocol, it must be handled by the application.

One of the most important requirements for delivering live video and voice over the network is that the data continues to flow quickly. Live video and voice applications can tolerate some data loss with minimal or no noticeable effect, and are perfectly suited to UDP.

The blocks of communication in UDP are called datagrams, or segments. These datagrams are sent as best effort by the transport layer protocol.

The UDP header is far simpler than the TCP header because it only has four fields and requires 8 bytes (i.e., 64 bits). The figure shows the fields in a TCP header.

UDP Header Fields - 14.3.3

The table identifies and describes the four fields in a UDP header.

UDP Header Field	Description
Source Port	A 16-bit field used to identify the source application by port number.
Destination Port	A 16-bit field used to identify the destination application by port number.
Length	A 16-bit field that indicates the length of the UDP datagram header.
Checksum	A 16-bit field used for error checking of the datagram header and data.

Refer to
Online Course
for Illustration

Applications that use UDP - 14.3.4

There are three types of applications that are best suited for UDP:

- **Live video and multimedia applications** - These applications can tolerate some data loss, but require little or no delay. Examples include VoIP and live streaming video.

- **Simple request and reply applications** - Applications with simple transactions where a host sends a request and may or may not receive a reply. Examples include DNS and DHCP.

- **Applications that handle reliability themselves** - Unidirectional communications where flow control, error detection, acknowledgments, and error recovery is not required, or can be handled by the application. Examples include SNMP and TFTP.

The figure identifies applications that require UDP.

Although DNS and SNMP use UDP by default, both can also use TCP. DNS will use TCP if the DNS request or DNS response is more than 512 bytes, such as when a DNS response includes many name resolutions. Similarly, under some situations the network administrator may want to configure SNMP to use TCP.

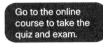

Go to the online course to take the quiz and exam.

Check Your Understanding - UDP Overview - 14.3.5

Port Numbers - 14.4

Refer to
Online Course
for Illustration

Multiple Separate Communications - 14.4.1

As you have learned, there are some situations in which TCP is the right protocol for the job, and other situations in which UDP should be used. No matter what type of data is being transported, both TCP and UDP use port numbers.

The TCP and UDP transport layer protocols use port numbers to manage multiple, simultaneous conversations. As shown in the figure, the TCP and UDP header fields identify a source and destination application port number.

The source port number is associated with the originating application on the local host whereas the destination port number is associated with the destination application on the remote host.

For instance, assume a host is initiating a web page request from a web server. When the host initiates the web page request, the source port number is dynamically generated by the host to uniquely identify the conversation. Each request generated by a host will use a different dynamically created source port number. This process allows multiple conversations to occur simultaneously.

In the request, the destination port number is what identifies the type of service being requested of the destination web server.. For example, when a client specifies port 80 in the destination port, the server that receives the message knows that web services are being requested.

A server can offer more than one service simultaneously such as web services on port 80 while it offers File Transfer Protocol (FTP) connection establishment on port 21.

Refer to
Online Course
for Illustration

Socket Pairs - 14.4.2

The source and destination ports are placed within the segment. The segments are then encapsulated within an IP packet. The IP packet contains the IP address of the source and destination. The combination of the source IP address and source port number, or the destination IP address and destination port number is known as a socket.

In the example in the figure, the PC is simultaneously requesting FTP and web services from the destination server.

In the example, the FTP request generated by the PC includes the Layer 2 MAC addresses and the Layer 3 IP addresses. The request also identifies the source port number 1305 (i.e., dynamically generated by the host) and destination port, identifying the FTP services on port 21. The host also has requested a web page from the server using the same Layer 2 and Layer 3 addresses. However, it is using the source port number 1099 (i.e., dynamically generated by the host) and destination port identifying the web service on port 80.

The socket is used to identify the server and service being requested by the client. A client socket might look like this, with 1099 representing the source port number: 192.168.1.5:1099

The socket on a web server might be 192.168.1.7:80

Together, these two sockets combine to form a *socket pair*: 192.168.1.5:1099, 192.168.1.7:80

Sockets enable multiple processes, running on a client, to distinguish themselves from each other, and multiple connections to a server process to be distinguished from each other.

The source port number acts as a return address for the requesting application. The transport layer keeps track of this port and the application that initiated the request so that when a response is returned, it can be forwarded to the correct application.

Port Number Groups - 14.4.3

The Internet Assigned Numbers Authority (IANA) is the standards organization responsible for assigning various addressing standards, including the 16-bit port numbers. The 16 bits used to identify the source and destination port numbers provides a range of ports from 0 through 65535.

The IANA has divided the range of numbers into the following three port groups.

Port Group	Number Range	Description
Well-known Ports	0 to 1,023	• These port numbers are reserved for common or popular services and applications such as web browsers, email clients, and remote access clients. • Defined well-known ports for common server applications enables clients to easily identify the associated service required.
Registered Ports	1,024 to 49,151	• These port numbers are assigned by IANA to a requesting entity to use with specific processes or applications. • These processes are primarily individual applications that a user has chosen to install, rather than common applications that would receive a well-known port number. • For example, Cisco has registered port 1812 for its RADIUS server authentication process.
Private and/or Dynamic Ports	49,152 to 65,535	• These ports are also known as *ephemeral ports*. • The client's OS usually assign port numbers dynamically when a connection to a service is initiated. • The dynamic port is then used to identify the client application during communication.

Note: Some client operating systems may use registered port numbers instead of dynamic port numbers for assigning source ports.

The table displays some common well-known port numbers and their associated applications.

Well-Known Port Numbers

Port Number	Protocol	Application
20	TCP	File Transfer Protocol (FTP) - Data
21	TCP	File Transfer Protocol (FTP) - Control
22	TCP	Secure Shell (SSH)
23	TCP	Telnet
25	TCP	Simple Mail Transfer Protocol (SMTP)
53	UDP, TCP	Domain Name Service (DNS)
67	UDP	Dynamic Host Configuration Protocol (DHCP) - Server
68	UDP	Dynamic Host Configuration Protocol - Client
69	UDP	Trivial File Transfer Protocol (TFTP)
80	TCP	Hypertext Transfer Protocol (HTTP)
110	TCP	Post Office Protocol version 3 (POP3)
143	TCP	Internet Message Access Protocol (IMAP)
161	UDP	Simple Network Management Protocol (SNMP)
443	TCP	Hypertext Transfer Protocol Secure (HTTPS)

Some applications may use both TCP and UDP. For example, DNS uses UDP when clients send requests to a DNS server. However, communication between two DNS servers always uses TCP.

Search the IANA website for port registry to view the full list of port numbers and associated applications.

The netstat Command - 14.4.4

Unexplained TCP connections can pose a major security threat. They can indicate that something or someone is connected to the local host. Sometimes it is necessary to know which active TCP connections are open and running on a networked host. Netstat is an important network utility that can be used to verify those connections. As shown below, enter the command **netstat** to list the protocols in use, the local address and port numbers, the foreign address and port numbers, and the connection state.

```
C:\> netstat

Active Connections

Proto    Local Address           Foreign Address            State

TCP      192.168.1.124:3126      192.168.0.2:netbios-ssn    ESTABLISHED

TCP      192.168.1.124:3158      207.138.126.152:http       ESTABLISHED

TCP      192.168.1.124:3159      207.138.126.169:http       ESTABLISHED

TCP      192.168.1.124:3160      207.138.126.169:http       ESTABLISHED

TCP      192.168.1.124:3161      sc.msn.com:http            ESTABLISHED

TCP      192.168.1.124:3166      www.cisco.com:http         ESTABLISHED
```

By default, the **netstat** command will attempt to resolve IP addresses to domain names and port numbers to well-known applications. The **-n** option can be used to display IP addresses and port numbers in their numerical form.

Go to the online course to take the quiz and exam.

Check Your Understanding - Port Numbers - 14.4.5

TCP Communication Process - 14.5

Refer to **Interactive Graphic** in online course

Refer to **Online Course** for Illustration

TCP Server Processes - 14.5.1

You already know the fundamentals of TCP. Understanding the role of port numbers will help you to grasp the details of the TCP communication process. In this topic, you will also learn about the TCP three-way handshake and session termination processes.

Each application process running on a server is configured to use a port number. The port number is either automatically assigned or configured manually by a system administrator.

An individual server cannot have two services assigned to the same port number within the same transport layer services. For example, a host running a web server application and a file transfer application cannot have both configured to use the same port, such as TCP port 80.

An active server application assigned to a specific port is considered open, which means that the transport layer accepts, and processes segments addressed to that port. Any incoming client request addressed to the correct socket is accepted, and the data is passed to the server application. There can be many ports open simultaneously on a server, one for each active server application.

Click each button for more information about TCP server processes.

Clients Sending TCP Requests

Client 1 is requesting web services and Client 2 is requesting email service using well-known ports (i.e., web services = port 80, email services = port 25).

Request Destination Ports

Requests dynamically generate a source port number. In this case, Client 1 is using source port 49152 and Client 2 is using source port 51152.

Request Source Ports

When the server responds to the client requests, it reverses the destination and source ports of the initial request.

Response Destination Ports

Notice that the Server response to the web request now has destination port 49152 and the email response now has destination port 51152.

Response Source Ports

The source port in the server response is the original destination port in the initial requests.

Refer to **Interactive Graphic** in online course

Refer to **Online Course** for Illustration

TCP Connection Establishment - 14.5.2

In some cultures, when two persons meet, they often greet each other by shaking hands. Both parties understand the act of shaking hands as a signal for a friendly greeting. Connections on the network are similar. In TCP connections, the host client establishes the connection with the server using the three-way handshake process.

Click each button for more information about each TCP connection establishment step.

Step 1. SYN

The initiating client requests a client-to-server communication session with the server.

Step 2. ACK and SYN

The server acknowledges the client-to-server communication session and requests a server-to-client communication session.

Step 3. ACK

The initiating client acknowledges the server-to-client communication session.

The three-way handshake validates that the destination host is available to communicate. In this example, host A has validated that host B is available.

Refer to **Interactive Graphic** in online course

Refer to **Online Course** for Illustration

Session Termination - 14.5.3

To close a connection, the Finish (FIN) control flag must be set in the segment header. To end each one-way TCP session, a two-way handshake, consisting of a FIN segment and an Acknowledgment (ACK) segment, is used. Therefore, to terminate a single conversation supported by TCP, four exchanges are needed to end both sessions. Either the client or the server can initiate the termination.

In the example, the terms client and server are used as a reference for simplicity, but any two hosts that have an open session can initiate the termination process.

Click each button for more information about the session termination steps.

Step 1. FIN

When the client has no more data to send in the stream, it sends a segment with the FIN flag set.

Step 2. ACK

The server sends an ACK to acknowledge the receipt of the FIN to terminate the session from client to server.

Step 3. FIN

The server sends a FIN to the client to terminate the server-to-client session.

Step 4. ACK

The client responds with an ACK to acknowledge the FIN from the server.

When all segments have been acknowledged, the session is closed.

Refer to
Online Course
for Illustration

TCP Three-way Handshake Analysis - 14.5.4

Hosts maintain state, track each data segment within a session, and exchange information about what data is received using the information in the TCP header. TCP is a full-duplex protocol, where each connection represents two one-way communication sessions. To establish the connection, the hosts perform a three-way handshake. As shown in the figure, control bits in the TCP header indicate the progress and status of the connection.

These are the functions of the three-way handshake:

- It establishes that the destination device is present on the network.

- It verifies that the destination device has an active service and is accepting requests on the destination port number that the initiating client intends to use.

- It informs the destination device that the source client intends to establish a communication session on that port number.

After the communication is completed the sessions are closed, and the connection is terminated. The connection and session mechanisms enable TCP reliability function.

The six bits in the Control Bits field of the TCP segment header are also known as flags. A flag is a bit that is set to either on or off.

The six control bits flags are as follows:

- **URG** - Urgent pointer field significant

- **ACK** - Acknowledgment flag used in connection establishment and session termination

- **PSH** - Push function

- **RST** - Reset the connection when an error or timeout occurs

- **SYN** - Synchronize sequence numbers used in connection establishment

- **FIN** - No more data from sender and used in session termination

Search the internet to learn more about the PSH and URG flags.

Refer to **Video**
in online course

Video - TCP 3-Way Handshake - 14.5.5

Click Play in the figure to see a video demonstration of the TCP 3-Way handshake, using Wireshark.

Go to the online course to take the quiz and exam.

Check Your Understanding - TCP Communication Process - 14.5.6

Reliability and Flow Control - 14.6

Refer to **Online Course** for Illustration

TCP Reliability - Guaranteed and Ordered Delivery - 14.6.1

The reason that TCP is the better protocol for some applications is because, unlike UDP, it resends dropped packets and numbers packets to indicate their proper order before delivery. TCP can also help maintain the flow of packets so that devices do not become overloaded. This topic covers these features of TCP in detail.

There may be times when TCP segments do not arrive at their destination. Other times, the TCP segments might arrive out of order. For the original message to be understood by the recipient, all the data must be received and the data in these segments must be reassembled into the original order. Sequence numbers are assigned in the header of each packet to achieve this goal. The sequence number represents the first data byte of the TCP segment.

During session setup, an initial sequence number (ISN) is set. This ISN represents the starting value of the bytes that are transmitted to the receiving application. As data is transmitted during the session, the sequence number is incremented by the number of bytes that have been transmitted. This data byte tracking enables each segment to be uniquely identified and acknowledged. Missing segments can then be identified.

The ISN does not begin at one but is effectively a random number. This is to prevent certain types of malicious attacks. For simplicity, we will use an ISN of 1 for the examples in this chapter.

Segment sequence numbers indicate how to reassemble and reorder received segments, as shown in the figure.

The receiving TCP process places the data from a segment into a receiving buffer. Segments are then placed in the proper sequence order and passed to the application layer when reassembled. Any segments that arrive with sequence numbers that are out of order are held for later processing. Then, when the segments with the missing bytes arrive, these segments are processed in order.

Refer to **Video** in online course

Video - TCP Reliability - Sequence Numbers and Acknowledgments - 14.6.2

One of the functions of TCP is to ensure that each segment reaches its destination. The TCP services on the destination host acknowledge the data that have been received by the source application.

Click Play in the figure to view a lesson on TCP sequence numbers and acknowledgments.

Refer to **Online Course** for Illustration

TCP Reliability - Data Loss and Retransmission - 14.6.3

No matter how well designed a network is, data loss occasionally occurs. TCP provides methods of managing these segment losses. Among these is a mechanism to retransmit segments for unacknowledged data.

Prior to later enhancements, TCP could only acknowledge the next byte expected. For example, in the figure, using segment numbers for simplicity, host A sends segments 1 through 10 to host B. If all the segments arrive except for segments 3 and 4, host B would reply with acknowledgment specifying that the next segment expected is segment 3. Host A has no idea if any other segments arrived or not. Host A would, therefore, resend segments 3 through 10. If all the resent segments arrived successfully, segments 5 through 10 would be duplicates. This can lead to delays, congestion, and inefficiencies.

Host operating systems today typically employ an optional TCP feature called selective acknowledgment (SACK), negotiated during the three-way handshake. If both hosts support SACK, the receiver can explicitly acknowledge which segments (bytes) were received including any discontinuous segments. The sending host would therefore only need to retransmit the missing data. For example, in the next figure, again using segment numbers for simplicity, host A sends segments 1 through 10 to host B. If all the segments arrive except for segments 3 and 4, host B can acknowledge that it has received segments 1 and 2 (ACK 3), and selectively acknowledge segments 5 through 10 (SACK 5-10). Host A would only need to resend segments 3 and 4.

Note: TCP typically sends ACKs for every other packet, but other factors beyond the scope of this topic may alter this behavior.

TCP uses timers to know how long to wait before resending a segment. In the figure, play the video and click the link to download the PDF file. The video and PDF file examine TCP data loss and retransmission.

Video - TCP Reliability - Data Loss and Retransmission - 14.6.4

Click Play in the figure to view a lesson on TCP retransmission.

TCP Flow Control - Window Size and Acknowledgments - 14.6.5

TCP also provides mechanisms for flow control. Flow control is the amount of data that the destination can receive and process reliably. Flow control helps maintain the reliability of TCP transmission by adjusting the rate of data flow between source and destination for a given session. To accomplish this, the TCP header includes a 16-bit field called the window size.

The figure shows an example of window size and acknowledgments.

The window size determines the number of bytes that can be sent before expecting an acknowledgment. The acknowledgment number is the number of the next expected byte.

The window size is the number of bytes that the destination device of a TCP session can accept and process at one time. In this example, the PC B initial window size for the TCP session is 10,000 bytes. Starting with the first byte, byte number 1, the last byte PC A can send without receiving an acknowledgment is byte 10,000. This is known as the send window of PC A. The window size is included in every TCP segment so the destination can modify the window size at any time depending on buffer availability.

The initial window size is agreed upon when the TCP session is established during the three-way handshake. The source device must limit the number of bytes sent to the destination device based on the window size of the destination. Only after the source device receives an acknowledgment that the bytes have been received, can it continue sending more data for the session. Typically, the destination will not wait for all the bytes for its window size to be received before replying with an acknowledgment. As the bytes are received and processed, the destination will send acknowledgments to inform the source that it can continue to send additional bytes.

For example, it is typical that PC B would not wait until all 10,000 bytes have been received before sending an acknowledgment. This means PC A can adjust its send window as it receives acknowledgments from PC B. As shown in the figure, when PC A receives an acknowledgment with the acknowledgment number 2,921, which is the next expected byte. The PC A send window will increment 2,920 bytes. This changes the send window from 10,000 bytes to 12,920. PC A can now continue to send up to another 10,000 bytes to PC B as long as it does not send more than its new send window at 12,920.

A destination sending acknowledgments as it processes bytes received, and the continual adjustment of the source send window, is known as sliding windows. In the previous example, the send window of PC A increments or slides over another 2,921 bytes from 10,000 to 12,920.

If the availability of the destination's buffer space decreases, it may reduce its window size to inform the source to reduce the number of bytes it should send without receiving an acknowledgment.

Note: Devices today use the sliding windows protocol. The receiver typically sends an acknowledgment after every two segments it receives. The number of segments received before being acknowledged may vary. The advantage of sliding windows is that it allows the sender to continuously transmit segments, as long as the receiver is acknowledging previous segments. The details of sliding windows are beyond the scope of this course.

Refer to **Online Course** for Illustration

TCP Flow Control - Maximum Segment Size (MSS) - 14.6.6

In the figure, the source is transmitting 1,460 bytes of data within each TCP segment. This is typically the Maximum Segment Size (MSS) that the destination device can receive. The MSS is part of the options field in the TCP header that specifies the largest amount of data, in bytes, that a device can receive in a single TCP segment. The MSS size does not include the TCP header. The MSS is typically included during the three-way handshake.

A common MSS is 1,460 bytes when using IPv4. A host determines the value of its MSS field by subtracting the IP and TCP headers from the Ethernet maximum transmission unit (MTU). On an Ethernet interface, the default MTU is 1500 bytes. Subtracting the IPv4 header of 20 bytes and the TCP header of 20 bytes, the default MSS size will be 1460 bytes, as shown in the figure.

Refer to **Online Course** for Illustration

TCP Flow Control - Congestion Avoidance - 14.6.7

When congestion occurs on a network, it results in packets being discarded by the overloaded router. When packets containing TCP segments do not reach their destination, they are left unacknowledged. By determining the rate at which TCP segments are sent but not acknowledged, the source can assume a certain level of network congestion.

Whenever there is congestion, retransmission of lost TCP segments from the source will occur. If the retransmission is not properly controlled, the additional retransmission of the

TCP segments can make the congestion even worse. Not only are new packets with TCP segments introduced into the network, but the feedback effect of the retransmitted TCP segments that were lost will also add to the congestion. To avoid and control congestion, TCP employs several congestion handling mechanisms, timers, and algorithms.

If the source determines that the TCP segments are either not being acknowledged or not acknowledged in a timely manner, then it can reduce the number of bytes it sends before receiving an acknowledgment. As illustrated in the figure, PC A senses there is congestion and therefore, reduces the number of bytes it sends before receiving an acknowledgment from PC B.

Notice that it is the source that is reducing the number of unacknowledged bytes it sends and not the window size determined by the destination.

Note: Explanations of actual congestion handling mechanisms, timers, and algorithms are beyond the scope of this course.

Go to the online course to take the quiz and exam.

Check Your Understanding - Reliability and Flow Control - 14.6.8

UDP Communication - 14.7

Refer to **Online Course** for Illustration

UDP Low Overhead versus Reliability - 14.7.1

As explained before, UPD is perfect for communications that need to be fast, like VoIP. This topic explains in detail why UDP is perfect for some types of transmissions. As shown in the figure, UDP does not establish a connection. UDP provides low overhead data transport because it has a small datagram header and no network management traffic.

Refer to **Online Course** for Illustration

UDP Datagram Reassembly - 14.7.2

Like segments with TCP, when UDP datagrams are sent to a destination, they often take different paths and arrive in the wrong order. UDP does not track sequence numbers the way TCP does. UDP has no way to reorder the datagrams into their transmission order, as shown in the figure.

Therefore, UDP simply reassembles the data in the order that it was received and forwards it to the application. If the data sequence is important to the application, the application must identify the proper sequence and determine how the data should be processed.

Refer to **Online Course** for Illustration

UDP Server Processes and Requests - 14.7.3

Like TCP-based applications, UDP-based server applications are assigned well-known or registered port numbers, as shown in the figure. When these applications or processes are running on a server, they accept the data matched with the assigned port number. When UDP receives a datagram destined for one of these ports, it forwards the application data to the appropriate application based on its port number.

Note: The Remote Authentication Dial-in User Service (RADIUS) server shown in the figure provides authentication, authorization, and accounting services to manage user access. The operation of RADIUS is beyond the scope for this course.

Refer to
Interactive Graphic
in online course

Refer to
Online Course
for Illustration

UDP Client Processes - 14.7.4

As with TCP, client-server communication is initiated by a client application that requests data from a server process. The UDP client process dynamically selects a port number from the range of port numbers and uses this as the source port for the conversation. The destination port is usually the well-known or registered port number assigned to the server process.

After a client has selected the source and destination ports, the same pair of ports are used in the header of all datagrams in the transaction. For the data returning to the client from the server, the source and destination port numbers in the datagram header are reversed.

Click each button for an illustration of two hosts requesting services from the DNS and RADIUS authentication server.

Clients Sending UDP Requests

Client 1 is sending a DNS request using the well-known port 53 while Client 2 is requesting RADIUS authentication services using the registered port 1812.

UDP Request Destination Ports

The requests of the clients dynamically generate source port numbers. In this case, Client 1 is using source port 49152 and Client 2 is using source port 51152.

UDP Request Source Ports

When the server responds to the client requests, it reverses the destination and source ports of the initial request.

UDP Response Destination

In the Server response to the DNS request is now destination port 49152 and the RADIUS authentication response is now destination port 51152.

UDP Response Source Ports

The source ports in the server response are the original destination ports in the initial requests.

Go to the online
course to take the
quiz and exam.

Check Your Understanding - UDP Communication - 14.7.5

Module Practice and Quiz - 14.8

Refer to **Packet
Tracer Activity**
for this chapter

Packet Tracer - TCP and UDP Communications - 14.8.1

In this activity, you will explore the functionality of the TCP and UDP protocols, multiplexing, and the function of port numbers in determining which local application requested the data or is sending the data.

What did I learn in this module? - 14.8.2

Transportation of Data

The transport layer is the link between the application layer and the lower layers that are responsible for network transmission. The transport layer is responsible for logical communications between applications running on different hosts. The transport layer includes TCP and UDP. Transport layer protocols specify how to transfer messages between hosts and is responsible for managing reliability requirements of a conversation. The transport layer is responsible for tracking conversations (sessions), segmenting data and reassembling segments, adding header information, identifying applications, and conversation multiplexing. TCP is stateful, reliable, acknowledges data, resends lost data, and delivers data in sequenced order. Use TCP for email and the web. UDP is stateless, fast, has low overhead, does not requires acknowledgments, do not resend lost data, and delivers data in the order it arrives. Use UDP for VoIP and DNS.

TCP Overview

TCP establishes sessions, ensures reliability, provides same-order delivery, and supports flow control. A TCP segment adds 20 bytes of overhead as header information when encapsulating the application layer data. TCP header fields are the Source and Destination Ports, Sequence Number, Acknowledgment Number, Header Length, Reserved, Control Bits, Window Size, Checksum, and Urgent. Applications that use TCP are HTTP, FTP, SMTP, and Telnet.

UPD Overview

UDP reconstructs data in the order it is received, lost segments are not resent, no session establishment, and UPD does not inform the sender of resource availability. UDP header fields are Source and Destination Ports, Length, and Checksum. Applications that use UDP are DHCP, DNS, SNMP, TFTP, VoIP, and video conferencing.

Port Numbers

The TCP and UDP transport layer protocols use port numbers to manage multiple simultaneous conversations. This is why the TCP and UDP header fields identify a source and destination application port number. The source and destination ports are placed within the segment. The segments are then encapsulated within an IP packet. The IP packet contains the IP address of the source and destination. The combination of the source IP address and source port number, or the destination IP address and destination port number is known as a socket. The socket is used to identify the server and service being requested by the client. There is a range of port numbers from 0 through 65535. This range is divided into groups: Well-known Ports, Registered Ports, Private and/or Dynamic Ports. There are a few Well-Known Port numbers that are reserved for common applications such at FTP, SSH, DNS, HTTP and others. Sometimes it is necessary to know which active TCP connections are open and running on a networked host. Netstat is an important network utility that can be used to verify those connections.

TCP Communications Process

Each application process running on a server is configured to use a port number. The port number is either automatically assigned or configured manually by a system administrator.

TCP server processes are as follows: clients sending TCP requests, requesting destination ports, requesting source ports, responding to destination port and source port requests. To terminate a single conversation supported by TCP, four exchanges are needed to end both sessions. Either the client or the server can initiate the termination. The three-way handshake establishes that the destination device is present on the network, verifies that the destination device has an active service and is accepting requests on the destination port number that the initiating client intends to use, and informs the destination device that the source client intends to establish a communication session on that port number. The six control bits flags are: URG, ACK, PSH, RST, SYN, and FIN.

Reliability and Flow Control

For the original message to be understood by the recipient, all the data must be received and the data in these segments must be reassembled into the original order. Sequence numbers are assigned in the header of each packet. No matter how well designed a network is, data loss occasionally occurs. TCP provides ways to manage segment losses. There is a mechanism to retransmit segments for unacknowledged data. Host operating systems today typically employ an optional TCP feature called selective acknowledgment (SACK), negotiated during the three-way handshake. If both hosts support SACK, the receiver can explicitly acknowledge which segments (bytes) were received including any discontinuous segments. The sending host would therefore only need to retransmit the missing data. Flow control helps maintain the reliability of TCP transmission by adjusting the rate of data flow between source and destination. To accomplish this, the TCP header includes a 16-bit field called the window size. The process of the destination sending acknowledgments as it processes bytes received and the continual adjustment of the source's send window is known as sliding windows. A source might be transmitting 1,460 bytes of data within each TCP segment. This is the typical MSS that a destination device can receive. To avoid and control congestion, TCP employs several congestion handling mechanisms. It is the source that is reducing the number of unacknowledged bytes it sends and not the window size determined by the destination.

UPD Communication

UDP is a simple protocol that provides the basic transport layer functions. When UDP datagrams are sent to a destination, they often take different paths and arrive in the wrong order. UDP does not track sequence numbers the way TCP does. UDP has no way to reorder the datagrams into their transmission order. UDP simply reassembles the data in the order that it was received and forwards it to the application. If the data sequence is important to the application, the application must identify the proper sequence and determine how the data should be processed. UDP-based server applications are assigned well-known or registered port numbers. When UDP receives a datagram destined for one of these ports, it forwards the application data to the appropriate application based on its port number. The UDP client process dynamically selects a port number from the range of port numbers and uses this as the source port for the conversation. The destination port is usually the well-known or registered port number assigned to the server process. After a client has selected the source and destination ports, the same pair of ports are used in the header of all datagrams used in the transaction. For the data returning to the client from the server, the source and destination port numbers in the datagram header are reversed

Go to the online
course to take the
quiz and exam.

Chapter Quiz - Transport Layer

Your Chapter Notes

CHAPTER 15

Application Layer

Introduction - 15.0

Why should I take this module? - 15.0.1

Welcome to Application Layer!

As you have learned, the transport layer is where data actually gets moved from one host to another. But before that can take place, there are a lot of details that have to be determined so that this data transport happens correctly. This is why there is an application layer in both the OSI and the TCP/IP models. As an example, before there was streaming video over the internet, we had to watch home movies in a variety of other ways. Imagine that you videotaped some of your child's soccer game. Your parents, in another city, only have a video cassette player. You have to copy your video from your camera onto the right type of video cassette to send to them. Your brother has a DVD player, so you transfer your video to a DVD to send to him. This is what the application layer is all about, making sure that your data is in a format that the receiving device can use. Let's dive in!

What will I learn to do in this module? - 15.0.2

Module Title: Application Layer

Module Objective: Explain the operation of application layer protocols in providing support to end-user applications.

Topic Title	Topic Objective
Application, Presentation, and Session	Explain how the functions of the application layer, presentation layer, and session layer work together to provide network services to end user applications.
Peer-to-Peer	Explain how end user applications operate in a peer-to-peer network.
Web and Email Protocols	Explain how web and email protocols operate.
IP Addressing Services	Explain how DNS and DHCP operate.
File Sharing Services	Explain how file transfer protocols operate.

Application, Presentation, and Session - 15.1

Application Layer - 15.1.1

Refer to
Online Course
for Illustration

In the OSI and the TCP/IP models, the application layer is the closest layer to the end user. As shown in the figure, it is the layer that provides the interface between the applications used to communicate, and the underlying network over which messages are transmitted. Application layer protocols are used to exchange data between programs running on the source and destination hosts.

Based on the TCP/IP model, the upper three layers of the OSI model (application, presentation, and session) define functions of the TCP/IP application layer.

There are many application layer protocols, and new protocols are always being developed. Some of the most widely known application layer protocols include Hypertext Transfer Protocol (HTTP), File Transfer Protocol (FTP), Trivial File Transfer Protocol (TFTP), Internet Message Access Protocol (IMAP), and Domain Name System (DNS) protocol.

Refer to
Online Course
for Illustration

Presentation and Session Layer - 15.1.2

Presentation Layer

The presentation layer has three primary functions:

- Formatting, or presenting, data at the source device into a compatible format for receipt by the destination device.

- Compressing data in a way that can be decompressed by the destination device.

- Encrypting data for transmission and decrypting data upon receipt.

As shown in the figure, the presentation layer formats data for the application layer, and it sets standards for file formats. Some well-known standards for video include Matroska Video (MKV), Motion Picture Experts Group (MPG), and QuickTime Video (MOV). Some well-known graphic image formats are Graphics Interchange Format (GIF), Joint Photographic Experts Group (JPG), and Portable Network Graphics (PNG) format.

Session Layer

As the name implies, functions at the session layer create and maintain dialogs between source and destination applications. The session layer handles the exchange of information to initiate dialogs, keep them active, and to restart sessions that are disrupted or idle for a long period of time.

Refer to
Interactive Graphic
in online course

TCP/IP Application Layer Protocols - 15.1.3

The TCP/IP application protocols specify the format and control information necessary for many common internet communication functions. Application layer protocols are used by both the source and destination devices during a communication session. For the communications to be successful, the application layer protocols that are implemented on the source and destination host must be compatible.

Click each application protocol type to learn more about each protocol.

Name System

DNS - Domain Name System (or Service)

- TCP, UDP client 53

- Translates domain names, such as cisco.com, into IP addresses.

Host Config

BOOTP - Bootstrap Protocol

- UDP client 68, server 67

- Enables a diskless workstation to discover its own IP address, the IP address of a BOOTP server on the network, and a file to be loaded into memory to boot the machine

- BOOTP is being superseded by DHCP

DHCP - Dynamic Host Configuration Protocol

- UDP client 68, server 67

- Dynamically assigns IP addresses to be re-used when no longer needed

Email

SMTP - Simple Mail Transfer Protocol

- TCP 25

- Enables clients to send email to a mail server

- Enables servers to send email to other servers

POP3 - Post Office Protocol

- TCP 110

- Enables clients to retrieve email from a mail server

- Downloads the email to the local mail application of the client

IMAP - Internet Message Access Protocol

- TCP 143

- Enables clients to access email stored on a mail server

- Maintains email on the server

File Transfer

FTP - File Transfer Protocol

- TCP 20 to 21

- Sets rules that enable a user on one host to access and transfer files to and from another host over a network

- FTP is a reliable, connection-oriented, and acknowledged file delivery protocol

TFTP - Trivial File Transfer Protocol

- UDP client 69

- A simple, connectionless file transfer protocol with best-effort, unacknowledged file delivery

- It uses less overhead than FTP

Web

HTTP - Hypertext Transfer Protocol

- TCP 80, 8080

- A set of rules for exchanging text, graphic images, sound, video, and other multimedia files on the World Wide Web

HTTPS - HTTP Secure

- TCP, UDP 443

- The browser uses encryption to secure HTTP communications

- Authenticates the website to which you are connecting your browser

Go to the online course to take the quiz and exam.

Check Your Understanding - Application, Session, Presentation - 15.1.4

Peer-to-Peer - 15.2

Refer to **Online Course** for Illustration

Client-Server Model - 15.2.1

In the previous topic, you learned that TCP/IP application layer protocols implemented on both the source and destination host must be compatible. In this topic you will learn about the client/server model and the processes used, which are in the application layer. The same is true for a peer-to-peer network. In the client/server model, the device requesting the information is called a client and the device responding to the request is called a server. The client is a hardware/software combination that people use to directly access the resources that are stored on the server.

Client and server processes are considered to be in the application layer. The client begins the exchange by requesting data from the server, which responds by sending one or more streams of data to the client. Application layer protocols describe the format of the requests and responses between clients and servers. In addition to the actual data transfer, this exchange may also require user authentication and the identification of a data file to be transferred.

One example of a client/server network is using the email service of an ISP to send, receive, and store email. The email client on a home computer issues a request to the email server of the ISP for any unread mail. The server responds by sending the requested email to the client. Data transfer from a client to a server is referred to as an upload and data from a server to a client as a download.

As shown in the figure, files are downloaded from the server to the client.

Refer to
Online Course
for Illustration

Peer-to-Peer Networks - 15.2.2

In the peer-to-peer (P2P) networking model, the data is accessed from a peer device without the use of a dedicated server.

The P2P network model involves two parts: P2P networks and P2P applications. Both parts have similar features, but in practice work quite differently.

In a P2P network, two or more computers are connected via a network and can share resources (such as printers and files) without having a dedicated server. Every connected end device (known as a peer) can function as both a server and a client. One computer might assume the role of server for one transaction while simultaneously serving as a client for another. The roles of client and server are set on a per request basis.

In addition to sharing files, a network such as this one would allow users to enable networked games or share an internet connection.

In a peer-to-peer exchange, both devices are considered equal in the communication process. Peer 1 has files that are shared with Peer 2 and can access the shared printer that is directly connected to Peer 2 to print files. Peer 2 is sharing the directly connected printer with Peer 1 while accessing the shared files on Peer 1, as shown in the figure.

Refer to
Online Course
for Illustration

Peer-to-Peer Applications - 15.2.3

A P2P application allows a device to act as both a client and a server within the same communication, as shown in the figure. In this model, every client is a server and every server is a client. P2P applications require that each end device provide a user interface and run a background service.

Some P2P applications use a hybrid system where resource sharing is decentralized, but the indexes that point to resource locations are stored in a centralized directory. In a hybrid system, each peer accesses an index server to get the location of a resource stored on another peer.

Refer to
Online Course
for Illustration

Common P2P Applications - 15.2.4

With P2P applications, each computer in the network that is running the application can act as a client or a server for the other computers in the network that are also running the application. Common P2P networks include the following:

- BitTorrent
- Direct Connect
- eDonkey
- Freenet

Some P2P applications are based on the Gnutella protocol, where each user shares whole files with other users. As shown in the figure, Gnutella-compatible client software allows users to connect to Gnutella services over the internet, and to locate and access resources shared by other Gnutella peers. Many Gnutella client applications are available, including µTorrent, BitComet, DC++, Deluge, and emule.

Many P2P applications allow users to share pieces of many files with each other at the same time. Clients use a torrent file to locate other users who have pieces that they need so that they can then connect directly to them. This file also contains information about tracker computers that keep track of which users have specific pieces of certain files. Clients ask for pieces from multiple users at the same time. This is known as a swarm and the technology is called BitTorrent. BitTorrent has its own client. But there are many other BitTorrent clients including uTorrent, Deluge, and qBittorrent.

Note: Any type of file can be shared between users. Many of these files are copyrighted, meaning that only the creator has the right to use and distribute them. It is against the law to download or distribute copyrighted files without permission from the copyright holder. Copyright violation can result in criminal charges and civil lawsuits.

Go to the online course to take the quiz and exam.

Check Your Understanding - Peer-to-Peer - 15.2.5

Web and Email Protocols - 15.3

Refer to
Interactive Graphic
in online course

Refer to
Online Course
for Illustration

Hypertext Transfer Protocol and Hypertext Markup Language - 15.3.1

There are application layer-specific protocols that are designed for common uses such as web browsing and email. The first topic gave you an overview of these protocols. This topic goes into more detail.

When a web address or Uniform Resource Locator (URL) is typed into a web browser, the web browser establishes a connection to the web service. The web service is running on the server that is using the HTTP protocol. URLs and Uniform Resource Identifiers (URIs) are the names most people associate with web addresses.

To better understand how the web browser and web server interact, examine how a web page is opened in a browser. For this example, use the http://www.cisco.com/index.html URL.

Click each button for more information.

Step 1

The browser interprets the three parts of the URL:

- http (the protocol or scheme)
- www.cisco.com (the server name)
- index.html (the specific filename requested)

Step 2

The browser then checks with a name server to convert www.cisco.com into a numeric IP address, which it uses to connect to the server. The client initiates an HTTP request to a server by sending a GET request to the server and asks for the index.html file.

Step 3

In response to the request, the server sends the HTML code for this web page to the browser.

Step 4

The browser deciphers the HTML code and formats the page for the browser window.

Refer to
Online Course
for Illustration

HTTP and HTTPS - 15.3.2

HTTP is a request/response protocol. When a client, typically a web browser, sends a request to a web server, HTTP specifies the message types used for that communication. The three common message types are GET (see figure), POST, and PUT:

- **GET** - This is a client request for data. A client (web browser) sends the GET message to the web server to request HTML pages.

- **POST** - This uploads data files to the web server, such as form data.

- **PUT** - This uploads resources or content to the web server, such as an image.

Although HTTP is remarkably flexible, it is not a secure protocol. The request messages send information to the server in plaintext that can be intercepted and read. The server responses, typically HTML pages, are also unencrypted.

For secure communication across the internet, the HTTP Secure (HTTPS) protocol is used. HTTPS uses authentication and encryption to secure data as it travels between the client and server. HTTPS uses the same client request-server response process as HTTP, but the data stream is encrypted with Secure Socket Layer (SSL) before being transported across the network.

Refer to
Online Course
for Illustration

Email Protocols - 15.3.3

One of the primary services offered by an ISP is email hosting. To run on a computer or other end device, email requires several applications and services, as shown in the figure. Email is a store-and-forward method of sending, storing, and retrieving electronic messages across a network. Email messages are stored in databases on mail servers.

Email clients communicate with mail servers to send and receive email. Mail servers communicate with other mail servers to transport messages from one domain to another. An email client does not communicate directly with another email client when sending email. Instead, both clients rely on the mail server to transport messages.

Email supports three separate protocols for operation: Simple Mail Transfer Protocol (SMTP), Post Office Protocol (POP), and IMAP. The application layer process that sends mail uses SMTP. A client retrieves email using one of the two application layer protocols: POP or IMAP.

Refer to
Interactive Graphic
in online course

Refer to
Online Course
for Illustration

SMTP, POP, and IMAP - 15.3.4

Click each button for more information.

SMTP

SMTP message formats require a message header and a message body. Although the message body can contain any amount of text, the message header must have a properly formatted recipient email address and a sender address.

When a client sends email, the client SMTP process connects with a server SMTP process on well-known port 25. After the connection is made, the client attempts to send the email to the server across the connection. When the server receives the message, it either places the message in a local account, if the recipient is local, or forwards the message to another mail server for delivery.

The destination email server may not be online, or may be busy, when email messages are sent. Therefore, SMTP spools messages to be sent at a later time. Periodically, the server checks the queue for messages and attempts to send them again. If the message is still not delivered after a predetermined expiration time, it is returned to the sender as undeliverable.

POP

POP is used by an application to retrieve mail from a mail server. With POP, mail is downloaded from the server to the client and then deleted on the server. This is the default operation of POP.

The server starts the POP service by passively listening on TCP port 110 for client connection requests. When a client wants to make use of the service, it sends a request to establish a TCP connection with the server, as shown in the figure. When the connection is established, the POP server sends a greeting. The client and POP server then exchange commands and responses until the connection is closed or aborted.

With POP, email messages are downloaded to the client and removed from the server, so there is no centralized location where email messages are kept. Because POP does not store messages, it is not recommended for a small business that needs a centralized backup solution.

POP3 is the most commonly used version.

IMAP

IMAP is another protocol that describes a method to retrieve email messages. Unlike POP, when the user connects to an IMAP-capable server, copies of the messages are downloaded to the client application, as shown in the figure. The original messages are kept on the server until manually deleted. Users view copies of the messages in their email client software.

Users can create a file hierarchy on the server to organize and store mail. That file structure is duplicated on the email client as well. When a user decides to delete a message, the server synchronizes that action and deletes the message from the server.

Go to the online
course to take the
quiz and exam.

Check Your Understanding - Web and Email Protocols - 15.3.5

IP Addressing Services - 15.4

Refer to
Interactive Graphic
in online course

Refer to
Online Course
for Illustration

Domain Name Service - 15.4.1

There are other application layer-specific protocols that were designed to make it easier to obtain addresses for network devices. These services are essential because it would be very time consuming to remember IP addresses instead of URLs or manually configure all of the devices in a medium to large network. The first topic in this module gave you an overview of these protocols. This topic goes into more detail about the IP addressing services, DNS and DHCP.

In data networks, devices are labeled with numeric IP addresses to send and receive data over networks. Domain names were created to convert the numeric address into a simple, recognizable name.

On the internet, fully-qualified domain names (FQDNs), such as http://www.cisco.com, are much easier for people to remember than 198.133.219.25, which is the actual numeric address for this server. If Cisco decides to change the numeric address of www.cisco.com, it is transparent to the user because the domain name remains the same. The new address is simply linked to the existing domain name and connectivity is maintained.

The DNS protocol defines an automated service that matches resource names with the required numeric network address. It includes the format for queries, responses, and data. The DNS protocol communications use a single format called a message. This message format is used for all types of client queries and server responses, error messages, and the transfer of resource record information between servers.

Click each button for more information.

Step 1
The user types an FQDN into a browser application Address field.

Step 2
A DNS query is sent to the designated DNS server for the client computer.

Step 3
The DNS server matches the FQDN with its IP address.

Step 4
The DNS query response is sent back to the client with the IP address for the FQDN.

Step 5
The client computer uses the IP address to make requests of the server.

DNS Message Format - 15.4.2

The DNS server stores different types of resource records that are used to resolve names. These records contain the name, address, and type of record. Some of these record types are as follows:

- **A** - An end device IPv4 address

- **NS** - An authoritative name server

- **AAAA** - An end device IPv6 address (pronounced quad-A)

- **MX** - A mail exchange record

When a client makes a query, the server DNS process first looks at its own records to resolve the name. If it is unable to resolve the name by using its stored records, it contacts other servers to resolve the name. After a match is found and returned to the original requesting server, the server temporarily stores the numbered address in the event that the same name is requested again.

The DNS client service on Windows PCs also stores previously resolved names in memory. The **ipconfig /displaydns** command displays all of the cached DNS entries.

As shown in the table, DNS uses the same message format between servers, consisting of a question, answer, authority, and additional information for all types of client queries and server responses, error messages, and transfer of resource record information.

DNS message section	Description
Question	The question for the name server
Answer	Resource Records answering the question
Authority	Resource Records pointing toward an authority
Additional	Resource Records holding additional information

Refer to
Online Course
for Illustration

DNS Hierarchy - 15.4.3

The DNS protocol uses a hierarchical system to create a database to provide name resolution, as shown in the figure. DNS uses domain names to form the hierarchy.

The naming structure is broken down into small, manageable zones. Each DNS server maintains a specific database file and is only responsible for managing name-to-IP mappings for that small portion of the entire DNS structure. When a DNS server receives a request for a name translation that is not within its DNS zone, the DNS server forwards the request to another DNS server within the proper zone for translation. DNS is scalable because hostname resolution is spread across multiple servers.

The different top-level domains represent either the type of organization or the country of origin. Examples of top-level domains are the following:

- **.com** - a business or industry

- **.org** - a non-profit organization

- **.au** - Australia

- **.co** - Colombia

The nslookup Command - 15.4.4

When configuring a network device, one or more DNS Server addresses are provided that the DNS client can use for name resolution. Usually the ISP provides the addresses to use for the DNS servers. When a user application requests to connect to a remote device by name, the requesting DNS client queries the name server to resolve the name to a numeric address.

Computer operating systems also have a utility called Nslookup that allows the user to manually query the name servers to resolve a given host name. This utility can also be used to troubleshoot name resolution issues and to verify the current status of the name servers.

In this figure, when the **nslookup** command is issued, the default DNS server configured for your host is displayed. The name of a host or domain can be entered at the **nslookup** prompt. The Nslookup utility has many options available for extensive testing and verification of the DNS process.

```
C:\Users> nslookup

Default Server:  dns-sj.cisco.com

Address:  171.70.168.183

> www.cisco.com

Server:  dns-sj.cisco.com

Address:  171.70.168.183

Name:     origin-www.cisco.com

Addresses:  2001:420:1101:1::a

            173.37.145.84

Aliases:  www.cisco.com

> cisco.netacad.net

Server:  dns-sj.cisco.com

Address:  171.70.168.183

Name:     cisco.netacad.net

Address:  72.163.6.223

>
```

Refer to
Interactive Graphic
in online course

Syntax Checker - The nslookup Command - 15.4.5

Practice entering the nslookup command in both Windows and Linux

Refer to
Online Course
for Illustration

Dynamic Host Configuration Protocol - 15.4.6

The Dynamic Host Configuration Protocol (DHCP) for IPv4 service automates the assignment of IPv4 addresses, subnet masks, gateways, and other IPv4 networking parameters. This is referred to as dynamic addressing. The alternative to dynamic addressing is static addressing. When using static addressing, the network administrator manually enters IP address information on hosts.

When a host connects to the network, the DHCP server is contacted, and an address is requested. The DHCP server chooses an address from a configured range of addresses called a pool and assigns (leases) it to the host.

On larger networks, or where the user population changes frequently, DHCP is preferred for address assignment. New users may arrive and need connections; others may have new computers that must be connected. Rather than use static addressing for each connection, it is more efficient to have IPv4 addresses assigned automatically using DHCP.

DHCP can allocate IP addresses for a configurable period of time, called a lease period. The lease period is an important DHCP setting, When the lease period expires or the DHCP server gets a DHCPRELEASE message the address is returned to the DHCP pool for reuse. Users can freely move from location to location and easily re-establish network connections through DHCP.

As the figure shows, various types of devices can be DHCP servers. The DHCP server in most medium-to-large networks is usually a local, dedicated PC-based server. With home networks, the DHCP server is usually located on the local router that connects the home network to the ISP.

Many networks use both DHCP and static addressing. DHCP is used for general purpose hosts, such as end user devices. Static addressing is used for network devices, such as gateway routers, switches, servers, and printers.

DHCP for IPv6 (DHCPv6) provides similar services for IPv6 clients. One important difference is that DHCPv6 does not provide a default gateway address. This can only be obtained dynamically from the Router Advertisement message of the router.

Refer to Online Course for Illustration

DHCP Operation - 15.4.7

As shown in the figure, when an IPv4, DHCP-configured device boots up or connects to the network, the client broadcasts a DHCP discover (DHCPDISCOVER) message to identify any available DHCP servers on the network. A DHCP server replies with a DHCP offer (DHCPOFFER) message, which offers a lease to the client. The offer message contains the IPv4 address and subnet mask to be assigned, the IPv4 address of the DNS server, and the IPv4 address of the default gateway. The lease offer also includes the duration of the lease.

The client may receive multiple DHCPOFFER messages if there is more than one DHCP server on the local network. Therefore, it must choose between them, and sends a DHCP request (DHCPREQUEST) message that identifies the explicit server and lease offer that the client is accepting. A client may also choose to request an address that it had previously been allocated by the server.

Assuming that the IPv4 address requested by the client, or offered by the server, is still available, the server returns a DHCP acknowledgment (DHCPACK) message that acknowledges to the client that the lease has been finalized. If the offer is no longer valid, then the selected server responds with a DHCP negative acknowledgment (DHCPNAK) message. If a DHCPNAK message is returned, then the selection process must begin again with a new DHCPDISCOVER message being transmitted. After the client has the lease, it must be renewed prior to the lease expiration through another DHCPREQUEST message.

The DHCP server ensures that all IP addresses are unique (the same IP address cannot be assigned to two different network devices simultaneously). Most ISPs use DHCP to allocate addresses to their customers.

DHCPv6 has a set of messages that is similar to those for DHCPv4. The DHCPv6 messages are SOLICIT, ADVERTISE, INFORMATION REQUEST, and REPLY.

Refer to **Lab Activity** for this chapter

Lab - Observe DNS Resolution - 15.4.8

In this lab, you will complete the following objectives:

- Part 1: Observe the DNS Conversion of a URL to an IP Address
- Part 2: Observe DNS Lookup Using the **nslookup** Command on a Web Site
- Part 3: Observe DNS Lookup Using the **nslookup** Command on Mail Servers

Go to the online course to take the quiz and exam.

Check Your Understanding - IP Addressing Services - 15.4.9

File Sharing Services - 15.5

Refer to **Online Course** for Illustration

File Transfer Protocol - 15.5.1

As you learned in previous topics, in the client/server model, the client can upload data to a server, and download data from a server, if both devices are using a file transfer protocol (FTP). Like HTTP, email, and addressing protocols, FTP is commonly used application layer protocol. This topic discusses FTP in more detail.

FTP was developed to allow for data transfers between a client and a server. An FTP client is an application which runs on a computer that is being used to push and pull data from an FTP server.

The client establishes the first connection to the server for control traffic using TCP port 21. The traffic consists of client commands and server replies.

The client establishes the second connection to the server for the actual data transfer using TCP port 20. This connection is created every time there is data to be transferred.

The data transfer can happen in either direction. The client can download (pull) data from the server, or the client can upload (push) data to the server.

Refer to **Online Course** for Illustration

Server Message Block - 15.5.2

The Server Message Block (SMB) is a client/server file sharing protocol that describes the structure of shared network resources, such as directories, files, printers, and serial ports. It is a request-response protocol. All SMB messages share a common format. This format uses a fixed-sized header, followed by a variable-sized parameter and data component.

Here are three functions of SMB messages:

- Start, authenticate, and terminate sessions.
- Control file and printer access.
- Allow an application to send or receive messages to or from another device.

SMB file-sharing and print services have become the mainstay of Microsoft networking. With the introduction of the Windows 2000 software series, Microsoft changed the underlying structure for using SMB. In previous versions of Microsoft products, the

SMB services used a non-TCP/IP protocol to implement name resolution. Beginning with Windows 2000, all subsequent Microsoft products use DNS naming, which allows TCP/IP protocols to directly support SMB resource sharing, as shown in the figure.

The SMB file exchange process between Windows PCs is shown in the next figure.

Unlike the file sharing supported by FTP, clients establish a long-term connection to servers. After the connection is established, the user of the client can access the resources on the server as though the resource is local to the client host.

The LINUX and UNIX operating systems also provide a method of sharing resources with Microsoft networks by using a version of SMB called SAMBA. The Apple Macintosh operating systems also support resource sharing by using the SMB protocol.

Go to the online course to take the quiz and exam.

Check Your Understanding - File Sharing Services - 15.5.3

Module Practice and Quiz - 15.6

What did I learn in this module? - 15.6.1

Application, Presentation, and Session

In the OSI and the TCP/IP models, the application layer is the closest layer to the end user. Application layer protocols are used to exchange data between programs running on the source and destination hosts. The presentation layer has three primary functions: formatting, or presenting, data at the source device into a compatible form for receipt by the destination device, compressing data in a way that can be decompressed by the destination device, and encrypting data for transmission and decrypting data upon receipt. The session layer creates and maintains dialogs between source and destination applications. The session layer handles the exchange of information to initiate dialogs, keep them active, and to restart sessions that are disrupted or idle for a long period of time. TCP/IP application layer protocols specify the format and control information necessary for many common internet communication functions. These protocols are used by both the source and destination devices during a session. The protocols implemented on both the source and destination host must be compatible.

Peer-to-Peer

In the client/server model, the device requesting the information is called a client and the device responding to the request is called a server. The client begins the exchange by requesting data from the server, which responds by sending one or more streams of data to the client. In a P2P network, two or more computers are connected via a network and can share resources without having a dedicated server. Every peer can function as both a server and a client. One computer might assume the role of server for one transaction while simultaneously serving as a client for another. P2P applications require that each end device provide a user interface and run a background service. Some P2P applications use a hybrid system where resource sharing is decentralized, but the indexes that point to resource locations are stored in a centralized directory. Many P2P applications allow users to share pieces of files with each other at the same time. Clients use a small file called a torrent file to locate other users who have pieces that they need so that they can connect directly to them. This file also contains information about tracker computers that keep track of which users have what pieces of which files.

Web and Email Protocols

When a web address or URL is typed into a web browser, the web browser establishes a connection to the web service. The web service is running on the server that is using the HTTP protocol. HTTP is a request/response protocol. When a client, typically a web browser, sends a request to a web server, HTTP specifies the message types used for that communication. The three common message types are GET, POST, and PUT. For secure communication across the internet, HTTPS uses the same client request-server response process as HTTP, but the data stream is encrypted with SSL before being transported across the network. Email supports three separate protocols for operation: SMTP, POP, and IMAP. The application layer process that sends mail uses SMTP. A client retrieves email using POP or IMAP. SMTP message formats require a message header and a message body. While the message body can contain any amount of text, the message header must have a properly formatted recipient email address and a sender address. POP is used by an application to retrieve mail from a mail server. With POP, mail is downloaded from the server to the client and then deleted on the server. With IMAP, unlike POP, when the user connects to an IMAP-capable server, copies of the messages are downloaded to the client application. The original messages are kept on the server until manually deleted.

IP Addressing Services

The DNS protocol matches resource names with the required numeric network address. The DNS protocol communications use a message format for all types of client queries and server responses, error messages, and the transfer of resource record information between servers. DNS uses domain names to form a hierarchy. Each DNS server maintains a specific database file and is only responsible for managing name-to-IP mappings for that small portion of the entire DNS structure. Computer OSs use Nslookup to allow the user to manually query the name servers to resolve a given host name. DHCP for IPv4 service automates the assignment of IPv4 addresses, subnet masks, gateways, and other IPv4 networking parameters. DHCPv6 provides similar services for IPv6 clients, except that it does not provide a default gateway address. When an IPv4, DHCP-configured device boots up or connects to the network, the client broadcasts a DHCPDISCOVER message to identify any available DHCP servers on the network. A DHCP server replies with a DHCPOFFER message, which offers a lease to the client. DHCPv6 has a set of messages that is similar to those for DHCPv4. The DHCPv6 messages are SOLICIT, ADVERTISE, INFORMATION REQUEST, and REPLY.

File Sharing Services

An FTP client is an application which runs on a computer that is being used to push and pull data from an FTP server. The client establishes the first connection to the server for control traffic using TCP port 21. The client establishes the second connection to the server for the actual data transfer using TCP port 20. The client can download (pull) data from the server, or the client can upload (push) data to the server. Here are three functions of SMB messages: start, authenticate, and terminate sessions, control file and printer access, and allow an application to send or receive messages to or from another device. Unlike the file sharing supported by FTP, clients establish a long-term connection to servers. After the connection is established, the user of the client can access the resources on the server as if the resource is local to the client host.

Go to the online
course to take the
quiz and exam.

Chapter Quiz - Application Layer

Your Chapter Notes

CHAPTER 16

Network Security Fundamentals

Introduction - 16.0

Why should I take this module? - 16.0.1

Welcome to Network Security Fundamentals!

You may have already set up a network, or you may be getting ready to do just that. Here is something to think about. Setting up a network without securing it is like opening all the doors and windows to your home and then going on vacation. Anyone could come by, gain entry, steal or break items, or just make a mess. As you have seen on the news, it is possible to break into *any* network! As a network administrator, it is part of your job to make it difficult for threat actors to gain access to your network. This module gives you an overview of types of network attacks and what you can do to reduce a threat actor's chances of succeeding. It also has Packet Tracer activities to let you practice some basic techniques for network security. If you have a network, but it is not as secure as possible, then you will want to read this module right now!

What will I learn to do in this module? - 16.0.2

Module Title: Network Security Fundamentals

Module Objective: Configure switches and routers with device hardening features to enhance security.

Topic Title	Topic Objective
Security Threats and Vulnerabilities	Explain why basic security measure are necessary on network devices.
Network Attacks	Identify security vulnerabilities.
Network Attack Mitigation	Identify general mitigation techniques.
Device Security	Configure network devices with device hardening features to mitigate security threats.

Security Threats and Vulnerabilities - 16.1

Refer to
Interactive Graphic
in online course

Refer to
Online Course
for Illustration

Types of Threats - 16.1.1

Wired and wireless computer networks are essential to everyday activities. Individuals and organizations depend on their computers and networks. Intrusion by an unauthorized person can result in costly network outages and loss of work. Attacks on a network can be devastating and can result in a loss of time and money due to damage, or theft of important information or assets.

Intruders can gain access to a network through software vulnerabilities, hardware attacks, or through guessing someone's username and password. Intruders who gain access by modifying software or exploiting software vulnerabilities are called threat actors.

After the threat actor gains access to the network, four types of threats may arise.

Click each button for information about each threat.

Information Theft

Information theft is breaking into a computer to obtain confidential information. Information can be used or sold for various purposes. Example: stealing an organization's proprietary information, such as research and development data.

Data Loss and Manipulation

Data loss and manipulation is breaking into a computer to destroy or alter data records. An example of data loss is a threat actor sending a virus that reformats a computer hard drive. An example of data manipulation is breaking into a records system to change information, such as the price of an item.

Identity Theft

Identity theft is a form of information theft where personal information is stolen for the purpose of taking over someone's identity. Using this information, a threat actor can obtain legal documents, apply for credit, and make unauthorized online purchases. Identify theft is a growing problem costing billions of dollars per year.

Disruption of Service

Disruption of service is preventing legitimate users from accessing services to which they are entitled. Examples: denial of service (DoS) attacks on servers, network devices, or network communications links.

Refer to
Interactive Graphic
in online course

Refer to
Online Course
for Illustration

Types of Vulnerabilities - 16.1.2

Vulnerability is the degree of weakness in a network or a device. Some degree of vulnerability is inherent in routers, switches, desktops, servers, and even security devices. Typically, the network devices under attack are the endpoints, such as servers and desktop computers.

There are three primary vulnerabilities or weaknesses: technological, configuration, and security policy. All three of these sources of vulnerabilities can leave a network or device open to various attacks, including malicious code attacks and network attacks.

Click each button for a table with examples and a description of each type of vulnerability.

Technological Vulnerabilities

Configuration Vulnerabilities

Policy Vulnerabilities

Refer to
Online Course
for Illustration

Physical Security - 16.1.3

An equally important vulnerable area of the network to consider is the physical security of devices. If network resources can be physically compromised, a threat actor can deny the use of network resources.

The four classes of physical threats are as follows:

- **Hardware threats** - This includes physical damage to servers, routers, switches, cabling plant, and workstations.

- **Environmental threats** - This includes temperature extremes (too hot or too cold) or humidity extremes (too wet or too dry).

- **Electrical threats** - This includes voltage spikes, insufficient supply voltage (brown-outs), unconditioned power (noise), and total power loss.

- **Maintenance threats** - This includes poor handling of key electrical components (electrostatic discharge), lack of critical spare parts, poor cabling, and poor labeling.

A good plan for physical security must be created and implemented to address these issues. The figure shows an example of physical security plan.

Go to the online
course to take the
quiz and exam.

Check Your Understanding - Security Threats and Vulnerabilities - 16.1.4

Network Attacks - 16.2

Refer to
Interactive Graphic
in online course

Types of Malware - 16.2.1

The previous topic explained the types of network threats and the vulnerabilities that make threats possible. This topic goes into more detail about how threat actors gain access to network or restrict authorized users from having access.

Malware is short for malicious software. It is code or software specifically designed to damage, disrupt, steal, or inflict "bad" or illegitimate action on data, hosts, or networks. Viruses, worms, and Trojan horses are types of malware.

Viruses

A computer virus is a type of malware that propagates by inserting a copy of itself into, and becoming part of, another program. It spreads from one computer to another, leaving infections as it travels. Viruses can range in severity from causing mildly annoying effects, to damaging data or software and causing denial of service (DoS) conditions. Almost all viruses are attached to an executable file, which means the virus may exist on a system but will not be active or able to spread until a user runs or opens the malicious host file or program. When the host code is executed, the viral code is executed as well. Normally, the host program keeps functioning after the virus infects it. However, some viruses overwrite other programs with copies of themselves, which destroys the host program altogether. Viruses spread when the software or document they are attached to is transferred from one computer to another using the network, a disk, file sharing, or infected email attachments.

Worms

Computer worms are similar to viruses in that they replicate functional copies of themselves and can cause the same type of damage. In contrast to viruses, which require the spreading of an infected host file, worms are standalone software and do not require a host program or human help to propagate. A worm does not need to attach to a program to infect a host and enter a computer through a vulnerability in the system. Worms take advantage of system features to travel through the network unaided.

Trojan Horses

A Trojan horse is another type of malware named after the wooden horse the Greeks used to infiltrate Troy. It is a harmful piece of software that looks legitimate. Users are typically tricked into loading and executing it on their systems. After it is activated, it can achieve any number of attacks on the host, from irritating the user (with excessive pop-up windows or changing the desktop) to damaging the host (deleting files, stealing data, or activating and spreading other malware, such as viruses). Trojan horses are also known to create back doors to give malicious users access to the system.

Unlike viruses and worms, Trojan horses do not reproduce by infecting other files. They self-replicate. Trojan horses must spread through user interaction such as opening an email attachment or downloading and running a file from the internet.

Click Play in the figure to view an animated explanation of the three types of malware.

Refer to
Interactive Graphic
in online course

Reconnaissance Attacks - 16.2.2

In addition to malicious code attacks, it is also possible for networks to fall prey to various network attacks. Network attacks can be classified into three major categories:

- **Reconnaissance attacks** - The discovery and mapping of systems, services, or vulnerabilities.

- **Access attacks** - The unauthorized manipulation of data, system access, or user privileges.

- **Denial of service** - The disabling or corruption of networks, systems, or services.

For reconnaissance attacks, external threat actors can use internet tools, such as the **nslookup** and **whois** utilities, to easily determine the IP address space assigned to a given corporation or entity. After the IP address space is determined, a threat actor can then ping the publicly available IP addresses to identify the addresses that are active. To help automate this step, a threat actor may use a ping sweep tool, such as **fping** or **gping**. This systematically pings all network addresses in a given range or subnet. This is similar to going through a section of a telephone book and calling each number to see who answers.

Click each type of reconnaissance attack tool to see an animation of the attack.

Internet Queries

Click Play in the figure to view an animation. The threat actor is looking for initial information about a target. Various tools can be used, including Google search, the websites of organizations, whois, and more.

Ping Sweeps

Click Play in the figure to view an animation. The threat initiates a ping sweep to determine which IP addresses are active.

Port Scans

Click Play in the figure to view an animation of a threat actor performing a port scan on the discovered active IP addresses.

Refer to
Interactive Graphic
in online course

Refer to
Online Course
for Illustration

Access Attacks - 16.2.3

Access attacks exploit known vulnerabilities in authentication services, FTP services, and web services to gain entry to web accounts, confidential databases, and other sensitive information. An access attack allows individuals to gain unauthorized access to information that they have no right to view. Access attacks can be classified into four types: password attacks, trust exploitation, port redirection, and man-in-the middle.

Click each button for an explanation of each type of attack.

Password Attacks

Threat actors can implement password attacks using several different methods:

- Brute-force attacks
- Trojan horse attacks
- Packet sniffers

Trust Exploitation

In a trust exploitation attack, a threat actor uses unauthorized privileges to gain access to a system, possibly compromising the target. Click Play in the figure to view an example of trust exploitation.

Port Redirection

In a port redirection attack, a threat actor uses a compromised system as a base for attacks against other targets. The example in the figure shows a threat actor using SSH (port 22) to connect to a compromised host A. Host A is trusted by host B and, therefore, the threat actor can use Telnet (port 23) to access it.

Man-in-the-Middle

In a man-in-the-middle attack, the threat actor is positioned in between two legitimate entities in order to read or modify the data that passes between the two parties. The figure displays an example of a man-in-the-middle attack.

Refer to
Interactive Graphic
in online course

Denial of Service Attacks - 16.2.4

Denial of service (DoS) attacks are the most publicized form of attack and among the most difficult to eliminate. However, because of their ease of implementation and potentially significant damage, DoS attacks deserve special attention from security administrators.

DoS attacks take many forms. Ultimately, they prevent authorized people from using a service by consuming system resources. To help prevent DoS attacks it is important to stay up to date with the latest security updates for operating systems and applications.

Click each button for an example of DoS and distributed DoS (DDoS) attacks.

DoS Attack

DoS attacks are a major risk because they interrupt communication and cause significant loss of time and money. These attacks are relatively simple to conduct, even by an unskilled threat actor.

Click Play in the figure to view the animation of a DoS attack.

DDoS Attack

A DDoS is similar to a DoS attack, but it originates from multiple, coordinated sources. For example, a threat actor builds a network of infected hosts, known as zombies. A network of zombies is called a botnet. The threat actor uses a command and control (CnC) program to instruct the botnet of zombies to carry out a DDoS attack.

Click Play in the figure to view the animation of a DDoS attack.

Go to the online
course to take the
quiz and exam.

Check Your Understanding - Network Attacks - 16.2.5

Refer to
Lab Activity
for this chapter

Lab - Research Network Security Threats - 16.2.6

In this lab, you will complete the following objectives:

- Part 1: Explore the SANS Website
- Part 2: Identify Recent Network Security Threats
- Part 3: Detail a Specific Network Security Threat

Network Attack Mitigations - 16.3

Refer to
Online Course
for Illustration

The Defense-in-Depth Approach - 16.3.1

Now that you know more about how threat actors can break into networks, you need to understand what to do to prevent this unauthorized access. This topic details several actions you can take to make your network more secure.

To mitigate network attacks, you must first secure devices including routers, switches, servers, and hosts. Most organizations employ a defense-in-depth approach (also known as a layered approach) to security. This requires a combination of networking devices and services working in tandem.

Consider the network in the figure. There are several security devices and services that have been implemented to protect its users and assets against TCP/IP threats.

All network devices including the router and switches are also hardened as indicated by the combination locks on their respective icons. This indicates that they have been secured to prevent threat actors from gaining access and tampering with the devices.

Keep Backups - 16.3.2

Backing up device configurations and data is one of the most effective ways of protecting against data loss. A data backup stores a copy of the information on a computer to removable backup media that can be kept in a safe place. Infrastructure devices should have backups of configuration files and IOS images on an FTP or similar file server. If the computer or a router hardware fails, the data or configuration can be restored using the backup copy.

Backups should be performed on a regular basis as identified in the security policy. Data backups are usually stored offsite to protect the backup media if anything happens to the main facility. Windows hosts have a backup and restore utility. It is important for users to back up their data to another drive, or to a cloud-based storage provider.

The table shows backup considerations and their descriptions.

Consideration	Description
Frequency	• Perform backups on a regular basis as identified in the security policy. • Full backups can be time-consuming, therefore perform monthly or weekly backups with frequent partial backups of changed files.
Storage	• Always validate backups to ensure the integrity of the data and validate the file restoration procedures.
Security	• Backups should be transported to an approved offsite storage location on a daily, weekly, or monthly rotation, as required by the security policy.
Validation	• Backups should be protected using strong passwords. The password is required to restore the data.

Refer to
Online Course
for Illustration

Upgrade, Update, and Patch - 16.3.3

Keeping up to date with the latest developments can lead to a more effective defense against network attacks. As new malware is released, enterprises need to keep current with the latest versions of antivirus software.

The most effective way to mitigate a worm attack is to download security updates from the operating system vendor and patch all vulnerable systems. Administering numerous systems involves the creation of a standard software image (operating system and accredited applications that are authorized for use on client systems) that is deployed on new or upgraded systems. However, security requirements change, and already deployed systems may need to have updated security patches installed.

One solution to the management of critical security patches is to make sure all end systems automatically download updates, as shown for Windows 10 in the figure. Security patches are automatically downloaded and installed without user intervention.

Refer to
Online Course
for Illustration

Authentication, Authorization, and Accounting - 16.3.4

All network devices should be securely configured to provide only authorized individuals with access. Authentication, authorization, and accounting (AAA, or "triple A") network security services provide the primary framework to set up access control on network devices.

AAA is a way to control who is permitted to access a network (authenticate), what actions they perform while accessing the network (authorize), and making a record of what was done while they are there (accounting).

The concept of AAA is similar to the use of a credit card. The credit card identifies who can use it, how much that user can spend, and keeps account of what items the user spent money on, as shown in the figure.

Refer to
Online Course
for Illustration

Firewalls - 16.3.5

A firewall is one of the most effective security tools available for protecting users from external threats. A firewall protects computers and networks by preventing undesirable traffic from entering internal networks.

Network firewalls reside between two or more networks, control the traffic between them, and help prevent unauthorized access. For example, the top topology in the figure illustrates how the firewall enables traffic from an internal network host to exit the network and return to the inside network. The bottom topology illustrates how traffic initiated by the outside network (i.e., the internet) is denied access to the internal network.

A firewall could allow outside users controlled access to specific services. For example, servers accessible to outside users are usually located on a special network referred to as the demilitarized zone (DMZ), as shown in the figure. The DMZ enables a network administrator to apply specific policies for hosts connected to that network.

Types of Firewalls - 16.3.6

Firewall products come packaged in various forms. These products use different techniques for determining what will be permitted or denied access to a network. They include the following:

- **Packet filtering** - Prevents or allows access based on IP or MAC addresses

- **Application filtering** - Prevents or allows access by specific application types based on port numbers

- **URL filtering** - Prevents or allows access to websites based on specific URLs or keywords

- **Stateful packet inspection (SPI)** - Incoming packets must be legitimate responses to requests from internal hosts. Unsolicited packets are blocked unless permitted specifically. SPI can also include the capability to recognize and filter out specific types of attacks, such as denial of service (DoS)

Endpoint Security - 16.3.7

An endpoint, or host, is an individual computer system or device that acts as a network client. Common endpoints are laptops, desktops, servers, smartphones, and tablets. Securing endpoint devices is one of the most challenging jobs of a network administrator because it involves human nature. A company must have well-documented policies in place and employees must be aware of these rules. Employees need to be trained on proper use of the network. Policies often include the use of antivirus software and host intrusion prevention. More comprehensive endpoint security solutions rely on network access control.

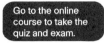

Go to the online course to take the quiz and exam.

Check Your Understanding - Network Attack Mitigation - 16.3.8

Device Security - 16.4

Cisco AutoSecure - 16.4.1

One area of networks that requires special attention to maintain security is the devices. You probably already have a password for your computer, smart phone, or tablet. Is it as strong as it could be? Are you using other tools to enhance the security of your devices? This topic tells you how.

The security settings are set to the default values when a new operating system is installed on a device. In most cases, this level of security is inadequate. For Cisco routers, the Cisco AutoSecure feature can be used to assist securing the system, as shown in the example.

```
Router# auto secure

                --- AutoSecure Configuration ---

*** AutoSecure configuration enhances the security of

the router but it will not make router absolutely secure

from all security attacks ***
```

In addition, there are some simple steps that should be taken that apply to most operating systems:

- Default usernames and passwords should be changed immediately.

- Access to system resources should be restricted to only the individuals that are authorized to use those resources.

- Any unnecessary services and applications should be turned off and uninstalled when possible.

Often, devices shipped from the manufacturer have been sitting in a warehouse for a period of time and do not have the most up-to-date patches installed. It is important to update any software and install any security patches prior to implementation.

Passwords - 16.4.2

To protect network devices, it is important to use strong passwords. Here are standard guidelines to follow:

- Use a password length of at least eight characters, preferably 10 or more characters. A longer password is a more secure password.

- Make passwords complex. Include a mix of uppercase and lowercase letters, numbers, symbols, and spaces, if allowed.

- Avoid passwords based on repetition, common dictionary words, letter or number sequences, usernames, relative or pet names, biographical information, such as birthdates, ID numbers, ancestor names, or other easily identifiable pieces of information.

- Deliberately misspell a password. For example, Smith = Smyth = 5mYth or Security = 5ecur1ty.

- Change passwords often. If a password is unknowingly compromised, the window of opportunity for the threat actor to use the password is limited.

- Do not write passwords down and leave them in obvious places such as on the desk or monitor.

The tables show examples of strong and weak passwords.

Weak Passwords

Weak Password	Why it is Weak
secret	Simple dictionary password
smith	Maiden name of mother
toyota	Make of a car
bob1967	Name and birthday of the user
Blueleaf23	Simple words and numbers

Strong Passwords

Strong Password	Why it is Strong
b67n42d39c	Combines alphanumeric characters
12^h u4@1p7	Combines alphanumeric characters, symbols, and includes a space

On Cisco routers, leading spaces are ignored for passwords, but spaces after the first character are not. Therefore, one method to create a strong password is to use the space bar and create a phrase made of many words. This is called a passphrase. A passphrase is often easier to remember than a simple password. It is also longer and harder to guess.

Additional Password Security - 16.4.3

Strong passwords are only useful if they are secret. There are several steps that can be taken to help ensure that passwords remain secret on a Cisco router and switch including these:

- Encrypting all plaintext passwords

- Setting a minimum acceptable password length

- Deterring brute-force password guessing attacks

- Disabling an inactive privileged EXEC mode access after a specified amount of time.

As shown in the sample configuration in the figure, the **service password-encryption** global configuration command prevents unauthorized individuals from viewing plaintext passwords in the configuration file. This command encrypts all plaintext passwords. Notice in the example, that the password "cisco" has been encrypted as "03095A0F034F".

To ensure that all configured passwords are a minimum of a specified length, use the **security passwords min-length** *length* command in global configuration mode. In the figure, any new password configured would have to have a minimum length of eight characters.

Threat actors may use password cracking software to conduct a brute-force attack on a network device. This attack continuously attempts to guess the valid passwords until one works. Use the **login block-for # attempts # within #** global configuration command to deter this type of attack. In the figure for example, the **login block-for 120 attempts 3 within 60** command will block vty login attempts for 120 seconds if there are three failed login attempts within 60 seconds.

Network administrators can become distracted and accidently leave a privileged EXEC mode session open on a terminal. This could enable an internal threat actor access to change or erase the device configuration.

By default, Cisco routers will logout an EXEC session after 10 minutes of inactivity. However, you can reduce this setting using the **exec-timeout** *minutes seconds* line configuration command. This command can be applied online console, auxiliary, and vty lines. In the figure, we are telling the Cisco device to automatically disconnect an inactive user on a vty line after the user has been idle for 5 minutes and 30 seconds.

```
Router(config)# service password-encryption

Router(config)# security password min-length 8

Router(config)# login block-for 120 attempts 3 within 60

Router(config)# line vty 0 4

Router(config-line)# password cisco

Router(config-line)# exec-timeout 5 30

Router(config-line)# transport input ssh

Router(config-line)# end

Router#

Router# show running-config | section line vty

line vty 0 4

 password 7 03095A0F034F
```

```
exec-timeout 5 30

login

Router#
```

Enable SSH - 16.4.4

Telnet simplifies remote device access, but it is not secure. Data contained within a Telnet packet is transmitted unencrypted. For this reason, it is highly recommended to enable Secure Shell (SSH) on devices for secure remote access.

It is possible to configure a Cisco device to support SSH using the following six steps:

Step 1. **Configure a unique device hostname.** A device must have a unique hostname other than the default.

Step 2. **Configure the IP domain name.** Configure the IP domain name of the network by using the global configuration mode command **ip-domain name.**

Step 3. **Generate a key to encrypt SSH traffic.** SSH encrypts traffic between source and destination. However, to do so, a unique authentication key must be generated by using the global configuration command **crypto key generate rsa general-keys modulus** *bits*. The modulus *bits* determines the size of the key and can be configured from 360 bits to 2048 bits. The larger the bit value, the more secure the key. However, larger bit values also take longer to encrypt and decrypt information. The minimum recommended modulus length is 1024 bits.

Step 4. **Verify or create a local database entry.** Create a local database username entry using the **username** global configuration command. In the example, the parameter **secret** is used so that the password will be encrypted using MD5.

Step 5. **Authenticate against the local database.** Use the **login local** line configuration command to authenticate the vty line against the local database.

Step 6. **Enable vty inbound SSH sessions.** By default, no input session is allowed on vty lines. You can specify multiple input protocols including Telnet and SSH using the **transport input [ssh | telnet]** command.

As shown in the example, router R1 is configured in the span.com domain. This information is used along with the bit value specified in the **crypto key generate rsa general-keys modulus** command to create an encryption key.

Next, a local database entry for a user named Bob is created. Finally, the vty lines are configured to authenticate against the local database and to only accept incoming SSH sessions.

```
Router# configure terminal

Router(config)# hostname R1

R1(config)# ip domain-name span.com

R1(config)# crypto key generate rsa general-keys modulus 1024

The name for the keys will be: R1.span.com % The key modulus size is
1024 bits

% Generating 1024 bit RSA keys, keys will be non-exportable...[OK]

•Dec 13 16:19:12.079: %SSH-5-ENABLED: SSH 1.99 has been enabled
```

```
R1(config)#
R1(config)# username Bob secret cisco
R1(config)# line vty 0 4
R1(config-line)# login local
R1(config-line)# transport input ssh
R1(config-line)# exit
R1(config)#
```

Disable Unused Services - 16.4.5

Cisco routers and switches start with a list of active services that may or may not be required in your network. Disable any unused services to preserve system resources, such as CPU cycles and RAM, and prevent threat actors from exploiting these services. The type of services that are on by default will vary depending on the IOS version. For example, IOS-XE typically will have only HTTPS and DHCP ports open. You can verify this with the **show ip ports all** command, as shown in the example.

```
Router# show ip ports all
Proto Local Address  oreign Address     State     PID/Program Name
TCB   Local Address  Foreign Address    (state)
tcp   :::443         :::*               LISTEN    309/[IOS]HTTP CORE
tcp   *:443          *:*                LISTEN    309/[IOS]HTTP CORE
udp   *:67           0.0.0.0:0                    387/[IOS]DHCPD Receive
Router#
```

IOS versions prior to IOS-XE use the **show control-plane host open-ports** command. We mention this command because you may see it on older devices. The output is similar. However, notice that this older router has an insecure HTTP server and Telnet running. Both of these services should be disabled. As shown in the example, disable HTTP with the **no ip http server** global configuration command. Disable Telnet by specifying only SSH in the line configuration command, **transport input ssh**.

```
Router# show control-plane host open-ports
Active internet connections (servers and established)
Prot    Local Address    Foreign Address        Service        State
 tcp        *:23              *:0               Telnet         LISTEN
 tcp        *:80              *:0               HTTP CORE      LISTEN
 udp        *:67              *:0           DHCPD Receive      LISTEN
Router# configure terminal
Router(config)# no ip http server
Router(config)# line vty 0 15
Router(config-line)# transport input ssh
```

Refer to **Packet Tracer Activity** for this chapter

Packet Tracer - Configure Secure Passwords and SSH - 16.4.6

The network administrator has asked you to prepare RTA and SW1 for deployment. Before they can be connected to the network, security measures must be enabled.

Refer to **Lab Activity** for this chapter

Lab - Configure Network Devices with SSH - 16.4.7

In this lab, you will complete the following objectives:

- Part 1: Configure Basic Device Settings
- Part 2: Configure the Router for SSH Access
- Part 3: Configure the Switch for SSH Access
- Part 4: SSH from the CLI on the Switch

Module Practice and Quiz - 16.5

Refer to **Packet Tracer Activity** for this chapter

Packet Tracer - Secure Network Devices - 16.5.1

In this activity you will configure a router and a switch based on a list of requirements.

Refer to **Lab Activity** for this chapter

Lab - Secure Network Devices - 16.5.2

In this lab, you will complete the following objectives:

- Part 1: Configure Basic Device Settings
- Part 2: Configure Basic Security Measures on the Router
- Part 3: Configure Basic Security Measures on the Switch

What did I learn in this module? - 16.5.3

Security Threats and Vulnerabilities

Attacks on a network can be devastating and can result in a loss of time and money due to damage or theft of important information or assets. Intruders who gain access by modifying software or exploiting software vulnerabilities are threat actors. After the threat actor gains access to the network, four types of threats may arise: information theft, data loss and manipulation, identity theft, and disruption of service. There are three primary vulnerabilities or weaknesses: technological, configuration, and security policy. The four classes of physical threats are: hardware, environmental, electrical, and maintenance.

Network Attacks

Malware is short for malicious software. It is code or software specifically designed to damage, disrupt, steal, or inflict "bad" or illegitimate action on data, hosts, or networks. Viruses, worms, and Trojan horses are types of malware. Network attacks can be classified into three major categories: reconnaissance, access, and denial of service. The four classes of physical threats are: hardware, environmental, electrical, and maintenance. The three types of reconnaissance attacks are: internet queries, ping sweeps, and port scans.

The four types of access attacks are: password (brute-force, Trojan horse, packet sniffers), trust exploitation, port redirection, and man-in-the-middle. The two types of disruption of service attacks are: DoS and DDoS.

Network Attack Mitigation

To mitigate network attacks, you must first secure devices including routers, switches, servers, and hosts. Most organizations employ a defense-in-depth approach to security. This requires a combination of networking devices and services working together. Several security devices and services are implemented to protect an organization's users and assets against TCP/IP threats: VPN, ASA firewall, IPS, ESA/WSA, and AAA server. Infrastructure devices should have backups of configuration files and IOS images on an FTP or similar file server. If the computer or a router hardware fails, the data or configuration can be restored using the backup copy. The most effective way to mitigate a worm attack is to download security updates from the operating system vendor and patch all vulnerable systems. To manage critical security patches, to make sure all end systems automatically download updates. AAA is a way to control who is permitted to access a network (authenticate), what they can do while they are there (authorize), and what actions they perform while accessing the network (accounting). Network firewalls reside between two or more networks, control the traffic between them, and help prevent unauthorized access. Servers accessible to outside users are usually located on a special network referred to as the DMZ. Firewalls use various techniques for determining what is permitted or denied access to a network including: packet filtering, application filtering, URL filtering and SPI. Securing endpoint devices is critical to network security. A company must have well-documented policies in place, which may include the use of antivirus software and host intrusion prevention. More comprehensive endpoint security solutions rely on network access control.

Device Security

The security settings are set to the default values when a new OS is installed on a device. This level of security is inadequate. For Cisco routers, the Cisco AutoSecure feature can be used to assist securing the system. For most OSs default usernames and passwords should be changed immediately, access to system resources should be restricted to only the individuals that are authorized to use those resources, and any unnecessary services and applications should be turned off and uninstalled when possible. To protect network devices, it is important to use strong passwords. A pass phrase is often easier to remember than a simple password. It is also longer and harder to guess. For routers and switches, encrypt all plaintext passwords, setting a minimum acceptable password length, deter brute-force password guessing attacks, and disable an inactive privileged EXEC mode access after a specified amount of time. Configure appropriate devices to support SSH, and disable unused services.

Go to the online course to take the quiz and exam.

Chapter Quiz - Network Security Fundamentals

Your Chapter Notes

CHAPTER 17

Build a Small Network

Introduction - 17.0

Why should I take this module? - 17.0.1

Welcome to Build a Small Network!

Hooray! You have come to the final module in the Introduction to Networks v7.0 course. You have most of the foundational knowledge needed to set up your own network. Where do you go from here? You build a network, of course. And not only do you build one, you verify that it is working, and even troubleshoot some common network problems. This module has labs and Packet Tracer activities to help you practice your new skills as a network administrator. Let's get going!

What will I learn to do in this module? - 17.0.2

Module Title: Build a Small Network

Module Objective: Implement a network design for a small network to include a router, a switch, and end devices.

Topic Title	Topic Objective
Devices in a Small Network	Identify the devices used in a small network.
Small Network Applications and Protocols	Identify the protocols and applications used in a small network.
Scale to Larger Networks	Explain how a small network serves as the basis of larger networks.
Verify Connectivity	Use the output of the ping and tracert commands to verify connectivity and establish relative network performance.
Host and IOS Commands	Use host and IOS commands to acquire information about the devices in a network.
Troubleshooting Methodologies	Describe common network troubleshooting methodologies
Troubleshooting Scenarios	Troubleshoot issues with devices in the network.

Devices in a Small Network - 17.1

Small Network Topologies - 17.1.1

Refer to
Online Course
for Illustration

The majority of businesses are small; therefore, it is not surprising that the majority of business networks are also small.

A small network design is usually simple. The number and type of devices included are significantly reduced compared to that of a larger network.

For instance, refer to the sample small-business network shown in the figure.

This small network requires a router, a switch, and a wireless access point to connect wired and wireless users, an IP phone, a printer, and a server. Small networks typically have a single WAN connection provided by DSL, cable, or an Ethernet connection.

Large networks require an IT department to maintain, secure, and troubleshoot network devices and to protect organizational data. Managing a small network requires many of the same skills as those required for managing a larger one. Small networks are managed by a local IT technician or by a contracted professional.

Refer to
Interactive Graphic
in online course

Device Selection for a Small Network - 17.1.2

Like large networks, small networks require planning and design to meet user requirements. Planning ensures that all requirements, cost factors, and deployment options are given due consideration.

One of the first design considerations is the type of intermediary devices to use to support the network.

Click each button for more information about the factors that must be considered when selecting network devices.

Cost

The cost of a switch or router is determined by its capacity and features. This includes the number and types of ports available and the backplane speed. Other factors that influence the cost are network management capabilities, embedded security technologies, and optional advanced switching technologies. The expense of cable runs required to connect every device on the network must also be considered. Another key element affecting cost considerations is the amount of redundancy to incorporate into the network.

Speed and Types of Ports/Interfaces

Choosing the number and type of ports on a router or switch is a critical decision. Newer computers have built-in 1 Gbps NICs. Some servers may even have 10 Gbps ports. Although it is more expensive, choosing Layer 2 devices that can accommodate increased speeds allows the network to evolve without replacing central devices.

Expandability

Networking devices are available in fixed and modular physical configurations. Fixed configuration devices have a specific number and type of ports or interfaces and cannot be expanded. Modular devices have expansion slots to add new modules as requirements evolve. Switches are available with additional ports for high-speed uplinks. Routers can be used to connect different types of networks. Care must be taken to select the appropriate modules and interfaces for the specific media.

Operating System Features and Services

Network devices must have operating systems that can support the organizations requirements such as the following:

- Layer 3 switching
- Network Address Translation (NAT)
- Dynamic Host Configuration Protocol (DHCP)
- Security
- Quality of service (QoS)
- Voice over IP (VoIP)

Refer to **Online Course** for Illustration

IP Addressing for a Small Network - 17.1.3

When implementing a network, create an IP addressing scheme and use it. All hosts and devices within an internetwork must have a unique address.

Devices that will factor into the IP addressing scheme include the following:

- End user devices - The number and type of connection (i.e., wired, wireless, remote access)
- Servers and peripherals devices (e.g., printers and security cameras)
- Intermediary devices including switches and access points

It is recommended that you plan, document, and maintain an IP addressing scheme based on device type. The use of a planned IP addressing scheme makes it easier to identify a type of device and to troubleshoot problems, as for instance, when troubleshooting network traffic issues with a protocol analyzer.

For example, refer to the topology of a small to medium sized organization in the figure.

The organization requires three user LANs (i.e., 192.168.1.0/24, 192.168.2.0/24, and 192.168.3.0/24). The organization has decided to implement a consistent IP addressing scheme for each 192.168.x.0/24 LAN using the following plan:

Device Type	Assignable IP Address Range	Summarized as ...
Default gateway (Router)	192.168.x.1 - 192.168.x.2	192.168.x.0/30
Switches (max 2)	192.168.x.5 - 192.168.x.6	192.168.x.4/30
Access points (max 6)	192.168.x.9 - 192.168.x.14	192.168.x.8/29
Servers (max 6)	192.168.x.17 - 192.168.x.22	192.168.x.16/29
Printers (max 6)	192.168.x.25 - 192.168.x.30	192.168.x.24/29
IP Phones (max 6)	192.168.x.33 - 192.168.x.38	192.168.x.32/29
Wired devices (max 62)	192.168.x.65 - 192.168.x.126	192.168.x.64/26
Wireless devices (max 62)	192.168.x.193 - 192.168.x.254	192.168.x.192/26

The figure displays an example of the 192.168.2.0/24 network devices with assigned IP addresses using the predefined IP addressing scheme.

For instance, the default gateway IP address is 192.168.2.1/24, the switch is 192.168.2.5/24, the server is 192.168.2.17/24, etc..

Notice that the assignable IP address ranges were deliberately allocated on subnetnetwork boundaries to simplify summarizing the group type. For instance, assume another switch with IP address 192.168.2.6 is added to the network. To identify all switches in a network policy, the administrator could specify the summarized network address 192.168.x.4/30.

Refer to Online Course for Illustration

Redundancy in a Small Network - 17.1.4

Another important part of network design is reliability. Even small businesses often rely heavily on their network for business operation. A failure of the network can be very costly.

In order to maintain a high degree of reliability, *redundancy* is required in the network design. Redundancy helps to eliminate single points of failure.

There are many ways to accomplish redundancy in a network. Redundancy can be accomplished by installing duplicate equipment, but it can also be accomplished by supplying duplicate network links for critical areas, as shown in the figure.

Small networks typically provide a single exit point toward the internet via one or more default gateways. If the router fails, the entire network loses connectivity to the internet. For this reason, it may be advisable for a small business to pay for a second service provider as backup.

Refer to Online Course for Illustration

Traffic Management - 17.1.5

The goal for a good network design, even for a small network, is to enhance the productivity of the employees and minimize network downtime. The network administrator should consider the various types of traffic and their treatment in the network design.

The routers and switches in a small network should be configured to support real-time traffic, such as voice and video, in an appropriate manner relative to other data traffic. In fact, a good network design will implement quality of service (QoS) to classify traffic carefully according to priority, as shown in the figure.

Go to the online course to take the quiz and exam.

Check Your Understanding - Devices in a Small Network - 17.1.6

Small Network Applications and Protocols - 17.2

Refer to Online Course for Illustration

Common Applications - 17.2.1

The previous topic discussed the components of a small network, as well as some of the design considerations. These considerations are necessary when you are just setting up a network. After you have set it up, your network still needs certain types of applications and protocols in order to work.

The network is only as useful as the applications that are on it. There are two forms of software programs or processes that provide access to the network: network applications and application layer services.

Network Applications

Applications are the software programs used to communicate over the network. Some end-user applications are network-aware, meaning that they implement application layer protocols and are able to communicate directly with the lower layers of the protocol stack. Email clients and web browsers are examples of this type of application.

Application Layer Services

Other programs may need the assistance of application layer services to use network resources like file transfer or network print spooling. Though transparent to an employee, these services are the programs that interface with the network and prepare the data for transfer. Different types of data, whether text, graphics or video, require different network services to ensure that they are properly prepared for processing by the functions occurring at the lower layers of the OSI model.

Each application or network service uses protocols, which define the standards and data formats to be used. Without protocols, the data network would not have a common way to format and direct data. In order to understand the function of various network services, it is necessary to become familiar with the underlying protocols that govern their operation.

Use the Task Manager to view the current applications, processes, and services running on a Windows PC, as shown in the figure.

Refer to
Online Course
for Illustration

Refer to
Interactive Graphic
in online course

Common Protocols - 17.2.2

Most of a technician's work, in either a small or a large network, will in some way be involved with network protocols. Network protocols support the applications and services used by employees in a small network.

Network administrators commonly require access to network devices and servers. The two most common remote access solutions are Telnet and Secure Shell (SSH). SSH service is a secure alternative to Telnet. When connected, administrators can access the SSH server device as though they were logged in locally.

SSH is used to establish a secure remote access connection between an SSH client and other SSH-enabled devices:

- **Network device** - The network device (e.g., router, switch, access point, etc.) must support SSH to provide remote access SSH server services to clients.

- **Server** - The server (e.g., web server, email server, etc.) must support remote access SSH server services to clients.

Network administrators must also support common network servers and their required related network protocols, as shown in the figure.

Click each button for more information about common network servers and their required related network protocols.

Web Server

- Web clients and web servers exchange web traffic using the Hypertext Transfer Protocol (HTTP).

- Hypertext Transfer Protocol Secure (HTTPS) is used for secure web communication.

Email Server

- Email servers and clients use Simple Mail Transfer Protocol (SMTP) to send emails.

- Email clients use Post Office Protocol (POP3) or Internet Message Access Protocol (IMAP) to retrieve email.

- Recipients are specified using the user@xyz.xxx format.

FTP Server

- File Transfer Protocol (FTP) service allows files to be downloaded and uploaded between a client and FTP server.

- FTP Secure (FTPS) and Secure FTP (SFTP) are used to secure FTP file exchange.

DHCP Server

Dynamic Host Configuration Protocol (DHCP) is used by clients to acquire an IP configuration (i.e., IP address, subnet mask, default gateway and more) from a DHCP server.

DNS Server

- Domain Name Service (DNS) resolves a domain name to an IP address (e.g., cisco.com = 72.163.4.185)

- DNS provides the IP address of a web site (i.e., domain name) to a requesting host.

Note: A server could provide multiple network services. For instance, a server could be an email, FTP, and SSH server.

These network protocols comprise the fundamental toolset of a network professional. Each of these network protocols define:

- Processes on either end of a communication session
- Types of messages
- Syntax of the messages
- Meaning of informational fields
- How messages are sent and the expected response
- Interaction with the next lower layer

Many companies have established a policy of using secure versions (e.g., SSH, SFTP, and HTTPS) of these protocols whenever possible.

Refer to
Online Course
for Illustration

Refer to
Interactive Graphic
in online course

Voice and Video Applications - 17.2.3

Businesses today are increasingly using IP telephony and streaming media to communicate with customers and business partners. Many organizations are enabling their employees to work remotely. As the figure shows, many of their users still require access to corporate software and files, as well as support for voice and video applications.

The network administrator must ensure the proper equipment is installed in the network and that the network devices are configured to ensure priority delivery.

Click each button for more information about the factors that a small network administrator must consider when supporting real-time applications.

Infrastructure

- The network infrastructure must support the real-time applications.

- Existing devices and cabling must be tested and validated.

- Newer networking products may be required.

VoIP

- VoIP devices convert analog telephone signals into digital IP packets.

- Typically, VOIP is less expensive than an IP telephony solution, but the quality of communications does not meet the same standards.

- Small network voice and video over IP can be solved using Skype and non-enterprise versions of Cisco WebEx.

IP Telephony

- An IP phone performs voice-to-IP conversion with the use of a dedicated server for call control and signaling.

- Many vendors provide small business IP telephony solutions such as the Cisco Business Edition 4000 Series products.

Real-Time Applications

- The network must support quality of service (QoS) mechanisms to minimize latency issues for real-time streaming applications.

- Real-Time Transport Protocol (RTP) and Real-Time Transport Control Protocol (RTCP) are two protocols that support this requirement.

Go to the online
course to take the
quiz and exam.

Check Your Understanding - Small Network Applications and Protocols - 17.2.4

Scale to Larger Networks - 17.3

Small Network Growth - 17.3.1

If your network is for a small business, presumably, you want that business to grow, and your network to grow along with it. This is called scaling a network, and there are some best practices for doing this.

Growth is a natural process for many small businesses, and their networks must grow accordingly. Ideally, the network administrator has enough lead-time to make intelligent decisions about growing the network in alignment with the growth of the company.

To scale a network, several elements are required:

- **Network documentation** - Physical and logical topology

- **Device inventory** - List of devices that use or comprise the network

- **Budget** - Itemized IT budget, including fiscal year equipment purchasing budget

- **Traffic analysis** - Protocols, applications, and services and their respective traffic requirements should be documented

These elements are used to inform the decision-making that accompanies the scaling of a small network.

Refer to **Online Course** for Illustration

Protocol Analysis - 17.3.2

As the network grows, it becomes important to determine how to manage network traffic. It is important to understand the type of traffic that is crossing the network as well as the current traffic flow. There are several network management tools that can be used for this purpose. However, a simple protocol analyzer such as Wireshark can also be used.

For instance, running Wireshark on several key hosts can reveal the types of network traffic flowing through the network. The following figure displays Wireshark protocol hierarchy statistics for a Windows host on a small network.

To determine traffic flow patterns, it is important to do the following:

- Capture traffic during peak utilization times to get a good representation of the different traffic types.

- Perform the capture on different network segments and devices as some traffic will be local to a particular segment.

Information gathered by the protocol analyzer is evaluated based on the source and destination of the traffic, as well as the type of traffic being sent. This analysis can be used to make decisions on how to manage the traffic more efficiently. This can be done by reducing unnecessary traffic flows or changing flow patterns altogether by moving a server, for example.

Sometimes, simply relocating a server or service to another network segment improves network performance and accommodates the growing traffic needs. At other times, optimizing the network performance requires major network redesign and intervention.

Refer to **Online Course** for Illustration

Employee Network Utilization - 17.3.3

In addition to understanding changing traffic trends, a network administrator must be aware of how network use is changing. Many operating systems provide built-in tools to display such information. For example, a Windows host provides tools such as the Task Manager, Event Viewer, and Data Usage tools.

These tools can be used to capture a "snapshot" of information such as the following:

- OS and OS Version
- CPU utilization
- RAM utilization
- Drive utilization
- Non-Network applications
- Network applications

Documenting snapshots for employees in a small network over a period of time is very useful to identify evolving protocol requirements and associated traffic flows. A shift in resource utilization may require the network administrator to adjust network resource allocations accordingly.

The Windows 10 Data Usage tool is especially useful to determine which applications are using network services on a host. The Data Usage tool is accessed using **Settings > Network & Internet > Data usage > network interface** (from the last 30 days).

The example in the figure is displaying the applications running on a remote user Windows 10 host using the local Wi-Fi network connection.

Go to the online course to take the quiz and exam.

Check Your Understanding - Scale to Larger Networks - 17.3.4

Verify Connectivity - 17.4

Refer to Online Course for Illustration

Verify Connectivity with Ping - 17.4.1

Whether your network is small and new, or you are scaling an existing network, you will always want to be able to verify that your components are properly connected to each other and to the internet. This topic discusses some utilities that you can use to ensure that your network is connected.

The **ping** command is the most effective way to quickly test Layer 3 connectivity between a source and destination IP address. The command also displays various round-trip time statistics.

Specifically, the **ping** command uses the Internet Control Message Protocol (ICMP) echo (ICMP Type 8) and echo reply (ICMP Type 0) messages. The **ping** command is available in most operating systems including Windows, Linux, macOS, and Cisco IOS.

On a Windows 10 host, the **ping** command sends four consecutive ICMP echo messages and expects four consecutive ICMP echo replies from the destination.

For example, assume PC A pings PC B. As shown in the figure, the PC A Windows host sends four consecutive ICMP echo messages to PC B (i.e., 10.1.1.10).

The destination host receives and processes the ICMP echos. As shown in the figure, PC B responds by sending four ICMP echo reply messages to PC A.

As shown in the command output, PC A has received echo replies from PC-B verifying the Layer 3 network connection.

```
C:\Users\PC-A> ping 10.1.1.10

Pinging 10.1.1.10 with 32 bytes of data:

Reply from 10.1.1.10: bytes=32 time=47ms TTL=51

Reply from 10.1.1.10: bytes=32 time=60ms TTL=51

Reply from 10.1.1.10: bytes=32 time=53ms TTL=51

Reply from 10.1.1.10: bytes=32 time=50ms TTL=51

Ping statistics for 10.1.1.10:

    Packets: Sent = 4, Received = 4, Lost = 0 (0% loss),

Approximate round trip times in milli-seconds:

    Minimum = 47ms, Maximum = 60ms, Average = 52ms

C:\Users\PC-A>
```

The output validates Layer 3 connectivity between PC A and PC B.

A Cisco IOS **ping** command output varies from a Windows host. For instance, the IOS ping sends five ICMP echo messages, as shown in the output.

```
R1# ping 10.1.1.10

Type escape sequence to abort.

Sending 5, 100-byte ICMP Echos to 10.1.1.10, timeout is 2 seconds:

!!!!!

Success rate is 100 percent (5/5), round-trip min/avg/max = 1/1/2 ms

R1#
```

Notice the !!!!! output characters. The IOS **ping** command displays an indicator for each ICMP echo reply received. The table lists the most common output characters from the **ping** command.

IOS Ping Indicators

Element	Description
!	• Exclamation mark indicates successful receipt of an echo reply message.
	• It validates a Layer 3 connection between source and destination.
.	• A period means that time expired waiting for an echo reply message.
	• This indicates a connectivity problem occurred somewhere along the path.
U	• Uppercase U indicates a router along the path responded with an ICMP Type 3 "destination unreachable" error message.
	• Possible reasons include the router does not know the direction to the destination network or it could not find the host on the destination network.

Note: Other possible ping replies include Q, M, ?, or &. However, the meaning of these are out of scope for this module.

Refer to
Online Course
for Illustration

Extended Ping - 17.4.2

A standard **ping** uses the IP address of the interface closest to the destination network as the source of the **ping**. The source IP address of the **ping 10.1.1.10** command on R1 would be that of the G0/0/0 interface (i.e., 209.165.200.225), as illustrated in the example.

The Cisco IOS offers an "extended" mode of the **ping** command. This mode enables the user to create special type of pings by adjusting parameters related to the command operation.

Extended ping is entered in privileged EXEC mode by typing **ping** without a destination IP address. You will then be given several prompts to customize the extended **ping**.

Note: Pressing **Enter** accepts the indicated default values.

For example, assume you wanted to test connectivity from the R1 LAN (i.e., 192.168.10.0/24) to the 10.1.1.0 LAN. This could be verified from the PC A. However, an extended **ping** could be configured on R1 to specify a different source address.

As illustrated in the example, the source IP address of the extended **ping** command on R1 could be configured to use the G0/0/1 interface IP address (i.e., 192.168.10.1).

The following command output configures an extended **ping** on R1 and specifies the source IP address to be that of the G0/0/1 interface (i.e., 192.168.10.1).

```
R1# ping
Protocol [ip]:
Target IP address: 10.1.1.10
Repeat count [5]:
Datagram size [100]:
Timeout in seconds [2]:
Extended commands [n]: y
Ingress ping [n]:
Source address or interface: 192.168.10.1
DSCP Value [0]:
Type of service [0]:
Set DF bit in IP header? [no]:
Validate reply data? [no]:
Data pattern [0x0000ABCD]:
Loose, Strict, Record, Timestamp, Verbose[none]:
Sweep range of sizes [n]:
Type escape sequence to abort.
Sending 5, 100-byte ICMP Echos to 10.1.1.1, timeout is 2 seconds:
Packet sent with a source address of 192.168.10.1
!!!!!
Success rate is 100 percent (5/5), round-trip min/avg/max = 1/1/1 ms
R1#
```

Note: The **ping ipv6** command is used for IPv6 extended pings.

Refer to
Online Course
for Illustration

Verify Connectivity with Traceroute - 17.4.3

The **ping** command is useful to quickly determine if there is a Layer 3 connectivity problem. However, it does not identify where the problem is located along the path.

Traceroute can help locate Layer 3 problem areas in a network. A trace returns a list of hops as a packet is routed through a network. It could be used to identify the point along the path where the problem can be found.

The syntax of the trace command varies between operating systems, as illustrated in the figure.

The following is a sample output of **tracert** command on a Windows 10 host.

```
C:\Users\PC-A> tracert 10.1.1.10

Tracing route to 10.1.10 over a maximum of 30 hops:

  1     2 ms      2 ms      2 ms    192.168.10.1

  2     *         *         *       Request timed out.

  3     *         *         *       Request timed out.

  4     *         *         *       Request timed out.

^C

C:\Users\PC-A>
```

Note: Use **Ctrl-C** to interrupt a **tracert** in Windows.

The only successful response was from the gateway on R1. Trace requests to the next hop timed out as indicated by the asterisk (*), meaning that the next hop router did not respond. The timed out requests indicate that there is a failure in the internetwork beyond the LAN, or that these routers have been configured to not respond to echo requests used in the trace. In this example there appears to be a problem between R1 and R2.

A Cisco IOS **traceroute** command output varies from the Windows **tracert** command. For instance, refer to the following topology.

The following is a sample output of traceroute command from R1.

```
R1# traceroute 10.1.1.10

Type escape sequence to abort.

Tracing the route to 10.1.1.10

VRF info: (vrf in name/id, vrf out name/id)

  1 209.165.200.226 1 msec 0 msec 1 msec

  2 209.165.200.230 1 msec 0 msec 1 msec

  3 10.1.1.10 1 msec 0 msec

R1#
```

In this example, the trace validated that it could successfully reach PC B.

Timeouts indicate a potential problem. For instance, if the 10.1.1.10 host was not available, the **traceroute** command would display the following output.

```
R1# traceroute 10.1.1.10

Type escape sequence to abort.

Tracing the route to 10.1.1.10

VRF info: (vrf in name/id, vrf out name/id)

  1 209.165.200.226 1 msec 0 msec 1 msec

  2 209.165.200.230 1 msec 0 msec 1 msec

  3  *   *   *

  4  *   *   *

  5  *
```

Use **Ctrl-Shift-6** to interrupt a **traceroute** in Cisco IOS.

Note: Windows implementation of traceroute (tracert) sends ICMP Echo Requests. Cisco IOS and Linux use UDP with an invalid port number. The final destination will return an ICMP port unreachable message.

Refer to
Online Course
for Illustration

Extended Traceroute - 17.4.4

Like the extended **ping** command, there is also an extended **traceroute** command. It allows the administrator to adjust parameters related to the command operation. This is helpful in locating the problem when troubleshooting routing loops, determining the exact next-hop router, or determining where packets are getting dropped or denied by a router or firewall.

The Windows **tracert** command allows the input of several parameters through options in the command line. However, it is not guided like the extended traceroute IOS command. The following output displays the available options for the Windows **tracert** command.

```
C:\Users\PC-A> tracert /?

Usage: tracert [-d] [-h maximum_hops] [-j host-list] [-w timeout]

               [-R] [-S srcaddr] [-4] [-6] target_name

Options:

    -d                 Do not resolve addresses to hostnames.

    -h maximum_hops    Maximum number of hops to search for target.

    -j host-list       Loose source route along host-list (IPv4-only).

    -w timeout         Wait timeout milliseconds for each reply.

    -R                 Trace round-trip path (IPv6-only).

    -S srcaddr         Source address to use (IPv6-only).

    -4                 Force using IPv4.

    -6                 Force using IPv6.

C:\Users\PC-A>
```

The Cisco IOS extended **traceroute** option enables the user to create a special type of trace by adjusting parameters related to the command operation. Extended traceroute is entered in privileged EXEC mode by typing **traceroute** without a destination IP address. IOS will guide you through the command options by presenting a number of prompts related to the setting of all the different parameters.

Note: Pressing **Enter** accepts the indicated default values.

For example, assume you want to test connectivity to PC B from the R1 LAN. Although this could be verified from PC A, an extended **traceroute** could be configured on R1 to specify a different source address.

As illustrated in the example, the source IP address of the extended **traceroute** command on R1 could be configured to use the R1 LAN interface IP address (i.e., 192.168.10.1).

```
R1# traceroute
Protocol [ip]:
Target IP address: 10.1.1.10
Ingress traceroute [n]:
Source address: 192.168.10.1
DSCP Value [0]:
Numeric display [n]:
Timeout in seconds [3]:
Probe count [3]:
Minimum Time to Live [1]:
Maximum Time to Live [30]:
Port Number [33434]:
Loose, Strict, Record, Timestamp, Verbose[none]:
Type escape sequence to abort.
Tracing the route to 192.168.10.10
VRF info: (vrf in name/id, vrf out name/id)
  1 209.165.200.226 1 msec 1 msec 1 msec
  2 209.165.200.230 0 msec 1 msec 0 msec
  3  *
    10.1.1.10 2 msec 2 msec
R1#
```

Network Baseline - 17.4.5

One of the most effective tools for monitoring and troubleshooting network performance is to establish a network baseline. Creating an effective network performance baseline is accomplished over a period of time. Measuring performance at varying times and loads will assist in creating a better picture of overall network performance.

The output derived from network commands contributes data to the network baseline. One method for starting a baseline is to copy and paste the results from an executed **ping**, **trace**, or other relevant commands into a text file. These text files can be time stamped with the date and saved into an archive for later retrieval and comparison.

Among items to consider are error messages and the response times from host to host. If there is a considerable increase in response times, there may be a latency issue to address.

For example, the following **ping** output was captured and pasted into a text file.

August 19, 2019 at 08:14:43

```
C:\Users\PC-A> ping 10.1.1.10

Pinging 10.1.1.10 with 32 bytes of data:

Reply from 10.1.1.10: bytes=32 time<1ms TTL=64

Reply from 10.1.1.10: bytes=32 time<1ms TTL=64

Reply from 10.1.1.10: bytes=32 time<1ms TTL=64

Reply from 10.1.1.10: bytes=32 time<1ms TTL=64

Ping statistics for 10.1.1.10:

    Packets: Sent = 4, Received = 4, Lost = 0 (0% loss),

Approximate round trip times in milli-seconds:

    Minimum = 0ms, Maximum = 0ms, Average = 0ms

C:\Users\PC-A>
```

Notice the **ping** round-trip times are less than 1 ms.

A month later, the ping is repeated and captured.

September 19, 2019 at 10:18:21

```
C:\Users\PC-A> ping 10.1.1.10

Pinging 10.1.1.10 with 32 bytes of data:

Reply from 10.1.1.10: bytes=32 time=50ms TTL=64

Reply from 10.1.1.10: bytes=32 time=49ms TTL=64

Reply from 10.1.1.10: bytes=32 time=46ms TTL=64

Reply from 10.1.1.10: bytes=32 time=47ms TTL=64

Ping statistics for 10.1.1.10:

    Packets: Sent = 4, Received = 4, Lost = 0 (0% loss),

Approximate round trip times in milli-seconds:

    Minimum = 46ms, Maximum = 50ms, Average = 48ms

C:\Users\PC-A>
```

Notice this time that the **ping** round-trip times are much longer indicating a potential problem.

Corporate networks should have extensive baselines; more extensive than we can describe in this course. Professional-grade software tools are available for storing and maintaining baseline information. In this course, we cover a few basic techniques and discuss the purpose of baselines.

Cisco's best practices for baseline processes can be found by searching the internet for "Baseline Process Best Practices".

Refer to
Lab Activity
for this chapter

Lab - Test Network Latency with Ping and Traceroute - 17.4.6

In this lab, you will complete the following objectives:

- Part 1: Use Ping to Document Network Latency
- Part 2: Use Traceroute to Document Network Latency

Host and IOS Commands - 17.5

Refer to
Online Course
for Illustration

IP Configuration on a Windows Host - 17.5.1

If you have used any of the tools in the previous topic to verify connectivity and found that some part of your network is not working as it should, now is the time to use some commands to troubleshoot your devices. Host and IOS commands can help you determine if the problem is with the IP addressing of your devices, which is a common network problem.

Checking the IP addressing on host devices is a common practice in networking for verifying and troubleshooting end-to-end connectivity. In Windows 10, you can access the IP address details from the **Network and Sharing Center**, as shown in the figure, to quickly view the four important settings: address, mask, router, and DNS.

However, network administrators typically view the IP addressing information on a Windows host by issuing the **ipconfig** command at the command line of a Windows computer, as shown in the sample output.

```
C:\Users\PC-A> ipconfig

Windows IP Configuration

(Output omitted)

Wireless LAN adapter Wi-Fi:

    Connection-specific DNS Suffix  . :

    Link-local IPv6 Address . . . . . : fe80::a4aa:2dd1:ae2d:a75e%16

    IPv4 Address. . . . . . . . . . . : 192.168.10.10

    Subnet Mask . . . . . . . . . . . : 255.255.255.0

    Default Gateway . . . . . . . . . : 192.168.10.1

(Output omitted)
```

Use the **ipconfig /all** command to view the MAC address, as well as a number of details regarding the Layer 3 addressing of the device, as shown in the example output.

```
C:\Users\PC-A> ipconfig /all

Windows IP Configuration

      Host Name . . . . . . . . . . . . : PC-A-00H20

      Primary Dns Suffix  . . . . . . . : cisco.com

      Node Type . . . . . . . . . . . . : Hybrid

      IP Routing Enabled. . . . . . . . : No

      WINS Proxy Enabled. . . . . . . . : No

      DNS Suffix Search List. . . . . . : cisco.com

(Output omitted)

Wireless LAN adapter Wi-Fi:

      Connection-specific DNS Suffix  . :

      Description . . . . . . . . . . . : Intel(R) Dual Band Wireless-AC
8265

      Physical Address. . . . . . . . . : F8-94-C2-E4-C5-0A

      DHCP Enabled. . . . . . . . . . . : Yes

      Autoconfiguration Enabled . . . . : Yes

      Link-local IPv6 Address . . . . . : fe80::a4aa:2dd1:ae2d:a75e%16
(Preferred)

      IPv4 Address. . . . . . . . . . . : 192.168.10.10(Preferred)

      Subnet Mask . . . . . . . . . . . : 255.255.255.0

      Lease Obtained. . . . . . . . . . : August 17, 2019 1:20:17 PM

      Lease Expires . . . . . . . . . . : August 18, 2019 1:20:18 PM

      Default Gateway . . . . . . . . . : 192.168.10.1

      DHCP Server . . . . . . . . . . . : 192.168.10.1

      DHCPv6 IAID . . . . . . . . . . . : 100177090

      DHCPv6 Client DUID. . . . . . . . :
00-01-00-01-21-F3-76-75-54-E1-AD-DE-DA-9A

      DNS Servers . . . . . . . . . . . : 192.168.10.1

      NetBIOS over Tcpip. . . . . . . . : Enabled
```

If a host is configured as a DHCP client, the IP address configuration can be renewed using the **ipconfig /release** and **ipconfig /renew** commands, as shown in the sample output.

```
C:\Users\PC-A> ipconfig /release

(Output omitted)

Wireless LAN adapter Wi-Fi:

      Connection-specific DNS Suffix  . :

      Link-local IPv6 Address . . . . . : fe80::a4aa:2dd1:ae2d:a75e%16

      Default Gateway . . . . . . . . . :

(Output omitted)
```

```
C:\Users\PC-A> ipconfig /renew

(Output omitted)

Wireless LAN adapter Wi-Fi:

    Connection-specific DNS Suffix  . :

    Link-local IPv6 Address . . . . . : fe80::a4aa:2dd1:ae2d:a75e%16

    IPv4 Address. . . . . . . . . . . : 192.168.1.124

    Subnet Mask . . . . . . . . . . . : 255.255.255.0

    Default Gateway . . . . . . . . . : 192.168.1.1

(Output omitted)

C:\Users\PC-A>
```

The DNS Client service on Windows PCs also optimizes the performance of DNS name resolution by storing previously resolved names in memory. The **ipconfig /displaydns** command displays all of the cached DNS entries on a Windows computer system, as shown in the example output.

```
C:\Users\PC-A> ipconfig /displaydns

Windows IP Configuration

(Output omitted)

    netacad.com

    ----------------------------------------

    Record Name . . . . . : netacad.com

    Record Type . . . . . : 1

    Time To Live  . . . . : 602

    Data Length . . . . . : 4

    Section . . . . . . . : Answer

    A (Host) Record . . . : 54.165.95.219

(Output omitted)
```

IP Configuration on a Linux Host - 17.5.2

Refer to Online Course for Illustration

Verifying IP settings using the GUI on a Linux machine will differ depending on the Linux distribution (distro) and desktop interface. The figure shows the **Connection Information** dialog box on the Ubuntu distro running the Gnome desktop.

On the command line, network administrators use the **ifconfig** command to display the status of the currently active interfaces and their IP configuration, as shown in the output.

```
[analyst@secOps ~]$ ifconfig

enp0s3    Link encap:Ethernet  HWaddr 08:00:27:b5:d6:cb

          inet addr: 10.0.2.15  Bcast:10.0.2.255  Mask: 255.255.255.0

          inet6 addr: fe80::57c6:ed95:b3c9:2951/64 Scope:Link

          UP BROADCAST RUNNING MULTICAST  MTU:1500  Metric:1
```

```
        RX packets:1332239 errors:0 dropped:0 overruns:0 frame:0

        TX packets:105910 errors:0 dropped:0 overruns:0 carrier:0

        collisions:0 txqueuelen:1000

        RX bytes:1855455014 (1.8 GB)  TX bytes:13140139 (13.1 MB) lo:
flags=73   mtu 65536

        inet 127.0.0.1  netmask 255.0.0.0

        inet6 ::1  prefixlen 128  scopeid 0x10

        loop  txqueuelen 1000  (Local Loopback)

        RX packets 0  bytes 0 (0.0 B)

        RX errors 0  dropped 0  overruns 0  frame 0

        TX packets 0  bytes 0 (0.0 B)

        TX errors 0  dropped 0 overruns 0  carrier 0  collisions 0
```

The Linux **ip address** command is used to display addresses and their properties. It can also be used to add or delete IP addresses.

Note: The output displayed may vary depending on the Linux distribution.

Refer to **Online Course** for Illustration

IP Configuration on a macOS Host - 17.5.3

In the GUI of a Mac host, open **Network Preferences > Advanced** to get the IP addressing information, as shown in the figure.

However, the **ifconfig** command can also be used to verify the interface IP configuration a shown in the output.

```
MacBook-Air:~ Admin$ ifconfig en0
en0: flags=8863 mtu 1500
        ether c4:b3:01:a0:64:98
        inet6 fe80::c0f:1bf4:60b1:3adb%en0 prefixlen 64 secured scopeid 0x5
        inet 10.10.10.113 netmask 0xffffff00 broadcast 10.10.10.255
        nd6 options=201
        media: autoselect
        status: active
MacBook-Air:~ Admin$
```

Other useful macOS commands to verify the host IP settings include **networksetup -listallnetworkservices** and the **networksetup -getinfo** <*network service*>, as shown in the following output.

```
MacBook-Air:~ Admin$ networksetup -listallnetworkservices
An asterisk (*) denotes that a network service is disabled.
iPhone USB
```

```
Wi-Fi

Bluetooth PAN

Thunderbolt Bridge

MacBook-Air:~ Admin$

MacBook-Air:~ Admin$ networksetup -getinfo Wi-Fi

DHCP Configuration

IP address: 10.10.10.113

Subnet mask: 255.255.255.0

Router: 10.10.10.1

Client ID:

IPv6: Automatic

IPv6 IP address: none

IPv6 Router: none

Wi-Fi ID: c4:b3:01:a0:64:98

MacBook-Air:~ Admin$
```

Refer to
Online Course
for Illustration

The arp Command - 17.5.4

The **arp** command is executed from the Windows, Linux, or Mac command prompt. The command lists all devices currently in the ARP cache of the host, which includes the IPv4 address, physical address, and the type of addressing (static/dynamic), for each device.

For instance, refer to the topology in the figure.

The output of the **arp -a** command on the Windows PC-A host is displayed.

```
C:\Users\PC-A> arp -a

Interface: 192.168.93.175 --- 0xc

    Internet Address        Physical Address        Type

    10.0.0.2                d0-67-e5-b6-56-4b        dynamic

    10.0.0.3                78-48-59-e3-b4-01        dynamic

    10.0.0.4                00-21-b6-00-16-97        dynamic

    10.0.0.254              00-15-99-cd-38-d9        dynamic
```

The **arp -a** command displays the known IP address and MAC address binding. Notice how IP address 10.0.0.5 is not included in the list. This is because the ARP cache only displays information from devices that have been recently accessed.

To ensure that the ARP cache is populated, **ping** a device so that it will have an entry in the ARP table. For instance, if PC-A pinged 10.0.0.5, then the ARP cache would contain an entry for that IP address.

The cache can be cleared by using the **netsh interface ip delete arpcache** command in the event the network administrator wants to repopulate the cache with updated information.

Note: You may need administrator access on the host to be able to use the **netsh interface ip delete arpcache** command.

Refer to
Interactive Graphic
in online course

Common show Commands Revisited - 17.5.5

In the same way that commands and utilities are used to verify a host configuration, commands can be used to verify the interfaces of intermediary devices. The Cisco IOS provides commands to verify the operation of router and switch interfaces.

The Cisco IOS CLI **show** commands display relevant information about the configuration and operation of the device. Network technicians use **show** commands extensively for viewing configuration files, checking the status of device interfaces and processes, and verifying the device operational status. The status of nearly every process or function of the router can be displayed using a **show** command.

Commonly used **show** commands and when to use them are listed in the table.

Click the buttons to see example output from each of these show commands. Note: The output of some commands has been edited to focus on pertinent settings and reduce content.

show running-config

Verifies the current configuration and settings

```
R1# show running-config

(Output omitted)

!

version 15.5

service timestamps debug datetime msec

service timestamps log datetime msec

service password-encryption

!

hostname R1

!

interface GigabitEthernet0/0/0

 description Link to R2

 ip address 209.165.200.225 255.255.255.252

 negotiation auto

!

interface GigabitEthernet0/0/1

 description Link to LAN

 ip address 192.168.10.1 255.255.255.0

 negotiation auto

!

router ospf 10
```

```
 network 192.168.10.0 0.0.0.255 area 0
 network 209.165.200.224 0.0.0.3 area 0
!
banner motd ^C Authorized access only! ^C
!
line con 0
 password 7 14141B180F0B
 login
line vty 0 4
 password 7 00071A150754
 login
 transport input telnet ssh
!
end
R1#
```

show interfaces

Verifies the interface status and displays any error messages

```
R1# show interfaces
GigabitEthernet0/0/0 is up, line protocol is up
  Hardware is ISR4321-2x1GE, address is a0e0.af0d.e140 (bia a0e0.af0d.
e140)
  Description: Link to R2
  Internet address is 209.165.200.225/30
  MTU 1500 bytes, BW 100000 Kbit/sec, DLY 100 usec,
     reliability 255/255, txload 1/255, rxload 1/255
  Encapsulation ARPA, loopback not set
  Keepalive not supported
  Full Duplex, 100Mbps, link type is auto, media type is RJ45
  output flow-control is off, input flow-control is off
  ARP type: ARPA, ARP Timeout 04:00:00
  Last input 00:00:01, output 00:00:21, output hang never
  Last clearing of "show interface" counters never
  Input queue: 0/375/0/0 (size/max/drops/flushes); Total output drops: 0
  Queueing strategy: fifo
  Output queue: 0/40 (size/max)
  5 minute input rate 0 bits/sec, 0 packets/sec
  5 minute output rate 0 bits/sec, 0 packets/sec
```

```
        5127 packets input, 590285 bytes, 0 no buffer

        Received 29 broadcasts (0 IP multicasts)

        0 runts, 0 giants, 0 throttles

        0 input errors, 0 CRC, 0 frame, 0 overrun, 0 ignored

        0 watchdog, 5043 multicast, 0 pause input

        1150 packets output, 153999 bytes, 0 underruns

        0 output errors, 0 collisions, 2 interface resets

        0 unknown protocol drops

        0 babbles, 0 late collision, 0 deferred

        1 lost carrier, 0 no carrier, 0 pause output

        0 output buffer failures, 0 output buffers swapped out
GigabitEthernet0/0/1 is up, line protocol is up
(Output omitted)
```

show ip interface

Verifies the Layer 3 information of an interface

```
R1# show ip interface
GigabitEthernet0/0/0 is up, line protocol is up
  Internet address is 209.165.200.225/30
  Broadcast address is 255.255.255.255
  Address determined by setup command
  MTU is 1500 bytes
  Helper address is not set
  Directed broadcast forwarding is disabled
  Multicast reserved groups joined: 224.0.0.5 224.0.0.6
  Outgoing Common access list is not set
  Outgoing access list is not set
  Inbound Common access list is not set
  Inbound  access list is not set
  Proxy ARP is enabled
  Local Proxy ARP is disabled
  Security level is default
  Split horizon is enabled
  ICMP redirects are always sent
  ICMP unreachables are always sent
  ICMP mask replies are never sent
  IP fast switching is enabled
```

```
                    IP Flow switching is disabled

                    IP CEF switching is enabled

                    IP CEF switching turbo vector

                    IP Null turbo vector

                    Associated unicast routing topologies:

                            Topology "base", operation state is UP

                    IP multicast fast switching is enabled

                    IP multicast distributed fast switching is disabled

                    IP route-cache flags are Fast, CEF

                    Router Discovery is disabled

                    IP output packet accounting is disabled

                    IP access violation accounting is disabled

                    TCP/IP header compression is disabled

                    RTP/IP header compression is disabled

                    Probe proxy name replies are disabled

                    Policy routing is disabled

                    Network address translation is disabled

                    BGP Policy Mapping is disabled

                    Input features: MCI Check

                    IPv4 WCCP Redirect outbound is disabled

                    IPv4 WCCP Redirect inbound is disabled

                    IPv4 WCCP Redirect exclude is disabled
          GigabitEthernet0/0/1 is up, line protocol is up

          (Output omitted)
```

show arp

Verifies the list of known hosts on the local Ethernet LANs

```
R1# show arp

Protocol  Address             Age (min)  Hardware Addr    Type  Interface

Internet  192.168.10.1            -       a0e0.af0d.e141  ARPA
GigabitEthernet0/0/1

Internet  192.168.10.10          95       c07b.bcc4.a9c0  ARPA
GigabitEthernet0/0/1

Internet  209.165.200.225         -       a0e0.af0d.e140  ARPA
GigabitEthernet0/0/0

Internet  209.165.200.226        138      a03d.6fe1.9d90  ARPA
GigabitEthernet0/0/0

R1#
```

show ip route

Verifies the Layer 3 routing information

```
R1# show ip route
Codes: L - local, C - connected, S - static, R - RIP, M - mobile, B - BGP
       D - EIGRP, EX - EIGRP external, O - OSPF, IA - OSPF inter area
       N1 - OSPF NSSA external type 1, N2 - OSPF NSSA external type 2
       E1 - OSPF external type 1, E2 - OSPF external type 2
       i - IS-IS, su - IS-IS summary, L1 - IS-IS level-1, L2 - IS-IS
level-2
       ia - IS-IS inter area, * - candidate default, U - per-user static
route
       o - ODR, P - periodic downloaded static route, H - NHRP, l - LISP
       a - application route
       + - replicated route, % - next hop override, p - overrides from
PfR

Gateway of last resort is 209.165.200.226 to network 0.0.0.0

O*E2  0.0.0.0/0 [110/1] via 209.165.200.226, 02:19:50,
GigabitEthernet0/0/0
      10.0.0.0/24 is subnetted, 1 subnets
O         10.1.1.0 [110/3] via 209.165.200.226, 02:05:42,
GigabitEthernet0/0/0
      192.168.10.0/24 is variably subnetted, 2 subnets, 2 masks
C         192.168.10.0/24 is directly connected, GigabitEthernet0/0/1
L         192.168.10.1/32 is directly connected, GigabitEthernet0/0/1
      209.165.200.0/24 is variably subnetted, 3 subnets, 2 masks
C         209.165.200.224/30 is directly connected, GigabitEthernet0/0/0
L         209.165.200.225/32 is directly connected, GigabitEthernet0/0/0
O         209.165.200.228/30
            [110/2] via 209.165.200.226, 02:07:19, GigabitEthernet0/0/0
R1#
```

show protocols

Verifies which protocols are operational

```
R1# show protocols
Global values:
  Internet Protocol routing is enabled
GigabitEthernet0/0/0 is up, line protocol is up
  Internet address is 209.165.200.225/30
```

```
GigabitEthernet0/0/1 is up, line protocol is up
   Internet address is 192.168.10.1/24
Serial0/1/0 is down, line protocol is down
Serial0/1/1 is down, line protocol is down
GigabitEthernet0 is administratively down, line protocol is down
R1#
```

show version

Verifies the memory, interfaces, and licences of the device

```
R1# show version
Cisco IOS XE Software, Version 03.16.08.S - Extended Support Release
Cisco IOS Software, ISR Software (X86_64_LINUX_IOSD-UNIVERSALK9-M),
Version 15.5(3)S8, RELEASE SOFTWARE (fc2)
Technical Support: http://www.cisco.com/techsupport
Copyright (c) 1986-2018 by Cisco Systems, Inc.
Compiled Wed 08-Aug-18 10:48 by mcpre
(Output omitted)
ROM: IOS-XE ROMMON
R1 uptime is 2 hours, 25 minutes
Uptime for this control processor is 2 hours, 27 minutes
System returned to ROM by reload
System image file is "bootflash:/isr4300-universalk9.03.16.08.S.155-3.
S8-ext.SPA.bin"
Last reload reason: LocalSoft
(Output omitted)
Technology Package License Information:
-----------------------------------------------------------------
Technology    Technology-package
              Current       Type          Next reboot
-----------------------------------------------------------------
appxk9        appxk9        RightToUse    appxk9
uck9          None          None          None
securityk9    securityk9    Permanent     securityk9
ipbase        ipbasek9      Permanent     ipbasek9
cisco ISR4321/K9 (1RU) processor with 1647778K/6147K bytes of memory.
Processor board ID FLM2044W0LT
2 Gigabit Ethernet interfaces
```

```
2 Serial interfaces

32768K bytes of non-volatile configuration memory.

4194304K bytes of physical memory.

3207167K bytes of flash memory at bootflash:.

978928K bytes of USB flash at usb0:.

Configuration register is 0x2102

R1#
```

Refer to
Online Course
for Illustration

The show cdp neighbors Command - 17.5.6

There are several other IOS commands that are useful. The Cisco Discovery Protocol (CDP) is a Cisco proprietary protocol that runs at the data link layer. Because CDP operates at the data link layer, two or more Cisco network devices, such as routers that support different network layer protocols, can learn about each other even if Layer 3 connectivity has not been established.

When a Cisco device boots, CDP starts by default. CDP automatically discovers neighboring Cisco devices running CDP, regardless of which Layer 3 protocol or suites are running. CDP exchanges hardware and software device information with its directly connected CDP neighbors.

CDP provides the following information about each CDP neighbor device:

- **Device identifiers** - The configured host name of a switch, router, or other device

- **Address list** - Up to one network layer address for each protocol supported

- **Port identifier** - The name of the local and remote port in the form of an ASCII character string, such as FastEthernet 0/0

- **Capabilities list** - For example, whether a specific device is a Layer 2 switch or a Layer 3 switch

- **Platform** - The hardware platform of the device--for example, a Cisco 1841 series router.

Refer to the topology and the **show cdp neighbor** command output.

```
R3# show cdp neighbors

Capability Codes: R - Router, T - Trans Bridge, B - Source Route Bridge

                S - Switch, H - Host, I - IGMP, r - Repeater,
P - Phone,

                D - Remote, C - CVTA, M - Two-port Mac Relay

Device ID    Local Intrfce    Holdtme    Capability    Platform    Port ID
S3           Gig 0/0/1        122                  S I WS-C2960+ Fas 0/5
Total cdp entries displayed : 1

R3#
```

The output displays that the R3 GigabitEthernet 0/0/1 interface is connected to the FastEthernet 0/5 interface of S3, which is a Cisco Catalyst 2960+ switch. Notice that R3 has not gathered information about S4. This is because CDP can only discover directly connected Cisco devices. S4 is not directly connected to R3 and therefore is not listed in the output.

The **show cdp neighbors detail** command reveals the IP address of a neighboring device, as shown in the output. CDP will reveal the IP address of the neighbor regardless of whether or not you can ping that neighbor. This command is very helpful when two Cisco routers cannot route across their shared data link. The **show cdp neighbors detail** command will help determine if one of the CDP neighbors has an IP configuration error.

As helpful as CDP is, it can also be a security risk because it can provide useful network infrastructure information to threat actors. For example, by default many IOS versions send CDP advertisements out all enabled ports. However, best practices suggest that CDP should be enabled only on interfaces that are connecting to other infrastructure Cisco devices. CDP advertisements should be disabled on user-facing ports.

Because some IOS versions send out CDP advertisements by default, it is important to know how to disable CDP. To disable CDP globally, use the global configuration command **no cdp run**. To disable CDP on an interface, use the interface command **no cdp enable**.

The show ip interface brief Command - 17.5.7

One of the most frequently used commands is the **show ip interface brief** command. This command provides a more abbreviated output than the **show ip interface** command. It provides a summary of the key information for all the network interfaces on a router.

For example, the **show ip interface brief** output displays all interfaces on the router, the IP address assigned to each interface, if any, and the operational status of the interface.

```
R1# show ip interface brief
```

Interface	IP-Address	OK?	Method	Status	Protocol
GigabitEthernet0/0/0	209.165.200.225	YES	manual	up	up
GigabitEthernet0/0/1	192.168.10.1	YES	manual	up	up
Serial0/1/0	unassigned	NO	unset	down	down
Serial0/1/1	unassigned	NO	unset	dow	down
GigabitEthernet0	unassigned	YES	unset	administratively down	down

```
R1#
```

Verify Switch Interfaces

The **show ip interface brief** command can also be used to verify the status of the switch interfaces, as shown in the output.

```
S1# show ip interface brief
```

Interface	IP-Address	OK?	Method	Status	Protocol
Vlan1	192.168.254.250	YES	manual	up	up
FastEthernet0/1	unassigned	YES	unset	down	down
FastEthernet0/2	unassigned	YES	unset	up	up
FastEthernet0/3	unassigned	YES	unset	up	up

The VLAN1 interface is assigned an IPv4 address of 192.168.254.250, has been enabled, and is operational.

The output also shows that the FastEthernet0/1 interface is down. This indicates that either no device is connected to the interface or the device that is connected has a network interface that is not operational.

In contrast, the output shows that the FastEthernet0/2 and FastEthernet0/3 interfaces are operational. This is indicated by both the status and protocol being shown as up.

Refer to **Video** in online course

Video - The show version Command - 17.5.8

The **show version** command can be used to verify and troubleshoot some of the basic hardware and software components used during the boot process. Click Play to view a video from earlier in the course, which reviews an explanation of the **show version** command.

Refer to **Packet Tracer Activity** for this chapter

Packet Tracer - Interpret show Command Output - 17.5.9

This activity is designed to reinforce the use of router **show** commands. You are not required to configure, but rather examine, the output of several show commands.

Troubleshooting Methodologies - 17.6

Basic Troubleshooting Approaches - 17.6.1

In the previous two topics, you learned about some utilities and commands that you can use to help identify problem areas in your network. This is an important part of troubleshooting. There are many ways to troubleshoot a network problem. This topic details a structured troubleshooting process that can help you to become a better network administrator. It also provides a few more commands to help you resolve problems. Network problems can be simple or complex, and can result from a combination of hardware, software, and connectivity issues. Technicians must be able to analyze the problem and determine the cause of the error before they can resolve the network issue. This process is called troubleshooting.

A common and efficient troubleshooting methodology is based on the scientific method.

The table shows the six main steps in the troubleshooting process.

Step	Description
Step 1. Identify the Problem	• This is the first step in the troubleshooting process. • Although tools can be used in this step, a conversation with the user is often very helpful.
Step 2. Establish a Theory of Probable Causes	• After the problem is identified, try to establish a theory of probable causes. • This step often yields more than a few probable causes to the problem.

Step	Description
Step 3. Test the Theory to Determine Cause	• Based on the probable causes, test your theories to determine which one is the cause of the problem. • A technician will often apply a quick procedure to test and see if it solves the problem. • If a quick procedure does not correct the problem, you might need to research the problem further to establish the exact cause.
Step 4. Establish a Plan of Action and Implement the Solution	After you have determined the exact cause of the problem, establish a plan of action to resolve the problem and implement the solution.
Step 5. Verify Solution and Implement Preventive Measures	• After you have corrected the problem, verify full functionality. • If applicable, implement preventive measures.
Step 6. Document Findings, Actions, and Outcomes	• In the final step of the troubleshooting process, document your findings, actions, and outcomes. • This is very important for future reference.

To assess the problem, determine how many devices on the network are experiencing the problem. If there is a problem with one device on the network, start the troubleshooting process at that device. If there is a problem with all devices on the network, start the troubleshooting process at the device where all other devices are connected. You should develop a logical and consistent method for diagnosing network problems by eliminating one problem at a time.

Resolve or Escalate? - 17.6.2

In some situations, it may not be possible to resolve the problem immediately. A problem should be escalated when it requires a manager decision, some specific expertise, or network access level unavailable to the troubleshooting technician.

For example, after troubleshooting, the technician concludes a router module should be replaced. This problem should be escalated for manager approval. The manager may have to escalate the problem again as it may require the approval of the financial department before a new module can be purchased.

A company policy should clearly state when and how a technician should escalate a problem.

The debug Command - 17.6.3

OS processes, protocols, mechanisms and events generate messages to communicate their status. These messages can provide valuable information when troubleshooting or verifying system operations. The IOS **debug** command allows the administrator to display these messages in real-time for analysis. It is a very important tool for monitoring events on a Cisco IOS device.

All **debug** commands are entered in privileged EXEC mode. The Cisco IOS allows for narrowing the output of **debug** to include only the relevant feature or subfeature. This is important because debugging output is assigned high priority in the CPU process and it can render the system unusable. For this reason, use **debug** commands only to troubleshoot specific problems.

For example, to monitor the status of ICMP messages in a Cisco router, use **debug ip icmp**, as shown in the example.

```
R1# debug ip icmp
ICMP packet debugging is on
R1#
R1# ping 10.1.1.1
Type escape sequence to abort.
Sending 5, 100-byte ICMP Echos to 10.1.1.1, timeout is 2 seconds:
!!!!!
Success rate is 100 percent (5/5), round-trip min/avg/max = 1/1/2 ms
R1#
*Aug 20 14:18:59.605: ICMP: echo reply rcvd, src 10.1.1.1, dst
209.165.200.225,topology BASE, dscp 0 topoid 0
*Aug 20 14:18:59.606: ICMP: echo reply rcvd, src 10.1.1.1, dst
209.165.200.225,topology BASE, dscp 0 topoid 0
*Aug 20 14:18:59.608: ICMP: echo reply rcvd, src 10.1.1.1, dst
209.165.200.225,topology BASE, dscp 0 topoid 0
*Aug 20 14:18:59.609: ICMP: echo reply rcvd, src 10.1.1.1, dst
209.165.200.225,topology BASE, dscp 0 topoid 0
*Aug 20 14:18:59.611: ICMP: echo reply rcvd, src 10.1.1.1, dst
209.165.200.225,topology BASE, dscp 0 topoid 0
R1#
```

To list a brief description of all the debugging command options, use the **debug ?** command in privileged EXEC mode at the command line.

To turn off a specific debugging feature, add the **no** keyword in front of the **debug** command:

```
Router# no debug ip icmp
```

Alternatively, you can enter the **undebug** form of the command in privileged EXEC mode:

```
Router# undebug ip icmp
```

To turn off all active debug commands at once, use the **undebug all** command:

```
Router# undebug all
```

Be cautious using some **debug** command. Commands such as **debug all** and **debug ip packet** generate a substantial amount of output and can use a large portion of system resources. The router could get so busy displaying **debug** messages that it would not have enough processing power to perform its network functions, or even listen to commands to turn off debugging. For this reason, using these command options is not recommended and should be avoided.

The terminal monitor Command - 17.6.4

Connections to grant access to the IOS command line interface can be established in the following two ways:

- **Locally** - Local connections (i.e., console connection) require physical access to the router or switch console port using a rollover cable.

- **Remotely** - Remote connections require the use of Telnet or SSH to establish a connection to an IP configured device.

Certain IOS messages are automatically displayed on a console connection but not on a remote connection. For instance, **debug** output is displayed by default on console connections. However, **debug** output is not automatically displayed on remote connections. This is because **debug** messages are log messages which are prevented from being displayed on vty lines.

In the following output for instance, the user established a remote connection using Telnet from R2 to R1. The user then issued the **debug ip icmp** command. However, the command failed to display **debug** output.

```
R2# telnet 209.165.200.225

Trying 209.165.200.225 ... Open

 Authorized access only!

User Access Verification

Password:

R1> enable

Password:

R1# debug ip icmp

ICMP packet debugging is on

R1# ping 10.1.1.1

Type escape sequence to abort.

Sending 5, 100-byte ICMP Echos to 10.1.1.1, timeout is 2 seconds:

!!!!!

Success rate is 100 percent (5/5), round-trip min/avg/max = 1/1/2 ms

R1#
```

To display log messages on a terminal (virtual console), use the **terminal monitor** privileged EXEC command. To stop logging messages on a terminal, use the **terminal no monitor** privileged EXEC command.

For instance, notice how the **terminal monitor** command has now been entered and the **ping** command displays the **debug** output.

```
R1#  terminal monitor

R1# ping 10.1.1.1

Type escape sequence to abort.
```

```
Sending 5, 100-byte ICMP Echos to 10.1.1.1, timeout is 2 seconds:

!!!!!

Success rate is 100 percent (5/5), round-trip min/avg/max = 1/1/2 ms

R1#

*Aug 20 16:03:49.735: ICMP: echo reply rcvd, src 10.1.1.1, dst
209.165.200.225,topology BASE, dscp 0 topoid 0

**Aug 20 16:03:49.737: ICMP: echo reply rcvd, src 10.1.1.1, dst
209.165.200.225,topology BASE, dscp 0 topoid 0

**Aug 20 16:03:49.738: ICMP: echo reply rcvd, src 10.1.1.1, dst
209.165.200.225,topology BASE, dscp 0 topoid 0

**Aug 20 16:03:49.740: ICMP: echo reply rcvd, src 10.1.1.1, dst
209.165.200.225,topology BASE, dscp 0 topoid 0

**Aug 20 16:03:49.741: ICMP: echo reply rcvd, src 10.1.1.1, dst
209.165.200.225,topology BASE, dscp 0 topoid 0

R1# no debug ip icmp

ICMP packet debugging is off

R1#
```

Note: The intent of the **debug** command is to capture live output for a short period of time (i.e., a few seconds to a minute or so). Always disable **debug** when not required.

Check Your Understanding - Troubleshooting Methodologies - 17.6.5

Go to the online course to take the quiz and exam.

Troubleshooting Scenarios - 17.7

Duplex Operation and Mismatch Issues - 17.7.1

Refer to **Online Course** for Illustration

Many common network problems can be identified and resolved with little effort. Now that you have the tools and the process for troubleshooting a network, this topic reviews some common networking issues that you are likely to find as a network administrator.

In data communications, *duplex* refers to the direction of data transmission between two devices.

There are two duplex communication modes:

■ **Half-duplex** - Communication is restricted to the exchange of data in one direction at a time.

■ **Full-duplex** - Communications is permitted to be sent and received simultaneously.

The figure illustrates how each duplex method operates.

Interconnecting Ethernet interfaces must operate in the same duplex mode for best communication performance and to avoid inefficiency and latency on the link.

The Ethernet autonegotiation feature facilitates configuration, minimizes problems and maximizes link performance between two interconnecting Ethernet links. The connected devices first announce their supported capabilities and then choose the highest performance mode supported by both ends. For example, the switch and router in the figure have successfully autonegotiated full-duplex mode.

If one of the two connected devices is operating in full-duplex and the other is operating in half-duplex, a duplex mismatch occurs. While data communication will occur through a link with a duplex mismatch, link performance will be very poor.

Duplex mismatches are typically caused by a misconfigured interface or in rare instances by a failed autonegotiation. Duplex mismatches may be difficult to troubleshoot as the communication between devices still occurs.

IP Addressing Issues on IOS Devices - 17.7.2

IP address-related problems will likely keep remote network devices from communicating. Because IP addresses are hierarchical, any IP address assigned to a network device must conform to that range of addresses in that network. Wrongly assigned IP addresses create a variety of issues, including IP address conflicts and routing problems.

Two common causes of incorrect IPv4 assignment are manual assignment mistakes or DHCP-related issues.

Network administrators often have to manually assign IP addresses to devices such as servers and routers. If a mistake is made during the assignment, then communications issues with the device are very likely to occur.

On an IOS device, use the **show ip interface** or **show ip interface brief** commands to verify what IPv4 addresses are assigned to the network interfaces. For example, issuing the **show ip interface brief** command as shown would validate the interface status on R1.

```
R1# show ip interface brief

Interface            IP-Address       OK? Method Status                Protocol
GigabitEthernet0/0/0 209.165.200.225  YES manual up                          up
GigabitEthernet0/0/1 192.168.10.1     YES manual up                          up
Serial0/1/0          unassigned       NO  unset  down                      down
Serial0/1/1          unassigned       NO  unset  down                      down
GigabitEthernet0     unassigned       YES unset  administratively down down
R1#
```

IP Addressing Issues on End Devices - 17.7.3

In Windows-based machines, when the device cannot contact a DHCP server, Windows will automatically assign an address belonging to the 169.254.0.0/16 range. This feature is called Automatic Private IP Addressing (APIPA) and is designed to facilitate communication within the local network. Think of it as Windows saying, "I will use this address from the 169.254.0.0/16 range because I could not get any other address".

Often, a computer with an APIPA address will not be able to communicate with other devices in the network because those devices will most likely not belong to the 169.254.0.0/16 network. This situation indicates an automatic IPv4 address assignment problem that should be fixed.

Note: Other operating systems, such Linux and OS X, will not assign an IPv4 address to the network interface if communication with a DHCP server fails.

Most end devices are configured to rely on a DHCP server for automatic IPv4 address assignment. If the device is unable to communicate with the DHCP server, then the server cannot assign an IPv4 address for the specific network and the device will not be able to communicate.

To verify the IP addresses assigned to a Windows-based computer, use the **ipconfig** command, as shown in the output.

```
C:\Users\PC-A> ipconfig

Windows IP Configuration

(Output omitted)

Wireless LAN adapter Wi-Fi:

    Connection-specific DNS Suffix   .  :
    Link-local IPv6 Address . . . . . : fe80::a4aa:2dd1:ae2d:a75e%16
    IPv4 Address. . . . . . . . . . . : 192.168.10.10
    Subnet Mask . . . . . . . . . . . : 255.255.255.0
    Default Gateway . . . . . . . . . : 192.168.10.1

(Output omitted)
```

Default Gateway Issues - 17.7.4

The default gateway for an end device is the closest networking device that can forward traffic to other networks. If a device has an incorrect or nonexistent default gateway address, it will not be able to communicate with devices in remote networks. Because the default gateway is the path to remote networks, its address must belong to the same network as the end device.

The address of the default gateway can be manually set or obtained from a DHCP server. Similar to IPv4 addressing issues, default gateway problems can be related to misconfiguration (in the case of manual assignment) or DHCP problems (if automatic assignment is in use).

To solve misconfigured default gateway issues, ensure that the device has the correct default gateway configured. If the default address was manually set but is incorrect, simply replace it with the proper address. If the default gateway address was automatically set, ensure the device can communicate with the DHCP server. It is also important to verify that the proper IPv4 address and subnet mask were configured on the interface of the router and that the interface is active.

To verify the default gateway on Windows-based computers, use the **ipconfig** command as shown.

```
C:\Users\PC-A> ipconfig

Windows IP Configuration

(Output omitted)

Wireless LAN adapter Wi-Fi:
```

```
       Connection-specific DNS Suffix  . :

       Link-local IPv6 Address . . . . . : fe80::a4aa:2dd1:ae2d:a75e%16

       IPv4 Address. . . . . . . . . . . : 192.168.10.10

       Subnet Mask . . . . . . . . . . . : 255.255.255.0

       Default Gateway . . . . . . . . . : 192.168.10.1
(Output omitted)
```

On a router, use the **show ip route** command to list the routing table and verify that the
default gateway, known as a default route, has been set. This route is used when the destination address of the packet does not match any other routes in its routing table.

For example, the output verifies that R1 has a default gateway (i.e., Gateway of last resort)
configured pointing to IP address 209.168.200.226.

```
R1# show ip route | begin Gateway

Gateway of last resort is 209.165.200.226 to network 0.0.0.0

O*E2  0.0.0.0/0 [110/1] via 209.165.200.226, 02:19:50,
GigabitEthernet0/0/0

       10.0.0.0/24 is subnetted, 1 subnets

O        10.1.1.0 [110/3] via 209.165.200.226, 02:05:42,
GigabitEthernet0/0/0

       192.168.10.0/24 is variably subnetted, 2 subnets, 2 masks

C        192.168.10.0/24 is directly connected, GigabitEthernet0/0/1

L        192.168.10.1/32 is directly connected, GigabitEthernet0/0/1

       209.165.200.0/24 is variably subnetted, 3 subnets, 2 masks

C        209.165.200.224/30 is directly connected, GigabitEthernet0/0/0

L        209.165.200.225/32 is directly connected, GigabitEthernet0/0/0

O        209.165.200.228/30

         [110/2] via 209.165.200.226, 02:07:19, GigabitEthernet0/0/0
R1#
```

The first highlighted line basically states that the gateway to any (i.e., 0.0.0.0) should be sent to
IP address 209.165.200.226. The second highlighted displays how R1 learned about the default
gateway. In this case, R1 received the information from another OSPF-enabled router.

Troubleshooting DNS Issues - 17.7.5

Domain Name Service (DNS) defines an automated service that matches names, such as
www.cisco.com, with the IP address. Although DNS resolution is not crucial to device
communication, it is very important to the end user.

It is common for users to mistakenly relate the operation of an internet link to the availability of the DNS. User complaints such as "the network is down" or "the internet is
down" are often caused by an unreachable DNS server. While packet routing and all
other network services are still operational, DNS failures often lead the user to the wrong

conclusion. If a user types in a domain name such as www.cisco.com in a web browser and the DNS server is unreachable, the name will not be translated into an IP address and the website will not display.

DNS server addresses can be manually or automatically assigned. Network administrators are often responsible for manually assigning DNS server addresses on servers and other devices, while DHCP is used to automatically assign DNS server addresses to clients.

Although it is common for companies and organizations to manage their own DNS servers, any reachable DNS server can be used to resolve names. Small office and home office (SOHO) users often rely on the DNS server maintained by their ISP for name resolution. ISP-maintained DNS servers are assigned to SOHO customers via DHCP. Additionally, Google maintains a public DNS server that can be used by anyone and it is very useful for testing. The IPv4 address of Google's public DNS server is 8.8.8.8 and 2001:4860:4860::8888 for its IPv6 DNS address.

Cisco offers OpenDNS which provides secure DNS service by filtering phishing and some malware sites. You can change your DNS address to 208.67.222.222 and 208.67.220.220 in the Preferred DNS server and Alternate DNS server fields. Advanced features such as web content filtering and security are available to families and businesses.

Use the **ipconfig /all** as shown to verify which DNS server is in use by the Windows computer.

```
C:\Users\PC-A> ipconfig /all

(Output omitted)

Wireless LAN adapter Wi-Fi:

    Connection-specific DNS Suffix  . :

    Description . . . . . . . . . . . : Intel(R) Dual Band Wireless-AC
8265

    Physical Address. . . . . . . . . : F8-94-C2-E4-C5-0A

    DHCP Enabled. . . . . . . . . . . : Yes

    Autoconfiguration Enabled . . . . : Yes

    Link-local IPv6 Address . . . . . : fe80::a4aa:2dd1:ae2d:a75e%16
(Preferred)

    IPv4 Address. . . . . . . . . . . : 192.168.10.10(Preferred)

    Subnet Mask . . . . . . . . . . . : 255.255.255.0

    Lease Obtained. . . . . . . . . . : August 17, 2019 1:20:17 PM

    Lease Expires . . . . . . . . . . : August 18, 2019 1:20:18 PM

    Default Gateway . . . . . . . . . : 192.168.10.1

    DHCP Server . . . . . . . . . . . : 192.168.10.1

    DHCPv6 IAID . . . . . . . . . . . : 100177090

    DHCPv6 Client DUID. . . . . . . . :
00-01-00-01-21-F3-76-75-54-E1-AD-DE-DA-9A

    DNS Servers . . . . . . . . . . . : 208.67.222.222

    NetBIOS over Tcpip. . . . . . . . : Enabled

(Output omitted)
```

The **nslookup** command is another useful DNS troubleshooting tool for PCs. With **nslookup** a user can manually place DNS queries and analyze the DNS response. The **nslookup** command shows the output for a query for www.cisco.com. Notice you can also simply enter an IP address and **nslookup** will resolve the name.

```
C:\Users\bvachon> nslookup
Default Server:  Home-Net
Address:  192.168.1.1

> cisco.com
Server:  Home-Net
Address:  192.168.1.1

Non-authoritative answer:
Name:    cisco.com
Addresses:  2001:420:1101:1::185
            72.163.4.185

> 8.8.8.8
Server:  Home-Net
Address:  192.168.1.1

Name:    dns.google
Address:  8.8.8.8

>

> 208.67.222.222
Server:  Home-Net
Address:  192.168.1.1

Name:    resolver1.opendns.com
Address:  208.67.222.222

>
```

Refer to Lab Activity for this chapter

Lab - Troubleshoot Connectivity Issues - 17.7.6

In this lab, you will complete the following objectives:

- Identify the Problem
- Implement Network Changes
- Verify Full Functionality
- Document Findings and Configuration Changes

Refer to Packet Tracer Activity for this chapter

Packet Tracer - Troubleshoot Connectivity Issues - 17.7.7

The objective of this Packet Tracer activity is to troubleshoot and resolve connectivity issues, if possible. Otherwise, the issues should be clearly documented and so they can be escalated.

Module Practice and Quiz - 17.8

Refer to
Lab Activity
for this chapter

Lab - Design and Build a Small Business Network - 17.8.1

In this lab, you will design and build a network.

Refer to **Packet Tracer Activity**
for this chapter

Packet Tracer - Skills Integration Challenge - 17.8.2

In this Packet Tracer activity, you will use all the skills you have acquired over throughout this course.

Refer to **Packet Tracer Activity**
for this chapter

Packet Tracer - Troubleshooting Challenge - 17.8.3

In this Packet Tracer activity, you will troubleshoot and resolve a number of issues in an existing network.

What did I learn in this module? - 17.8.4

Devices in a Small Network

Small networks typically have a single WAN connection provided by DSL, cable, or an Ethernet connection. Small networks are managed by a local IT technician or by a contracted professional. Factors to consider when selecting network devices for a small network are cost, speed and types of ports/interfaces, expandability, and OS features and services. When implementing a network, create an IP addressing scheme and use it on end devices, servers and peripherals, and intermediary devices. Redundancy can be accomplished by installing duplicate equipment, but it can also be accomplished by supplying duplicate network links for critical areas. The routers and switches in a small network should be configured to support real-time traffic, such as voice and video, in an appropriate manner relative to other data traffic. In fact, a good network design will implement quality of service (QoS) to classify traffic carefully according to priority.

Small Network Applications and Protocols

There are two forms of software programs or processes that provide access to the network: network applications and application layer services. Some end-user applications implement application layer protocols and are able to communicate directly with the lower layers of the protocol stack. Email clients and web browsers are examples of this type of application. Other programs may need the assistance of application layer services to use network resources like file transfer or network print spooling. These are the programs that interface with the network and prepare the data for transfer. The two most common remote access solutions are Telnet and Secure Shell (SSH). SSH service is a secure alternative to Telnet. Network administrators must also support common network servers and their required related network protocols such as web server, email server, FTP server, DHCP server, and DNS server. Businesses today are increasingly using IP telephony and streaming media to communicate with customers and business partners. These are real-time applications. The network infrastructure must support VoIP, IP telephony, and other real-time applications.

Scale to Larger Networks

To scale a network, several elements are required: network documentation, device inventory, budget, and traffic analysis. Know the type of traffic that is crossing the network as well as the current traffic flow. Capture traffic during peak utilization times to get a good representation of the different traffic types and perform the capture on different network segments and devices as some traffic will be local to a particular segment. Network administrators must know how network use is changing. Usage details of employee computers can be captured in a 'snapshot' with such tools as the Windows Task Manager, Event Viewer, and Data Usage.

Verify Connectivity

The **ping** command is the most effective way to quickly test Layer 3 connectivity between a source and destination IP address. The command also displays various round-trip time statistics. The Cisco IOS offers an "extended" mode of the ping command which lets the user create special types of pings by adjusting parameters related to the command operation. Extended ping is entered in privileged EXEC mode by typing ping without a destination IP address. Traceroute can help locate Layer 3 problem areas in a network. A trace returns a list of hops as a packet is routed through a network. It is used to identify the point along the path where the problem can be found. In Windows, the command is **tracert**. In Cisco IOS the command is **traceroute**. There is also an extended **traceroute** command. It allows the administrator to adjust parameters related to the command operation. The output derived from network commands contributes data to the network baseline. One method for starting a baseline is to copy and paste the results from an executed ping, trace, or other relevant commands into a text file. These text files can be time stamped with the date and saved into an archive for later retrieval and comparison.

Host and IOS Commands

Network administrators view the IP addressing information (address, mask, router, and DNS) on a Windows host by issuing the **ipconfig** command. Other necessary commands are **ipconfig /all**, **ipconfig /release** and **ipconfig /renew**, and **ipconfig /displaydns**. Verifying IP settings by using the GUI on a Linux machine will differ depending on the Linux distribution (distro) and desktop interface. Necessary commands are **ifconfig**, and **ip address**. In the GUI of a Mac host, open Network Preferences > Advanced to get the IP addressing information. Other IP addressing commands for Mac are **ifconfig**, and **networksetup -listallnetworkservices** and **networksetup -getinfo** *<network service>*. The **arp** command is executed from the Windows, Linux, or Mac command prompt. The command lists all devices currently in the ARP cache of the host, which includes the IPv4 address, physical address, and the type of addressing (static/dynamic), for each device. The **arp -a** command displays the known IP address and MAC address binding. Common **show** commands are **show running-config**, **show interfaces**, **show ip address**, **show arp**, **show ip route**, **show protocols**, and **show version**. The **show cdp neighbor** command provides the following information about each CDP neighbor device: identifiers, address list, port identifier, capabilities list, and platform. The **show cdp neighbors detail** command will help determine if one of the CDP neighbors has an IP configuration error. The **show ip interface brief** command output displays all interfaces on the router, the IP address assigned to each interface, if any, and the operational status of the interface.

Troubleshooting Methodologies

Step 1.   Identify the problem

Step 2.   Establish a theory of probably causes.

Step 3.   Test the theory to determine the cause.

Step 4.   Establish a plan of action and implement the solution.

Step 5.   Verify the solution and implement preventive measures.

Step 6.   Document findings, actions, and outcomes.

A problem should be escalated when it requires a the decision of a manager, some specific expertise, or network access level unavailable to the troubleshooting technician. OS processes, protocols, mechanisms and events generate messages to communicate their status. The IOS **debug** command allows the administrator to display these messages in real-time for analysis. To display log messages on a terminal (virtual console), use the **terminal monitor** privileged EXEC command.

Troubleshooting Scenarios

There are two duplex communication modes: half-duplex and full-duplex. If one of the two connected devices is operating in full-duplex and the other is operating in half-duplex, a duplex mismatch occurs. While data communication will occur through a link with a duplex mismatch, link performance will be very poor.

Wrongly assigned IP addresses create a variety of issues, including IP address conflicts and routing problems. Two common causes of incorrect IPv4 assignment are manual assignment mistakes or DHCP-related issues. Most end devices are configured to rely on a DHCP server for automatic IPv4 address assignment. If the device is unable to communicate with the DHCP server, then the server cannot assign an IPv4 address for the specific network and the device will not be able to communicate.

The default gateway for an end device is the closest networking device that can forward traffic to other networks. If a device has an incorrect or nonexistent default gateway address, it will not be able to communicate with devices in remote networks. Because the default gateway is the path to remote networks, its address must belong to the same network as the end device.

DNS failures often lead the user to conclude that the network is down. If a user types in a domain name such as www.cisco.com in a web browser and the DNS server is unreachable, the name will not be translated into an IP address and the website will not display.

Go to the online course to take the quiz and exam.

Chapter Quiz - Build a Small Network

Your Chapter Notes

Internet Protocol version 4 (IPv4), 57
Internet Protocol version 6 (IPv6), 57
internet protocols, 57
internet queries, 285
internet standards, 59
intranets, 8
  subnetting, 195–196
intrusion prevention systems (IPS), 18
IOS. *See* Cisco IOS
IoT (Internet of Things), 208
IP (Internet Protocol)
  characteristics, 137–138
    best effort, 137
    connectionless, 137
    media independent, 137–138
  encapsulation, 136–137
IP (Internet Protocol) addresses, 3, 40–41
  configuration, 42–43
    automatic configuration, 42
    on Linux host, 314–315
    on macOS host, 315–316
    manual configuration, 42
    SVI configuration, 43
    on Windows host, 312–314
  discovery, 151–153
  as Layer 3 logical addresses, 64–65
  naming system protocols, 273–275
  in small networks, 299–300
  troubleshooting
    on end devices, 330–331
    on IOS devices, 330
ip address command, 216, 315
ip default-gateway command, 173
IP telephony, 303
ipconfig /all command, 312, 333
ipconfig command, 221, 312, 331
ipconfig /displaydns command, 274, 314
ipconfig /release command, 313
ipconfig /renew command, 313
IPS (intrusion prevention systems), 18
IPv4 (Internet Protocol version 4), 57
IPv4 addresses, 40–41
  ARP (Address Resolution Protocol) and, 153–157
  assignment of, 187
  binary number system and, 93–94
  coexistence with IPv6, 208–209
  converting binary to/from decimal, 95–100
  limitations, 139, 207–208
  network segmentation, 187–189. *See also* subnetting
  number systems in, 100
  structure of, 178–182
    broadcast addresses, 181
    determining with logical AND operation, 179–180
    host addresses, 181
    host portion, 178
    network addresses, 180–181
    network portion, 178
    prefix length, 178–179
    subnet masks, 178
  subnetting, 189–198
    with /8 prefix, 194
    with /16 prefix, 192–194
    minimizing unused host addresses, 197–198
    on octet boundary, 189–191
    public versus private address space, 195–197
    structured design, 201–203

VLSM, 199–201
    within octet boundary, 191–192
  types of, 184–187
    broadcast addresses, 182–183
    classful addressing, 186–187
    internet routing, 184–185
    link-local addresses, 186
    loopback addresses, 185–186
    multicast addresses, 183
    private addresses, 184
    public addresses, 184
    unicast addresses, 182
IPv4 packets, 138–139
IPv4 routing tables, viewing, 146–147
IPv6 (Internet Protocol version 6), 57
ipv6 address command, 216, 218
IPv6 addresses, 41
  benefits over IPv4, 139–140, 207–208
  coexistence with IPv4, 208–209
  configuration
    dynamic GUA configuration, 218–222
    dynamic LLA configuration, 222–224
    static GUA configuration, 216–217
    static LLA configuration, 217–218
    verifying, 224–226
  hexadecimal number system and, 100–101
  Neighbor Discovery (ND) protocol, 157–159
  representation of, 209–212
    double colon (::), 211–212
    omit leading zeros, 210–211
    preferred format, 209–210
  subnetting, 227–229
  types of, 212–216
    anycast addresses, 213
    GUA (Global Unicast Address), 213–215
    LLA (Link-local Address), 213, 215–216
    multicast addresses, 213, 226–227
    prefix length, 213
    unicast addresses, 212–213
    unique local addresses, 213–214
IPv6 packets, 139–141
ipv6 unicast-routing command, 219
ISN (initial sequence number), 257
IT professionals, 19
  CCNA certification, 19
  jobs for, 19
ITU-T (International Telecommunications Union-
  Telecommunication Standardization Sector), 59

J

jobs for IT professionals, 19

K

keywords for commands, 30

L

LANs (Local Area Networks), 6–7
  data link frames, 115
  physical topologies, 109–110
latency, 77
Layer 2 physical addresses. *See* data link layer addresses

network applications in small networks, 301
network architecture, 11–12
network attacks, 283–286
  access attacks, 285–286
  denial of service attacks, 286
  malware, 283–284
  mitigations for, 286–289
    AAA, 288
    backups, 287
    defense-in-depth approach, 286–287
    endpoint security, 289
    firewalls, 288
    security patches, 287–288
  reconnaissance attacks, 284–285
network communications protocols, 53
network infrastructure security, 13
Network Interface Cards (NICs), 4, 74
network layer addresses, role of, 66
network layer (OSI), 61
  address types, 64
  characteristics, 135–138
  host routing, 141–143
    default gateway, 142
    forwarding methods, 141
    viewing routing table, 142–143
  IPv4 packets, 138–139
  IPv6 packets, 139–141
  routing, 143–147
    dynamic routing, 145
    forwarding methods, 143–144
    IP router routing tables, 144
    static routing, 144–145
    viewing IPv4 routing table, 146–147
network media, 4, 41–42
network performance baseline, 310–312
network portion
  of IPv4 addresses, 178
  of IPv6 addresses, 213
network protocols. *See* protocols
network security protocols, 53
network utilization tools, 304–305
networks
  components, 2–4
    end devices, 3
    hosts, 2–3
    intermediary devices, 4
    network media, 4
    peer-to-peer, 3
  reliability, 11–13
    fault tolerance, 12
    network architecture, 11–12
    QoS (Quality of Service), 12–13
    scalability, 12
    security, 13
  representations, 4–5
  security, 17–19
    solutions, 18
    threats, 17–18
  segmenting, 187–189. *See also* subnetting
  sizes of, 5–6
  topology diagrams, 5
  trends, 13–17
    BYOD (Bring Your Own Device), 14
    cloud computing, 14–15
    online collaboration, 14

powerline networking, 16
smart home technology, 15–16
video communications, 14
wireless broadband, 17
WISP (Wireless Internet Service Provider), 16
  types of, 5–8
    internet, 7
    intranets/extranets, 8
    LANs/WANs, 6–7
  usefulness of, 2
networksetup -getinfo command, 315
networksetup -listallnetworkservices command, 315
NICs (Network Interface Cards), 4, 74
no cdp enable command, 324
no cdp run command, 324
no debug command, 327
no hostname command, 34
no ip directed-broadcasts command, 183
no ip http server command, 293
no shutdown command, 165
node icon, 53
nodes, 106
NS (Neighbor Solicitation) messages, 158, 235–236
nslookup command, 275, 334
number systems
  binary, 93–95
    conversion to/from decimal, 95–100
    IPv4 addresses and, 93–94
    positional notation, 94–95
  decimal
    conversion to/from binary, 95–100
    conversion to/from hexadecimal, 101–102
    positional notation, 94–95
  hexadecimal, 100–102
    conversion to/from decimal, 101–102
    IPv6 addresses and, 100–101
  in IPv4 addresses, 100

O

octet boundaries
  subnetting on, 189–191
  subnetting within, 191–192
octets, 94, 100, 209
online collaboration, 14
Open Shortest Path First (OSPF), 57
open standards, 58
operating systems, 25–26
  purpose, 26–27
optical fiber. *See* fiber-optic cabling
ordered delivery with TCP, 257
OSI reference model, 60–61
  comparison with TCP/IP model, 61–62
  physical layer
    bandwidth, 76–78
    encoding, 76
    physical components, 75
    purpose, 73–74
    signaling, 76
    standards, 74–75
OSPF (Open Shortest Path First), 57
out-of-band access, 27